Sanskrit Drama
With Special Reference to Prahasana and Vīthī

Sanskrit Drama

With Special Reference to Prahasana and Vīthī

S. Ramaratnam

With a Foreword by
Satyavrat Shastri

PRINTWORLD
Publishers of Indian Traditions

Cataloging in Publication Data — DK
[Courtesy: D.K. Agencies (P) Ltd. <docinfo@dkagencies.com>]

Ramaratnam, S.
Sanskrit drama : with special reference to prahasana and vīthī / S. Ramaratnam.
p. cm.
Includes bibliographical references (p.) and index.
ISBN 13: 9788124606551

1. Sanskrit farces — History and criticism.
2. Sanskrit drama — History and criticism.
I. Title.

DDC 891.2209 23

First published in India, 2014
ISBN 13: 978-81-246-0655-1

Printed and published by:
D.K. Printworld (P) Ltd.
Regd. office : *Vedaśrī*, F-395, Sudarshan Park
(Metro Station: Ramesh Nagar)
New Delhi – 110 015
Phones : (011) 2545 3975; 2546 6019; *Fax* : (011) 2546 5926
E-mail: indology@dkprintworld.com
Web: www.dkprintworld.com

Foreword

IT is indeed a great pleasure going through the learned work "Prahasana and Vīthī in Sanskrit Literature" (coming under the generic title *Sanskrit Drama*) by Prof S. Ramaratnam. Being a comprehensive survey of the *prahasana* and the *vīthī* literature in Sanskrit, it deserves a warm welcome of scholars.

As a prelude to noticing *prahasana*s and *vīthī*s in Sanskrit, the author subjects a considerable corpus of ancient Sanskrit literature from the Veda down to the Upaniṣads, the *Rāmāyaṇa* and the *Mahābhārata* and the works of the classical period, to a searching scrutiny to trace the element of humour in it, thus offering the rebuttal to the viewpoint of a section of the critics that Sanskrit literature, infact has been, and still is, far too serious to admit in it comic relief, with the exception of Sanskrit plays, where it surfaces in crude form in the antics of jester (*vidūṣaka*) who is introduced in them for the specific purpose of producing it. The ancient Sanskrit literature, infact, has enough evidence of it, as very ably brought out by our author, with a plethora of instances culled from it, in all its varieties of wit, satire and parody. Indian society has always been as robust as any other to indulge in the lighter side of life in its approach to live life in all its fullness.

Humour has two broad divisions, subtle and gross/crude. While the instances in the ancient literature point to its subtle variety, that in the *prahasana*s by and large, with few honourable exceptions, point to its gross/crude variety. The real humour is one that does not give the appearance of an effort behind it. That indication robs it of much of its sheen and may not appeal to more sophisticated taste, particularly in the modern times. The Sanskrit poets and playwrights of the modern period who have taken to humorous writing have been/are more careful in this regard. The humour in their creations, in quite a number of them, is more natural, flowing out of the situations and not a contrived one.

Humour is represented by the term *hāsya* in Sanskrit literature. The impact of it is noticeable in the form of smile or laughter. The rhetoricians in India have been at pains to notice the shades in them, in all their minutae, thus proving their sharpness in understanding and appreciating them. It is debatable whether critics in any other language would have been so sharp and keen-eyed to notice them and detail them in their works.

It is to the keen insight of Prof S. Ramaratnam to have brought out such a thorough and comprehensive study of an important branch of Sanskrit dramatic literature. He has done a commendable job in collecting and presenting an account of many unpublished *prahasana* manuscripts. His account of the *vīthī* and the *vīthyaṅga*s is equally praiseworthy. The appendices and the exhaustive bibliography further enhance the value of the work. His sharp intellect and critical approach are noticeable in another of his work too, the work on an altogether different subject of management principles as gleaned from Sanskrit literature. I am pretty certain that he would, over a period of time, produce more of such works which will do the country proud.

New Delhi **Satyavrat Shastri**
12 December 2012

Preface

In the pages that follow, an attempt is made for the first time, at presenting a detailed account of the Sanskrit dramatic literature with special reference to the *prahasana* and the *vīthī*. The *prahasana* part of the present work represents the research work done by me during the period 1975-79, first in the Department of Sanskrit, Ramakrishna Mission Vivekananda College, Chennai, and later in the Sanskrit Department of the University of Madras, under the supervision of Dr. M. Narasimhachary, former Reader in Sanskrit, who subsequently became the Professor and Head of the Department of Vaishnavism, University of Madras. The *vīthī* portion was written by me while functioning as the UGC Emeritus Professor at the Post-graduate and Research Department of Sanskrit, Rajah's College of Sanskrit and Tamil Studies, Tiruvaiyaru, Tamil Nadu during 2005-07.

Prahasana and the *vīthī* are two of the ten major types of Sanskrit drama, the other eight being *nāṭaka, prakaraṇa, bhāṇa, ḍima, vyāyoga, samavakāra, aṅka* and *īhāmṛga. Nāṭaka* (popular play) and *prakaraṇa* (social play) are the most perfected varieties, depicting all the sentiments and possessing varied characters. The other play-forms differ from one another in the main sentiment that is delineated and the type of characters introduced. Thus, the *prahasana* has the comic as its predominant sentiment and generally depicts the corrupt practices of certain sections of the society. The *prahasana* is useful in the sense that it cautions the good against the possible exploitation by the unscrupulous elements in the society. The *vīthī* has a sprinkling of all the sentiments but has just two or three characters in it. It has a simple theme and can be presented as a street play. Thus, its message can reach the masses directly.

Though studies on some individual *prahasana*s and the *vīthī*s have appeared from time to time in research journals, no detailed study has yet been made to analyse them in a cogent fashion. The present study thus, is an attempt for the first time to present a large body of *prahasana*s and the *vīthī*s covering all important aspects of their theory and practice. In doing so, no effort has been spared in collecting relevant manuscripts, microfilms and transcripts of the original works from different sources, though still a few could not be traced or procured.

The first chapter is introductory in nature, dealing with the important aspects of Sanskrit drama, such as its origin, the different types and their salient features. The second chapter gives a brief account of the theories of *rasa*-realization and a detailed treatment of the *hāsya rasa* with suitable illustrations. Other connected problems, like whether or not *hāsya* forms a secondary *rasa*, its relation to the other *rasa*s and its scope in wider Sanskrit literature have been discussed in this chapter.

The third chapter deals with the Sanskrit *prahasana* in theory and practice. The salient points discussed in this chapter are — the origin of the *prahasana*, its theoretical features as sanctioned in the dramaturgical works and the presence of such features in the available specimens.

The fourth and the fifth chapters analyse the *śuddha* and the *saṁkīrṇa* types of *prahasana*s respectively. The latter has two sub-sections — the well-known *prahasana*s and the minor ones.

The sixth chapter discusses the theoretical aspects of the *vīthī*. This is followed by a detailed account of the available *vīthī* specimens, in the seventh chapter. In the penultimate chapter (Chapter 8), the scope of the *vīthyaṅga*s in Sanskrit drama is discussed. The last chapter (Chapter 9) gives a retrospective resume of the study made in the preceding chapters. In addition to this, the relation of the *vīthī* to the Indian Folk Theatre is also discussed in this chapter. The scope of this work is limited to the specimens up to the nineteenth century. However a brief account of the works of the twentieth century writers is given in the appendix. The influence of Sanskrit *prahasana* and *vīthī* over the dramatic literature in other Indian languages, and a brief account of the farces in English literature are also presented in the appendix.

While rendering the verses, some of the long compounds have been split for the sake of easy readability. This has resulted in violation of the metrical rules in some places. I may be pardoned for the same. Some of the verses are the *chāyā* of the corresponding Prākṛt verses, and hence, they may also suffer from the loss of metre. Short lines in prose are rendered in roman style for the sake of convenience. While identifying the prose lines in the footnotes, references to their abutting verse numbers are given. For example, Act II, 10-11 means that the relevant passage occurs in between verses 10 and 11 in Act II.

I have extreme pleasure in expressing my deep gratitude to Prof Satyavrat Shastri, the scholar par excellence, who agreed to write a Foreword to this volume. In spite of his very busy schedule and indifferent health he spared his valuable time for this purpose, just out of love for me. I was not fortunate enough to have been either his student or his colleague but he condescended to my request readily. I fondly remember the hospitality extended to me by Prof Shastri and Dr Usha when I visited them a few months ago.

I am deeply indebted to Dr M. Narasimhachary, former Head of the Department of Vaishnavism, University of Madras, who has been my mentor all along. He was my guide for my PhD way back in the 1970s and he continues to be a lifelong guiding spirit for me. Scholars of his stature are generally inaccessible but Dr Acharya is an exception. He goes all out to help his students. Simplicity is his forte. I cannot forget the five years we spent together as colleagues in the Sanskrit Department of Vivekananda College. We used to be called as inseparables. I cherish my association with him.

I place on record my heartfelt thanks to Prof J.L. Brockington who wrote the Foreword for my *prahasana* thesis when it was printed. I could send him only the incomplete proof of the work at that time, but he was kind enough to go through it and provide the Foreword. When I apologized for the shortcoming he wrote back saying that he was only concerned about the quality of the work and not the peripherals. That speaks very high of him.

I had the pleasure of studying under Dr K. Kunjunni Raja at the University of Madras when I was doing M.A. He was the Head of the Department when I submitted my thesis. He introduced me to his colleagues saying "Ramaratnam has written his thesis very well, he is sure to get his PhD". He wrote a few lines in appreciation of the work when it was printed. I somehow did not get the opportunity to study under Dr V. Raghavan, but I have immensely benefited from his scholarly writings.

I also remember with profound gratitude the help, support and encouragement extended by scholars like Dr N. Veezhinathan, former Professor and Head of the Department of Sanskrit, University of Madras, Dr S.S. Janaki, former Director of Kuppuswami Shastri Research Institute, Dr Venkateswaran, former Professor of Sanskrit, Annamalai University, Dr V. Varadachari, former Director of French Institute of Indology, Pondicherry, and Prof M.D. Vasantaraj, Professor of Sanskrit and Prakrit, University of Mysore (who helped me with his Prakrit). I remember with devotion, Prof Kalyanasundara Shastrigal, Prof V. Rajagopalan and Prof S. Viswanathan, my beloved teachers in Vivekananda College.

My sincere thanks are also due to the following government organizations/institutions for helping me to carry out the *prahasana* project successfully.

i. University Grants Commission, Govt. of India, New Delhi.
ii. Higher Education Department, Government of Tamil Nadu.
iii. Ramakrishna Mission Vivekananda College, Chennai.
iv. University of Madras.

I am thankful to the UGC again for selecting me as Emeritus Professor for the period 2005-07. My thanks are due to the authorities of Rajah's College of Sanskrit and Tamil Studies, Tiruvaiyaru, for having given me an opportunity to work under the scheme in the Post-graduate and Research Department of Sanskrit of their institution. I am particularly thankful to Dr T.N. Aravamudhan, my former student and currently the principal of the college for having persuaded me to apply for the scheme and for having provided me with all the facilities during the tenure of the project.

I thank the members of my family for their constant encouragement and support in all my academic activities.

I shall be failing in my duty if I do not thank two important people who are involved in the publication of my books.

The first one is Shri Murthy who was the proprietor of Kavyalaya Publishers, Mysore, and who brought out my *prahasana* book in 1987. The second is Susheel Mittal, the Director of D.K. Printworld, Delhi. The latter is one of the leading International publishers of Indological books. Susheel Mittal is doing a great service to the cause of Oriental Studies by bringing out quality books in Sanskrit and Indology from time to time. He brought out my *Management Mantras* in 2010. I am grateful to him for bringing out the present volume as well.

Last but not the least, I submit my obeisance at the lotus feet of my *iṣṭa devatā* Lord Kṛṣṇa whose loving grace keeps me in good stead. My humble *praṇāma*s are due to my *guru*s, Jagadguru Kripaluji Maharaj and Swami Mukundanandaji.

Chennai, 12 December 2012 **Ramaratnam**

Contents

Views of Scholars*

It gives me great pleasure to provide a Foreword to Ramaratnam's study of *Prahasana in Sanskrit Literature.* Having first learnt at the end of 1980 that he was engaged in research on this topic, I am naturally delighted now to see the finished results, which amount to a major contribution to our appreciation of Sanskrit literature. The genre of *prahasana* (farce), has been relatively neglected by scholars, despite having remained, as Dr Ramaratnam so ably shows, much more of a living form than most types of dramatic presentation; this is no doubt due to the *prahasana*'s broad popular appeal.

Dr Ramaratnam first provides us with the necessary background through a concise survey of the origin and types of Sanskrit drama in his first chapter and a study of the *rasa* theory, in particular, the *hāsya rasa,* in his second chapter. He shows himself throughout to be well acquainted with the Sanskrit theoreticians, as well as with the views of modern scholars, all of which he discusses in a succinct and lucid fashion. With his third chapter on the theory and practice of the *prahasana,* he provides us with an excellent overview of the genre as a whole, before surveying in the next two substantial chapters the extant examples. These two chapters then divide the extant *prahasana*s into two types, *śuddha* and *saṁkīrṇa,* propounded by Bharata in the *Nāṭyaśāstra* and very broadly corresponding to their chronological production. He shows a proper caution in assigning the earliest example, the

* Extract from *Prahasana in Sanskrit Literature* by the present author, published by Kavyalaya Publishers, Mysore, 1987.

Bhagavadajjukīya, to the sixth century CE, a much more plausible date than that implied by Warder, who appears to date it in the third century CE (*Indian Kavya Literature*, vol. 2 1974, p. 335). This and Mahendravarman's *Mattavilāsa-prahasana* are justly famous for their literary qualities, as well as being important social documents. Dr Ramaratnam's excellent summaries of all the plays, together with the further analysis of various features of the *śuddha* examples and the better known among the *saṁkīrṇa* type, enable us to get a real flavour of their style and subject matter. He has put us all in his debt particularly by providing such summaries of even the minor *saṁkīrṇa* specimens, many of which are available only in manuscript; the perseverance and industry needed to track down and read all these in their various locations is most commendable.

To complete the picture, he has also furnished us, in two appendices with a list of *prahasanas* that are no longer available and a select bibliography of the twentieth-century examples, when the genre has enjoyed something of a renaissance after falling, as Dr Ramaratnam demonstrates, into a rather sorry state in the previous period. I personally am pleased to see that the latter includes one of the many productions for the stage of the late Prof V. Raghavan, the most eminent of Madras Sanskritists, whose acquaintance I was privileged to make through our common interest in the *Rāmāyaṇa*. The enthusiasm and scholarly concern for the Sanskrit dramatic tradition flourishing in Madras through his efforts, including the establishment of the Saṁskṛta Raṅga, has found another worthy proponent in the person of Dr S. Ramaratnam on the evidence of this volume. I am pleased to have been given the opportunity of commending it to the readers and congratulate him on its production.

Edinburgh, September 1987 **J.L. Brockington**

(Former Head of the Department of Sanskrit
University of Edinburgh)

I have great pleasure in introducing the comprehensive and thorough study on *Prahasana in Sanskrit Literature* by Prof S. Ramaratnam, Head of the Department of Sanskrit, Vivekananda College, Madras, to the world of Sanskrit scholars. Substantially, it forms his doctoral thesis prepared during 1975-79, under the direction of Prof M. Narasimhachary in the Department of Sanskrit, University of Madras.

. . . Regarding *lāsyāṅga*s — ten in number, performed by female dancers and suited to *śṛṅgāra* — and their role in the *prahasana*s, there is some difference of opinion among scholars. The *Daśarūpaka* associates the *lāsyāṅga*s with the *bhāṇa*, and its commentator Dhanika says that the *prahasana* too has the *lāsyāṅga*s. Dr Raghavan rejected this view, and stated that the *lāsyāṅga*s have no place in *bhāṇa* and *prahasana* where *hāsya* is the main sentiment. Dr Ramaratnam disagrees with this view and says that though *prahasana* has *hāsya* as the predominant sentiment, still it has some scope for *śṛṅgāra* and the *lāsyāṅga*s as is clear in the *Bhagavadajjukīya*.

The available *prahasana*s have been described in detail under two headings with full documentation. The appendix gives a "List of Non-available Prahasanas", "Select Bibliography of the Twentieth Century Prahasanas", "Prahasanas in Other Indian Languages" and "The Farce in English Literature".

I am sure that this book will be favourably received by all lovers of Sanskrit and Indian theatre.

Madras, September 1987 **(Late) K. Kunjunni Raja**

(Former Professor and Head of the Department of Sanskrit University of Madras)

The *prahasana*, recognized as a play-form right from Bharata's times, has a rich literature. Full-fledged works, however, appear from the fifth or sixth century CE of which the *Bhagavadajjukīya* and *Mattavilāsaprahasana* deserve special mention. The *prahasana* was used as an important medium to expose the weakness of the contemporary society. Though the earlier and the medieval *prahasana*s carried out this task with commendable decency and dignity, some later *prahasana*s degraded themselves by indulging in objectionable vulgarity, meaningless repetition and lack-lustre presentation. In the twentieth century this trend has been reversed, thanks to the prevailing sense of human dignity and literary aesthetics.

All along, scholars have been content to treat the *prahasana*s in a general manner and no serious attempt seems to have been made to present a cogent and complete account of all the available *prahasana*s in Sanskrit. The long-felt desideratum has been filled up by Dr Ramaratnam, in this all-encompassing study under my guidance, which won him the Doctorate Degree from the University of Madras in 1979.

Apart from the printed *prahasana*s, Dr Ramaratnam has collected and studied more than twenty unpublished manuscripts; the problem of the *prahasana* has been studied by him in theory and practice, which lends the study, a harmonious blend of precision and completeness. A detailed analysis of the sentiment of *hāsya,* the *prahasana*-elements, the *vīthyaṅga*s and their application have been carried out by the author with clarity of thought and lucidity of expression backed by an amazing mastery in the subject. The painstaking thoroughness with which each and every *prahasana* has been studied is quite commendable. The author has also included in the appendix useful material on the modern *prahasana*s in Sanskrit and a few Indian vernaculars.

The present study is certainly a mine of information for both students and teachers interested in the study, growth and development of Sanskrit plays in general, and those of *prahasana*s in particular. The study also forms a model for similar studies by aspiring scholars in future.

Madras, September 1987 **M. Narasimhachary**

(Former Reader, Department of Sanskrit,
and Former Professor and Head of the Department of Vaishnavism,
University of Madras)

Abbreviations

AB	*Ātmabodha*
Abhi.	*Abhinavabhāratī*
ABORI	*Annals of Bhandarkar Oriental Research Institute*
AIOC	All India Oriental Conference
Aufrecht	Aufrecht's *Catalogue Catalogorum*
AV	*Atharvaveda*
Ava	*Avaloka*
BA	*Bhagavadajjukīya*
Bāl	*Bālarāmāyaṇa*
BG	*Bhagavad-Gītā*
BORI	Bhandarkar Oriental Research Institute
BP	*Bhāvaprakāśana*
BṛUp.	*Bṛhadāraṇyaka Upaniṣad*
Capeller	Capeller's resume in *Gurupūjākaumudī*, Leipzig
CC	*Catalogus Catalogorum*
ChāUp.	*Chāndogya Upaniṣad*
CSS	Chowkhamba Sanskrit Series

Dhv	*Dhvanyāloka*
Din	*Dinmātrapradarśinī*
DR	*Daśarūpaka*
GOS	Gaekwad Oriental Series
Hall	Hall's edition of *Daśarūpaka*
Hā.Cū.	*Hāsyacūḍāmaṇi*
HCSL	*History of Classical Sanskrit Literature*
IOL	India Office Library, London
Insc.	Inscription
JBORS	*Journal of Bihar and Orissa Research Society*
JBRS	*Journal of Bihar Research Society*
JOR	*Journal of Oriental Research*, Madras
Kām	*Kāmasūtra*
Kar	*Karpūramañjarī*
KaṭhUp.	*Kaṭhopaniṣad*
KauṣUp.	*Kauṣītaki Upaniṣad*
KD	*Kāvyādarśa*
Keith	A.B. Keith's *Sanskrit Drama*
KM	Kāvyamālā series
Konow	Konow's *Indian Drama*
KP	*Kāvyaprakāśa*
KS	*Kāvyānuśāsana*
Ku	*Kumārasambhava*
Māl	*Mālavikāgnimitra*

Man.	*Manusmṛti*
MB	*Mahābhāṣya*
Mbh	*Mahābhārata*
MKC	*Madanaketucarita*
Mṛc.	*Mṛcchakaṭika*
MuṇḍUp.	*Muṇḍakopaniṣad*
MV	*Mattavilāsaprahasana*
NC	*Nāṭakacandrikā*
NCC	*New Catalogus Catalogorum*
ND	*Nāṭyadarpaṇa*
NLRK	*Nāṭakalakṣaṇa Ratnakośa*
NŚ	*Nāṭyaśāstra*
NS Press	Nirnaya Sagar Press
Pāda	*Pādatāḍitaka*
Pāṇḍ	*Pāṇḍavānanda*
PR	*Pratāparudrīya*
Prabh	*Prabodha Candrodaya*
Pras.	*Prasannarāghava*
Raghu	*Raghuvaṁśa*
RASB	Royal Asiatic Society of Bengal
Rat	*Ratnāvalī*
RC	*Raghuvīracarita*
RG	*Rasagaṅgādhara*
RS	*Rasārṇavasudhākara*

Śāk.	*Abhijñāna Śākuntala*
ŚB	*Śatapatha Brāhmaṇa*
Schuyler	Schuyler's *Bibliography of Sanskrit Drama*
SD	*Sāhityadarpaṇa*
Śṛ.Pra.	*Śṛṅgāraprakāśa*
Subhā	*Subhāṣitāvalī*
S*ūk*	*Sūktimuktāvalī*
TB	*Tāṇḍya Brāhmaṇa*
TSS	Trivandrum Sanskrit Series
URC	*Uttara Rāmacarita*

1

Sanskrit Dramaturgy

Introduction

MAN derives pleasure in reviewing and visualising his own mental states in different situations of life. He does not stop with that. He tries to give expression to those states through different means like language, gesticulations and symbolic representation, which emerge as poetry, dance, painting and sculpture. Drama is one such expression of human mind.[1]

Drama is evidently the most popular form of literature in any language. The popularity of the drama can be gauged from such expressions as, "नाटकान्तं हि साहित्यम्", "काव्यस्यान्तं हि नाटकम्" and "काव्येषु नाटकं रम्यम्". The reason for this is that drama is the only art which combines poetry, music and dance and appeals to the ear and the eye simultaneously. It depicts different situations of human life and gives expression to the hopes, emotions and conduct of men.[2] When different aspects of human nature with its joys and sorrows are reproduced on the stage through gestures, words, costumes and the like, it is called drama.[3]

---

1. नाट्यम् भावानुकीर्तनम् — *Nāṭyaśāstra* (*NŚ*), ch. I, śl. 106, ed. Ghosh.
2. Ibid., śl. 111, नानाभावोपपन्नं नानावस्थान्तरात्मकम् ।
   लोकवृत्तानुकरणं . . . ॥
3. Ibid., śl. 121, कृतानुकरणं लोके नाट्यमित्यभिधीयते ।
   योऽयं स्वभावो लोकस्य सुखदुःखसमन्वितः ॥

There is nothing that is not found in a drama — worldly knowledge, fine arts, different activities — in fact, everything concerning human life finds a place in it.

न तज्ज्ञानं न तच्छिल्पं न सा विद्या न सा कला।
न स योगो न तत् कर्म नाट्येऽस्मिन् यन्न दृश्यते ॥[4]

क्वचिद्धर्मः क्वचित्क्रीडा क्वचिदर्थः क्वचिच्छमः।
क्वचिद्धास्यं क्वचित् युद्धं क्वचित् कामः क्वचिद्वधः ॥[5]

Drama is an education in itself, since it shows why the actions of the noble are to be emulated and those of the wicked are to be avoided. It upholds the moral codes and confers courage, amusement and happiness.

hitopadeśajananaṁ dhṛtikriḍāsukhādikṛt ॥[6]

It imparts a sense of duty to those who are against it, carries instructions on love for those who are eager for its fulfilment, chastises the ill-bred or unruly; promotes self-restraint in those who are disciplined, gives courage to the cowardly and energy to the heroic. It enlightens men of poor intellect and gives wisdom to the learned.[7] This is what Kālidāsa has beautifully summarised as

nāṭyaṁ bhinnarucer-janasya bahudhāpyekaṁ samārādhanam.[8]

Origin of Sanskrit Drama

It is well known that tradition assigns a mythological origin for Sanskrit drama. The *Ṛk*, *Yajus*, *Sāma* and *Atharvaveda* contributed dialogues, gestures, music and sentiment to the

4. *Nāṭyaśāstra* (*NŚ*), ch. I, śl. 116.
5. Ibid., śl. 107.
6. Ibid., śl. 112.
7. Ibid., śls. 108-9.
8. *Mālavikāgnimitra*, I. 4.

drama. Lord Śiva and his consort Pārvatī originated the Tāṇḍava and Lāsya types of dances while Lord Viṣṇu evolved the four dramatic styles *Kaiśikī, Ārabhaṭī, Bhāratī* and *Sātvatī*. Other gods contributed many other dramatic artifices. Sage Bharata was entrusted with the stage direction.[9]

With all its mythical colouring, the traditional theory cannot be brushed aside as totally unacceptable. It points to the fact that music and dance formed an integral part of early Sanskrit drama. The Saṁvāda-Sūktas[10] of the *Ṛgveda* reveal traces of dramatic element. The musical style of the *Sāmaveda* recitations is quite significant. The epics with their vast treasure of interesting stories might have given a new impetus to the dramatic traditions in India. Though references to drama and dramatic traditions are found in the *Aṣṭādhyāyī* of Pāṇini[11] and the *Mahābhāṣya* of Patañjali[12] Sanskrit drama did not take its full shape until about Bhāsa's time (second century BCE). We do not have any specimen of Sanskrit drama prior to Bhāsa's time, preserved.

The rather late evolution of Sanskrit drama has led many Western scholars[13] to believe that it was influenced by the Greek drama after Alexander's invasion of India. The word *yavanikā* (the curtain used in Sanskrit dramas) according to them, is derived from "Yavana", which means the Greeks. They further argue that Yavana girls were employed as servant-maids at the courts of Indian kings. Moreover, there

9. *NŚ*, ch. I, śls. 41-46.

10. I.165, 170, 179; III.33; IV.18; VII.33; VIII.100; X.11, 28, 51, 53, 86, 95, 108.

11. *Aṣṭādhyāyī*, 4.3.110.

12. *Mahābhāṣya*, 3.1.26.

13. Prof. Windish and Prof. Weber, for instance, see Keith, *Sanskrit Drama*, p. 57.

are certain structural similarities between Sanskrit drama and the Greek drama. But this theory is untenable because the points of contrast are far too many. Two of the main aspects of the Greek drama, viz. the Tragedy and the three Unities (of Time, Place and Action) are absent in Sanskrit drama.

According to Sten Konow,

> Sanskrit drama came into existence as a result of coalescence of two elements, viz. on the one side, the recitation of the epic legends, and in the other, the display of the shadow images concomitantly with the manifestations of the features of the mimic art.[14]

Konow's theory presupposes the existence of the popular stage where pantomimic shows and shadow plays were in vogue. The three terms connected with Sanskrit drama, *naṭa* (actor), *nāṭaka* (drama) and *nāṭya* (dance) — all proceed from the same root, *nṛt*, to dance, and dancing is the most important function of the pantomime. The stage director of the Sanskrit drama is called *sūtradhāra* (holder of the strings) which again supports the theory that Sanskrit drama had an indigenous origin. Similarly the tradition of the shadow play is also very old. Chāyānāṭaka has been mentioned even in the *Mahābhārata*.[15] In ancient India, the recitation of the epics before the spectators used to be accompanied by the depiction of the relevant stories through shadow images.[16] The general term referring to Sanskrit drama, *rūpaka*, is connected to *rūpa* which indicates the display of figures in a shadow play.[17]

---

14. *Indian Drama*, Preface, p. iii, pp. 74-75.

15. Cf. ibid.

16. Ibid., pp. 69ff.

17. Ibid., pp. 71ff.

Konow's theory has been criticised by Prof. Keith in his *Sanskrit Drama*.[18] According to Keith, there does not occur any authentic information regarding the performance of the mimes prior to the origin of Sanskrit drama.[19] Keith also observes that the term *chāyānāṭaka* does not refer to the shadow play. It only refers to the play within the play. The origin of *rūpaka* from *rūpa* is also untenable since *rūpa* just refers to a visible performance and not particularly to the shadow play.[20] According to Keith, the recitation of the epic stories provided the necessary base for Sanskrit drama. The dramatic action has an independent origin from the religious contests and only the union of these two produced the drama.[21] I. Shekar opines on the basis of the findings at Mohenjo-Daṛo and Haṛappā[22] that the Sanskrit drama owes its origin to the native Indian tradition of the Dravidians.

The hoary tradition of the Sanskrit drama, however, renders it difficult to put forward any conclusive evidence with regard to its origin. As for the mimic plays, which according to Keith, could not have existed in ancient India, it has to be kept in mind that this art is still preserved in our country in some form or other. It is quite probable that what we have now is only a legacy left by the ancient form of this particular art. It may be difficult to adduce literary proofs for all that is obtained now. But absence of such proofs cannot lead to an outright negation or denial of this possibility. It therefore appears reasonable that there is truth in some of the theories put forth by scholars, since drama, after all, combines

18. See *Sanskrit Drama*, p. 25.

19. Ibid., p. 49.

20. Ibid., p. 54.

21. Ibid., p. 73.

22. See, I. Shekar, *Sanskrit Drama: Its Origin and Decline*, ch. I.

in itself elements from different sources. Thus the dialogue portion would have been inspired by the "Saṁvāda-Sūktas" of the *Ṛgveda*; epic stories could have provided the necessary base; religious contests could have been responsible for the action part of drama. The mimic art, shadow play, etc. would also have contributed their own mite for the overall development of the Sanskrit drama.

Side by side with the dramas, there arose a well-defined system of dramaturgy in Sanskrit literature. It was a two-way process — dramatists observing rules of dramaturgy provided by earlier writers on dramaturgy and the latter, framing rules on the basis of the available plays.

Types of Sanskrit Drama

Sanskrit drama is referred to by the general term, *rūpaka*.[23] There are ten kinds of *rūpaka*s — Nāṭaka, Prakaraṇa, Bhāṇa, Prahasana, Ḍima, Vyāyoga, Samavakāra, Vīthī, Aṅka and Īhāmṛga. The Nāṭaka and the Prakaraṇa are the most perfected and more popular of all these forms. The characteristic features of the *rūpaka*s have been dealt with elaborately in the works on dramaturgy. We shall, however, present below some of the most important features of these, for the purpose of a full and cogent account of the subject on hand.

NĀṬAKA

The plot in a *nāṭaka* is chiefly drawn from a well-known episode (*prakhyāta*).[24] It has all the five *sandhi*s (junctures) and the main sentiment in it shall be *śṛṅgāra* or *vīra*.[25] It may have acts ranging

23. *rūpakam tat samāropāt* — It is called "representation" (*rūpaka*) because of the assumption of roles by actors, *Daśarūpaka*, I.9.

24. *NŚ*, XVIII.10 Edn. NS-KM; *DR*, III.21, Edn. Hall; *SD*, VI.7. edn. NS Press.

25. *DR*, III.30; *SD*, VI.10.

from five to ten.[26] The hero shall be a noble character[27] belonging to one of the four types — *dhīrodātta, dhīroddhata, dhīralalita* and *dhīraśānta*.[28] A *nāṭaka* shall have as its end one of the first three *puruṣārthas* — *dharma, artha* or *kāma*.[29] All the four *vṛttis* (styles of expression), *kaiśikī, ārabhaṭī, bhāratī* and *sātvatī* shall be employed in it.[30]

Model Plays: *Abhijñānaśākuntala* and *Veṇīsaṁhāra*.

PRAKARAṆA[31]

The Prakaraṇa has a social theme which is invented by the poet himself (*utpādya*). Like Nāṭaka the Prakaraṇa too has all the five *sandhis*. It has acts ranging from five to ten, has all the five *vṛttis* and may have *śṛṅgāra* as its main sentiment. The hero should be a minister, a brāhmaṇa or a merchant adhering to *dharma*. The heroine is either a woman from a noble family or a harlot. Slaves, *viṭas* and *śreṣṭhins* play a significant role in a Prakaraṇa.

Model Play: *Mṛcchakaṭika*.

BHĀṆA[32]

Bhāṇa again has an invented theme. It has only the *mukha* and the *nirvahaṇa sandhis*. *Kaiśikī* and *ārabhaṭī vṛttis* are prohibited in it. The main sentiment is *śṛṅgāra* with *hāsya* ranking next. The peculiarity of Bhāṇa is that it is purely a monologue play

---

26. *NŚ*, XVIII.105 ff; *DR*, III.34; *SD*, VI.8.
27. *NŚ*, XVIII.11.
28. *SD*, VI.9.
29. *NŚ*, XVIII.11.
30. Ibid., XVIII.4.
31. *NŚ*, XVIII.98.100; *DR*, III.35.36; *SD*, VI.224.26.
32. *NŚ*, XVIII.159ff; *DR*, III.44.46; *SD*, VI.227ff.

enacted by a single actor, a *viṭa*. The dramatic device known as *ākāśabhāṣita* is employed in the narrative.

Model Plays: The *Caturbhāṇī-Padmaprābhṛtaka, Pādatāḍitaka, Dhūrtaviṭasaṁvāda* and *Ubhayābisārikā*.

PRAHASANA[33]

The Prahasana (farce) too has an *utpādya* theme. It generally derides the evils of the society. It follows the Bhāṇa with respect to the *sandhis* and the *vṛttis*. *Hāsya* is the predominant sentiment in it. The *Nāṭyaśāstra* speaks of two varieties — the *śuddha* and the *saṁkīrṇa*. *Daśarūpaka* adds one more variety, namely, the *vikṛta*. The difference between these is mainly based on the nature of the characters employed. Ascetics, brāhmaṇas and others appear in the *śuddha* variety while the *saṁkīrṇa* has eunuchs, parasites and rogues. The *vikṛta* has a free mix-up of these characters and has the Vīthyaṅgas.

Model Plays: *Bhagavadajjukīya* and *Laṭakamelaka*.

ḌIMA[34]

The Ḍima has a *prakhyāta* theme. It may have four acts. *Ārabhaṭī* and *sātvatī* are extensively employed. *Vimarśa sandhi* is generally avoided. *Raudra* is the predominant sentiment; *śṛṅgāra* and *hāsya* are prohibited. Gods, *gandharvas*, *rākṣasas* and the like figure in a Ḍima. Natural calamities, violent fights, witchcraft and the like may also find place here.

Model Play: *Tripuravijaya* of Vatsarāja.

VYĀYOGA[35]

Vyāyoga too derives its plot from a known source (*prakhyāta*).

---

33. *NŚ*, XVIII.153ff; *DR*, III.49ff, *SD*, VI.264ff.
34. *NŚ*, XVIII.135ff; *DR*, III.51ff; *SD*, VI.241ff.
35. *NŚ*, XVIII.141ff; *DR*, III.54.55; *SD*, VI.231ff.

The incidents described in it should not extend beyond the span of a single day. There will be no women characters in it. Battles and boastings of the warriors form its main theme. *Kaiśikī vṛtti*, the *garbha* and *vimarśa sandhi*s and *śṛṅgāra* and *hāsya rasa*s are to be avoided in it.

Model Play: *Madhyamavyāyoga* of Bhāsa.

SAMAVAKĀRA[36]

The Samavakāra again derives its theme from a *prakhyāta* source. Battle scenes form the subject matter and gods and demons figure in it. *Vīra* and *raudra* shall be the main sentiments. It may have three acts. *Vimarśa sandhi* and the *kaiśikī vṛtti* are to be excluded.

Model Play: *Samudramanthana* of Vatsarāja.

VĪTHĪ[37]

The Vīthī has an *utpādya* theme and is an one-act play. Only two or three characters appear in it. *Śṛṅgāra* shall be the main sentiment. *Mukha* and *nirvahaṇa sandhi*s alone are to be employed. *Ākāśabhāṣita* may be introduced.

Model Play: *Līlāvatīvīthī* of Rāmapāṇivāda.

AṄKA[38]

The theme of an Aṅka may either be *prakhyāta* or *utpādya*, dealing with the death of a hero and the lamentations of women. *Bhāratī vṛtti* shall be mainly employed. Only *mukha* and *nirvahaṇa sandhi*s occur in it. The chief sentiment in it is *karuṇa*.

Model Play: *Ūrūbhaṅga* of Bhāsa.

---

36. *NŚ*, XVIII.114ff; *DR*, III.56ff; SD, VI.234ff.

37. *NŚ*, XVIII.163ff; *DR*, III.62ff; *SD*, VI.253ff.

38. *NŚ*, XVIII.145ff; *DR*, III.64ff; *SD*, VI.250ff.

ĪHĀMṚGA[39]

The theme of Īhāmṛga is partly *prakhyāta* and partly *utpādya*. This play form is so called because its hero longs for a maiden who is difficult to be obtained like a gazelle. *Kaiśikī vṛtti* is to be avoided. Only *mukha, pratimukha* and *nirvahaṇa sandhi*s occur in it. It may have four acts.

Model Play: *Rukmiṇīharaṇa* of Vatsarāja.

Apart from these major varieties, there are minor dramatic pieces known as the *uparūpaka*s.[40] The *nāṭikā* (e.g. the *Ratnāvalī*) and the *saṭṭaka* (e.g. the *Karpūramañjarī*) are the popular play forms among the *uparūpaka*s.

Different features of the drama like the *nāndī*, the *prastāvanā*, *viṣkambhaka*, and *praveśaka*, the types of the hero and the heroine, nature of the theme, the five *sandhi*s, etc. have been discussed elaborately in books on Sanskrit drama and dramaturgy[41] and hence they are not taken up for a detailed analysis but a brief account of them is given here for the sake of general readers.

Every play is expected to begin with one or more benedictory stanzas called *nāndī*. At the end of *nāndī*, the stage manager (*sūtradhāra*) enters the stage along with one of the actresses or the jester of the play to discuss about the nature of the play. This part of the play is called *prastāvanā* (prelude). Some details about the author, the occasion on which the play is staged and certain other preliminary details are given during the conversation. At the end of the prelude, enters the main

39. *NŚ*, XVIII.129ff; *DR*, III.66ff; *SD*, VI.246ff.

40. On *uparūpakas*, see article by V. Raghavan, *Saṁskṛta Raṅga Annual*, no. V.

41. See, for instance, *Sanskrit Drama* by Keith, and *Laws and Practice of Sanskrit Drama* by S.N. Sarma.

character following a veiled remark about him, and the play properly begins. The connection between one act and another is maintained by means of interludes called *praveśaka* or *viṣkambhaka* (there is not much of difference between excepting the nature of the characters employed). Sometimes there will be announcements behind the curtain and this device is called *cūlikā*. There are two other devices; one is called *aṅkāsya* which is an actual indication of the succeeding event by the last outgoing character, the other one being *aṅkāvatāra* where an unbroken continuity is maintained. The plot of the drama is carried on through five different stages of development which are called the *sandhis*; they are *mukha sandhi, pratimukha sandhi, garbha sandhi, avamarśa sandhi* and *nirvahaṇa sandhi*. The play ends with a benedictory stanza called *bharata-vākya*.

The most important and abiding factor in a *rūpaka* is, of course, *rasa* or the sentiment. The main sentiment of the play form called the *Prahasana*, now taken up for a detailed study, is *hāsya* (comic). A detailed account of the nature of *hāsya*, its subdivisions, its relation to the other *rasa*s and allied topics are dealt with in the next chapter. A brief survey of the *rasa* theory is also given at the beginning of chapter 2 with a view to placing *hāsya* in its proper setting.

2

Theory of Rasa: Hāsya Rasa

The Rasa

THE word *rasa* primarily means "taste" or "flavour" but metaphorically it means "the emotional experience of beauty in poetry and drama".[1] Poetry and drama carry an emotional appeal to the connoisseur's mind. We witness a drama and enjoy it because it frees us from all worldly worries and distractions. It also arouses our dormant pleasurable instincts (*bhāva*s), which, when enjoyed, give us unalloyed pleasure and this is known as *rasāsvāda*. The purpose of poetry and drama is to evolve this *rasa* and hence *rasa* is considered to be their soul. But for *rasa*, there is nothing worthwhile in a literary work.[2] The principal *rasa* runs like a connnecting thread in a drama.[3] The theory of evolution of *rasa* has been dealt with at length by a number of *ālaṁkārika*s starting from Bharata.

There are what are known as *sthāyī bhāva*s (permanent mental conditions, e.g. *rati* and *hāsa*) in our mind. These are aroused by certain "causes" called *vibhāva*s like the hero and the heroine (*ālaṁbana vibhāva*) and the stimulant factors like the seasons, moon and surroundings (*uddīpana vibhāva*). There

1. See P.V. Kane, *History of Sanskrit Poetics*, p. 356.
2. *NŚ*, GOS edn., vol. I, p. 274. *na hi rasādṛte kaścidarthaḥ pravartate.*
3. *Abhinavabhāratī*, vol. I, p. 273:
एक एव तावत् परमार्थतो रसः सूत्रस्थानीयत्वेन रूपके प्रतिभाति।

are again external expression of the inner feeling called the *anubhāvas*, such as the roving side glances, smile and the like. There are also transitory mental conditions called *vyabhicāri* (*sañcāri*) *bhāvas*, like despair, fatigue and anxiety. All these mingle together to evoke a particular *rasa*.

विभाव-अनुभाव-व्यभिचारि-संयोगाद् रसनिष्पत्तिः ।[4]

This seemingly simple *Rasasūtra* of Bharata has been variously interpreted by different schools of criticism, the most important of them being the "Rasotpattivāda" of Bhaṭṭa Lollaṭa, the "Rasānumitivāda" of Śrīśaṅkuka, the "Rasabhukti-vāda" of Bhaṭṭanāyaka and the "Rasābhivyaktivāda" of Abhinavagupta. Jagannātha Paṇḍita has summed up these theories and added the *navya* view also in his *Rasagaṅgādhara*.

According to Bhaṭṭa Lollaṭa, *rasa* is generated only in the original characters; the actors, by their clever gesticulations make the spectators feel, wrongly though, that they (actors) possess those emotions. This invalid cognition makes the spectators enjoy *rasa*. According to Bhaṭṭa Lollaṭa the word *saṁyoga* in Bharata's *sūtra* means "the relation between cause and effect", i.e. *utpādya-utpādaka-bhāva* and the word *niṣpatti* means *utpatti* or generation. But this theory is rejected on the ground that it goes against the general rule that the cause and the effect should co-exist in a single substratum (*sāmānādhikaraṇya*). In other words, if *rasa* exists in the original character or the actor, it cannot be pleasurable to the spectator.

Śrīśaṅkuka explains *rasa*-realisation through inferential knowledge (*anumāna*). On witnessing a drama, a spectator infers that the *rasas* of the original characters exist in the actors also and this inferential knowledge leads to pleasure. The word *saṁyoga* in Bharata's *Rasasūtra* means *anumāpya-anumāpaka-bhāva*,

4. *NŚ*, p. 274, GOS, edn., vol. I.

the relation between a thing that is inferred and the thing that forms that ground of the inference. The word *niṣpatti* should be interpreted as *anumiti* or inference. Śrīśaṅkuka's theory has the same defect as the previous one, namely lack of *sāmānādhikaraṇya* or co-ordination of cause and effect.

Bhaṭṭanāyaka who comes next, removes the anomalies of the two previous theories and expounds the theory of *rasabhukti*. Bhaṭṭanāyaka recognises three functions known as (i) *abhidhāyakatva-vyāpāra* (ii) *bhāvakatva-vyāpāra* and (iii) *bhojakatva-vyāpāra*. By the first *vyāpāra* the original characters are stripped of their individual traits and by the second, viz. the *bhāvakatva-vyāpāra*, they become universalised. Śakuntalā, for instance, is taken not as the consort of Duṣyanta but as a lovely young woman. This helps the spectator get rid of the feeling of *agamyatva* when he looks at Śakuntalā. Then by the *bhojakatva-vyāpāra*, the spectator forgets his own individual traits and enjoys the sentiment. In this process, the *rajas* and *tamas* constituents of his mind are overpowered by the *sattva* which is responsible for the happiness experienced by him. This final enjoyment of *rasa* of the spectator is impersonal in character and is different from *laukika ānanda* (ordinary pleasure). The word *saṁyoga* in the *Rasasūtra* is understood as *bhojyabhojaka bhāva*, "the relation between the enjoyer and a thing that is enjoyed" and the "universalisation" through *bhāvanā-vyāpāra*. The word *niṣpatti* here means *bhukti* or enjoyment.

Commenting on Bhaṭṭanāyaka's theory, Abhinavagupta points out that there is neither the need nor an authority for assuming two separate functions, viz. *bhāvakatva* and *bhojakatva*, for they are implicitly included in the idea of *rasavyañjanā* and its ultimate *āsvāda*. The so-called *bhāvakatva*, according to Abhinavagupta, consists in nothing more than a suitable use of *guṇa* and *alaṁkāra* for the ultimate purpose of awakening *rasa* through the suggestive power of word and sense. As there cannot be any process other than *rasapratīti* or realisation of *rasa, bhojakatva* becomes redundant and hence useless.

This *pratīti* of *rasa,* Abhinavagupta maintains, results from its *abhivyakti* or manifestation by the power of suggestion and consists of a state of relish known as *vāsanā, āsvāda* or *carvaṇa.* According to him everybody has in his heart permanently, the *vāsanā*s or latent impressions of the *sthāyī bhāva*s (permanent moods). On witnessing a drama, this *sthāyī* is aroused by the *vibhāva*s, etc., which are taken in their general form without specific connections. The *vibhāva*s, therefore, are generalised not by *bhāvakatva-vyāpāra* as Bhaṭṭanāyaka supposed, but generally through the suggestive power of sound and sense, and specifically through a skilful use of *guṇa* and *alaṁkāra* in poetry and clever representation in drama. In the same way, the *sthāyī bhāva* which is the source of *rasa,* is also generalised because the germ in it is already existent in the mind of the *sahṛdaya* in the form of latent impression. This together with the beauty of the generalised representation of the *vibhāva*s etc. removes all temporal and spatial limitations and leads to the enjoyment of *rasa.* Abhinavagupta interprets the work *saṁyoga* in Bharata's *Rasasūtra* as *vyaṅgya-vyañjaka bhāva,* the relation between a revealer and the revealed. The word *niṣpatti* should be interpreted as *vyakti,* suggestion or revelation.[5]

In the realisation of *rasa,* there is complete absorption (*cittaniṣpandatā*) for the *sahṛdaya,* a condition of bliss and in which there is complete cessation from all activities. This negative aspect of bliss in *rasa*-realisation has been modified by later *ālaṁkārika*s like Jagannātha. The soul, according to the Vedāntins, is of the form of eternal consciousness and supreme bliss. To the soul are presented, in the course of *rasa*-realisation,

5. See S.K. De, *History of Sanskrit Poetics,* vol. II, pp. 133-34.

the mental impressions in their intensified and generalised *alaukika* form. And then the veil or *āvaraṇa* of *avidyā* is lifted up and the blissful *Ātman* is realised along with *sthāyī bhāva*. Just as a light, when cleared of its cover, reveals itself and the objects nearby, so also the effulgent *Ātman*, when its veil of *avidyā* is removed reveals itself and the *sthāyī bhāva*s along with their *vibhāva*s, etc. Hence *rasa* is nothing but the *sthāyībhāva* illumined by the inner *caitanya* when it is freed from its *āvaraṇa*.[6]

We shall now take up for discussion, *hāsya rasa*, the comic sentiment.

Hāsya Rasa

The comic sentiment has as its *sthāyī bhāva*, *hāsa* (laughter). The *vibhāva*s that evoke *hāsa* are unseemly dress and ornaments, impudence, greediness, quarrel, deformity, use of irrelevant words, fault-finding nature and the like, noticed in others.

अथ हास्यो नाम हासस्थायिभावात्मकः। स च विकृतपरवेषालङ्कार-धार्ष्ट्यलौल्य-कुहक-असत्प्रलाप-व्यङ्ग्यदर्शनदोषोदाहरणादिभिः विभावैः उत्पाद्यते ॥[7]

Hāsya is to be represented on this stage by *anubhāva*s like throbbing of the lips, nose and cheeks, opening the eyes wide or contracting them, perspiration and holding both the sides, with hands.

तस्योष्ठनासाकपोलस्पन्दनदृष्टिव्याकोशाकुञ्चनस्वेदास्यरागपार्श्वं-ग्रहणादिभिः अनुभावैः अभिनयः प्रयोक्तव्यः।[8]

---

6. Vide V.A. Ramaswamy Śāstry, *Jagannātha Paṇḍita: A Study*, pp. 94-95.
7. *NŚ*, GOS, edn., vol. I, p. 312.
8. Ibid.

Its *vyabhicāri bhāvas* are indolence, dissimilation, drowsiness, sleep, dreaming, insomnia, envy and the like.

व्यभिचारिणश्चास्य अवहित्था-आलस्य-तन्द्रा-निद्रा- स्वप्नप्रबोध-असूयादयः ।[9]

Jagannātha has illustrated *hāsya* with the following verse:

> श्रीतातपादैर्निहिते निबन्धे निरूपिता नूतनयुक्तिरेषा ।
> अङ्गं गवां पूर्वमहो पवित्रं कथं न वा रासभधर्मपत्न्याः ॥[10]
>
> In the work composed by my revered father, the following new argument is introduced — The front part of the body of the cow is sacred. Why is that of a female ass not so?

Here the son of the logician is the *ālambana vibhāva*, his assertion without a tinge of doubt is *uddīpana vibhāva*, the showing of his teeth, etc. and his inquisitive nature, which we have to imagine, are the *anubhāva* and the *vyabhicāri bhāva* respectively. All these contribute to the delineation of *hāsya*.

According to Bharata, *hāsya* is of two kinds, *ātmastha* (self-centred) and *parastha* (centred in others). When a person himself laughs, it is *ātmastha*; but when he makes other laugh, it is *parastha*.

> द्विविधश्चायमात्मस्थः परस्थश्च । यदा स्वयं हसति तदा तु आत्मस्थः । यदा तु परं हासयति तदा परस्थः ॥[11]

The *sthāyī bhāvas* which develop into different *rasas* are directly related to the four *puruṣārthas*, viz. *dharma*, *artha*, *kāma* and *mokṣa*. For instance, *rati* is connected with *kāma*, *dharma* and *artha*; *krodha* with *artha*, *utsāha* with *kāma* and *dharma*, and *śama* with *dharma* and *mokṣa*. Laughter, etc. also contribute to the attainment of the *puruṣārthas*, by being accessories to the other

---

9. *NŚ*, GOS, edn., vol. I, p. 312.
10. *Rasagaṅgādhara*, p. 182 (Chowkhamba edn.), 1970.
11. *NŚ*, ch. VI, preceding *śl.* 54, Ghosh edn.

sthāyī bhāvas, viz. *rati, krodha, utsāha* and *śama*.[12] *Hāsa, śoka, bhaya* and the like are "common" *sthāyins* in the sense that they are found in abundance even in laymen. Even an unsophisticated person laughs, feels grief and experiences fear. Bharata says, *strī-nīcaprakṛtaveṣa bhūyiṣṭhaṁ dṛśyate rasaḥ*.[13]

Six Kinds of Laughter

Laughter is of six kinds according to Bharata.[14]

स्मितमथ हसितं विहसितमुपहसितं चापहसितमतिहसितम् ।
द्वौ द्वौ भेदौ स्यातामुत्तममध्यमाधमप्रकृतौ ॥

> *Smitam* (gentle smile) and *hasitam* (smile) belong to persons of superior type. *Vihasitam* (gentle laughter) and *upahasitam* (deriding laughter) belong to ordinary people. *Apahasitam* (indecent laughter) and *atihasitam* (reeling laughter) belong to the inferior type of people.

The *gentle* smile of people of the superior type is characterised by slightly blown cheeks and elegant glances. In it, the teeth are not visible. The *Rasārṇavasudhākara* gives illustrations for these six kinds of laughter.[15] The smile (*hasita*) should be distinguished by blooming eyes, face and cheeks and in it the teeth would be slightly visible. The "gentle laughter" (*vihasita*) produces some sweet sound and should be suitable to the occasion and in it eyes and cheeks would be contracted and face appears beaming. In the "deriding laughter" (*upahasita*) nose would be expanded, eyes would be quinting and the shoulder and head would be bent. *Apahasitam* is the laughter

---

12. See Har Dutt Sarma, "Hāsya as a Rasa in Sanskrit Rhetoric and Literature". *ABORI*, vol. XXII, 1941.
13. *NŚ*, ch. VI.
14. Ibid., *śls*. 54-59, Ghosh edn.
15. For details see *Rasārṇavasudhākara*, pp. 193 ff., TSS, edn.

produced on occasion not suited for it. It is marked by tears in the eyes or by the shoulder and the head violently shaking. "Reeling laughter" (*atihasita*) is that in which the eyes are expanded and tearful, sound is loud and excessive, and the sides are held by hands.

Hāsya may be subjected to another sixfold classification also, viz. (i) *ātmastha* of the *uttama* people; (ii) *ātmastha* of the *madhyama* people; (iii) *ātmastha* of the *adhama* people; (iv) *parastha* of the *uttama* people; (v) *parastha* of the *madhyama* people; and (vi) *parastha* of the *adhama* people.

We may recall here that according to Bharata, if one laughs for himself, it is *ātmastha* and if he makes others laugh it is called *parastha*. Abhinavagupta criticises this view. He says:

आत्मस्थैर्विभावैर्विकृतवेषादिभिः विदूषकः स्वयं हसति, स आत्मस्थः,
देवीं च हासयति इति तस्याः परस्थः, तदिदम् असत्।
एवं हि, विभावानां आत्मस्थत्वविभागः ... स्यात् , न हासस्य।[16]

If by *parastha* is meant the feature of making others experience the sentiment one has, then it is common for all the sentiments and it need not be a special trait of *hāsya* alone. For example, the master's grief is shared by his subordinates too. So the *ātmastha* and *parastha* distinction which is peculiar to *hāsya* alone, according to Bharata, is to be understood in a different way, says Abhinavagupta. If one laughs at oneself it is *ātmastha*. If one laughs due to some other extraneous reason, it is *parastha*. The following example will make this distinction clear.

आत्मस्थो यथा —
पाणौ कङ्कणमुत्फणः फणिपतिर्नेत्रं ज्वलत्पावकम्
कण्ठः कूष्टितकालकूटकुटिलो वस्त्रं गजेन्द्राजिनम्।

16. *Abhinavabhāratī*, GOS edn., vol. I, p. 312.

गौरीलोचनलोभनाय सुभगो वेषो वरस्यैष मे
गण्डोल्लासविभावितः पशुपतेर्हास्योद्गमः पातु वः ॥[17]

Here Lord Śiva, getting ready as bridegroom, looks at the incongruence of his dress and ornaments and laughs at Himself. This is an example of *ātmastha hāsya*.

परस्थो यथा —
कनककलशस्वच्छे राधापयोधरमण्डले
नवजलधरश्यामामात्मद्युतिं प्रतिबिम्बिताम् ।
असितसिचयप्रान्तभ्रान्त्या मुहुर्मुहुरुत्क्षिपन्
जयति जनितव्रीडाहासः प्रियाहसितो हरिः ॥[18]

This is an example of *parastha hāsya*, since here Rādhā experiences *hāsya*, looking at the confusion into which Kṛṣṇa is thrown.

Is Hāsya a Secondary Rasa?

Bharata considers the sentiments of *śṛṅgāra*, *raudra*, *vīra* and *bībhatsa* as primary in nature and the rest as secondary, being derived from them. Thus *hāsya* is derived from *śṛṅgāra*, *karuṇa* from *raudra*, *adbhuta* from *vīra*, and *bhayānaka* from *bībhatsa*.

शृङ्गाराद्धि भवेद्धात्यो रौद्राच्च करुणो रसः ।
वीराच्चैवाद्भुतोत्पत्तिः बीभत्साच्च भयानकः ॥[19]

Let us take up for instance, the question of *hāsya* arising out of *śṛṅgāra*.[20] Bharata explains this phenomenon thus:

17. Quoted in *Kāvyānuśāsana*, Nirnayasagar Press edn., p. 89.

18. Quoted in *KS*, p. 89.

19. *NŚ*, Ch. VI. *śls*. 40ff.

20. *Bhāvaprakāśana*, GOS edn., p. 57 gives the following mythological origin for the evolution of *hāsya* from *śṛṅgāra*.

जटाजिनधरो भोगिभूषणः साग्निलोचनः ।
भस्माङ्गरागश्च यदा देव्या कामयते रतिम् ॥

तदा सखीनां देव्याश्च हासः समुदभून्महान् ।
तस्माद्धास्यसमुत्पत्तिः शृङ्गारादिति कथ्यते ॥

शृङ्गारानुकृतिर्या तु स हास्यस्तु प्रकीर्तितः ।[21]

The imitation of *śṛṅgāra* leads to *hāsya*. In a drama, while the hero's love for the heroine is taken seriously, the *vidūṣaka*'s love affair evokes only laughter. The *vidūṣaka*'s love is never considered as evoking *śṛṅgāra*. It is a mere imitation of *śṛṅgāra* which leads to *hāsya*. It is not *śṛṅgārānukāra* alone that leads to *hāsya*. The *ābhāsa* (semblance) of *śṛṅgāra* also leads to *hāsya*. *Rasābhāsa* (semblance of *rasa*) is caused by *anaucitya* or impropriety.

अनौचित्यप्रवृत्तत्त्व आभासो रसभावयोः ।[22]

Bhāvaprakāśana discusses the *rasābhāsa* case in great detail.[23] Only mutual love between the *nāyaka* and the *nāyikā* gives rise to *śṛṅgāra*. In the case of unequal love or one-sided love there would be only *vibhāvābhāsa*, *anubhāvābhāsa* and *vyabhicāri-ābhāsa*. They work upon *ratyābhāsa* and the *rasa* evolved in such a case would only be *śṛṅgārābhāsa* but not *śṛṅgāra*. This *śṛṅgārābhāsa* which does not have the sublimity of love turns out to be base and sensual in character, giving rise to *hāsya*.[24] Abhinavagupta offers the following illustration:

दूराकर्षनमोहमन्त्र इव ते तन्नाम्नि याते श्रुतिं
चेतः कालकलामपि प्रहसते नानास्थितिं तां विना ।
एतैराकुलितस्य विक्षतरतेरङ्गैरनङ्गातुरैः
सम्पद्येत कथं तदाप्तिसुखमित्येतन्न वेद्मि स्फुटम् ॥[25]

---

21. *NŚ*, ch. VI, *śls.* 40 ff.

22. Cf. *Sāhitya-Darpaṇa*, ch. III, 262.
Cf. also *Dhvanyāloka*, ch. III.
अनौचित्यादृते नान्यद् रसभङ्गस्य कारणम् ।

23. See p. 132, GOS edn.

24. Cf. *Raghuvaṁśa*, XII, 36a:
संरम्भं मैथिलीहासः क्षणसौम्यां निनाय ताम् ।

25. *Abhinavabhāratī*, vol. I, p. 296, GOS edn.

Rāvaṇa's love for Sītā is expressed in this verse. This is a case of *śṛṅgārābhāsa*. Now the question is: Is there any *hāsya* in this verse? The above words of Rāvaṇa may not evoke any laughter at once. But one must take into consideration the situation in full view, the *vibhāvas*, *anubhāvas* and *vyabhicāri bhāvas*, the anxiety, infatuation, weakness and the like, which are opposed to the age, nature and stature of Rāvaṇa and the *anubhāvas* like tears, lamentation, etc. and the resulting impropriety (*anaucitya*) which are evident here, evoke laughter.

It is not the *ābhāsa* of *śṛṅgāra* alone that generates laughter. The *ābhāsa* of every other *rasa* too leads to *hāsya*. When a coward acts like a brave man he becomes a butt of ridicule. When a pseudo-religious monk behaves as though he is a true monk, there is *śāntābhāsa*, which again evokes laughter. Even *hāsyābhāsa* leads to *hāsya*. Abhinavagupta gives an illustration.

लोकोत्तराणि चरितानि न लोक एष सम्मन्यते यदि किमङ्ग वदाम नाम।
यत्त्वत्र हासमुखरत्वममुष्य तेन पार्श्वोपपीडमिह को न विजाहसीति ॥[26]

> If people appreciate things which deserve praise, there is nothing to say about it. But if anyone laughs at a serious thing, who will not burst into laughter at this?

Thus every *rasa* gives rise to *hāsya*: *etena sarve rasāḥ hāsye antarhitāḥ iti darśitam.*[27] It may be noted that Bhoja[28] also objects to Bharata's statement *śṛṅgāráddhi bhaveddhāsyaḥ*, since *hāsya* arises not only from *śṛṅgāra* but from other *rasas* as well.[29]

---

26. *Abhi. Bhā.* vol. I, p. 297.

27. Ibid., vol. I, p. 297, GOS edn.

28. Cf. V. Raghavan, *Bhoja's Śṛṅgāraprakāśa*, p. 435.

29. Ibid.
अथोच्यते शृङ्गारानुकृतिर्येह स हास्यो रस इष्यते।
तर्हि वीरस्यानुकृतिर्येह सोऽपि हास्य इतीष्यताम् ॥

From *śṛṅgāra* can arise not only *hāsya* but other *rasa*s as well. The *vipralambha śṛṅgāra,* as for instance, the Rativilāpa in *Kumārasambhava,* Canto IV, leads to *karuṇa.* The so-called *prakṛtirasa śṛṅgāra* may itself be an offshoot of *vīra* as in the case of *Draupadī Svayaṁvara.* So the theory, *śṛṅgārāddhi bhaveddhāsyaḥ* does not hold ground.[30]

Dasarūpaka (IV.43) holds that *citta* has four states: *vikāsa, vistara, kṣobha* and *vikṣepa,* corresponding to the four *rasas, śṛṅgāra, vīra, bībhatsa* and *raudra.* From these four, four others arise, for they are of the same mental condition *vikāsa,* etc. respectively. Thus *śṛṅgāra* and *hāsya* have *vikāsa; vīra* and *adbhuta, vistara; bībhatsa* and *bhayānaka, kṣobha;* and *raudra* and *karuṇa, vikṣepa.* But *bhaya* does not have the same *kṣobha* as *bībhatsa; raudra* is not a *vikṣepa* but is *dīpti,* similar to the *vistara* of *adbhuta. Karuṇa* is similar to *vipralambha śṛṅgāra* and is the height of *druti.* Thus there seems to be no justification in the classification of *rasa*s as primary and secondary on the basis to the respective identity of the mental states of these *rasa*s.[31] It is reasonable therefore to grant independent status to *hāsya;* and to all other *rasa*s. Bharata's text must be taken to mean as indicating a study of *rasa*s from the point of view of their interrelation of how emotions are closely related and how one leads to another.[32]

It their treatment of *hāsya,* most of the *ālaṁkārika*s have followed Bharata closely.[33] *Rasārṇavasudhākara* mentions *narman*

---

30. Cf. V. Raghavan, *Bhoja*'s *Śṛṅgāraprakāśa,* p. 435.

31. *Bhoja*'s *Śṛṅgāraprakāśa,* p. 435.

32. Ibid.

33. *DR* and *Avaloka,* (ch. IV, *śl.* 75, p. 108, Nirṇayasagar edn.).
SD, III, *śl*s. 241 ff.
BP, GOS edn. pp. 33 ff.
KS, Nirṇayasagar edn., pp. 89 ff.
PR, V. Raghavan edn., p. 152. →

also as a source of *hāsya*. *Narman* is one of the four elements of the *kaiśikī vṛtti*, the other three being *narmasphoṭa, narmasphūñja* and *narmagarbha*. *Narman* is defined as *parihāsa* which is not *grāmya* or coarse. *Narman* may be caused by *śṛṅgārahāsya*, *śuddhahāsya* or *bhayahāsya*. These again have subdivisions and altogether there are eighteen varieties. Siṁhabhūpāla has illustrated all these varieties of *narman* which give rise to *hāsya*.[34] We may note only one illustration here.

वाचा शुद्धहास्यजं नर्म यथा —
अर्चिष्मन्ति विदार्य वक्त्रकुहराण्यासृक्वतो वासुकेः
तर्जन्या विषकर्बुरान् गणयतः संस्पृश्य दन्ताङ्कुरान्।
एकं त्रीणि नवाष्ट सप्त षडिति व्यत्यस्तसंख्याक्रमा
वाचः क्रौञ्चरिपोः शिशुत्वविकलाः श्रेयांसि पुष्णन्तु वः॥

Position of Hāsya among the Rasas

It has already been noted that the *ābhāsa* or *anukṛti* of every *rasa* can lead to *hāsya*.[35] The sphere of *hāsya* is therefore much wider than that of any other sentiment.[36] Now the question is: Is *hāsya* a noble sentiment at all? We laugh at the physical deformities of the *vidūṣaka* in the play we witness. If laughter is aroused at the expense of sufferings of another, how can it occupy a unique place among *rasa*s?

It is to be understood in this context that the physical deformities of others evoke laughter only when presented in a particular situation in the drama but not in real life. In

→ *RS*, TSS edn., p. 193.
KP, ch. IV, śl. 37, p. 84 (Motilal Banarsidass edn.).
RG, Chowkhamba edn., vol. I, pp. 182 ff.

34. *RS*, pp. 74 ff, TSS edn.

35. See above, pp. 20-21.

36. See, Satindranath Sengupta, "The Sentiment of Laughter", *JBRS*, vol. XXXIX, pt. 4, p. 377.

practical life, the physical deformities may evoke only sympathy and not laughter. When we laugh at the physical deformities of the *vidūṣaka*, we know for certain that the character is not really suffering from these deformities. But it is his skilled feigning of the deformity that produces laughter. Hence there is no stigma attached to *hāsya* and it is as noble as any other *rasa*.

Whatever may be the cause of laughter, it cannot be denied that it makes one happy as long as it lasts. In it, we find an expression of the spirit of man. *Bhaya, jugupsā,* etc., on the other hand, make one shrink with horror or disgust. *Śṛṅgāra* is also responsible for *vikāsa* or expansion of the mind but it is only in privacy that it finds fuller expression.[37] Its *vikāsa* is confined to two persons only. Laughter, on the other hand, is more social in its nature and is much wider in its field of operation. It requires only two to make love, but one hundred can join together in laughter.[38] Anger always has an undesirable element in it and its consequences are also bitter. Anger can never compare with laughter in its popular appeal. Courage is a noble quality, no doubt; but it has an element of risk; and excessive courage may lead to rashness and danger. It is always easier to make people laugh than to instil courage in them. Wonder has a thrill in it, but it presupposes our incapacity to understand and explain the nature of such a phenomenon. Sorrow is heart-rending, but it also indicates our weakness. Humour, thus seems to be rather free from the limitations of other primary emotions. In addition to its psychological advantage, laughter contributes to our physical well-being also. While all other *rasa*s may cause worry or concern in some form

---

37. Cf. *Mṛcchakaṭika*, VIII.30: *vivikta-visraṁbha-raso hi kāmaḥ*.
38. For a fuller treatment, see Satindranath Sengupta, "The Sentiment of Laughter", *JBRS*, vol. XXXIX, pt. 4, pp. 377 ff.

or other, it is only *hāsya* which is free from all such constraints.[39] Humour has a place even in grim places like the hospital, the law-court or even the battlefield (Humour in Uniform). Pathos and other sentiments cannot compete with humour in terms of universal appeal.

The Definition of Hāsya: A Re-appraisal

There is something special about Bharata's definition of *hāsya* which runs thus: *hāsyo nāma hāsasthāyibhāvātmakaḥ*.[40] *Hāsya* is the very essence of its *sthāyin, hāsa* (laughter). The relation between the *sthāyī* and the *rasa* in the case of *hāsya* is very close indeed and the transition from the *sthāyī*-state to the *rasa*-state is very smooth and almost imperceptible. Even the close relationship between the two words *hāsya* and *hāsa* speaks of the unique nature of humour. The word *ātmaka* (of very essence of) in Bharata's definition brings out clearly the closeness between the states of the *sthāyī* and the *rasa* with regard to *hāsya*. The significance of the term might be understood much better when we compare the definition of *hāsya* with those of other *rasa*s.

शृङ्गारो नाम रतिस्थायिभावप्रभवः[41];
करुणो नाम शोकस्थायिभावप्रभवः।[42]

---

39. Cf. *Pādatāḍitakam, śl.* 5.

    न प्राप्नुवन्ति यतयो रुदितेन मोक्षं स्वर्गायतिं न परिहासकथा रुणद्धि।
    तस्मात् प्रतीतमनसा हसितव्यमेव वृत्तिं बुधेन खलु कौरुकुचीं विहाय॥

    "Ascetics do not attain *mokṣa* by weeping. Humorous stories do not obstruct the future attainment of heaven. Therefore a wise man should laugh with an appreciative mind abandoning the mean modes of life."

40. *NŚ*, ch. VI, bet. *śl*s. 48 and 49; GOS edn.

41. Ibid., bet. *śl*s. 44 and 45.

42. Ibid., bet. *śl*s. 61 and 62.

While other *rasa*s are produced (*prabhavaḥ*) from their respective *sthāyī bhāvas*, *hāsya* is the very essence of its *sthāyī*, says Bharata. The *rati*, *śoka*, etc. of the characters represented on the stage do not produce the feelings of love or sorrow in the spectator. But *hāsya* that is represented on the stage, makes the spectator to laugh. This is the essential difference between *hāsya* and the other *rasa*s. Another speciality of *hāsya* is that, irrespective of the mood of the comic character in the play we witness — he may be angry, may be terrified or may fall in love or even experience grief — we, from a position of detachment, enjoy only *hāsya*. This sense of detachment which is the criterion for a fuller enjoyment, is more pronounced in *hāsya* than in other sentiments.

The Divinity and the Colour Symbolising Hāsya

Bharata has allocated colours and divinities presiding over different sentiments.[43] According to him Pramatha is the Lord of *hāsya*. Pramatha is one of the lower orders of divinities attending on Lord Śiva. Pramatha (from *math* to churn) refers to the act of churning or stirring up. *Hāsya* stirs up our spirits and revamps our mental condition and transposes us to a totally different state of happiness. This, probably, is the significance of associating Pramatha with *hāsya*.

The colour that symbolises *hāsya*, according to Bharata, is white; and this is perhaps due to the whiteness of the teeth noticed when people laugh. That smile is white in colour is one of the popular *kavisamaya*s.

In this connection it may be noted that whiteness suggests *sattva guṇa*, the principle of light, purity and goodness. *Hāsya* is a noble *rasa* and has *sattva* as its fundamental quality. There is nothing like the harshness of *raudra* or the undesirability

43. *NŚ*, ch. VI, GOS edn., bet. *śl*s. 42 and 45.

of *bībhatsa* in it. At times *hāsya* may relate to the rough side of life also. Occasionally it may have a touch of vulgarity. But these are not the faults of the *rasa* as such. It is only the method adopted by a writer to evoke this *rasa* that may be found fault with. But good *hāsya*, true to its fundamental quality of *sattva*, expands and revitalises the spirit and hence its association with white colour. Further, whiteness has in it all the colours blended, in *hāsya* likewise all other *rasa*s are blended together.[44]

A Brief Survey of Hāsya in Sanskrit Literature

The origin of *hāsya* in Sanskrit literature can be traced to the Vedic period. In the Frog Hymn, the croaking of the frogs is compared to the monotonous recitation of the Vedic hymns by the priests.[45] Humour in the form of self-criticism is found in the ninth Maṇḍala of the *Ṛgveda*,[46] where the Vedic bard says that though a priest, he is towing the ways of the world in running after material benefits. In a similar hymn[47] the bard admits that he took to different professions in the hope of getting some material gains. In the Gambler Hymn[48] where humour is mixed with a tinge of pathos, the gambler says, "No better use I see for a gambler than for a costly horse worn out and aged". The dialogue between the celibate and the virgin in the *Atharvaveda*[49] is another illustration of humour in early period.

There are a number of legends in the *Śatapatha* and *Aitareya Brāhmaṇa* which reveal traces of humour; e.g. the argument

44. See above — "The Divinity and the Colour Symbolising Hāsya".
45. *Ṛgveda* VII. 103.
46. Ibid., IX. 112.
47. Ibid., X. 97.
48. Ibid., X. 34.
49. *AV* IX. 134.

between the trader and his customers,[50] and a part of Hariścandra's story where the king cites a number of pretexts for the postponement of the sacrifice of his son.[51] The story of the Śiśu in the *Tāṇḍya Brāhmaṇa* opens with a touch of humour when all the elders are addressed "Oh, children".[52]

Though philosophical in outlook, the Upaniṣads also reveal traces of humour here and there. The *Bṛhadāraṇyaka*, for instance, has a satire at the greedy nature of the brāhmaṇas when it says: "The brāhmaṇas desire only cows. They do not know about *Brahman*."[53]

Even a pure Śāstra, like grammar, offers scope for humour. Patañjali compares the consonants with an actress *vyañjanāni naṭabhāryāvat*.[54] Many of the *nyāya*s used in Vedānta reveal traces of humour, as for instance, the maxim of "the opium addict and the boatman" and *kākadantaparīkṣā* and logical fallacies like "the son of Bhīṣma is strong because he is kṣatriya" and *vandhyādauhitrasmaraṇa* — the barren woman recollecting her grandson. Sureśvarācārya gives an interesting collection of such fallacies in his *Vārttika* on Śaṅkara's *Bṛhadāraṇyaka Bhāṣya*:

मृगतृष्णाम्भसि स्नातः खपुष्पकृतशेखरः ।
एष वन्ध्यासुतो याति शशशृङ्गधनुर्धरः ॥[55]

The epics too show traces of humour here and there. The description of the disfigured demonesses surrounding Sītā in the Aśokavana[56] and the description of Kumbhakarṇa being

50. *ŚB* III.iii.

51. *Aitareya Brāhmaṇa* VII.Vii.3.

52. *TB*, 1.i.

53. *Bṛ. Upa.*, 3.1.2.

54. *Mahābhāṣya*, VI.i.2 (*Mahābhāṣyaśabdakośa* edn. Poona: BORI, 1927).

55. See C. on *Pañcadaśī*, V.24

56. Sundara Kāṇḍa, XVII, N.S. Press, edn. Bombay.

aroused from his slumber and his enormous meal,[57] the monkeyish *ceṣṭās* of the overjoyed Hanumān when he mistakes Mandodarī for Sītā[58] may be cited as instances of *hāsya* in the *Rāmāyaṇa*. From the *Mahābhārata* we can see Duryodhana's plight in the Mayasabhā;[59] the Gṛdhra-Gomāyu episode,[60] etc. as instances of *hāsya*. There is an instance of gnomic wisdom expressed with humour, when Vidura says that there are six kinds of people flourishing at the cost of others — thieves on the heedless, physicians on the sick, women on the sensuous people, priests on the worshippers, kings on the litigants and the wise on the fools.[61] The Buddhist and the Jaina liteatures too abound in humour. Many Buddhist Jātaka stories impart wisdom through humorous episodes. The Jaina text *Sūyagaḍaṅga* ridicules the plight of men who, being caught in the snares of women, hold babies and wash their clothes like washermen.[62] There is an anonymous verse quoted in the *Subhāṣitāvalī*, which ridicules the dubious character of certain Jaina monks.[63]

The classical period provided much wider scope for humour. Aśvaghoṣa's *Saundarānanda* reveals the poet's sense of humour at least in one place where the Buddha asks Nanda

---

57. Yuddha Kāṇḍa LX. 62. 63.

58. Sundara Kāṇḍa, X.54.

59. Sabhā Parvan, I, Poona: BORI edn., 1971.

60. Śānti Parvan, CLIII.

61. *Mbh*, V.33.7.

62. See S.K. Dey, "Wit, Humour and Satire in Sanskrit Literature", *Our Heritage*, vol. III, 1955.

63. *Subhāṣitāvalī*, no. 2402:

भिक्षो कन्था श्लथा ते, ननु शफरवधे जालिकैषा, अत्सि मत्स्यान्
तेऽमी मद्यावंदशाः, पिबसि मधु, समं वेश्यया, यासि वेश्याम्।
दत्त्वाऽरीणां गलेङ्घ्रिं किमु तव रिपवो, भित्तिभेत्तास्मि येषां
चोरस्त्वं द्यूतहेतोः, कथमसि कितवो येन दासीसुतोऽस्मि॥

if his (Nanda's) beloved is more beautiful than the one-eyed ape.[64] Kālidāsa has a delicate touch of humour. One cannot read without a smile, the arguments and counter-arguments between the disguised Śiva (as *brahmacārin*) and Pārvatī in *Kumārasambhava* (Canto V).

The numerous puns and *double entendre* in *Kirātārjunīya* and *Śiśúpālavadha* do elicit a smile even from a most sober reader. Canto XVI of *Naiṣadha,* dealing with the marriage of Nala and Damayantī abounds in humour, though vulgar at times. The description of the Jaraddraviḍadhārmika in *Kādambarī* is introduced by Bāṇa, for a comic relief. The *Daśakumāracarita* excels in humour — the story of Upahāravarman standing out as a prominent example. The vast fable literature aims at educating the society through humorous stories. Isolated humorous stanzas can be noticed in almost every lyric.

In the whole range of Sanskrit literature, it is the drama which offers an important place for *hāsya.* In fact, the comedian *vidūṣaka* is an indispensable character in a Sanskrit drama. His humorous remarks and actions not only provide the necessary comic relief for the audience, but they are also vital for the development of the plot.

Bhāsa has a very high sense of humour. His *vidūṣaka*s in the *Avimāraka, Pratijñāyaugandharāyaṇa* and *Svapnavāsavadattā* are delightful comedians. The *vidūṣaka* in Avimāraka finds fault with his master thus, "Since you are very close to me, you mock at me. People who know nothing about my wisdom, praise me highly." But it is in the Cārudatta that the poet excels as a humourist. The prologue of the Cārudatta, and the brāhmaṇa burglar's remark that his sacred thread is useful as a measuring line during nights, are but two of the many

64. *Saundarānanda* X.

humorous places in the play. Sage Nārada (in *Bālacarita*) is disgusted with the peace in heaven and feels that he must go to earth and rake up some quarrel and make himself happy. Kālidāsa's humour is at once dignified and enjoyable. Śakuntalā, when compared to a creeper clinging to a tree, appreciates Priyaṁvadā that she has a befitting name; Priyaṁvadā explaining Śakuntalā's admiration for Vanajyotsnā (Act I), the *praveśaka* in Act II, *vidūṣaka*'s innocent query whether he is to help the king in the act of eating sweetmeats and a number of other places in the course of the conversation between the king and the *vidūṣaka* in the same act, are but a few instances of *hāsya* in the *Abhijñānaśākuntala*. The *vidūṣaka* comparing himself with Urvaśī and his fumbling with the love-letter of Purūravā in the Act II, his gluttony (even the orb of the moon reminds him of the half-bitten pancake) provide good comic relief in an otherwise serious drama, *Vikramorvaśīya*. The *vidūṣaka* in the *Mālavikāgnimitra* is cleverer than his counterparts in the other two plays. He is very resourceful and secures the love of Mālavikā for the king by his own efforts. His alleged fault in the dance perfomance of Mālavikā, his clever covering up of his desire to quench his hunger (by saying that, according to the doctor's advice, one should not transgress the dinner time unduly), his remark about Mālavikā's plight in Act IV (King: How is Mālavikā? Vidūṣaka: As happy as a cuckoo seized by a cat), etc. are some instances of good humour.

Another dramatist who handles the sentiment of humour in a masterly fashion is Śūdraka. Maitreya's exchange of question and answer with Śakāra in Act I, and with Kumbhīlaka in Act V, his topsy-turvy arrangements of words in haste (*kim bhaṇasi? coram kartayitvā sandhiḥ niṣkrāntaḥ*?) and his humorous remarks about himself (compared to a beaten-up donkey) and about *gaṇikās* (*gaṇikā nāma pādukāntarapraviṣṭeva loṣṭukā duḥkhena punarnirākriyate*) and the whole of the *dyūtakarasaṁvāhakāṅka* in the *Mṛcchakaṭika* are remarkable for their humour.

All the three plays of King Harṣa have humour to a considerable extent. The *vidūṣaka*'s ignorance about the types of dances (Act I), his mistaking the rumblings of Sārikā to be the utterances of some ghost and attributing his own fear to the king (Act II), his inability to distinguish between the *Ṛk* stanzas and the *Gāthā*, his folly in revealing the *citraphalaka* to the queen, his boasting that he can surpass even Bṛhaspati in intelligence (Act III), his comparison of the queen's arrival to the *akālavātāvalī* when the king rejoices over finding Sāgarikā (*vayasya, seyam anabhrā vṛṣṭiḥ*) in the *Ratnāvalī* are but a few of such humorous scenes. The whole of Act III in *Nāgānanda* is a delightful piece of comedy. Other humorous scenes in the play include the *vidūṣaka*'s comparing himself to Madana (Act I) and the conversation between the heroine and the *ceṭī* in Act II. The *vidūṣaka*'s ignorance of the exact number of Vedas, his revelation of the secrets in his drowsy condition, his pretension as a doctor and demand for fee, etc. in the Priyadarśikā are worth noting.

Bhavabhūti is often criticised for his lack of humour. But we can still find a few instances of humour in his plays — the teasing remarks of Sītā's friends in Act II of the *Mahāvīracarita*, Makaranda appearing in the guise of Mālatī in Act VI of *Mālatīmādhava*, and Sītā asking Lakṣmaṇa about Urmilā in the *Uttararāmacarita* Act I (*vatsa, iyam khalu aparā kā*?) and the description of the horse by the hermit boys in Act IV of the same play.

With the general decline of dramatic art in later times, *hāsya* too suffered and lost its identity and almost went into oblivion. There was a partial revival of *hāsya* at the hands of

Murāri and Rājaśekhara but one fails to see true comedians on the lines of those created by Bhāsa, Kālidāsa, Śūdraka or Harṣa.

Though thus *hāsya* occupies a significant place in the *nāṭaka* and the *prakaraṇa*s, the field where it is of pivotal importance is the *prahasana*. An account of the origin and development of the *prahasana* will be useful not only in terms of the chief sentiment *hāsya* but for the general understanding of the society and culture of India from the seventh century down to the modern times. A study of its theoretical aspects from the point of view of the different *ālaṁkārika*s is a necessary prelude to the study of *prahasana*s, which will be taken up in the following chapter.

3

Theory and Practice of Sanskrit Prahasanas

Origin and Development

RIGHT from Bharata, all the writers on Sanskrit dramaturgy have recognised *prahasana* as a distinct play form and have dealt with its theoretical aspects. On the basis of the general rule that the *lakṣya* precedes the *lakṣaṇa* we may presume that the *prahasana* must have existed long before Bharata's time. Among the ten types of Sanskrit drama, the *nāṭaka* and the *prakaraṇa* have been accepted as the most perfected forms. It is reasonable to hold that this perfection in the dramatic art must have been achieved only after much experimentation with the smaller varieties of drama. In the absense of proper stage facilities and auditorium, the earliest Sanskrit drama must have been staged in the streets and might have thus attained the name *vīthī*. The street drama called *terukkūttu* (*teru* means street and *kūttu* means play) was a popular play form in ancient Tamil country also and it was in vogue till about a few decades ago. Even today one can witness this, sporadically though, in some villages and towns of Tamil Nadu. Short and well-known episodes blended with folk music and folk dance formed the main theme of the *vīthī*. The number of characters in this play form must have been the bare minimum for lack of experienced actors and necessary co-ordination. With the passage of time, there must have been a flair for original themes and this must have resulted in a play form with a preponderance of comic element which is universal in appeal and entertaining in character. That is how the play form called *prahasana*, would have taken shape. With the rise of *prahasana*, the *vīthī* must have died out lending its elements to the former. That is why the *vīthyaṅgas*[1] figure prominently in the *prahasana*. Such experiments in the dramatic art must have continued with varying degrees of stress on the length of the play as also different sentiments and corresponding themes. An attempt to present almost the same *prahasana*-theme as a monologue play resulted in a separate play form called the *bhāṇa*. Even according to the theory given by Bharata, the *prahasana* and the *bhāṇa* share many common features.[2] At a time when tribal wars were quite common, heroic exploits of the battle must have engaged the attention of the playwrights who wrote short plays with *vīra* as the predominant sentiment and this gave rise to the other play forms *ḍima, vyāyoga* and *samavakāra*. A natural sequel of valour and victory of one side is the defeat and the lamentation of the opposite ranks. An attempt to depict this unpleasant aspect of the battle scene — viz. the story of the defeated and the deceased must have given rise to the short one-act play *aṅka*, with *karuṇa* as the predominant sentiment. There must have been much hesitation in depicting a private sentiment as *śṛṅgāra* on the stage publicly. A cautious experiment in this direction must have resulted in another one-act play form, the *īhāmṛga*. Much time must have elapsed before all the characteristics of these play forms were blended together and presented in the popular play form *nāṭaka* and the social play form *prakaraṇa*. Thus in the history of Sanskrit drama, the *prahasana* represents one of

---

1. See below in this chapter for an account of the *vīthyaṅgas*.
2. See below in this chapter — The Relation between the *Prahasana* and other *Rūpakas*.

the earliest stages of development. It appears to have soon become popular with the masses, as evidenced by Bharata's statement, *sarvalokaṁ prahasanaiḥ bādhante nāṭyasaṁśrayaiḥ*.[3]

Characteristics of the Prahasana

The earliest dramaturgical text dealing with the theory of the *prahasana* (as also the other *rūpaka* varieties) is, of course, Bharata's *Nāṭyaśāstra*. Given below are the stanzas dealing with the *prahasana* features as found in the GOS edition of *Nāṭyaśāstra*, which is by far the most authentic among the editions of Bharata's text. Variant readings found in the other editions are also given below for reference:

> प्रहसनमतःपरमहं सलक्षणं सम्प्रवक्ष्यामि ।
> प्रहसनमपि विज्ञेयं द्विविधं शुद्धं तथा च[i] संकीर्णम् ।
> वक्ष्यामि तयोर्युक्त्या[ii] पृथक् पृथक् लक्षणविशेषम् ॥[iii]
> भगवत्तापसविप्रैरन्यैरपि हास्यवादसम्बद्धम्[iv] ॥
> कापुरुष[v]सम्प्रयुक्तं परिहासाभाषणप्रायम् ॥
> अविकृतभाषाचारं विशेषभावो[vi]पपन्नचरित[vii]पदम्[viii] ।
> नियतगतिवस्तुविषयं शुद्धं ज्ञेयं प्रहसनं तु ॥
> वेश्याचेटनपुंसकविटधूर्ता बन्धकी च यत्र स्युः ।
> अनिभृतवेषपरिच्छदचेष्टितकरणैस्तु[ix] संकीर्णम् ॥
> लोकोपचारयुक्ता या वार्ता यश्च दम्भसंयोगः ।
> स प्रहसने प्रयोज्यो[x] धूर्तप्रविवादसम्पन्नः[xi] ॥
> वीथ्यङ्गैः सम्युक्तं कर्तव्यं प्रहसनं यथायोगम्[xii] ॥

i. Kāśī, Ghosh — तथैव

ii. Kāśī, Ghosh — तस्य व्यख्यास्येऽहम्

---

3. *NŚ*, ch. XXXVI, *śl*. 29; see also V. Raghavan, "A Note on the Daśarūpaka", *JOR*, vol. VII, 1933; *KSS* reads it as . . . *bādhyante hāsyasaṁśrayaiḥ*.

iii. Kāśī, Ghosh — विशेषान्

iv. Kāśī, Ghosh — भिक्षुश्रोत्रियविप्रातिहाससंयुक्तम्

v. Kāśī, Ghosh — नीचजन

vi. Kāśī, Ghosh — हास्योपहास

vii. KM, Kāśī, Ghosh— रचित

viii. *Kāvyānuśāsana* of Hemacandra (Nirṇayasāgar edn., p. 442) — मिदम्

ix. Kāśī, Ghosh — चेष्टाकरणात्तु

x. KM — तत्प्रहसनेषु योज्यं
Kāśī, Ghosh — तत्प्रहसने प्रयोज्यं

xi. KM — धूर्तोक्तविवादसंयुक्तम्
Kāśī, Ghosh — धूर्तविवादसम्पन्नम्

xii. Kāśī — उद्धात्यकादिभिरिदं वीथ्यङ्गैः मिश्रितं भवेन्मिश्रम्।

GOS . . . Gaekwad Oriental Series edition, *NŚ* — vol. II, ch. XVIII, *śl*s. 101-06.

KM . . . Kāvyamālā edition, ch. XVIII, *śl*s. 154-59.

Kāśī . . . Kāśī Sanskrit Series edition, ch. XX, 106-11.

Ghosh. . . . Manmohan Ghosh edition, ch. XX. *śl*s. 101-07.

Bharata speaks of two varieties of the *prahasana* — the *śuddha* and the *saṁkīrṇa*. The difference between them lies only in the nature of characters introduced.

The *śuddha* (pure) type consists of humorous speeches of holy men, ascetics, brāhmaṇas and others. It may also have the cunning and the wicked characters (*kāpuruṣāḥ*). It is full of humorous speeches with no artificiality either in language or behaviour. The words in it should be full of emotion and its plot should have a fixed goal. In the *saṁkīrṇa* variety (the mixed), harlots, servants, eunuchs, parasites and cheats have a leading role who put on coarse dress, gestures, etc. Popular episodes or a story full of coarse speech may form the theme for a *prahasana*. It has the *vīthyaṅgas* also.

There are several references to the *prahasana* in the *Nāṭyaśāstra* itself, apart from the section on "Daśarūpaka".

(i) वीथी . . . प्रहसनं डिमः ।
कैशिकीवृत्तिहीनानि रूपाण्येतानि कारयेत् ॥[4]

Kaiśikī, ārabhaṭī, bhāratī and *sāttvatī* are the four styles of expression. *Kaiśikī* is soft and gentle and is suited for *śṛṅgāra*. *ārabhaṭī* which is the opposite of it is used for representing conflict, rage, frenzy and the like. Virtue, courage, self-sacrifice and the like are best expressed through the *sātvatī* style. *Bhāratī* is the eloquent style which can be used in any situation (*vṛttiḥ sarvatra bhāratī*).[5] Of all the *rūpakas* the *nāṭaka*, and the *prakaraṇa* are called the *pūrṇavṛttirūpakas*, since they can accommodate all the four *vṛttis*. *Prahasana* and the other *rūpakas* are devoid of the *kaiśikī vṛtti*, since they have very little scope for *śṛṅgāra* and its outward expression through song, dance, coquetry and the like.[6]

(ii) द्विसन्धि तु प्रहसनं वीथ्यङ्कौ भाण एव च ।
मुखनिर्वहणे स्यातां तेषां वृत्तिश्च भारती ॥[7]

Bharata points out that the *bhāratī vṛtti* shall be mainly employed in a *prahasana* and that the *prahasana* as also the *bhāṇa vīthī* and *aṅka* shall have only two *sandhis*, viz. the *mukha* (opening) and the *nirvahaṇa* (denouement). This is evidently

4. *NŚ*, ch. XVIII, *śl*. 7, Kāvyamālā edn.
5. *DR*, II, *śl*. 62, N.S. Press edn.
6. Ibid., II, *śl*. 47, — गीतनृत्यविलासाद्यैर्मृदुः शृङ्गारचेष्टितैः ।
7. *NŚ*, XXI, *sl*. 47, Kāśī edn.

due to the simplicity of the plot and structure of these play forms.

(iii) नाटके सप्रकरणे भाणे प्रहसने तथा।
मृदङ्गं पणवं चैव दर्दरं चैव वादयेत् ॥[8]

Percussion instruments like the *mṛdaṅga*, *paṇava* and *dardara* shall be played during the performance of a *prahasana*, *nāṭaka*, *prakaraṇa* and *bhāṇa*.

(iv) भेदास्तस्यास्तु विज्ञेयाश्चत्वारो अङ्गत्वमागताः।
प्ररोचना आमुखं चैव वीथी प्रहसनं तथा।[9]

What Bharata means here is that the *bhāratī* style shall be employed in the *prahasana* and the *vīthī* and in the parts of the prologue, viz. *prarocanā* and *āmukha*. Many later writers on dramaturgy incuding Dhanañjaya have confused the issue by taking all these four names as constituting the *aṅga*s of the *bhāratī vṛtti*, which shall be employed in the prologue. Further they explain the term *prahasana* here as a short comic speech to be employed in the prologue. Prof. Raghavan has clarified this point in his *Bhoja's Śṛṅgāraprakāśa*, and also in his papers on *vṛtti*s.[10] By the expression *aṅgatvamāgataḥ*, Bharata just means "find expression in". "*Bhāratī* is a style of expression and it finds use in *prahasana*, *vīthī*, etc.", is the proper way of construing the above statement.

(v) On the question of the scope of *hāsya* (which is the main sentiment in the *prahasana*) Bharata says, *strīnīcaprakṛtāveṣa bhūyiṣṭham dṛśyate rasaḥ*.[11] Abhinavagupta takes this into consideration while commenting on the *prahasana āryas*.

8. *NŚ*, ch. XXXIV, *śl.* 295, GOS edn., vol. IV.
9. Ibid., ch. XX, *śl.* 26, GOS edn.
10. *JOR*, vol. VI and VII.
11. *NŚ*, ch. VI, *sl.* 52.

उत्सृष्टिकाङ्कप्रहसनभाणास्तु करुणहास्यविस्मय-प्रधानत्वात्
रञ्जकरस प्रधानाः। तत एवात्र स्त्रीबालमूर्खादिः अधिकारी।
न च विततं अत्रेतिवृत्तम्। इतिवृत्तिवैचित्र्यं अपि तत्र नास्ति।[12]

It has already been noted that *hāsya* has a much wider application than the other *rasas*.[13] It is the commonest of the *rasas* with an entertaining nature. Hence it is called *rañjaka rasa*.

Since *prahasana* is *rañjaka-rasa-pradhāna*, its chief beneficiaries are women, children and the gullible. Another characteristic of the *prahasana* is the simplicity of its plot. A simple and straightforward theme alone is used in a *prahasana* and there may not be any secondary episodes like the *patākā* or the *prakarī* in it. There are no surprise turns (*vaicitrya*), or gripping climaxes in it.

The *Daśarūpaka* speaks of the *śuddha*, *vikṛta* and *saṁkīrṇa* classes in *prahasana*. Of these the *śuddha* is the same as in the *NŚ* and the *vikṛta* is the *saṁkīrṇa* type of Bharata. The *saṁkīrṇa* of Dhanañjaya corresponds to the one that is mixed with the *vīthyaṅgas*.[14]

तद्वत् प्रहसनं त्रेधा शुद्ध-विकृत-संकरैः।
पाखण्डिविप्रप्रभृति चेटचेटीविटाकुलम्।
चेष्टितं वेषभाषाभिः शुद्धं हास्यवचोन्वितम्।
कामुकादिवचोवेषैः षण्डकञ्चुकितापसैः।
विकृतं संकराद्वीथ्या संकीर्णं धूर्तसंकुलम्।

Another reference to *prahasana* is found in chapter II of the *Daśarūpaka*[15] — *raktaiva tvaprahasane naiṣā divyanṛpāśraye*. A *gaṇikā*

12. *Abhinavabhāratī*, GOS edn., vol. II, p. 451.
13. See above in chapter 2 — Position of *Hāsya* among the *Rasas*.
14. *DR*, III, *sl*s. 54-56a, N.S. Press edn.
15. *DR*, N.S. Press edn., II, *sl*. 23.

can be depicted as in love with a hero in a play form other than the *prahasana*. This, in Dhanika's words, means *prahasane tvaraktāpi hāsyahetutvāt*. In a *prahasana*, a harlot need not be presented as loving the hero. In a number of available *prahasanas* the scene of activity is the house of a *gaṇikā*, where her customers meet and clash with one another to win her favour. In certain cases it turns out to be the mother *gaṇikā* who wins a lover (as Danturā in the *Laṭakamelaka*). In view of the predominence of such hilarious scenes the theory of one lady for one man (*gaṇikā* or otherwise) does not always hold good in a *prahasana*.

The *Sāhitya-Darpaṇa* states that the *prahasana* should be devoid of the *ārabhaṭī vṛtti*, and the *praveśaka* or *viṣkambhaka*.[16] According to Viśvanātha, the *śuddha* type of *prahasana* has its plot revolving round a single rogue and one *Kandarpakeli prahasana* is given as an instance, which however has not come down to us.[17]

एको यत्र भवेत् धृष्टो हास्यं तत् शुद्धमुच्यते।
आश्रित्य कञ्चन जनं संकीर्णमिति तद्विदुः॥

The *saṁkīrṇa prahasana* has many rogues. *Dhūrtacarita*, another lost play, belongs to this type. The *saṁkīrṇa*, according to Viśvanātha, may have two acts, which means that the *śuddha* variety may have only one act.[18] The *Laṭakamelaka* is mentioned as an instance of a two-act *saṁkīrṇa* type of *prahasana*. Viśvanātha justifies Bharata's inclusion of the *vikṛta* in the *saṁkīrṇa* type, thus disagreeing with Dhanañjaya's addition of the third type.

---

16. *SD*, *śls*. 264-68, N.S. Press edn., 1910.
    अत्र नारभटी नापि विष्कम्भप्रवेशकौ

17. Ibid.

18. *SD*, pp. 344-45.
    तत् पुनर्भवति द्व्यङ्कमथवैकाङ्कनिर्मितम्।

विकृतन्तु विदुर्यत्र षण्डकञ्चुकितापसाः।
भुजङ्गचारणभटप्रभृतेर्वेषवाग्युतः॥
इदं तु संकीर्णेनैव गतार्थमिति मुनिना न पृथक् उक्तम्।[19]

Abhinavagupta's Views on Prahasana

It has already been stated that holy men, ascetics and brāhmaṇas are the main characters in a *prahasana*. Is it not improper to make these noble men the butt of ridicule on the stage? Abhinavagupta analyses this problem. The activities of the holy men, etc. are not by themselves subject to any criticism or disapproval. It is only when rogues or men of dubious character try to assume the roles of these men, that we have a case for *prahasana*.

ये तु स्वभावतः न गर्हिता भगवत्तापसादिचेष्टाविशेषैस्तेषां प्राकृतपुरुष-संक्रान्ति दौरात्म्योदितां अन्यसम्बन्धदूष्यमानतया प्रहसनीयतां याताः[20]

As for the number of *vīthyaṅga*s to be employed in a *prahasana*, Abhinava says that there is no hard and fast rule.[21] With regard to the number of acts in a *prahasana*, Abhinava says — शुद्धं एकाङ्कं, संकीर्णं तु अनेकाङ्कम्, वेश्यादिचरित संख्याबलादिति केचित्।[22]

Abhinava also answers the question whether it is worthwhile to present on the stage a *prahasana* which generally depicts the life of the degraded persons. He says that the *prahasana* too has its moral appeal in that it shows how one should not act. If the association of the rogues can corrupt the minds of even the holy men, ascetics and the brāhmaṇas, it is needless to say what effect it would have on common men. On witnessing the *prahasana*, a wise man would become wiser and would learn to avoid the wicked.

---

19. *SD*, pp. 344-45.
20. *Abhinavabhāratī*, pp. 447ff., GOS edn., vol. II.
21. Ibid. — तेषां सम्प्रयोगे संख्यायाः क्रमस्य तु न कश्चिन्नियम इति दर्शयति।
22. Ibid.

तद्विषये यः प्रकृष्टो विवादः विरुद्धतया अवभासनेन फलभूतेन संपाद्यतया यदुक्तं प्रहस्यमान तत् तथाभूतचरितावलोकनेन हि सम्स्कृतमतिः व्युत्पाद्यो न भूयस्तान् वञ्चकानुपसर्पति इति।[23]

Nāṭyadarpaṇa follows *Abhinavabhāratī* in interpreting the definition of *prahasana* found in the *Nāṭyaśāstra*. The new point that *ND* mentions is with regard to the statement, *atra strībāla-mūrkhādiḥ adhikārī*.[24] Does it mean that the regular connoisseurs of art (*sahṛdaya*s) are prohibited from seeing a *prahasana*? *Prahasana*, being simple in theme and replete with comic situations, will invariably appeal to women, children and the innocent at once. They are thus trained in the art of witnessing dramas and analysing them critically. In course of time, they too can become full-fledged connoisseurs of art like others and can witness and enjoy the perfected play forms, the *nāṭaka* and the *prakaraṇa*. The *prahasana*, according to *ND*, marks the first stage in the art of appreciating the popular play form, *nāṭaka*.

प्रहसनेन च बालस्त्रीमूर्खाणां हास्यप्रदर्शनेन नाट्ये प्ररोचना क्रियते।
ततः सञ्जात-नाट्यरुचयः शेषरूपकैः धर्मार्थकामेषु व्युत्पाद्यन्ते॥[25]

The Prahasana Elements

Among other dramaturgical texts dealing with the definition of *prahasana*, *Rasārṇavasudhākara* of Śiṅgabhūpāla deserves special mention. The author gives a list of ten new elements of *prahasana* and illustrates[26] them from *Ānandakośa Prahasana* which is yet to be traced. The ten elements are:

---

23. *Abhinavabhāratī*, pp. 447ff.
24. See above in this chapter, fn. 13
25. *ND*, GOS edn., no. XLVIII, vol. I, 1928, p. 128.
26. *RS*, ch. III, pp. 290 ff., TSS edn., no. L, 1916. The definitions of the *prahasana* elements given above are from this edition only. All the illustrations given are from *Ānandakośa Prahasana* quoted therein, unless otherwise stated.

अवलगितमवस्कन्दो व्याहारो विप्रलम्भ उपपत्तिः।
भयमनृतं विभ्रान्तिः गद्गदवाक् च प्रलापश्च॥

(i) *Avalagitam*: *Avalagitam* consists in decrying (दूषण) or abandoning (त्यजन) one's earlier decision, out of delusion.

पूर्वमात्मगृहीतस्य समाचारस्य मोहतः।
दूषणं त्यजनं चात्र द्विधा अवलगितं मतम्॥

e.g. यानि घ्नन्ति गलादधः सुकृतिनो लोम्नां च तेषां स्थितं।
यान्यूर्ध्वं परिपोषयन्ति पुरुषास्तेषां मुहुः खण्डनम्॥
कृत्वा सर्वजगद् विरुद्धविधिना सञ्चारिणां मादृशां।
श्रीगीता च हरीतकी च हरतो हन्तोपभोग्यं वयः॥

Since the monk here is presented as decrying his ascetic life, this is an illustration of *avalagitam* comprising *dūṣaṇa*. Another illustration is from the *Prabodhacandrodaya*,[27] where a *kṣapaṇaka* desires to take up another religious order, giving up his own (*tyajana*).

अहो कापालिकदर्शनमेवैकं सौख्यमोक्षसाधनम्। भो कापालिक, अहं तव साम्प्रतं दासः संवृत्तः। ममापि महाभैरवानुशासने दीक्षय।

(ii) *Avaskandaḥ*: *Avaskanda* is the one where several persons offer different and absurd interpretations to a given phenomenon, according to their own bent of mind.

अवस्कन्दस्तु अनेकेषां अयोग्यस्य एकवस्तुनः।
सम्बन्धाभासकथनात् स्वस्वयोग्यत्वयोजना॥

e.g. यतिः : साक्षाद्भूतं वदति कुचयोरन्तरं द्वैतवादं
बौद्धः : भावो बोधक्षणिकमहिमा सौगते दत्तपादः।
जैनः : बाह्वोर्मूले नयति शुचितामार्हती काचिदीक्षा
सर्वे : नाभेर्मूलं प्रथयति फलं सर्वसिद्धान्तसारम्॥

27. *Prabodhacandrodaya*, III, bet. *śls*. 19 and 20.

Here the adherents of different faiths try to read their own philosophical truths, wrongly though, in the physical configuration of a harlot.

(iii) *Vyāhāraḥ*: *Vyāhāra* is a humorous conversation between two or three persons.

e.g. "व्याहारः स्वसंवादो द्वित्राणां हास्यकारणम् ।"
बौद्धः — (यतिं विलोक्य) कुतो मुण्डः एकदण्डी ।

मिथ्यातीर्थः — (विलोक्य, दृष्टिं अपकर्षन्, आत्मगतं) क्षणिकवादी न संभाषणीय एव । तथाऽपि दण्डं अन्तर्धाय निरुत्तरं करोमि ।
(प्रकाशं) अये शून्यवादिन्, अदण्डो मुण्डोऽहं आगलादस्मि ।

जैनः — (आत्मगतं) नूनमसौ मायावादी । भवतु, अहमपि किमपि अन्तर्धाय प्रस्तुतं पृच्छामि । (प्रकाशं) अये महापरिणामवादिन् बृहद्बीज, लोम्नां समानजातीयत्वेऽपि केषाञ्चित् संकर्तनम्, अन्येषां संरक्षणमिति व्यवस्थितेः किं कारणम्?

मिथ्यातीर्थः — जीवदमेध्यमङ्गं धारको नरपिशाचोऽयं अन्तर्धायापि न संभाषणीयः ।

सनिष्कच्छकीर्तिः — (सादरं) सखे, आर्हतमुने, वादे त्वया अयं अप्रतिपत्तिं नाम निग्रहस्थानमारोपितो मायावादी ।

मिथ्यातीर्थः — (आत्मगतं) नूनमिमावपि मादृशावेव लिङ्गधारणमात्रेण कुक्षिम्भरी स्याताम् ।

This humorous conversation between the followers of different religious schools is an instance of *vyāhāra*.

(iv) *Vipralambhaḥ*: *Vipralambha* is frightening and deceiving others by pretending possession by an evil spirit and the like. This is illustrated by another passage from *Ānandakośa*, where a *gaṇikā* pretends possession of a *yakṣiṇī* and deceives others.

(v) *Upapatti*: *Upapatti* is offering a humorous explanation for a well-known phenomenon or concept on the basis of another well-known observation.

उपपत्तिस्तु सा प्रोक्ता यत प्रसिद्धस्य वस्तुनः।
लोकप्रसिद्धया युक्त्या साधनं हास्यहेतुना॥

e.g. मिथ्यातीर्थः — (पुरोऽवलोक्य) अये उपसरित्तीरं पिप्पलनामा वनस्पतिः यश्च गीतासु भगवता निजविभूतितया निर्दिष्टः।

(विचिन्त्य) कथमस्य तरोः इयं अतिमहिमसंभावना ? (विमृश्य) उपपद्यत एव —

तत्पदं तनुमध्याया येनाश्वत्थदलोपमम्।
तदश्वत्थोऽस्मि वृक्षाणामित्यूचे भगवान् हरिः॥

अत्र लोकप्रसिद्धेन अश्वत्थदलोरुमूलयोः साम्येन हेतुना लोकप्रसिद्धस्यैव भगवदश्वत्थयोरैक्यस्य साधनं हास्यकारणं उपपत्तिः।

(vi) *Bhayam*: *Bhayam* is the fear caused by the arrival of the policemen, etc.

स्मृतं भयं तु नगरशोधकादिकृतोदयम्।

This *prahasana* element is illustrated by a scene from *Ānandakośa* again, where the sudden arrival of the policemen throws the pseudo-ascetics out of gear.

(vii) *Anr̥tam*: *Anr̥tam* is an utterance of false praise or flattery.

अनृतं तु भवेत् वाक्यं असत्यस्तुतिगुम्फितम्।
तदेव अनृतं इत्याहुः अपरे स्वमतस्तुतिः॥

e.g. बालातपेन परिमृष्टमिवारविन्दं माञ्जिष्टचेलमिव मान्मथमातपत्रम्।
सालक्तलेखमिव सौख्यकरण्डमद्य यूनां मुदे तरुणि तत्पदमार्तवं ते॥

स्वमतं तु यथा कर्पूरमञ्जर्यां —

रण्डा चण्डा दीक्षिता धर्मदारा मद्यं मांसं पीयते खाद्यते च।
भिक्षा भोज्यं चर्मखण्डं च शय्या कौलो धर्मः कस्य नो भाति रम्यः॥

(viii) *Vibhrāntiḥ*: *Vibhrānti* is the delusion caused by the similarity of features between two things.

वस्तुसाम्यकृतो मोहो विभ्रान्तिरिति गीयते।

e.g. बौद्धः — (पुरोऽवलोक्य)

हेमकुम्भवती रम्यतोरणा चारुदर्पणा।
काऽपि गन्धर्वनगरी दृश्यते भूमिचारिणी॥

जैनः — अयि, क्षणभङ्गवादिन्, एतदुत्पातफलं प्रथमदर्शिनो भवत एव परिणमते (इति लोचने निमीलयति)

बौद्धः — (पुनर्निर्वर्ण्य) हन्त, किमपदे भ्रान्तोऽस्मि।
न पुरीयं विशालाक्षी न तोरणमिमे भ्रुवौ।
न दर्पणमिमौ गण्डौ न च कुम्भाविमौ स्तनौ॥

(ix) *Gadgadavāk*: *Gadgadavāk* is faltering of speech due to feigned crying.

असत्यरुदितोन्मिश्रं वाक्यं गद्गदवाक् भवेत्।

e.g. (भगिन्यौ परस्परमाश्लिष्य रुदत इव)

गुह्यग्राही (आत्मगतं)

अनुपात्तबाष्पकणिकं गद्गदनिःश्वासकलितमव्यक्तम्।
अनयोरसत्यरुदितं सुरतान्तदशां व्यनक्तीव।

(x) *Pralāpa*: *Pralāpa* is welcoming an unworthy act as a worthy one.

प्रलापः स्यात् अयोग्यस्य योग्यत्वेनानुमोदनम्।
राजाः — (सौदार्योद्रेकम्) अये बिडालाक्ष। अस्मदीये नगरे विषये च

पतिहीना च या नारी जायाहीनश्च यः पुमान्।
तौ दम्पती यथाकामं भवेतामिति घोष्यताम्॥

बिडालाक्षः — देवः प्रमाणम्। (इति सानुचरो निष्क्रान्तः)

गुह्यग्राही — (सश्लाघागौरवम्)

नष्टाश्वभग्नशकटन्यायेन प्रतिपादितम्।
उचिता ते महाराज सेयं कारुण्यघोषणा॥

अपि च —

मन्वादयो महीपालाः गामपालयन्।
न केनापि कृतो मार्गः एवमाश्चर्यसौख्यदः॥

The Vīthyaṅgas

Since writers like Bharata and others prescribe the presence of the *vīthyaṅga*s in the *prahasana*, a brief description of them may not be out of place here. Bharata has stated and defined them.[28] Other dramaturgical texts like the *Daśarūpaka* offer illustrations too, mostly culled out from well-known plays. The most striking illustrations and their appropriate definitions chosen from various texts, are given below. The *vīthyaṅga*s are thirteen in number. They are:

उद्घात्यकावलगिते प्रपञ्चत्रिगते छलम्।
वाक्केल्यधिबले गण्डं अवस्यन्दित नालिके।
असत्प्रलापव्याहार मृदवानि त्रयोदश।[29]

(i) उद्घात्यक (Speech with a hidden meaning).

गूढार्थपदपर्यायमाला प्रश्नोत्तरस्य वा।
यत्रान्योन्यं समालापो द्वेधा उद्घात्यं तदुच्यते॥[30]

Uddhātyaka is of two kinds — (i) a series of successive words with a hidden meaning and (ii) a series of questions and answers.

Illustration for the first kind

विदूषकः — भो वयस्य, क एष कामो येन त्वमपि दूयसे? स किं पुरुषो अथवा स्त्रीति?

राजाः — सखे,
मनोजातिरनाधीना सुखेष्वेव प्रवर्तते।
स्नेहस्य ललितो मार्गः काम इत्यभिधीयते॥

विदूषकः — एवमपि न जानामि।

राजाः — वयस्य, इच्छाप्रभवः स इति।

28. *NŚ*, ch. XVII, *śl*s. 104-05.

29. *DR*, ch. III, *śl*s. 12-13a, N.S. Press edn.

30. Ibid., pp. 65ff.

विदूषकः — किं यो यदिच्छति स तत् कामयति?

राजाः — अथ किम्?

विदूषकः — तज्ज्ञातम्, यथाऽहं सूपकारशालायां भोजनमिच्छामि।

The Avaloka wrongly states that this passage is from the *Vikramorvaśīya*. Prof. Raghavan points out that this is from a *vīthī* called *Mālatikā* which is also quoted by Bhoja in his *Śṛṅgāraprakāśa* (*SṛPr*).[31]

Illustration for the second kind of उद्घात्यक

का श्लाघ्या गुणिनां क्षमा, परिभवः को, यः स्वकुल्यैः कृतः
किं दुःखं, परसंश्रयो, जगति कः श्लाघ्यो, य आश्रीयते।
को मृत्युर्व्यसनं शुचं जहति के, यैर्निर्जिताः शत्रवः
कैर्विज्ञातमिदं, विराटनगरे छन्नस्थितैः पाण्डवैः॥[32]

(ii) अवलगितम् (Unexpected turn)

यत्रान्यस्मिन् समावेश्य कार्यमन्यत् प्रसाध्यते।
तच्चावलगितं नाम विज्ञेयं नाटचयोक्तृभिः॥[33]

Avalagitam consists in an unexpected turn in events.

Illustration: *Sṛ.Pra.* cites the following passage from the चित्रफलक episode in Act II of *Ratnāvalī*.[34]

सुसङ्गता - सखि, यस्य कृते त्वमागता सोऽयं ते पुरतस्तिष्ठति।
सागरिका - (सासूयम्) सुसङ्गते कस्य कृते अहमागता?
सुसङ्गता - (विहस्य) अलं अन्यशङ्कितेन, ननु चित्रफलकस्य।

Here the clever Susaṅgatā indirectly refers to the love Sāgarikā has for the king in a way that is quite unexpected.

---

31. See *DR*; V. Raghavan, *Bhoja's Śṛṅgāraprakāśa*; pp. 872-73, ed. author, 1978.
32. From *Pāṇḍavānanda*, quoted in *Avaloka*, N.S. Press edn., pp. 65ff.
33. *Śr. Pr.* Josyer edn., vol. II, pp. 492ff.
34. *Ratnāvalī*, ed. C.S.R. Sastry, Madras, p. 61.

(iii) *Prapañca* (Unworthy praise)

असद्भूतं मिथःस्तोत्रं प्रपञ्चो हास्यकृन्मतः ।[35]

Prapañca is unworthy praise that evokes laughter. The Avaloka quotes the *Karpūramañjarī* verse, *raṇḍā caṇḍā* ...[36] as an illustration of *prapañca.*

(iv) *Trigatam* (Triple explanation)

श्रुतिसाम्यात् अनेकार्थयोजनं त्रिगतं त्विह ।[37]

If, based on similarity, three different explanations are offered regarding the exact nature of a particular sound heard, we have *trigata.*

Illustration:

वाणीमुरजक्कणितं श्रुतिसुभगं किं सुधामुचः स्तनितम् ।
जलदस्य किमाज्ञातं तव मधुरगभीरवाग्विलासोऽयम् ।[38]

Here the sweet and resonant words of the *sūtradhāra* are variously understood by his assistant as the sound produced by the drum or the cloud or the speech of Sarasvatī herself.

(v) *Chalam* (Deception)

प्रियाभैरप्रियैर्वाक्यैर्विलोभ्यछलनाच्छलम् ।[39]

Chalam arises from the desire to deceive or mislead others with unfriendly words that seem friendly.

---

35. *DR*, pp. 65ff.
36. See above, *Prahasanāṅga anṛtam*
37. *DR*, pp. 65ff.
38. Verse from *Abhirāmarāghava*, quoted by *RS*, pp. 238ff.
39. *DR*, p. 66.

Illustration:

विद्वानसौ कलावानपि रसिको बहुविधप्रयोगज्ञः ।
इति च भवन्तं विद्मो निर्व्यूढं साधु तत् त्वया सर्वम् ॥[40]

These words of the assistant, though apparently praising the talents of the *sūtradhāra*, are only sarcastic in nature and hence form the illustration for *chala*.

(vi) *Vākkelī* (Witty retort)

वाक्केली हास्यसम्बन्धो द्वित्रिप्रत्युक्तितो भवेत् ।[41]

Vākkelī arises from a comic dialogue comprising two or more sets of questions and answers.

Illustration: *SD* quotes the following verse as an instance of वाक्केली

मिक्षो मांसनिषेवणं प्रकुरुषे? किं तेन मद्यं विना
मद्यं चापि तव प्रियं? प्रियमहो वाराङ्गनाभिः सह ।

वेश्याप्यर्थरुचिः, कुतस्तव धनं? द्यूतेन चौर्येण वा
चौर्यद्यूतपरिग्रहोऽपि भवतो? नष्टस्य काऽन्या गतिः ॥[42]

(vii) अधिबलम् (Outvying)
अन्योन्य वाक्याधिक्योक्तिः स्पर्धयाऽधिबलं भवेत् ।[43]

Adhibalam is a dialogue in emulation or battle of wits among persons where each one outwits the other.

Illustration: Viśvanātha cites a passage from his own work *Prabhāvatī*:[44]

---

40. Verse from *Abhirāmarāghava*, quoted by *RS*, pp. 238ff.

41. *SD*, p. 218, Motilal Banarsidass edn., 1977.

42. *SD*.

43. Ibid.

44. *SD*, The full name of the work is probably *Prabhāvatī-Pradyumna*.

वज्रनाभः — अस्य वः क्षणेनैव निर्मथ्य गदयानया।
लीलया उन्मूलयाम्येष भुवनद्वयमद्य वः॥

प्रद्युम्नः — अरे रे, असुरापसद, अलममुना बहुप्रलापेन, . . .

(viii) गण्डम् (Abrupt remark)
गण्डः प्रस्तुतसम्बन्धि भिन्नार्थं सहसोदितम्।[45]

Gaṇḍa is a statement suddenly introduced in the middle of another statement as a sort of dramatic irony, which has some connection with the context on hand.

Illustration: Avaloka quotes the following passage from *Uttararāmacarita*:[46]

रामः— इयं गेहे लक्ष्मीः . . . परमसह्यस्तु विरहः।
प्रतीहारी — देव उपस्थितः।
रामः— अयि कः?
प्रतीहारी — देवस्यासन्न परिचारकः दुर्मुखः।

(ix) अवस्यन्दित (Re-interpretation)
रसोक्तस्य अन्यथा व्याख्या यत्रावस्यन्दितं हि तत्।[47]

Avasyanditam consists in re-interpreting certain words uttered earlier emotionally.

Illustration: The Avaloka cites an illustration from *Chalitarāma*:[48]

सीता — जात, कल्यं खलु युवाभ्यां अयोध्यायां गन्तव्यं।
तर्हिस राजा विनयेन नमितव्यः।
लवः — अम्ब, किमावाभ्यां राजोपजीविभ्यां भवितव्यम्।
सीता — जात, स खलु युवयोः पिता।
लवः — किमावयोः रघुपतिः पिता।

45. *DR*, pp. 65ff.

46. *URC*, I, pp. 38ff.

47. *DR*, pp. 65ff.

48. Ibid., छलितराम is one of the lost Rāma plays.

सीता — (साशङ्कम्) जात, न खलु परं युवयोः, सकलाया एव पृथिव्याः।

Here the statement that Rāma is the father of Lava and Kuśa, made first in an emotional sway is re-interpreted by Sītā that he is the father of the entire earth.

(x) नालिका (Riddle)

सोपहासा निगूढार्था नालिकैव प्रहेलिका।[49]

Nālikā is an enigmatic remark with a hidden meaning, meant for evoking laughter. It is of two kinds —

(i) अन्तर्लाप, and

(ii) बहिर्लाप

Illustration for अन्तर्लाप

प्रत्यङ्कमङ्कुरित-सर्व-रसावतारन्नव्योल्लसत्-कुसुमराजिविराजिबन्धम्।
घर्मेतरांशुमिव वक्रतयाभिरम्यं नाट्यप्रबन्धमतिमञ्जुलसंविधानम्॥[50]

Some of the letters used in this verse combine to give the name of the play, viz. प्रसन्नराघवम् (syllables underlined).

Illustration for बहिर्लाप

क्रमवर्धमानविलासं रसातले किं करोति कन्दर्पः।
सूत्रधारः — अये, प्रश्नोत्तरं सेयमस्मत्प्रीतिरिति दैवादेशः। तत् स्वयमेव वाचयामि।
निर्भरगुरुर्व्यधत्त च वाल्मीकिकथां किमनुसृत्य॥[51]

The answer to the riddle posed in the verse above is बालरामायण which is the name of the play to be presented by the सूत्राधार.

49. *DR*, pp. 65ff.

50. Quoted in *RS*, pp. 238ff, *Prasannarāghava*, I.7.

51. Quoted in *RS*, *Bālarāmāyaṇa*, I.4.

(xi) असत्प्रलापः (Incoherent talk)
असम्बद्ध-कथाप्रायं असत्प्रलापो यथोत्तरः।[52]

Illustration: *ND* cites the following verse[53] as an illustration of *asatpralāpa*

अर्चिष्मन्ति विदार्य वक्त्रकुहराण्यासृक्वतो वासुकेः
तर्जन्या विषकर्बुरान् गणयतः सम्पृश्य दन्ताङ्कुरान्।
एकं त्रीणि नवाष्ट सप्त षडिति व्यत्यस्तसंख्याक्रमा
वाचः क्रौञ्चरिपोः शिशुत्व-विकलाः श्रेयांसि पुष्णन्तु वः॥

Here the incoherent talk and the wrong way in which child Kumāra counts the cardinal numbers, is an instance of Asatpralāpa.

(xii) व्याहारः (Humorous speech)
अन्यार्थ एव व्याहारो हास्यलोभकरं वचः।[54]

Vyāhāra is a remark made with a different purpose while it is understood by others as having a different motive. This evokes laughter and may have a basis in greed or undue desire.

Illustration: *DR* cites *vidūṣaka*'s remark from the *lāsya-prayoga* scene of *Mālavikāgnimitra*.[55]

(मालविका गन्तुमिच्छति)

विदूषकः — मा तावत्। उपदेशशुद्धा गमिष्यसि।

गणदासः — (विदूषकं प्रति) आर्य, उच्यतां यस्त्वया क्रमभेदो लक्षितः।

विदूषकः — प्रथमं प्रत्यूषे ब्राह्मणस्य पूजा भवति, सा तया लङ्घिता।

(मालविका स्मयते)

---

52. *DR*, pp. 65ff.
53. *ND*, pp. 133ff, GOS edn.
54. *DR*, pp. 65ff.
55. *Mālavikāgnimitra*, Act II, dialogue after *śl*. 5.

Here what *vidūṣaka* meant by *upadeśaśuddhā* is that he must be honoured first while Gaṇadāsa thought that Mālavikā was wrong in her performance.

(xiii) मृदवम् (Euphemism)
दोषा गुणा गुणा दोषा यत्र स्युः मृदवं हि तत्।[56]

Mṛdava is that in which defects become merits or vice versa.

Illustration: *ND* quotes the following verse:[57]

सन्तः सच्चरितोदयव्यसनिनः प्रादुर्भवद्यन्त्रणाः
सर्वत्रैव जनापवादचकितास्तिष्ठन्ति दुःखान् सदा।

अव्युत्पन्नमतिः कृतेन न सता नैवासता व्याकुलो
युक्तायुक्तविवेकशून्यहृदयो धन्यो जनः प्राकृतः॥

Prahasana Elements and the Vīthyaṅgas in Other Forms of Literature

Before going into the question of *prahasana* elements in other forms of literature, it is necessary to distinguish them from the general *hāsya* elements.[58] A passage may be said to contain a particular *prahasana* element only if it is *hāsyaprāya*. But the contrary is not true. Not all passages which are *hāsya*-oriented can be said to have a *prahasana* element. A *prahasana* element is that, which, while being *hāsya*-oriented, is dramatic in nature and is full of action and gesticulations. *Hāsya*, plain and simple, may evoke *smita* (gentle smile) or *hasita* (smile), but a *prahasana* element is boisterously farcical evoking *apahasita* (loud laughter) or *atihasita*[59] (reeling laughter). The *prahasana* element

---

56. *DR*, pp. 65ff.

57. *ND*, p. 133.

58. On *hāsya rasa*, see above in chapter 2, under *Hāsya Rasa*.

59. On *smita*, *hasita*, etc., see above in chapter 2 under "Six Kinds of Laughter".

may be based on pun and other types of wordplay, ridiculing of physical deformities, vain quarrel, improper speech, impertinence, roundabout talk, misquoting of scriptures or well-established sayings, exaggeration, deception and the like. The scene in the *Uttararāmacarita* (Act I), where Sītā, pointing to Urmilā's picture and asking Lakṣmaṇa who she is, is plain humour. Such elements of humour should be contrasted with *prahasana* elements and the *vīthyaṅga*s described above.

It may be noted that there are one or two overlappings between the *prahasana*-elements and the *vīthyaṅga*s. For instance, the *prahasana* element *anṛtam* is similar to the *vīthyaṅga, prapañca*. False praise is the basis for both. The *Karpūramañjarī* verse, *raṇḍā caṇḍā* . . . etc. which is offered as an illustration for the *vīthyaṅga, prapañca,* is cited as an instance of his *anṛtam* by Śiṅgabhūpāla. The *prahasana* element *gadgadavāk*, resembles the *vīthyaṅga asatpralāpa*. Again some of the *prahasana* elements and the *vīthyaṅga*s have similar names but their features differ. Thus we have *avalagitam* in both, the *vīthyaṅga, avalagitam* is an action taking place unexpectedly while its namesake, as a *prahasana* element, consists in repenting for an earlier decision. Thus the *prahasana* elements *avaskanda* and *vyāhāra* resemble the *vīthyaṅga*s *avasyandita* and *vyāhāra* respectively, in name only.

The origin of the *prahasana* elements can be traced to the Ṛgvedic period. The following conversation between Indra and his wife Indrāṇī from the tenth Maṇḍala of the *Ṛgveda*[60] may be cited as an illustration of the *prahasana* element *vyāhāra* which is a humorous conversation between two or three persons.

---

60. *Ṛgveda*, X.86. Translation of the relevent hymns are based on Wilson's edition.

Indra : They have neglected the "Soma pressing". They have not praised me in the sacrifice and Vṛṣākapi is rejoicing over this.

Indrāṇī : Though much annoyed at Vṛṣākapi's action, thou hastenest towards him and bestowest on him prosperity. The *kapi* has spoiled the oblations of *ghee*. May the dog which chases the boar seize him by the ear and devour him.

Indra : Why are you angry with our friend Vṛṣākapi?

Indrāṇī : This savage beast despises me as one who has no male offspring, though I am the mother of male offspring.

Indra : I am not happy, Indrāṇī, without my friend Vṛṣākapi.

Indrāṇī : The man who is impotent begets not progeny, but the one who is endowed with vigour.

Indra : He who is endowed with vigour begets not progeny but he who is an impotent.

The name Vṛṣākapi (male monkey) in the above passage may evoke a sense of humour. The pun on the word *kapi* (ref. to (i) monkey, (ii) shortened form of "Vṛṣākapi") and Indra controverting Indrāṇī on the question of progeny may also be noted for their humour. Coming to the classical period, the Śūrpaṇakhā episode in the *Rāmāyaṇa* and the Gṛdhra-Gomāyu episode in the *Mahābhārata* may be cited as instances of humour in the *prahasana* style.

The *prahasana* elements find their extensive usage only in the dramatic literature. The *nāṭaka*, *prakaraṇa*, *bhāṇa*, *prahasana*, *vīthī* and the *uparūpaka* varieties, viz. the *nāṭikā* and the *saṭṭaka* provide a number of instances of the *prahasana* elements. The illustrations of the *vīthyaṅgas* from the *Mālatikā Vīthī*, *Pāṇḍavānanda*, *Ratnāvalī* (a *nāṭikā*), *Karpūramañjarī* (a *saṭṭaka*), *Mālavikāgnimitra* and *Uttararāmacarita* (*nāṭakas*) and some of the lost Rāma-plays like *Abhirāmarāghava* and *Chalitarāma* have been already referred to.[61] Illustrations for the *prahasana* elements have been mostly drawn by Śiṅgabhūpāla from the non-available *prahasana Ānandakośa*.

The Relation between the Prahasana and Other Rūpakas

It has been already pointed out that the *nāṭaka* and the *prakaraṇa* are the most perfected forms of the *rūpakas* and they contain all the features of the rest of the *rūpakas*.[62] The prologue of Bhāsa's *Cārudatta*, the opening scene of Act I of Kālidāsa's *Abhijñānaśakuntala*, the Dyūtakarasaṁvāhakāṅka (Act II) of *Mṛcchakaṭika* and Act V of *Prabodhacandrodaya*, for instance, themselves stand out as small independent *prahasanas*. The *vidūṣaka*, who figures prominently in the *nāṭaka* and the *prakaraṇa* appears in the *prahasana* too. *Prahasana* bears close resemblance to the *bhāṇa* with regard to the dramaturgical aspects like the *sandhis* and the *vṛttis*. The *viṭa* who is an indispensable character in the *bhāṇa*, may appear in a *prahasana*. In fact, certain portions from well-known *bhāṇas* like the *Caturbhāṇi-Padmaprābhṛtaka*,[63] when recast in the dialogue form, will turn out to be excellent *prahasanas*. The theme is *utpādya* (invented) in both the *prahasana* and the *bhāṇa*. *Hāsya* is the main *rasa* in the *prahasana* and generally so in the *bhāṇa* too. On the stage, of course, the *bhāṇa* differs from the *prahasana*, and also from every other *rūpaka*, in being a monologue play. *Aṅka* is totally

---

61. See above in this chapter under "Prahasana Elements".

62. See above in the beginning of this chapter.

63. Śūdraka's *Padmaprābhṛtaka*, Īśvaradatta's *Dhūrtaviṭasaṁvāda*, Vararuci's *Ubhayābhisārika* and Śyāmilaka's *Pādatāḍitaka*.

different from the *prahasana*, since it is full of tragic element, with no room for humour. The *ihāmṛga*, which comes later to the *prahasana* in the evolution of Sanskrit drama,[64] also contains *prahasana* elements. It has been already pointed out that the *prahasana* has taken into its fold the limbs of *vīthī*.[65] The heroic types of *ḍima*, *vyāyoga* and *samavakāra*, have little scope for humour in their theme, but their prologues doubtless contain some *prahasana* elements since light comedy will be useful in heightening the effect of a serious sentiment that follows. Thus the *prahasana* element is essential in one form or other in every kind of *rūpaka*.

Characters Appearing in the Prahasanas

The characters in the *prahasana* are drawn from all strata of society. The *Bhagavān*, an enlightened *yogin* is seen only in two *prahasanas* *Bhagavadajjukīya* and the *Madanaketucarita*. Monks belonging to different religious orders appear in a number of *prahasanas* but all of them turn out to be unscrupulous cheats with "false outer robes and amorous inner inclinations". The Kāpālika in Mattavilāsa is one such specimen. Kāpālikas, Pāśupatas and Śākteyas — all belong to different Tāntric sects.[66] Emancipation, for a Kāpālika, results through meditation on the Supreme Being as abiding in the female organ. He besmears his body with the ashes of the burnt-off bodies from the cemetery. He adorns himself with the garlands of human bones. A human skull is used by him as his begging bowl. He eats human flesh and drinks wine contained in a cow's horn. He worships Mahābhairava with human sacrifice and offers oblations of human flesh. The Kāpālikas come under the Kaula

64. See above in the beginning of this chapter.

65. Ibid.

66. *The Tantras*, Chintaharan Chakravarti, ch. VII, pp. 50-58.

system and they worship Śiva and Śakti. The Kaulas have sects — Pūrva Kaulas, Uttara Kaulas, Digambaras, Kāpālikas and Kṣapaṇakas. The Pūrva Kaulas take recourse to the symbolic representations while the other four sects practise crude worship of the sex organ. They also follow the leftist form of worship *vāmācāra* as opposed to the Pūrva Kaulas, who follow the *dakṣiṇācāra* worship. Persons belonging to all these four sects of the Kaulas appear in different *prahasana*s.

All the *prahasana*s that have come down to us were written at a time when Buddhism and Jainism were already on the decline due to various reasons, one of them being the erosion of moral values. There is dig at such practices even in the *Bhagavadajjukīya*. *Mattavilāsa* (*MV*) is open with the criticism of certain corrupt practices of the Buddhists of its time. The Buddhist monk in *MV* even hopes to revise the Buddhist scriptures by unearthing and revealing to the world the necessary authority permitting the enjoyment of women and wine. Following *MV*, many later *prahasana*s ridicule the corrupt practices of not only the Buddhists but other religious sects as well.

The plight of the kings in the *prahasana*s is rather pitiable. They do not have a hall in their "palace" big enough to conduct their assembly. For fear that the roof might collapse anytime over their heads, the inmates of the royal household sleep only in the open (*Hāsyārṇava*). Everything is topsy-turvy in the territories of these kings. They are served by foolish ministers. Their Army Generals are cowards of the first order. A horse is useful for them only to flee from the battlefield (*Laṭakamelaka*). They are sacred of seeing anything that is red in colour, and will swoon at the sight of blood in the battlefield (*Hās.*). The doctors appearing in the *prahasana*s are mere quacks. They prescribe medicines that only aggravate the malady. Even nectar becomes poison when prescribed by them (*Laṭaka.*).

What is more, they themselves are the abodes of all diseases (*Hās. śl.* 30). Other characters in the *prahasana*s who look ill-suited for their professions are the illiterate *paṇḍit*s, hypocritic teachers, impertinent students, ignorant astrologers, greedy *purohit*s, dastardly police chiefs and the like.

*Viṭa*s and *vidūṣaka*s have been sanctioned by the theory itself and they do, of course, appear in the *prahasana*s. They are the chief counsellors of the cultured citizens (*nāgaraka*s) and the courtesans. The *Pādatāḍitaka bhāṇa* defines a *viṭa* thus,

> He is the one who, regardless of his life, protects his friends and their interests and whom a courtesan, smitten with love, approaches for help and whose wealth is always laid open to the needy.[67]

The *viṭa*s, generally, speak in Sanskrit and sparkle in wit and humour. They are very clever in extracting important personal secrets from others. Fraudulent by nature, they can easily detect duplicity in others.

While the *vidūṣaka* has a major role to play in the *nāṭaka*, the *prakaraṇa* and the *nāṭikā* and is generally the only character through whom humour is introduced,[68] he is only a minor character in the *prahasana*. The *vidūṣaka* has hideous dress, ludicrous behaviour and speech, excessive fondness for the pleasures of the table and has funny mannerisms.[69] As an actor, he appears on the stage with the *sūtradhāra* in the prologue and carries on with him a witty conversation. He is a close companion of the hero and acts as his *kāmasaciva* and tries to win his beloved for him (as in *Mālavikāgnimitra*). He is normally a brāhmaṇa but knows very little about the significance of the

67. *Pādatāḍitaka*, verse 16.

68. See *Bhāvaprakāśana*, p. 94, *hāsyakṛt syāt vidūṣakaḥ*.

69. Cf. J.T. Parikh, *Vidūṣaka in Theory and Practice*, Surat, 1953.

scriptures. He has some physical deformity or other, which offers scope for others to make fun of him.[70] In the *prahasana*, however, he appears only as a messenger of love for a *gaṇikā*, a *nāgaraka* or a pseudo-religious monk.[71]

Gaṇikās and their mothers play a prominent role in the *prahasanas*. The *Kāmasūtra* devotes four entire chapters (book VI, ch. i-iv) for *vaiśika*, the courtesan's art. It deals with how a courtesan should conduct herself and how she should cleverly extract money from her customers, at the same time, pretending to shower all love on them. The *Nāṭyaśāstra* (ch. xxiv) speaks of three classes of prostitutes — *kumbhadāsī*, *rūpājīvā* and *gaṇikā*. The *kumbhadāsīs* are low-class maid-servants having clandestine love affairs with the master of the house they are serving in. The *rūpājīvās* are also non-professional prostitutes, dependent on their youth and beauty to entice their lovers. The *rūpājīvās* are grouped under six heads — (i) *paricārikā*, lady-in-waiting in respectable families, (ii) *kulaṭā*, a married woman seeking a secret lover without the knowledge of her husband, (iii) *svairiṇī*, a married woman going after her paramour on the very face of her husband, (iv) *naṭī*, an actress by profession but often indulging in prostitution, (v) *śilpakārikā*, wife of an artisan who indulges in adultery, and (vi) *prakāśavinaṣṭā*, a woman belonging to any caste or class having indiscriminate affairs with any man who suits her purpose, money and temperament.

Gaṇikās, the third category of *veśyās*, are professional prostitutes[72] serving in temples, and royal courts. They may run their own brothels. They are generally skilled in dancing

---

70. See *Nāṭyaśāstra*, ch. XXIV, *śl.* 103: *vāmano danturaḥ kubjaḥ* . . .

71. See *Kāmasūtra*, I.4.47: *veśyānām nāgarakāṇām ca mantriṇah sandhivigrahaniyuktāḥ*.

72. Cf. Sinha and Basu, *History of Prostitution in India*, vol. I.: Ancient.

and other fine arts. They are youthful, charming and skilled in the art of love. It is their mother who shapes their career. The mother should guard her daughter against the overtures and indiscriminate association of the youths. She should, of course, invite the accomplished youths of the society to her house on an auspicious day and announce that her daughter is ready to enter the family profession. The first taste of her youth would be given to the most eligible man of the city who would also be required to pay a huge sum of money. The mother should give her daughter's hand amidst pseudo-nuptial ceremony to the person who agrees to pay the stipulated amount. Or the mother should connive for a time at her daughter's relationship with an accomplished youth and afterwards bring the whole matter to the notice of the wise elders for deciding how much money the man ought to pay as penal contribution. Or in case there be no one available to perform her daughter's "first nuptials" and the necessity for initiating her daughter in amatory subjects has arisen, the mother should allow her to be trained in these matters by a suitable master who is well-versed in Kāmaśāstra. After the girl has thus gained the rudimentary knowledge of practical erotics, her mother should proclaim her as a lovely girl in the prime of her youth open to negotiation and try to attract all voluptuous rich youths around her. The *Hāsyārṇava*, for instance, has a pseudo-nuptial ceremony conducted in the house of a *gaṇikā*.

Other characters who figure in the *prahasana*s are the *ceṭa*s, *ceṭi*s (male and female attendants) and the *bhujaṅga*s (eunuchs). The influence of the Mohammedan rule in India is found reflected in the *prahasana*s too. Mohammedan characters appear in many later *prahasana*s like *Kuhanābhaikṣava* and *Kukṣimbharabhaikṣava*. The *Kukṣimbharabhaikṣava* has Europeans too in its cast.

Paradoxical Names of Characters in the Prahasanas

One of the principal features responsible for *hāsya* in the *prahasana* is the choice of names for the characters. These names which are paradoxical in nature may be grouped thus:

(i) Names standing for something good or noble but the actions of the persons so named being quite contrary to the significance of the name.

(ii) Names of the characters befitting their actions.

(iii) Names suggestive of some physical deformity (*aṅgavikāra*).

(iv) Names indicative of some base animal nature.

(v) Names referring to some eatables of which the character is fond.

(vi) Names referring to some other weakness of the character.

(vii) Names referring to a certain branch of Śāstra, which the character is supposed to have specialised in.

(viii) Allegorical names.

Of the first two types of names we have, Jñānarāśi (Heap of Knowledge) in *Hāsyacūḍāmaṇi* who professes to know the "Kevalī Jñāna" but is a hoax in reality. On the other hand, we have Ajñānarāśi (Heap of Ignorance) in the *Laṭakamelaka*, whose actions justify his name. Names referring to *aṅgavikāra* are many, as for instance Dīrghadanta, Vakranāsa, Dīrghaśepha and Laṁbavṛṣaṇa. With regard to names referring to certain animal characteristics, we have Ulūkākṣaḥ and Uṣṭrāsyaḥ or names referring to some animal like Biḍālaḥ, Mārjārāḥ, Biḍālaka Jambukaḥ, Śṛgālaḥ, etc. In the *Palāṇḍumaṇḍana* of Harijīvanamiśra, there are characters named after some vegetables or edible substances of which they are fond, i.e.

Palāṇḍumaṇḍana (fond of red onion), Pūrṇapolikā (fond of *poli*, a kind of sweetmeat) and Laśunapantaḥ (fond of garlic). As for names indicating the weakness of a character, we have Varṇagāminī, Parihāsalatā, Nijastrītyāgiśāstrin and Parastrīgrāhīśāstrin. In the *Vibudhamohana* of Harijīvanamiśra, we come across names like Tarkakarkaśa, Pātañjalanātha and Vaiśeṣikabhaṭṭācārya, which refer to branches of knowledge the character is supposed to have specialised in. It is again Harijīvanamiśra who in his *Sahṛdayānanda*, gives allegorical names to his characters like, Vyañjanā, Abhidhā, Lakṣaṇā and Rasapratibandhaka — all connected with Alaṁkāraśāstra.

Hero and Heroine in the Prahasana

In Sanskrit dramas, the hero is expected to be young, energetic, handsome, noble and virtuous. But contrary to this, we have only old monks, ascetics and rogues as the leading characters in the *prahasana*. Now the question is whether these people can be called as heroes at all. According to Kohala, quoted by Abhinavagupta, an *adhama* character cannot be the hero in a play. This view is refuted by Abhinava. According to him, hero is one "who figures prominently in a play and is closely associated with the main theme and the effect (*kārya*)". Since the main sentiment in a *prahasana* is *hāsya*, which is evoked by unseemly dress, speech, etc., its hero can justifiably be an *adhama* character.[73] There is no age restriction also for one to be qualified as a hero in the *prahasana*. The Parivrājaka in the *Bhagavadajjukīya*, the Kāpālika in the *Mattavilāsa-prahasana*, and the ascetic Jñānarāśi in the *Hāsyacūḍāmaṇi*, all seem to be well past their youth and are perhaps on the wrong side of sixty. Abhinava's definition of a hero is true with a heroine too. Thus a heroine is one who is closely associated with the main

73. *Abhinavabhāratī*, vol. I, p. 173, GOS edn.

theme and consummation of the play. She need not even be the consort or fiancee of the hero. Generally *gaṇikā*s figure as heroines in the *prahasana*s, as for instance, Vasantasenā in *Bhagavadajjukīya* and Devasomā in *Mattavilāsa*. Sometimes the mothers of the *gaṇikā*s have a more prominent role to play than their own daughters. In the *Laṭakamelaka*, the young *gaṇikā* Madanamañjarī is just a passive spectator, while her mother Danturā figures prominently throughout the play, outwitting her visitors by her speech and action. Similarly Kapaṭakeli has a more prominent role to play than her daughter, Madanasundarī, in the *Hāsyacūḍāmaṇi*.

Vulgarity in the Prahasanas

In accordance with the nature of the hero (an *adhama*) and the *rasa* that is delineated, viz. *hāsya*, there are passages bordering on vulgarity in most of the *prahasana*s. This tendency is particularly noticeable in most of the later *prahasana*s starting with the *Laṭakamelaka*. The *Lambodaraprahasana* and *Caṇḍānurañjana*, however, exceed all limits of decency and are deplorably vulgar. But in the other *prahasana*s the sexy element is well within the limits, heightening the comic effect in general. After all, some overtones of *śṛṅgāra* go well with the comic. Even in our day-to-day life we come across such private jokes. In fact, such a freedom to include jokes associated with sex, has already been wielded by poets like Śrīharṣa.[74]

We must also take into consideration the social conditions that existed during the medieval period in India, when most of these *prahasana*s came into existence. Due to various reasons child marriage was quite common and a boy attained his married status directly from his childhood.

74. Cf. *Naiṣadham*, Canto, XVI, *śls*. 50-54.

The problems of adolescence were unknown and the chances of young boys and girls getting corrupted due to pornography was almost nil. Hence a joke or two connected with sex were not frowned upon, if not welcomed. In the light of these observations, the modern reader need not get appalled at the so-called vulgarity in the *prahasana*s, but may just wink at and it leaves it at that.

Prākṛt in Prahasanas

The presence of low characters in the *prahasana*s necessitates the usage of different dialects of the Prākṛt in the dialogues. Most of the printed editions of the *prahasana*s contain the Sanskrit *chāyā*, except the *Nāṭavāṭa-prahasana*. In many later *prahasana*s, the Prākṛt has only a conventional usage with no relevance to the times in which they were composed. While there is no appreciable difference in the roles of the disciple and the Vidūṣaka in some of the *prahasana*s, a difference is brought in through the language used — Sanskrit for the former and Prākṛt for the latter. A woman character very often switches over to Sanskrit, as in *Hāsyārṇava* and *Dhūrtasamāgama*, such change being indicated by the stage direction, *Saṁskṛtamāśritya*. The different dialects like Śaurasenī and Mahārāṣṭrī, intended to make certain distinctions between some of the characters, get very often mixed up. The Prākṛt is almost absent in the twentieth-century *prahasana*s.

Rasas Other than Hāsya in the Prahasanas

In *prahasana*s, the *hāsya* is presented through several means — the *ātmastha* and *parastha* varieties, the *rasābhāsa*, the *vīthyaṅga*s and the *prahasana* elements. But the predominance of *hāsya* does not exclude the scope of other *rasa*s like *śṛṅgāra*, *adbhuta* and even *karuṇa*. It may be noted that[75] *śṛṅgāra* figures in the

75. See below in chapter 4 under "Rasas other than Hāsya".

love songs of *Bhagavadajjukīya* and *Dhūrtasamāgama*. The *Hāsyacūḍāmaṇi* and *Madanaketucarita* too have enough scope for *śṛṅgāra*. The transmigration of souls in *Bhagavadajjukīya* and the *Madanaketucarita* has an element of *adbhuta*. The lament of Mṛgāṅkalekhā in the *Hāsyārṇava* is an instance of *karuṇa*. One may also notice traces of *raudra* in *prahasana*s where some of the characters clash on issues like religious beliefs and love preferences.

Number of Acts in the Prahasanas

Bharata does not prescribe the number of acts for *prahasana*. *Sāhitya-Darpaṇa* states that the *saṁkīrṇa* variety of *prahasana* may have two acts,[76] which means that a *śuddha* piece may have only one act. The available *śuddha* type of *prahasana*s satisfy this condition. Some of the *vikṛta* (or *saṁkīrṇa*) *prahasana*s have more than two acts. The *Adbhutataraṅga* and the *Muṇḍita Prahasana* have three acts. There is one other play, *Sāndrakutūhala*, which has four acts, but it is doubtful whether its first three acts can be taken as part of the genuine text of the *prahasana* at all.

Lāsyāṅgas in Prahasanas

Lāsya is a gentle type of dance suited to *śṛṅgāra*, performed by female dancers on the stage. It has ten limbs or *aṅga*s. *Nāṭyaśāstra* defines them[77] and states that *lāsya* like *bhāṇa*, is *ekapātrahārya*, i.e. presented by a single actor on the stage.[78] The *Daśarūpaka*, however, associates the ten *lāsyāṅga*s, with the *bhāṇa* and the Avaloka remarks that[79] the *prahasana* too has the *lāsyāṅga*s. Pointing out the mistake in associating the

76. See above in this chapter.

77. *NŚ*, ch. XX, p. 136.

78. *NŚ*, ch. XX, p. 116: *bhāna iva ekaprayojyāni, bhāṇakṛtivat lāsyam*.

79. See under *DR*, ch. III, *sl.* 54.

lāsyāṅgas with the *bhāṇa*, Prof. Raghavan states that the *lāsyāṅgas* find a place only in major play forms like the *nāṭaka*, the *śuddha prakaraṇa*, the *nāṭikā*, the *troṭaka* and the *saṭṭaka*.[80] Since *bhāṇa* is a monologue play performed by a single male actor on the stage, there is no scope for *lāsya* in it. *Aṅka* has *karuṇa* as its main sentiment and so *lāsya* which is *śṛṅgāra*-oriented has no place in it. The *ḍima*, the *vyāyoga*, and the *samavakāra* are all heroic plays and so *lāsya* cannot figure in them also. The *prahasana* with *hāsya* as its main sentiment cannot have *lāsya* and its *aṅgas*. *Lāsyāṅgas* may, however, figure in the prologues of all the *sukumāra* varieties of *rūpakas*, viz. the *nāṭaka*, *prakaraṇa*, *bhāṇa* and *prahasana*.

While we agree with Prof. Raghavan that the *lāsyāṅgas* cannot find a place in the *bhāṇa*, it is rather difficult to accept his view on the relationship between the *lāsyāṅgas* and the *prahasana*. *Prahasana* has, of course, *hāsya* as its predominant sentiment. Still it has enough scope for *śṛṅgāra*. We have in the available *prahasana* specimens, delightful young pairs of lovers like for instance, Rāmilaka and Vasantasenā in the *Bhagadavadajjukīya*, Kalākaraṇḍaka and Madanasundarī in the *Hāsyacūḍāmaṇi*. If the main *rasa* in a play form alone is the criterion for the inclusion of *lāsya*, then even a *nāṭaka* with *vīra* as its main sentiment cannot have *lāsya*. Hence it would be reasonable to suppose that the *prahasana* may also have the *lāsyāṅga*. For instance the *Bhagavadajjukīya* has two beautiful love songs rendered by the heroine (*śls*. 28 and 29) which may illustrate the *lāsyāṅga*, *āsīnapāṭhya*.[81] The Maithila version of the *Dhūrtasamāgama prahasana* has twenty delightful songs for which the author fixed the *rāga* and the *tāla* too,[82] and hence

80. See V. Raghavan, *Bhoja's Śṛṅgāraprakāśa*, p. 175.

81. For definition of *āsinapāṭhya*, see *NŚ*, ch. XVIII, pp. 180-89.

82. See S.S. Janaki, "Two Farces from East India", *Samskṛta Raṅga*, vol. VI.

they are also fit for *lāsya* dance.

Nāṭyadharmī and Lokadharmī

Since drama is a representation of the actions of the men there is bound to be a good amount of "realism" in it relating to the ways of the world. This realistic representation is technically called *lokadharmī*. When the vast and varied interests of the world are to be represented on the stage, certain improvisations and techniques are to be employed and this is called *nāṭyadharmī*. Suggestive and symbolic language, soliloquies and asides to reveal the character's thoughts, etc., music suited to different *rasas*, the make-up, the peculiar convention called *kakṣyāvibhāga* or apportioning several parts of the stage for representing several geographical regions, personification of inanimate things (e.g. *samudrarāja* appearing in person to represent the ocean) — all go under the name *nāṭyadharmī*. Dialects suited to different characters, *pravṛtti* or the local manners and customs, dress according to the age, gait to suit that, speech in accordance with the gait and action in harmony with the speech are some of the *lokadharmī* devices. Among the ten *rūpakas*, the *nāṭaka* is more imaginative and it is a *nāṭyadharmī* play. *Prahasana* along with the *prakaraṇa* and the *bhāṇa* is predominantly *lokadharmī*; yet introduction of some of the *nāṭyadharmī* devices may be necessary. For instance, the *janāntika* technique (aside) is used extensively in the *Hāsyacūḍāmaṇi* and has a very important function in the play since it covers up the weakness of the recluse and helps to preserve his image before other characters. Significant hand gestures and international changes will have to be affected while staging the *Bhagavadajjukīya*, indicating the transmigration of the souls.

Theatrical Aspects

Bharata gives a threefold classification of theatre, based upon its size[83] — *jyeṣṭha* (big), *madhyama* (medium) and *kanīyas* (small).

83. *NŚ*, ch. II.

Commenting on this passage, Abhinava says that the *ḍima* with divine characters shall be performed in a *jyeṣṭha* type of theatre. *Nāṭaka* with royal characters requires a *madhyama* theatre, and for the rest of the play form, the *kanīyas* type of theatre would suffice. Thus a *prahasana* can be enacted even in a small theatre since it does not require much of theatrical sophistication or large scene settings. Most of the *prahasana*s are short plays and some of them have only one act, confined to a single setting such as the house of a *gaṇikā* or the *maṭha* room of a recluse. Some scenic settings may however be needed while staging some of the *prahasana*s. For instance, there is a scene in the *Hāsyacūḍāmaṇi* in which the disciple of a recluse jumps from a tree. There is a similar scene in the *Kukṣimbharibhaikṣava* too. A few *prahasana*s like the *Madanaketucarita* require elaborate court scenes with all paraphernalia.

Instrumentation

It has already been pointed out that percussion instruments like *mṛdaṅga*, *paṇava* and *dardara* are played when a *prahasana* is staged.[84] At least two of the available *prahasana*s *Bhagavadajjukīya* and the *Dhūrtasamāgama* have references to songs.[85] In the *Hāsyārṇava* we find a reference to *tālayugala*, *jhillī* and *mardala*. The harlot-mother, Bandhurā, asks her *bhujaṅga*s to welcome King Anayasindhu with songs accompanied by the aforesaid instruments and accordingly the *bhujaṅga*s sing and dance.[86] In the prologue of the *Laṭakamelaka*[87] the *sūtradhāra* says that he hears the sounding of the instruments *ḍiṇḍima*, *gomukha*, *jhillī*

---

84. See above (iii) under "Characteristics of the Prahasana" in this chapter.

85. See above under "Lāsyāṅgas in Prahasanas" in this chapter.

86. *Hāsyārṇava*, p. 14, Chowkhamba edn.

87. *Laṭakamelaka*, *śl.*, 11, Act. I, Chowkhamba edn.

and *mṛdaṅga* and then learns that it is the *bhujaṅga* music emanating from the house of the *gaṇikā* Danturā.

Nāndī and the Prologue

In addition to serving the usual purpose of benediction, the *nāndī* in the *prahasanas* indicates the main *rasa* that is going to be delineated, i.e. the *hāsya*. As in a majority of *nāṭakas*, the *nāndī* in most of the *prahasanas* deals with the Śiva-Pārvatī theme. The five faces of Śiva vying with each other to kiss the face of Pārvatī (in the *Nāṭavāṭa*), the agitation of the Ganges and the moon on the continued dalliance of Śiva and Pārvatī (in the *Laṭakamelaka*), Śiva's daughter on seeing Heramba mistaking the moonlight from Śiva's head to be waters of the Ganges (in the *Hāsyacūḍāmaṇi*), the refusal of Pārvatī's friends to apply the *kastūrī* on her breasts on the ground that it is anyhow going to be wiped out by the embrace of the ash-besmeared body of Śiva (in the *Madanaketucarita*) and Śiva's teasing Pārvatī that her face is going to be devoured by Rāhu by mistake due to its similarity with the moon (in the *Hāsyārṇava*) — all have an element of *hāsya* in them. In some of the later *prahasanas*, this type of fun at the expense of gods is overdone amounting to obscenity as in the case of the *Lambodara* and the *Gaurīdigambara prahasanas*.

The prologue in most of the *prahasanas* is carried out in the usual style, the *sūtradhāra* and his associates discussing the merits of the play. Excepting the *Bhagavadajjukīya*, all other *prahasanas* contain some references to the author and his attainments. The prologue of the *Nāṭavāṭa* is unique in the sense that the *sūtradhāra* performs it as a monologue in the *bhāṇa* style with the aid of *ākāśabhāṣita*. Some of the old conventions are broken in a few of the later *prahasanas*. For example, in the *Vibudhamohana*, before the conventional *nāndyante praviśati sūtradhāraḥ*, there is a long interlude wherein figure, verses culled out from various sources like *Ratnāvalī, Mālatīmādhava, Rasagaṅgādhara, Nalacampū* and the *Hitopadeśa*. According to Viśvanātha, *prahasana* should not have the *viṣkambha* at all. As a rule, it should not appear in the beginning of the first act of any kind of *rūpaka*. But in the *Madanaketucarita* and *Kukṣimbharibhaikṣava*, we have *viṣkambha* in the beginning of the first act itself.

Most of the *prahasana*s refer to the seasons in which they are staged. The action in most of the *prahasana*s last for a day. There are exceptions as in the case of *Hāsyārṇava*, where the course of action is spread over two days.

The Bharatavākya

Most of the *prahasana*s end with the conventional Bharatavākya. The Bhagavadajjukīya is an exception. It just ends with the description of the sunset. The Bharatavākya, in the well-known *nāṭaka*, generally follows the set expression, *tathāpīdamastu*. But the *Madanaketucarita, Mattavilāsa, Nāṭavāṭa* and *Laṭakamelaka* do not contain such an expression. The *Madanaketucarita* has an epilogue after the Bharatavākya. The *Hāsyārṇava* breaks the convention in not having a Bharatavākya at all.

Stage Worthiness

The prologues in many of the *prahasana*s give details with regard to when and where the plays were first presented — during a certain temple festival or at the king's court. But these details need not be taken seriously since it became a matter of routine for the dramatists to refer to such occasions even though the plays were not actually staged. Plays like *Lambodaraprahasana* and *Caṇḍānurañjana* would never have been staged, though their prologues mention that they were put on boards on such and such an occasion.

But the *Bhagavadajjukīya* and the *Mattavilāsa* have long been associated with the Kerala stage in the Kūḍiyāṭṭam tradition, and are being staged even today in many parts of the country.[88] *Hāsyacūḍāmaṇi* and *Madanaketucarita* are also fit to be staged.[89] *Laṭakamelaka, Hāsyārṇava* and *Dhūrtasamāgama* may need a bit of editing before they are put on boards. Most of the later *prahasana*s ridiculing certain practices of several religious sects may not appeal to the modern audience since sects like the Kāpālikas and the Kālāmukhas have almost become extinct now. Another difficulty which presents itself in staging some of the later *prahasana*s is, of course, the obscenity which does not receive the approbation of cultured audience.

It has already been noted that while *Nāṭyaśāstra* divides the *prahasana* into two classes, the *Daśarūpaka* adds one more variety, viz. the one with the *vīthyaṅgas*.[90] The *vīthyaṅga*s are certain dramatic situations and can be included in any play form including the *śuddha* and the *saṁkīrṇa* varieties of the *prahasana*. Thus there seems to be no justification in having a separate class of *prahasana* with the *vīthyaṅga*s.

Sāhitya-Darpaṇa follows the *Nāṭyaśāstra* and classifies the *prahasana* only into two classes[91] — the *śuddha*, with higher characters and the *saṁkīrṇa*, with the lower characters. This classification will be followed in the present study of the *prahasana*s. On the basis of this classification, only four of the available *prahasana*s can be brought under the *śuddha* type —

---

88. *BA* was staged during the "Indian History Congress" on 30 December, 1976.

89. *Hāsyacūḍāmaṇi* was presented by the *Saṁskṛta Raṅga*, Madras, in 1960.

90. See above, under "Characteristics of the Prahasana" in this chapter.

91. Ibid.

the *Bhagavadajjukīya*, the *Mattavilāsa*, the *Hāsyacūḍāmaṇi* and the *Madanaketucarita*. Rest of the *prahasanas* are rather coarse and are fit to be included only in the *saṁkīrṇa* class. A study of the four *śuddha prahasanas* will be taken up in the next chapter.

4

The Śuddha Type of Prahasanas

Introduction

UNLIKE the *Caturbhāṇī-Padmaprābhr̥taka* all of which belong to almost the same period and have much in common between them with respect to style and state of society represented, the four important *prahasana*s, the *Bhagavadajjukīya* (*BA*), the *Mattavilāsa* (*MV*), the *Hāsyacūḍāmaṇi* (*Hā.Cū.*) and the *Madanaketucarita* (*MKC*) provide a contrasting picture. *BA* is of doubtful authorship, *MV* came from the pen for a royal monarch (Mahendrapallava), *Hā.Cū.* was written by a minister (Vatsarāja) and *MKC* was written by a court-poet, Rāmapāṇivāda. These four works are also far removed from one another by time. While the date of *BA* is uncertain, the other three belong to the seventh, thirteenth and eighteenth centuries respectively. All these four works, in contrast to the other *prahasana*s are free from vulgarity. The *BA* and *MKC* have true *yogin*s in their cast and deal with a noble theme, viz. mending the ways of an erring man. Though no such exalted motive is openly expressed in *MV* and *Hā.Cū.*, the two are free from coarseness and obscenity. Though there is not much of a story-value in *MV*, its plot is simple and straightforward with minimum number of characters, and the dialogues in it are crisp and sharp. *Hā.Cū.* has a very interesting plot and is full of humorous dialogues and situations. Though of late origin, *MKC* has all the ingredients of a classical drama, and is noted for its lucid verses and racy dialogues. An account of these four *prahasanas*, which can rightly be called the *śuddha prahasanas*, as given in the following pages, will bring out how closely they are connected with one another. On account of its prime importance, the *BA* is taken up first for a study.

The Bhagavadajjukīya

The *BA* is undoubtedly the most popular of all the *prahasanas*. It has seen four editions so far[1] and a number of adaptations and translations into vernaculars.[2] It is probably the most widely staged *prahasana*.[3] The *Nāṭakalakṣaṇaratnakoṣa* makes a special mention of it.[4] The earliest references to the *BA* is found in the controversial Māmaṇḍūr inscription,[5] dating back to the seventh century CE. The *BA* has been quite popular in the Kūḍiyāṭṭam tradition of the Kerala stage. A twelfth-century work called the *Kūḍiāṭṭakrama* describes the method to be followed while staging this play.[6]

AUTHORSHIP OF THE BHAGAVADAJJUKĪYA

One of the most intriguing problems with regard to the *BA* is its authorship. Unfortunately the prologue of the play does

---

1. *BA* editions: (i) ed. Prof. A. Banerji Sastri, *Journal of Bihar and Orissa Research Society*, March and June, 1924; (ii) ed. Anujan Achan, Trichur, 1925; (iii) ed. Lockwood and Vishnubhatt, Christian Literature Society, Madras, 1978; (iv) Vanitha Press, Madras.
2. For Tamil transl., see *Saṁskṛta Raṅga Annual* no. 5.
3. Staging of this play at least on two important occasions are known (i) All India Drama Festival at Trichur, 1971; (ii) 37th Session of Indian History Congress, Calicut, 1976.
4. *NLRK*, Chowkhamba edn., p. 276.
5. *South India Inscription*, vol. IV, no. 38 of 88.
6. *BA*, ed. Anujan Achan, Introduction, p. xviii.

not contain any reference to the author. Two of its MSS and also the only available commentary give the name of the author as Bodhāyana Kavi.[7] Winternitz observes, "I see no reason to doubt that this is the name of the poet".[8] The Māmaṇḍūr inscription (portion of line 6) which has led to many misunderstandings and misconceptions, runs thus:

व्यासकल्पस्य . . . (भग) वदज्जुकम् ।
. . . स्यं मत्तविलासादिपदं प्रहसनोत्तमम् ॥

The mention of *BA* along with *MV* in this inscription has led many scholars to believe that Mahendravarman Pallava, the author of *MV*, is also the author of *BA*. Michael Lockwood, in the Madras edition of the text,[9] puts forth the following arguments in support of the common authorship of the *BA* and *MV*.

(i) The Nirnayasagar Press edition (1911) of Jalhaṇa's *Sūktimuktāvalī* refers to these as Mahendravarman's works.[10]

(ii) The word "Indra" in the *nāndī* refers to the author Mahendra and the whole verse is indicative of the author's devotion to Lord Rudra. Mahendravarman was a devout Śaivite in the later years of his life.

(iii) The repetitive puns on the word "Pallava" occur in five places in the play.

(iv) Words like *atimāna, vidhiḥ* and *akaruṇa* which are some

7. *BA*, ed. Anujan Achan, Introduction, p. vi.

8. Ibid.

9. Pp. 2ff.

10. Vide *hāsyapradhāna evaṁ tu nāṭyam prahasanaṁ sadā īti mattvaiva rājendro mahendraḥ kṛtavān kṛtī nāṭyam mattavilāsam ca nāṭyam bhagavadajjukam sarvānandakarau granthau sarvalokasukhapradau.*

of the titles of King Mahendravarman Pallava, occur in the text.

However, we may offer the following arguments in reply:

(i) It is doubtful whether the *Sūktimuktāvalī* verses mentioned above are authentic, for they do not appear in the GOS edition of the text.

(ii) The word "Indra" in the *nāndī* verse,[11] need not be taken in any special sense (as referring to Mahendra). It does not even refer to "Indra" as translated by the editors in their Madras edition.[12] The term *Indracārumaṇi* refers to the *Indranīlamaṇi* or the blue diamond, as explained by the commentary in the Trichur edition.[13] Moreover, the whole verse is to be explained with a philosophical significance and the author of the play seems to be well-versed in different systems of Indian philosophy. This is evident from a number of stanzas dealing with the concepts of Sāṁkhya, Yoga, etc. in the course of the play. The word *pāda* in the verse refers to the *yogin* in the play. Religious teachers and venerable persons are generally addressed as *pūjyapādāḥ*. *Lakṣaṇa* refers to the "True Knowledge". "Rāvaṇa" refers to the troublesome worldly life (*rāvayati iti rāvaṇah*). The word *rudra* indirectly refers to the disciple, who weeps at the death of his master (*rodanāt rudraḥ*). The implied meaning of

---

11. Vide *tvām pātu lakṣaṇāḍhyas-suravaramukuṭendra-cārumaṇighṛṣṭaḥ rāvaṇanamitāṅguṣṭho rudrāya sadārcitaḥ pādaḥ*.

12. Of excellent attributes, being rubbed by the beautiful gem
In the crown of the foremost of gods, Indra's diadem,
And having the toe which supressed Rāvaṇa too,
May the ever worshipped foot of Rudra protect you.

13. Vide Commentary, pp. 1-2.

the whole verse is "May the venerable teacher, a repository of spiritual knowledge and one who is fit to be worshipped even by the gods, save you, pitiable soul, from the fetters of the dangerous and wretched worldly life." True to the significance of the *nāndī* explained this way, the disciple Śāṇḍilya, who runs after the mundane pleasures, is refined by the teacher at the end. And after all, the *nāndī* is expected to refer to some character of the play.

(iii) As for the repeated occurrence of the word *pallava* in the text, in all the places where the word occurs, it conveys only the usual meaning, viz. "shoot" or "foliage" and there seems to be no scope for any veiled reference to the Pallava dynasty. This will be clear if the passages where the word *pallava* occurs are read without any pre-conceived notion.

(iv) Similarly the words *atimāna*, *vidhi* and *akaruṇa* also would seem to carry some special significance only if they are taken out of context. But there is no reason why they should be denied the import which is quite natural to them on the basis of the context.

The following grounds will justify that the two plays in question cannot be of the same authorship.

(i) Had Mahendravarman been the author of *BA*, he would have definitely mentioned his name, at least in the prologue of the play. The prologue of *MV* makes a direct mention of not only the author but some of his titles too.

(ii) *MV* contains the usual Bharatavākya, but *BA* does not have a Bharatavākya. It just ends with a description of the evening. This clearly brings out the different styles of composition of the two plays.

(iii) *MV* generally abides by the rules of dramaturgy laid down by Bharata. *BA*, on the other hand, violates some of the rules of dramaturgy as for instance, in introducing a death scene.

(iv) *MV* carries open attacks on Buddhism, whereas the *BA* shows a more tolerant attitude towards it.

(v) Buddhist society seems to have been far more degraded at the time of *MV*, than it appears to be at the time of *BA*.

(vi) The author of *BA* seems to be well-versed in Sāṁkhya and Yoga philosophies, which the author of *MV* cannot boast of.

(vii) The author of *BA*, like any other professional poet, expects royal patronage. The prologue says that the play is inaugurated at a king's court. But the author of *MV*, being a king himself, just states in the prologue that a new play is going to be staged.

(viii) The Prākṛt of *BA* seems to be more archaic than that of *MV*.

In the light of these arguments, it is reasonable to accept the independent authorship of *BA*. In his prefaces to the Kerala edition, Winternitz points out the essential difference between the *BA* and the *MV*.

> It (*BA*) is certainly quite different from *MV*. The *MV*, like all other *prahasana*s, hitherto known, is a real farce and a satire. The comic effect is produced by the characters rather than by the plot. On the other hand, *BA* is rather a comedy in our sense of the word than a farce. The *parivrājaka* in *BA* is a true ascetic, a *yogin* and a very learned man not to be compared with the low type ascetics who are ridiculed in other *prahasana*s. Even Śāṇḍilya (the disciple) has nothing in

> common with this type of religious men. He is by no means a bad character like the Kapālin or the Śākyabhikṣu in the *MV*.[14]

Hence *BA* seems to be older than *MV* in many respects. Certain similarities of expression and the reference to Buddhist doctrines have to be explained as due to the influence of *BA* over *MV*. King Mahendravarman has indeed tried to emulate the author of *BA* in presenting a *prahasana*. As a mark of his indebtedness to his predecessor, he has mentioned the *BA* in the Māmaṇḍūr inscription. Kuppuswami Sastri has suggested a reconstructed reading of the mutilated inscription as below:

> व्यासकल्पस्य सुकवेः जेतुं काव्यं भगवदज्जुकम् ।
> हास्यं मत्तविलासादिपदं प्रहसनोत्तमम् ॥[15]

BODHĀYANA KAVI

The anonymous commentary of the play published along with the text in the Trichur edition,[16] clearly gives the name of the author as Bodhāyana Kavi. This Bodhāyana, of course, must be distinguished from the author of the *sūtra*s of the Baudhāyana school, and from the other Bodhāyana referred to by Śrī Rāmānuja as *vṛttikāra*, an early commentator on the *Brahma-Sūtra* of Bādarāyaṇa.[17] But it is certain that the poet belonged to the Baudhāyana school (of Sūtra) of south India.

---

14. Introduction, p. 11.
15. See the article "The Royal Artist Mahendrapallava" by T.N. Ramachandran, *JOR* VII, p. 236 wherein this reconstruction is referred to.
16. *Bhagavadajjukīya*, with commentary, ed. Anujan Achan, Mangalodayam Press, Trichur, Kerala, 1925. The references to the page number and *śloka* numbers in this book are only from this edition, unless otherwise specified.
17. Introduction, p. xx.

According to Kṛṣṇamācārya,[18] it is probably this poet who has been praised by Sukumāra in his *Raghuvīracarita*, a play of the twelfth century, thus: *yair bodhāyanavākya-puṣpakalikāḥ karṇāvataṁsīkṛtāḥ*. Whatever might have been the original name of the poet it is quite clear that he was well-versed in Sāṁkhya and Yoga systems, the *Bhagavad-Gītā* and in Sanskrit rhetorics and dramaturgy. His lucid poetry, easy and unsophisticated conventional style and high sense of humour remind the readers of the plays of Bhāsa and Kālidāsa.

DATE OF THE BHAGAVADAJJUKĪYA

The date of *BA* can be fixed only tentatively since the work does not contain any historical reference. The author does not give his name or other details of his personal life anywhere in the work. The lower limit for the date of the work can be easily fixed on the basis of the Māmaṇḍūr inscription, already referred to. It cannot therefore be later than CE 610. Kṛṣṇamācārya's view[19] that it must be assigned to the period between first century CE and fourth century CE seems to lack conviction. On the other hand, certain similarities that exist between *BA* and *MV* suggest that the former could have been earlier to the latter by not more than a few decades. Of course, *BA* exhibits certain deviations from the conventional practices. For instance, it does not have a Bharatavākya. This was probably due to the influence of a non-Bharata school of dramaturgy which the author of *BA* might have followed. Hence it is reasonable to assign the work to sixth century CE. The following observations made through a study of *BA*, would support this view.

(i) The references to Buddhism in the text reveal that it was quite popular in India during fifth-sixth centuries.

18. *History of Classical Samskrit Literature*, Para 589.

19. *HCSL*, para 589.

It may be noted that at the height of the Gupta era, that is, during third and fourth centuries, Buddhism was at a low ebb.

(ii) *BA* reveals that religious conversion was quite common among the people. History reveals that King Harṣa and King Mahendrapallava who flourished round about seventh century were religious converts. Perfect freedom in religious matters can be noticed here. That one could change one's religion to another and again switch back to one's first belief is clearly seen in the character of Śāṇḍilya.

(iii) References to the Sāṁkhya doctrines (p. 50, lines 4-6) found in *BA* can be traced to the *Tattvasamāsa*, a work on Sāṁkhya. The date of *Tattvasamāsa* has not been yet fixed beyond doubt, but it is generally accepted as later than fifth century CE.[20]

(iv) *BA* might have belonged to the post-Kālidāsan period. The reference to a detached soul getting relieved of the fetters of life and the simile thereon, viz. a valiant man crossing a lake infested with crocodiles, may be traced to the influence of the *Raghuvaṁśa* passage: *mārutiḥ sāgaram tīrṇaḥ samsāramiva nirmamaḥ* (XII.60).

THE PLAY

Dramatis Personae

Sūtradhāra/ Vidūṣaka	:	the stage director.
Parivrājaka	:	the *yogin*.
Śāṇḍilya	:	the disciple.
Vasantasenā	:	the *gaṇikā*.

20. See "A Note on the Date of Tattvasamāsa", *JOR* VII, p. 145ff.

Madhukarikā : the maid.

Parabhṛtikā : the maid.

Yamapuruṣa.

Vasantasenā's mother.

Rāmilaka : Vasantasenā's lover.

The doctor.

Plot

The theme centres round a *yogin* and his disciple, Śāṇḍilya, a wayward, who takes to asceticism as it is an easy means of fetching food. All the attempts of the teacher to educate his disciple spiritually, seem to fail. As the two retire to a garden nearby, Śāṇḍilya is struck by the sweet music emanating from another part of the garden. He comes to know that the songs were sung by a *gaṇikā* by name Vasantasenā, who was waiting there for her lover, Rāmilaka.

Meanwhile Yamapuruṣa enters and decides to take away the life of Vasantasenā under orders from his master. The death is caused by snake-bite. Śāṇḍilya is overcome with grief at the sight of the dead body of the *gaṇikā* and regrets that he did not get an opportunity of touching her beautiful body when she was alive. He turns towards his master and requests him to revive the *gaṇikā* by means of his yogic power. The *yogin* decides to bring in a sense of detachment in the mind of his disciple. By means of his yogic power, he stages the *parakāyapraveśa* and enters into the body of the *gaṇikā*. The *gaṇikā* now gets up as though from a slumber, but speaks and acts like the *yogin*, which surprises her lover and her mother who had arrived by then. They arrange to get a doctor who turns out to be a quack. The girl exposes the ignorance of the doctor who runs away to save his face.

The Yamapuruṣa now comes back since he had wrongly taken away the life of the *gaṇikā* instead of that of another lady also known as Vasantasenā. He wants to restore the life of the *gaṇikā*. But to his surprise, he finds that the girl is already revived. Realising that it must have been the work of the *yogin* he infuses the soul of the *gaṇikā* into the body of the *yogin*. Now the *yogin* starts behaving in a curious fashion, imitating the words and actions of the *gaṇikā*. Surprised at this the disciple Śāṇḍilya remarks: *naiva bhagavān naiva ajjukā, bhagavadjjukam nāma saṁvṛttam.*[21] Ultimately at the request of the Yamapuruṣa the *yogin* relinquishes the body of the *gaṇikā* and enters into his own. Being now infused with her own soul, the *gaṇikā* too behaves normally much to the satisfaction of her mother and lover. That Śāṇḍilya gets convinced about the transient nature of the worldly objects and becomes a true disciple, is left to the imagination of the readers.

CHARACTER STUDY

The Parivrājaka

As per the definition of a hero given earlier,[22] the Parivrājaka, addressed as "Bhagavān", is the hero of the *BA* since he is more closely connected with the denouement than any other character in the play. In the prologue, the *sūtradhāra* refers to him as *yogeśvara* and *dvijavṛṣa*. He is truly a detached soul. To his disciple's query *tvam tāvat kaḥ?* the *yogin* replies,

खपवनसलिलानां तेजसश्चैकदेशाद्-
उपचितचलमूर्तिः पार्थिवद्रव्यराशिः ।
श्रवण-नयन-जिह्वा-नासिका-स्पर्शवेदी
नर इति कृतसंज्ञः कोऽप्यहं प्राणिधर्मा ॥

— *śl.* 9

21. *BA*, p. 87.
22. See above, chapter 3 of this book, under "Hero and Heroine in the *prahasana*".

He is skilled in the art of *parakāyapraveśa*. This he does, not to demonstrate his prowess but to educate his erring disciple. The *yogin* is steeped in traditional learning and is a master of Sāṁkhya and Yoga. He is fully aware of the ephemeral nature of worldly life.

देहो रोगनिधिर्जरावशगतो लीनान्तकाधिष्ठितो
यो नित्य-प्रतिघातरुद्धविषयस्तीरे यथा पादपः।
तं लब्ध्वा सुकृतैः अनेकगुणितैः देहात्मना विस्मितो
मत्तो यो बलरूपयौवनगुणैः दोषान् न तान् पश्यति॥

— *śl.* 3

His kindness towards his disciple is amazing. He instructs him patiently and puts up with his silly questions and criticisms. With a view to putting him in the correct path, he stages the *parakāyapraveśa* and brings in a sense of remorse into his heart. Taking pity on his disciple who is enamoured of the *gaṇikā*, he says: *eṣa khalu tapasvī kartavyābodhyatayā āśramāpavādam na jānāti.*[23] He reprimands the doctor for his foolishness and exposes his ignorance. When the quack commits a grammatical blunder, *trīṇi sarpā bhavantyete,* while quoting from the Vaidyaśāstra, he corrects him immediately, *ayam apaśabdaḥ trayaḥ sarpā iti vaktavyam.*[24] When the doctor says that there are 100 symptoms of serpent bite, the *yogin* corrects him that they are only seven in number.

रोमाञ्चो मुखशोषश्च वैवर्ण्यं चैव वेपथुः।
हिक्का श्वासश्च, सम्मोहः सप्तैते विषविक्रियाः॥

— *śl.* 34

He is held in high esteem by other characters in the play. He towers like a giant over them but never exercises his powers unduly.

23. *BA*, p. 76.

24. Ibid., p. 92.

Śāṇḍilya the Disciple

Śāṇḍilya, the disciple, plays a pivotal role in the drama, in the sense that it is his attitude which needs a radical reformation, and the whole theme is about how this is brought about. He is young and fickle. Though born in a brāhmaṇa family, he switched over to Buddhism so as to be free from the worry of fetching the breakfast. This does not suit him since the Buddhists take food only once a day. So he again joins the Brāhmanical ascetic order. He makes it clear that his switch over to different religions is not out of any inquisitiveness to find out the ultimate Truth of life.

> न मामकोऽस्ति न भ्रातृको वा पिता कुतो मे भगवत्प्रसादः।
> एकोऽहमन्नहतत्वेन यष्टिं प्रविष्टो न खलु धर्मलोभात्॥
>
> — *śl.* 5

He taunts his master always with impertinent questions. He even abuses him, when advised not to lament over the death of the *gaṇikā*. At times he looks very innocent and gullible. He mistakes a peacock for a tiger and is frightened. Even a song from a distance would disturb his concentration. He is enamoured of even the dead body of the *gaṇikā* and laments that he could not touch her when she was alive. He calls her his *svajana* and requests his master to revive her. But he is not altogether a dull head. When asked by the master as to the nature of the *Ātman* and *karmātman*, he replies योऽजोऽच्छेद्योऽभेद्यः स आत्मा नाम,[25] which elicits the admiration of his master. He is eager to know the secrets of *ātmatattva* and *yoga*, and listens with rapt attention when his master explains. He has love and affection for his master. On seeing the body of his master bereft of life, he is overcome with terrible grief, and laments thus: *hā dhik, hā bhagavan, hā vācālaka, hā atiyogavittaka, hā*

25. *BA*, p. 29.

upādhyāya, . . .[26] Later he is happy to see his master regain life but becomes worried when the master behaves differently. He heaves a sigh of relief when the master regains normalcy and says: *eṣa bhagavān svabhāve paryavasthitaḥ*.[27]

Vasantasenā

Vasantasenā, the heroine of the play, is a charming young *gaṇikā* and possesses all the skills that are expected of a woman of her class. Even the Yamapuruṣa is captivated by her beauty and hesitates to snatch away her life.[28] The young disciple, Śāṇḍilya, is easily attracted to her ravishing beauty. Though a *gaṇikā* she is devoted to a single lover, Rāmilaka, to the extent that she forgives even his weakness for gambling. Just before her death and immediately after her revival also she thinks of her lover only.

Rāmilaka

Rāmilaka, the lover of Vasantasenā, has very little role in the play. He belongs to the rich *nāgaraka* class and spends most of his time in the *goṣṭhī* indulging in gambling and revelry. He has deep love for Vasantasenā. He is very much concerned when he learns that she is bitten by the serpent and immediately rushes to the spot, and arranges to bring the doctor. He is shocked to find his lady love talking philosophy and becomes relieved only when she calls him affectionately by name.

LITERARY MERITS IN THE PLAY

Bhagavadajjukīya occupies a unique place among the *prahasana* literature for its high literary merits. An account of the *rasa*,

26. *BA*, p. 78.
27. Ibid., p. 95.
28. Ibid., *śl*. 23.

alaṁkāras and other poetic merits of *BA* detailed below will exemplify this point.

THE SENTIMENT HĀSYA

Unlike other *prahasanas*, where *hāsya* is evoked by unseemly dress, speech and the like, the *BA* provides *hāsya* through really humorous situations. The topsy-turvy behaviour of the *gaṇikā* and the *yogin* when their souls are exchanged provides refreshingly original *hāsya*.

The *hāsya* in the play is at once dignified and delectable. For the disciple, the burning problem of the day is just how to get a day's meal without much effort. His way of offering salutation to the Buddha is quite funny: *āhārapramādaḥ sarvapramāda iti mantrayamāṇāya namo bhagavate buddhāya*. His mixing up of the Sāṁkhya and Śākyamata doctrines, his constant worry about food (*bhagavān susamāhito yogam cintayatu, aham susamāhita odanam cintayāmi*), his attempt to outwit his own teacher by quoting the moral codes,[29] his attempt to cover up his foolish fear on the mistaken identity of the peacock with a tiger[30] (*dāsyāḥ putraḥ vyāghraḥ madbhayena mayūrarūpam gṛhītvā palāyate*) . . . are some of the instances of good *hāsya*. The quack doctor is another humorous character in the play. He does not know even the rudiments of medicine. His grammatical blunder of treating *sarpa* as a neuter gender word and the consequent snubbing at the hands of the *gaṇikā* evokes laughter. Hurriedly remarking that the girl had been bitten by the "Grammarian serpent", he disappears from the scene before he is put to much severe ridicule.

PRAHASANA ELEMENTS IN THE BHAGAVADAJJUKĪYA

The opening speech of Śāṇḍilya where he repents for his

29. Cf. pp. 61, 62, *ayuktam pravrājakāṇām kopitum*.

30. Cf. p. 37.

life of asceticism and states the reason for his leaving Buddhism (since he cannot get food after midday) is an instance of the *prahasana* element known as *avalagitam*. Śāṇḍilya's fear at the imagined presence of a tiger in the garden is an instance of *bhayam* and the comparison of the *gaṇikā* to a *pravrājikā*[31] is an instance of *anṛtam*. When the doctor is asked to quote the relevant rules of Vaidyaśāstra, he struggles at the very first step and mutters some unintelligible sounds. This is called *gadgadavāk*. The conversation between the teacher and the disciple, in the garden may be cited as an instance of the *vīthyaṅga*, *udghātyaka*.

RASAS OTHER THAN HĀSYA IN THE BHAGAVADAJJUKĪYA

As already noticed,[32] *śṛṅgāra* ranks next to *hāsya* in importance, in the play. We have a delightful young pair of lovers in Rāmilaka and Vasantasenā.[33] The two love songs of Vasantasenā and Rāmilaka's appreciative words on the beauty of his love[34] are instances of *śṛṅgāra*. The disciple's love for the *gaṇikā* is *śṛṅgārābhāsa*, leading to *hāsya*. The other prominent *rasa* that figures in the play is *adbhuta* arising out of the exchange of the souls. Another *rasa* that strikes the mind of a discernible reader is *śānta*. The *vairāgya* of the *yogin* in the play and the references to the *anityatva* of the human body and the bondages of the worldly life, etc. contribute to the development of *śama* which is the *sthāyin* of *śānta rasa*.

ALAṀKĀRAS

Being a simple and small work, *BA* does not contain any

---

31. Cf. *BA*, p. 71.
32. See above in this book, chapter 3, under "Rasa Other than Hāsya in the Prahasanas".
33. *BA*, *śls*. 18 and 19.
34. Ibid., *śls*. 27 and 28.

complicated *alaṁkāras*. Instances of *upamā* are, of course, available in plenty, most of them on the lines of the Upaniṣadic similes. Human life is compared to a tree on a river bank ready to collapse and to a deep mire, dragging in the unsuspecting passers-by. The *śloka* in which the beauty of the heroine is described is outstanding for its simile.

सपल्लवैस्तप्तसुवर्णवर्णैरशोकपुष्पस्तबकैर्मनोज्ञैः ।
अन्तर्हिताभाति वराङ्गनैषा सन्ध्याभ्रजालैरिव चन्द्रलेखा ॥
— *śl.* 22

The conventional simile of the lover approaching his lady love like the bee seeking a lotus also finds its place in Rāmilaka's words.

इच्छामि तावदस्याः कलमधुरवचोमुखं विशालाक्ष्याः ।
मधुपव्रतोऽभिपातुं विकसितमिव कोमलं कमलम् ॥
— *śl.* 27

METRES

Though short, the *BA* uses a variety of metres, such as *āryā*, *anuṣṭubh*, *indravajrā*, *upendravajrā*, *vaṁśastha*, *praharṣiṇī*, *mālinī*, *vasantatilakā*, *śārdūlavikrīḍitam* and *sragdharā*.

PHILOSOPHICAL IDEAS PRESENT IN THE BHAGAVADAJJUKĪYA

In *BA*, we find the quintessence of Vedānta presented in a simple and sweet style. The permanence of the soul and the perishable nature of material world and the physical body are again and again pointed out.[35] Man thinks that his birth in the world is the result of good deeds done in his previous births and becomes enamoured of strength, youth and physical charm. He is never aware of his own defects and shortcomings.[36]

35. Cf. *śls.* 3 ff.

36. Ibid.

Man is just one among the several beings in the Universe, made up of the five elements — earth, water, fire, wind and ether.[37] It is the *karmātman* that experiences happiness and misery, sleeps, eats and does all things.[38] One must carry on his duties in a detached manner, controlling his lust.[39] One has to emulate the true *yogin*s who, free from conceit and concern, lead a simple life. One must seek the yogic knowledge which is the basis for all other types of knowledge, the essence of *tapas* and which puts an end to all sense of duality. This alone liberates an embodied soul,[40] from desire, hatred and other ill feelings. Yogic knowledge grants miraculous powers and even gods consider it as invaluable.[41] One must strive for attaining wisdom through a study of scriptures. The scriptural knowledge leads to higher knowledge (Supreme) which leads to self-control; self-control leads to penance which in turn leads to the attainment of yogic knowledge. The *yoga* brings in the knowledge of the past, present and future by which one realises the Ultimate Reality.[42] The aim of human life must be to attain the "True Knowledge" which is attained through meditation.[43] True Knowledge leads to the recognition and realisation of the unity between the individual and the Universal soul.[44] Those who are free from desire and are not touched by worldly miseries attain emancipation.[45] It is not

---

37. *Śl*. 9.
38. *Śl*. 8.
39. First half of *śl*. 6.
40. *Śl*. 15.
41. *Śl*. 14.
42. Passage between *śl*s. 13 and 14.
43. *Śl*s. 16, 17.
44. *Śl*. 17.
45. *Śl*. 11.

philosophy alone that the *BA* teaches. There are hints for practical wisdom and general ethics. One should abstain from things that are not within one's reach. No living being should be killed. One should desist from vain talk and untimely eating. One should maintain chastity and perform charities.[46] One should conquer pride and jealousy and should be free from bias and prejudices.[47] In times of doubt one must refer to the codes of conduct prescribed by the ancient seers which have stood the test of time and hence have become authentic.[48]

STYLE OF THE BHAGAVADAJJUKĪYA

BA has an archaic, simple and effective style of expression, reminding one of early writers like Bhāsa and Kālidāsa. The old style of drama, viz. verses for descriptions and prose for conversation — is generally followed, the practice of which is overlooked by later dramatists like Bhavabhūti who employs a large number of verses and long undramatic descriptions. The conversational style looks easy, natural and convincing, befitting stage requirements. The following conversation between the teacher and the disciple looks quite natural, bringing out the boyish impetuosity of the disciple and the mature wisdom of the teacher.[49]

परिव्राजकः — आगच्छ, वत्स अधीष्व तावत्।

शाण्डिल्यः — न तावदध्येष्ये (on another occasion he asks यद्यहं अधीये वा नाधीये वा किं तव मुक्तस्य?)

परिव्राजकः — किमर्थम्?

शाण्डिल्यः — अध्ययनस्य तावदर्थं श्रोतुं इच्छामि।

---

46. Passage between *śls*. 15 and 16.

47. Cf. *śl*. 12.

48. Cf. *śl*. 13.

49. Vide pp. 44-45.

परिव्राजकः — अधीताध्ययनैरपि कालान्तरविज्ञेया भवन्ति
अध्ययनार्थाः तस्माद् अधीष्व तावत् ।

Feminine curiosity and anxiety are well brought out in the conversation between Vasantasenā and her friends.[50] The words of the Yamapuruṣa very well bring out the haughtiness that is expected of him.

नानाराष्ट्रनदीवनाचलवतीं भूमिं समालोकयन्
मेघैस्तोयभरावनम्रनिचयैः प्रच्छाद्यमानो भृशम् ।
तीर्त्वा चारणसिद्धकिन्नरयुतं वातोद्धताभ्रं नभः
सम्प्राप्तोऽस्मि यमेन यत्र विहितस्तर्कादिवाहं पुरम् ॥
— *śl.* 21

The fussiness of the doctor is also quite appropriately brought out thus.

वैद्यः (उपविश्य मण्डलं रचयित्वा) कुण्डलकुटिलगामिनि, मण्डलं प्रविश, मण्डलम्, वासुकिपुत्र, तिष्ठ, शू, शू, यावच्छिरावेधं करिष्यामि ।
— p. 84

We do not have many descriptions in *BA*. The description of the garden and the sunset are however worth noting, of which the latter is outstanding for its imagery.

अस्तं गतो हि दिनकृत् गगनान्तलम्बी
मूषामुखस्थ इव तप्तसुवर्णराशिः ।
यस्य प्रभाभिरनुरञ्जितमेघवृन्दं
आलक्ष्यते दहनगर्भमिवान्तरिक्षम् ॥
— *śl.* 36

The setting sun, clinging to the end of the horizon, looks like the molten gold in a crucible. Being illumined by his rays, the clouds appear like the जठराग्नि of the sky.

---

50. Vide pp. 57-58.

DRAMATIC TECHNIQUE

Moulded in the classical drama style, *BA* may be said to follow the rules of dramaturgy reasonably well. At the same time it does not follow the rules blindly. The practical aspect of the play is given more attention to. One or two violations of the theory have not affected the reputation of the play and in fact such innovations speak for the originality of the playwright. Further, such exceptions may even indicate that the author followed some other texts on dramaturgy (i.e. other than the *NŚ*).

Nāndī and the Prologue

The *nāndī* in *BA* belongs to the *aṣṭapadī* type. As expected of a *nāndī*, the opening verse is a benedictory stanza dedicated to Lord Śiva and the verse also suggests the main theme of the play.[51] But it is doubtful whether the opening verse can be treated as the traditional *nāndī śloka*. The verse is found after the stage direction: *nāndyante tataḥ praviśati sūtradhāraḥ* and is recited by the *Sūtradhāra* himself. (In most of the classical dramas, we have *nāndī śloka* first and at the end of it, occurs the conventional stage direction *nāndyante tataḥ praviśati sūtradhāraḥ*.) This peculiar feature found in the *MV* also, is a characteristic feature of Bhāsa's plays. In the absence of any other benedictory stanza, the one we have as the opening verse, *tvām pāṭu lakṣaṇāḍhyaḥ* . . . etc. may be taken as the *nāndī śloka* for stage purposes.

The prologue is carried out by the *sūtradhāra* and the *vidūṣaka*. The *vidūṣaka* is most probably the disciple Śāṇḍilya in the main play, as is evident from his curiosity and inquisitiveness. The prologue of *BA* has a number of noteworthy features. Reference to the *siddhapuruṣa* and his

---

51. See above in this chapter fn. 3.

prediction (that the *sūtradhāra* is going to present a new play in the king's court on the seventh day) is suggestive of the character of the *yogin* and his miraculous powers. Then the *sūtradhāra* refers to ten kinds of play forms that have originated from *nāṭaka* and the *prakaraṇa*. This is definitely a new piece of information. The *nāṭaka* and the *prakaraṇa*, known to be the best forms of *rūpaka*s, are, in no work on dramaturgy, said to be the origin for the rest of the *rūpakas*. Of the ten *rūpaka*s that have sprung from the *nāṭaka* and the *prakaraṇa*, according to the *BA*, are two new varieties, *vāra* and *saṁlāpa*. *Saṁlāpa* at least is known through references in the dramaturgical works. The *Rasārṇavasudhākara* mentions it as one of the *uparūpaka*s. But the name *vāra* is totally unknown to Sanskrit dramatic tradition.

When the Vidūṣaka asks what a *prahasana* is, the *sūtradhāra* replies: *tena tu śikṣatu bhavān, na śakyam aśikṣitena kiñcidapi jñātum*. The reference to *śikṣaṇa* here is suggestive of the student-teacher theme in the main play. The prologue ends with a verse referring to the student following the teacher (the *yogin*) and the *parivrājaka* enters the stage at the end of the prologue. The entry of the character in the main body of the play thus belongs to the *proyogātiśaya* variety.

Vastu, Avasthā, Sādhana and Sandhis

The *vastu* in *BA* is *utpādya* or invented. The theme is *ādhikārika* in character and the play has only one act. Being simple in theme, a *prahasana* is expected to have only two *sandhis*, *mukha* and *nirvahaṇa*, the Opening and the Denouement. The *mukhasandhi* is indicated in the opening speech of the *yogin* where he refers to the ignorance of his disciple. His hope to reform his student is suggested through the words *tasmāt anaparāddhaḥ khalu ayam tapasvī. Punarapi samāhvānam kariṣye.*[52] The same is the *bīja* as also the *ārambha*. Midway between the *mukha* and the

52. *BA*, p. 8.

nirvahaṇa sandhis, occurs the *garbha sandhi* where a plan is envisaged to achieve the *kārya* and there is hope of success. Though not specifically sanctioned in theory, the *garbhasandhi* is clearly visible in the following statement of the *yogin*.

> *eṣa khalu tapasvī kartavyābodhyatayā āśramāpavādam na jānāti* ।
>
> *kiñcicchrutam maheśvarādibhiḥ yogācāryaiḥ śiṣyānukrośaḥ saṅgam na bādhata iti* ।
>
> *tadasya pratyayotpādanam kariṣyāmīdṛśo yoga iti, asyāḥ gaṇikāyāḥ śarīre ātmānam yojayāmi* ।[53]

The same passage accounts for *prāptyāśā* also. The achievement of the *kārya* is suggested. The student is no more interested in the *gaṇikā* and is happy to see his teacher regain his own soul. The suggestion is that the student is reformed. There is no *patākā* or *prakarī* in the play.

Texts on dramaturgy have made distinction between incidents that can be presented on the stage (*dṛśya*) and those that can be indicated (*sūcya*). *BA* has a peculiar problem. The Yamapuruṣa will have to appear on the stage but his form should not be visible to other characters on the stage. In order to make this scene realistic, the other characters must continue their conversation in the forefront while the Yamapuruṣa appears at the hinter part of the stage and announces the purpose of his visit. The setting near him (the cloud formation, for instance) must suggest that he is found in the sky. The snatching away of the life of the *gaṇikā* must be indicated by a thud of the foot and the hand gesticulating the snatch. Likewise, skilful gesticulation on the part of the characters of the *yogin* and the *gaṇikā* are necessary to represent the abnormal behaviour due to their exchanged souls. As mentioned earlier,

---

53. *BA*, p. 76.

BA breaks the dramatic convention by presenting a death scene on the stage. But the play does not have a tragic end since both the parties concerned come back to life later.[54]

As discussed earlier[55] there is scope for *lāsyāṅga* in *BA*. The two love songs sung by the *gaṇikā* can be represented by a *lāsya* dance.

Time Analysis

The incidents of *BA* last for a day from morning till evening. The disciple refers to breakfast in his opening speech: *ā eṣa duṣṭaliṅgī prātaraśanalobhena ekākī bhikṣāmāhiṇḍitum pūrva eva gataḥ iti tarkayami.*[56] The play comes to an end with a description of the evening thus completing a day of action.

Bharatavākya

As pointed out earlier[57] *BA* does not have a Bharatavākya in the conventional style. It just ends with a description of the evening. The editor of the Kerala edition adds the following note after the Bharatavākya,

> A (one of the manuscripts) adds after *niṣkrāntau* two verses, of which the first has appeared as one of the two Bharatavākyas in *Nāgānanda* (Bombay Edition).[58]

---

54. Ānandavardhana in his *Dhvanyāloka* allows death on the stage provided the persons dead revive within a reasonable period of time, *śṛṅgāre vā, maraṇasyādīrghakālapratyāpattisambhave kadācidupanibandho nāṭyantavirodhī* — cf. *Dhvanyāloka*, ch. III, p. 368, Chowkhamba edn.
55. See above chapter 3 in this book under "Lāsyāṅgas in Prahasanas".
56. *BA*, p. 9.
57. See above in this chapter under "Bharatavākya".
58. *BA*, p. 97.

THE INFLUENCE OF ŚRUTI AND SMṚTI TEXTS ON THE BHAGAVADAJJUKĪYA

The author of *BA* reveals his sound scholarship in different Śāstras through the *yogin* in the play. The text that seems to have influenced the author to a great extent is the *Bhagavad-Gītā*. The very first *śloka* in the main body of the play[59] which speaks of the impermanence of the human body reminds one of the *Gītā* passage (II.18) अन्तवन्त इमे देहाः नित्यस्योक्ताः शरीरिणः, etc. The same *śloka* states how man is foolishly proud of his birth and considers it a privilege to have possessed a body. A parallel idea can be found in the *Muṇḍaka Upaniṣad* (I.29):

अविद्यायां बहुधा वर्तमाना वयं कृतार्था इत्यभिमन्यन्ति बालाः

The *Mānavadharma-Śāstra* too speaks of the *anityatva* of the human body.

अस्थिस्थूणं स्नायुयुतं मांसशोणितलेपनम्।
चर्मावनद्धं दुर्गन्धि पूर्णं मूत्रपुरीषयोः॥

जराशोकसमाविष्टं रोगायतनमातुरम्।
रजस्वलमनित्यं च भूतावसमिमं त्यजेत्॥
— VI.76-77

The *BA* states that one must perform actions in this world in a detached style[60] which reflects the *Gītā* passage (II.48):

योगस्थः कुरु कर्माणि सङ्गं त्यक्त्वा धनञ्जय।

The *yogin*'s explanation of the state of *asaṅgatā* as *rāgadveṣayormadhyasthatā* . . . and the following verse:

सुखेषु दुःखेषु च नित्यतुल्यतां
भयेषु हर्षेषु च नातिरिक्तताम्।

---

59. Vide, *śl.* 3, *deho roganidhiḥ* . . . etc.

60. Vide *śl.* 6.

सुहृत्स्वमित्रेषु च भावतुल्यतां
वदन्ति तां तत्वविदो ह्यसङ्गताम्॥
— *śl.* 7

reminds us of the *Gītā* passage (II.38).

सुखदुःखे समे कृत्वा लाभालाभौ जयाजयौ।

Regarding the proper time for the ascetics to go for *bhikṣā*, the *yogin* in *BA* says,

न्यस्तमुसले व्यङ्गारे सर्वभुक्तजने काल इत्युपदेशः[61]

which corresponds to the relevant rule,

विधूमे सन्नमुसले व्यङ्गारे भुक्तवज्जने।
वृत्ते शरावसम्पाते भिक्षां नित्यं यतिश्चरेत्॥[62]

Distinguishing between the *antarātmā* and the *karmātmā*, the *BA* says that the *karmātmā* is the enjoyer of the different moods, कर्मात्मा श्रमसुखभाजनं नराणाम्[63]

which reflects the śāstric statement,

पञ्चप्राणमनोबुद्धि दशेन्द्रियसमन्वितम्।
अपञ्चीकृतभतोत्थं सूक्ष्माङ्गं भोगसाधनम्॥[64]

The *BA* warns that discontentment and lack of concentration will never lead to emancipation.[65] The positive aspect of the same idea is expressed in the *Gītā*.

युञ्जन्नेवं सदात्मानं योगी नियतमानसः।
शान्तिं निर्वाणपरमां मत्संस्थां अधिगच्छति॥
— VI.15

61. *BA*, p. 26.
62. Quoted in the Com., p. 26
63. *BA*, *śl.* 8.
64. Quoted in the Com., p. 29. See *Ātma-bodha of Śaṅkara*, V.13.
65. *BA*, śl. 11.

One must follow the codes of conduct prescribed by the wise and take them as *pramāṇa*, in times of doubt, says the *BA*[66] which reflects the *Gītā* passages,

यद्यदाचरति श्रेष्ठः तत्तदेव इतरो जनः[67]

and

तस्मात् शास्त्रं प्रमाणं ते[68]

On Yoga the *Kaṭhopaniṣad* says:

तां योगमिति मन्यन्ते स्थिरां इन्द्रियधारणाम् ।
अप्रमत्तस्तदा भवति योगो हि प्रभवाप्ययौ ॥

— VI.11

The following definition of the Yoga as given in *BA* corresponds to the above:

ज्ञानमूल तपःसारं सत्वस्थं द्वन्द्वनाशनम् ।
मुक्तं द्वेषाच्च रागाच्च योग इत्यभिधीयते ॥

— *śl.* 15

The reference to *dvandvanāśana* in the *BA* has parallel again, in the *Gītā* (II.45):

निर्द्वन्द्वो नित्यसत्वस्थो निर्योगक्षेम आत्मवान्

The *Kauṣītaki Upaniṣad* too stresses that the abandonment of the "pairs of opposites" is necessary for the realisation of the *Brahman*:

66. *BA*, *śl*s. 12 and 13.

67. *Gītā*, III, 21.

68. Cf. *Gītā*, XVI.24:

तस्माच्छास्त्रं प्रमाणं ते कार्याकार्यव्यवस्थितौ ।
ज्ञात्वा शास्त्रविधानोक्तं कर्म कर्तुं इहार्हसि ॥

Cf. also *Manusmṛti*, II.6:

वेदोऽखिलो धर्ममूलं स्मृतिशीले च तद्विदाम् ।
आचारश्चैव साधूनां आत्मनस्तुष्टिरेव च ॥

Cf. *Pūrvamīmāṁsā*, I.iii.7:

अपि वा कारणाग्रणे प्रयुक्तानि प्रतीयेरन् ॥

एवं सुकृत दुष्कृते सर्वाणि च द्वन्द्वानि, स एष
विसुकृतो विदुष्कृतो ब्रह्म विद्वान् ब्रह्मैवाभिप्रैति।

— I.4

The *BA* stresses the importance of *dhyāna* for the attainment of "True Knowledge", ध्यानमेतत् ज्ञानप्रयोजनम् which finds a parallel in the *Chāndogya Upaniṣad*.

अस्ति भगवो ध्यानात् भूय इति
यावद्ध्यानस्य गतं तत्रास्य यथा कामचारो भवति।

— VIII.6.2

Describing how one should control the senses and concentrate on the soul, the *BA* says:

सर्वं जगत् संक्षिप देहबन्धे यथेन्द्रियाण्यात्मनि योजयित्वा।
ज्ञानेन सत्वं समुपाश्रय त्वं देहात्मनात्मानमवेक्ष्य कृत्स्नम्॥

— *śl.* 17

The invincibility of the sense-organs and the need to control them has been very much dwelt upon in the *Gītā* and the Upaniṣads. The *Gītā* says:

यततो ह्यपि कौन्तेय पुरुषस्य विपश्चितः।
इन्द्रियाणि प्रमाथीनि हरन्ति प्रसभं मनः॥

तानि सर्वाणि सम्यम्य युक्त आसीत मत्परः।
वशे हि यस्येन्द्रियाणि तस्य प्रज्ञा प्रतिष्ठिता॥

— II.60-61

On the revolving cycle of birth and death, the *BA* says:

स्वकर्म भोक्तुं जायन्ते प्रायेणैव हि जन्तवः।
क्षीणे कर्मणि चान्यत्र पुनर्गच्छन्ति देहिनः॥

— *śl.* 24

This reminds us of the *śruti* passage quoted in the *Vedānta-paribhāṣā*:

तद्यथेह कर्मचितो लोकः क्षीयते, एवमेवामुत्र पुण्यकृतो लोकः क्षीयते[69]

INFLUENCE OF THE BHAGAVADAJJUKĪYA ON OTHER PRAHASANAS

BA has served as a model for all the *śuddha* type of *prahasana*s that appeared later. Its influence on the *MV* is evident from its quoting the Buddhistic code of conduct found in the former. The disciple in *Hāsyacūḍāmaṇi* has Śāṇḍilya as his model and the lovers Kalākaraṇḍaka and Madanasundarī therein are replicas of the pair in *BA*. The *prahasana* that has been influenced by *BA* to a greater extent is the *Madanaketucarita* (*MKC*) of Rāmapāṇivāda.[70]

As in *BA*, the reformation of an erring religious man is the central theme in *MKC*, and here too the *parakāyapraveśa* technique is employed by the *yogin*. The *gaṇikā* is again the cause of temptation in *MKC*, as in *BA*. The influence of *BA* over *MKC* as also *prahasana*s will be better understood when individual *prahasana*s are taken up for discussion in the subsequent portion of this book.

PRĀKṚT IN BHAGAVADAJJUKĪYA

In accordance with dramatic conventions here also the higher characters speak in Sanskrit and the lower characters in Prākṛt. The *sūtradhāra*, the *parivrājaka*, Rāmilaka and the Yamapuruṣa speak in Sanskrit, while all the women characters, the attendants, the doctor, the *vidūṣaka* and Śāṇḍilya use Prākṛt. The *gaṇikā*, infused with the soul of the *yogin* speaks in Sanskrit and likewise the *yogin* infused with the soul of the *gaṇikā* rightly speaks in Prākṛt. The two love songs rendered by the *gaṇikā* are in

69. *Chāndogya Upaniṣad* 8.1.6

70. Vide "Rāmapāṇivāda's indebtedness to the author of Bhagavadajjukīya" — paper submitted to the All India Oriental Conference, Poona, 1978, by the present writer.

Sanskrit. The Prākṛt employed in *BA* is generally Śaurasenī which is the closest to Sanskrit among the Prākṛt dialects, and hence poses no problem to follow.

THE COMMENTARY

The Trichur edition of the text contains a commentary named *Diṅmātradarśinī* by an anonymous Kerala writer. But it is evident that he was a disciple of the great Nārāyaṇa Bhaṭṭatiri, the author of *Nārāyaṇīya*.[71] The commentary can thus be assigned to the seventeenth century. (The commentator mentions that he wrote a commentary *Bhāvārthadīpikā*[72] on *Uttararāmacarita*.) It is this commentary which gives the name of the author of *BA* as "Bodhāyana Kavi". The commentator proposes to explain the inner meanings (*gūḍhārtha*)[73] of the original work and tries to interpret every line with a philosophical outlook. But sometimes even simple expressions are explained laboriously to suit his own plan. Nevertheless the importance of the commentary cannot be underestimated. He quotes appropriate Śruti and Smṛti texts here and there implied by the passages in the original work. He also gives the *chāyā* of the Prākṛt passages in the text. Some of the dialogues have been versified by the commentator. For instance, the conversation between the *gaṇikā* and her friend is rendered in a verse form thus:

प्रणयकोपपराङ्मुखवल्लभ-
प्रणयविह्वलधीर्मधु बोधिता।
इति जगाद ततो गणिका सखीं
क्व नु गतो बत रामिलको मम॥

— p. 56

71. Cf. *BA*, p. 41: *yathoktamasmadgurubhiḥ* . . . etc.

72. Vide *BA*, p. 98.

73. *BA*, p. 1

SOCIAL CONDITIONS OF THE STATE AT THE TIME OF BHAGAVADAJJUKĪYA

The social life in India at the time of *BA* seems to be one of peace and prosperity, marked by stable rule and religious tolerance. Kings patronised poets and scholars and encouraged fine arts and literature. There were weekly performances of drama, dance and music,[74] and artists were substantially rewarded.[75] The elite of the public lived in the main parts of the cities and at the outskirts of the cities there were beautiful gardens abutting forests. The ascetic teachers and their disciples used to resort to these gardens for privacy. There were hermitages of the Hindu monks and Buddhist monasteries in many parts, in and around the city. People lived in amity and peace. They were interested in fine arts and dramatic performances were generally welcomed. They believed in Astrology and approached the well-informed ascetics to know about their future.[76] There were big festivals and celebrations.[77] As in all ages in India, superstition had its sway over the common people.

The brāhmaṇas held key positions in society and were proud of their lineage,[78] though languishing in poverty at times. Enlightened sages lived in *āśrama*s and attracted students and devotees. They possessed miraculous yogic powers but demonstrated it only for a good cause.[79] The student-teacher relationship was generally smooth. The *gurukula* system of

74. Cf. the prologue of *BA*.
75. Cf. Ibid.
76. Cf. Prologue.
77. Cf. Śāṇḍilya's words, p. 15.
78. Ibid., pp. 8-9.
79. Cf. The Parivrājaka's words, p. 76.

education was in practice. Erring students were punished only with the aim of instilling discipline in them. Students were expected to memorise their lessons, the importance of which would be known to them only in later years.[80] The teachers were versatile scholars in different branches of learning — scriptures, philosophy and general knowledge. The ascetics ate very little, just to sustain themselves and the food was procured by begging.[81] Leaders of different religious sects lived in peace and amity. Conversion from one religion to the other was easy and devoid of rigid restrictions.[82] Buddhist monks had their own monasteries and observed strict rules with regard to congregation and food habits.[83]

Next to brāhmaṇas the *nāgarakas* (lit. elite citizens) occupied an important place in society. They moved among high circles and were usually rich. They lived an easy way of life and were given to the pleasures of life. They spent much of their time in *goṣṭhis*[84] where they gambled and drank liquor.

The *gaṇikās* had a special status in society. By virtue of their skills in dancing and music and of course, by their personal charm, they attracted the *nāgarakas*. There were also *gaṇikās* like Vasantasenā who were devoted to a single person.

The medical needs of the people were attended to by

80. Cf. The Parivrājaka's words, p. 44.

81. Ibid., p. 26.

82. Cf. Śāṇḍilya's words, pp. 8-9.

83. Ibid.

84. See *BA*, p. 57. On *Ghoṣṭi* Cf. *Kāmasūtra*, ch. IV, ed. CSS., 1964, p. 136: *veśyābhavane sabhāyām anyatamasya udvasite vā samāna vidyā buddhi śilavitta-vayasām saha vesyābhiḥ anurūpaiṅ ālāpaiḥ āsanbandhogoṣṭhī tatra madhu-maireya-surā-āsavān vividha lavaṇa-phalaharita-śāka-tikta-kaṭuka-āmla upadmaśān veśyāḥ, pāyayeyuh anupibeyusca.*

qualified physicians. Different kinds of ailments like *garbhasrāva* (abortion), *piṭakajvara* (typhoid), *karṇaroga* (ear infection), tumors of the heart, eye and brain were diagnosed and treated. Both oral and external applications were prescribed. Medicinal tablets were prepared afresh by the physicians themselves and given to the patients. Physicians cured snakebites also. More often spells and incantations were resorted to for curing the ailments. The physicians sometimes acted as exorcists in driving out the evil spirits. The doctors were paid handsomely. There also used to be quacks.

CONCLUSION

The *Bhagavadajjukīya* excels other *prahasanas* in every aspect and is one of the most interesting and original pieces in the whole range of Sanskrit drama. It is also one of the most frequently staged Sanskrit plays. The humour in *BA* is dignified and free from vulgarity. It has an excellent theme and thought-provoking moral instructions. Lofty philosophical ideas are presented in lucid verses, and illustrated with suitable similes. *BA* has influenced a number of later *prahasanas* and stands as a model play even for the writers of the present day.

The Mattavilāsa-prahasana[85]

Next in importance to the *BA*, is the *MV* of King Mahendravarman Pallava. "This *prahasana* is a remarkably smart production of genre, replete with mirth and satire. The characters are vigorously drawn throwing a flood of light on the contemporary life." Like the *BA*, *MV* has also been quite

---

85. Its editions: (i) Trivandrum Sanskrit Series, No. 55, 1917.
(ii) Chowkhamba Sanskrit Series.
(iii) Dr N.P. Unni, Trivandrum, 1973.

The page references in the following pages are from the edition referred to last.

popular with the Kerala stage-tradition of Kūḍiyāṭṭam. The popularity of *MV* can be assessed from the fact that it has gone through three editions and a number of translations in different languages both Indian and foreign, from time to time. It has been analysed by Professor Keith,[86] Mankad[87] and Krishnamachariar.[88] Dr Barnett took special interest in this work and published a translation of *MV*.[89] A number of articles have also appeared in research journals, dealing with some of the important problems connected with this play.[90]

AUTHOR AND DATE

Fortunately we do not have many problems with regard to the author and the date of *MV*. We have clear reference to the author's name in the prologue itself. Mention is made of some of the royal titles of Mahendravarman in the prologue as also in the Bharatavākya. The date of the work can be fixed as *c*. CE 610, on the basis of the Māmaṇḍūr inscription.[91]

Mahendravarman was a gifted poet. That he could spare time for his literary pursuits in spite of hectic political activity, speaks high of his love for literature. He succeeded his father Siṁhaviṣṇu to the Pallava throne and his reign is noteworthy in the history of south India for a number of reasons. Jainism

86. *Sanskrit Drama* by Keith, pp. 182-85.
87. *Types of Sanskrit Drama* by D.R. Mankad.
88. *History of Classical Sanskrit Literature*, by M. Krishnamachariar.
89. *Bulletin of the School of Oriental Studies*, 1930.
90. (i) *Die Streiche der Brauchten* by Dr Hortel, Leipzig, 1924.

    (ii) Article by T.A. Gopinatha Rao, *Madras Christian College Magazine*, 1917.

    (iii) "The Royal Artist Mahendrapallava" by T.N. Ramachandran, *Journal of Oriental Research*, Madras, vol. VII, pp. 235-37.
91. See above p. 79.

which held its sway in south India till the early part of his reign, lost its hold on society gradually. There was a revival of Hindu religions especially of Śaivism during the later part of his rule. Rock-cut temple architecture was given a new impetus during his reign. Architecture, music, dance, and other fine arts flourished under his rule.

Mahendravarman's period was one of political turmoil. The Pallava king faced constant threat from the powerful Cāḷukyan king, Pulakeśin II and there are conflicting accounts as to who conquered whom. The Kāsakkudi plates belonging to the period of Nandivarman II (CE 710-75) say that Mahendravarman defeated his enemy at a place called Pallalur near Kāñcīpuram.[92] But according to the Aihoḷe inscription,[93] Mahendravarman was confined within his fortress when the Cāḷukyan army besieged his capital. Anyhow it is clear that the Pallava capital could not be captured by the Cāḷukyan king and King Mahendravarman must have possessed considerable war tactics in halting the advancement of his powerful enemy.

Mahendravarman was the forerunner of the rock-cut temple architecture in south India. Rock-cut temples dedicated to deities of different religions took shape during his reign. The temples at Māmaṇḍūr, Mahendravāḍī, Singavaram and Nāmakkal are dedicated to Lord Viṣṇu while those at Siyamaṅgalam, Pallavapuram, Vallam, Dalavanur, Tirukazhukkunram and Trichinopoly are Śaivite in character. The temple at Mandagapaṭṭu is called Trimūrti Temple and the rock-cuts at Chitannavasal are Jaina temples.[94] The rock temples at Mahābalipuram near Madras are also attributed to him, though it is generally believed that his son,

92. Cf. *South India Inscriptions*, vol. II, p. 356.

93. Cf. *Epigraphia Indica*, vol. VI, p. 11.

94. *History of Pallavas*, p. 96, Madras: Saiva Siddhānta Publishers, 1971.

Narasiṁhavarman Pallava directed the construction of these temples.

Mahendravarman bore a number of titles, some of which appear paradoxical (e.g. *Mattavilāsa*). More than a dozen of his titles appear in various temple-inscriptions and works.[95] These titles which are in Sanskrit, Prākṛt, Tamil and Telugu are given below along with their English equivalents.

T — Trichy cave temple.

P — Pallavapuram cave temple.

K — Kāñcī Pillar (now in Madras Museum)

S — Siyamaṅgalam cave temple.

C — Chezarla slab inscription.

M — Mandagapaṭṭu cave temple.

1. *Akaruṇaḥ* — (T) Skt. Merciless.
2. *Anumānaḥ* — (TP) Skt. Logician.
3. *Abhimukhaḥ* — (TPK) Skt. Forward-looking.
4. *Avanibhājanaḥ* — (TPSC) Skt. Receptacle of the world.
5. *Iṣṭaduṣṭacaritaḥ* — (TP) Skt. Performer of good, bad and degenerate acts.
6. *Kaduntarambu* — (TP) Telugu, Fierce tidal wave.
7. *Caḷmbu* — (T) Telugu, Active, Charming.
8. *Citrakārappuli* — (TPK) Tamil, Tiger among artists.
9. *Ceththākkāri* — (TP) Old Tamil, Engraver of inscriptions.
10. *Tukānu* — (TP) Pkt. (?); One who looks after the distressed.

95. Cf. *Bhagavadajjukīya*, ed. M. Lockwood and A. Vishnu Bhat, Madras, 1978, Appendix D.

11. *Nirapekṣaḥ* — (T) One free from desires.
12. *Pravṛttamātraḥ* — (P) Skt. Devoted to welfare of the people.
13. *Mattavilāsaḥ* — (TP) Skt. One who sports with revelry.
14. *Mūrkhavijaya* — (TP) Pkt. One who has won over the rogues.
15. *Kakṣitaḥ* — (TPM) Skt. Distinguished.
16. *Lokavaśyaḥ* — (P) Skt. One who has controlled the world.
17. *Vicitracittaḥ* — (TP) Skt. One of an inventive mind.
18. *Vidhiḥ* — (T) Skt. Systematic, Creative Order.
19. *Vunātha* — (TPK) Pkt. (?) from Skt. Vināthaḥ, One without a master over himself.

Mahendravarman's contribution to literature is matching his achievement in other fields. The *Bhagavadajjukīya* is also attributed to him by some scholars, though it is difficult to accept the common authorship of these two *prahasanas*, as already discussed above.[96] A work called *Gandhamādana*, which is known only from references is attributed to him.[97] But it is *Mattavilāsa-prahasana* which has won him universal fame as a writer of a unique farce in Sanskrit literature.

THE PLOT

Dramatis Personae

Sūtradhāra	:	the stage manager.
Naṭī	:	an actress.
Satyasoma	:	a Kāpālika.

96. See above in this chapter under "The Bhagavadajjukīya".

97. See Introduction (p. 14) *Mattavilāsa-prahasana*, ed. N.P. Unni.

Devasomā	:	the fiancee of the Kāpālika.
Nāgasena	:	a Buddhist monk.
Babhrukalpa	:	a Pāśupata.
Unmattaka	:	a lunatic.

A Kāpālika, by name Satyasoma, enters the scene accompanied by his fiancee, Devasomā. Both are heavily drunken and in this state, the Kāpālika forgets the name of his companion and calls her Somadeva. Devasomā takes him to task for this *gotraskhalana*. Satyasoma asks for pardon and blames his own drunkenness for the mistake and vows to stop drinking. But Devasomā pleads with him not to stop drinking which she terms "sacred". After praising his own sect which permits drinking and throwing an attack on Buddhism, the Kāpālika wants to have another bout. They move to a nearby liquor shop which is compared to a sacrificial hall. The Kāpālika notices that his begging bowl is missing. He also laments that the loss of his bowl may lead to banishment from his religious order. The Kāpālika fears that it might have been stolen either by a dog or by a Buddhist monk since it contained a piece of roasted meat.

Then arrives a Buddhist monk, cursing the elderly monks of his order for prohibiting wine and women. He feels that originally there were portions in the sacred texts which permitted these things and that they have been deliberately suppressed by the old monks out of jealousy for the younger monks. He vows to trace the original text and thus render yeoman service to his religion. The sight of this monk hiding something inside of his cloak arouses the suspicion of the Kāpālika. He demands the monk to show the hidden object. The *bhikṣu* says that it is his own begging bowl but the Kāpālika charges him with stealing of his bowl. In the fight that ensues, the Kāpālika and his companion Devasomā are knocked down by the sturdy Buddhist monk. Enters then a Pāśupata who offers to mediate between them. The *bhikṣu* then shows up his bowl which is red in colour. But the Kāpālika says that the original black colour of his own bowl might have been turned red by the sticky reddish robe of the Buddhist monk.

Now comes a mad man carrying a bowl which he had snatched from a dog. The Kāpālika recognises it to be his own bowl. He tries to snatch it away from the lunatic who refuses to budge. Being called an *unmattaka* the lunatic requests the Kāpālika to show another *unmattaka* whom he is anxious to meet, and take the bowl as fee for his services. The Kāpālika directs the lunatic to look for the *unmattaka* behind a wall and the lunatic hurries behind, leaving the bowl. The Kāpālika feels elated at the recovery of his bowl. Devasomā remarks that her lover shines in the company of his bowl like the evening in conjuction with the moon. The play comes to an end with the conventional Bharatavākya.

CHARACTER STUDY

The Kāpālika

Satyasoma, the Kāpālika, satisfies the conditions of the *adhama* hero. He is the main character in the play. He is a degraded ascetic of the Kāpālika order and resides near the Ekāmranātha Temple in Kāñcī. He is, what we may term, an Epicurean by his faith. According to him,

पेया सुरा प्रियतमामुखमीक्षितव्यं
ग्राह्यः स्वभावललितो विकृतश्च वेषः।
येनेदमीदृशमदृश्यत मोक्षवर्त्म
दीर्घायुरस्तु भगवान् स पिनाकपाणिः ॥[98]

The liquor shop is the sacrificial ground for him.[99] At times

98. *MV*, *śl.* 7.

99. Ibid., pp. 45-56, N.P. Unni edn., Trivandrum, 1974.

he is disgusted with his own evil habit of drinking.[100] He is dogmatic in his religious beliefs and throws blistering attacks on Buddhists now and then.[101] According to him the Buddhists culled out portions from the *Mahābhārata* and Upaniṣads and compiled their own texts.

वेदान्तेभ्यो गृहीत्वार्थान् यो महाभारतादपि।
विप्राणां मिषतामेव कृतवान् कोशसञ्चयम् ॥

— *śl.* 12

Satyasoma is not altogether devoid of finer sentiments. His description of Kāñcī has the touch of an artist.[102] He has not also altogether neglected the study of the scriptures. He knows for instance, the expiatory ceremony performed by Lord Śiva after he crushed the head of Brahmā.[103] He has the genius of misrepresenting the true significance of the precepts and practices of his own sect.[104] For him the true sign of a Kāpālika is the begging bowl alone. Only when his lost bowl is recovered, he feels he becomes a Kāpālika again. *Bhagavatprasādāt punarapi kapālī samvṛttaḥ* (p. 65). He sees the manifestation of his Lord in his bowl.

तिरोहितः स तु सहसा सुखेन नः
त्वमद्य यत् कुशलि कपाल दृश्यसे।

— *śl.* 21-b

Devasomā

Devasomā is the heroine of the play. She is probably a *gaṇikā*. She was first associated with a Pāśupata but switched over to

100. *MV*, N.P. Unni edn., Trivandrum, p. 43.
101. Cf. ibid., *śl.* 8.
102. P. 45.
103. See ibid., *śl.* 17.
104. See ibid., *śl.* 6, *peyā surā* . . . etc.

the side of the Kāpālika expecting better benefits. She follows him to the liquor shops and drinks in good measure. She pleads with him not to give up drinking. For her, the city of Kāñcī is as sweet as liquor. *Bhagavan, bahagvatī vāruṇī iva anavagīta-madhurā kāñcī.*[105] She is quickwitted. As the Kāpālika compares the liquor shop to a sacrifice, she completes the simile saying that their *bhikṣā* is comparable to the portion set apart for Lord Śiva in the sacrifice.[106] She has full faith in the religion of her companion. She is very shrewd in spotting the suspect, the Buddhist monk, even on the crowded main road.[107] When it is the question of fighting she is up her sleeves. She calls the Buddhist monk *dāsyāḥputraḥ* and kicks him. She avoids the matter being taken to the court under the pretext that the Buddhist monk might bribe the concerned officers and get a judgement in his favour.[108]

The Buddhist Monk

The Buddhist monk Nāgasena represents the corrupt state of his religious sect during Mahendravarman's times. His very appearance is uncouth according to Devasomā (p. 50). He has not forsaken any pleasures of the world. He has a flair for non-vegetarian food and soft couches.[109] He is totally unhappy about the prohibition of wine and women in his religion. According to him, Lord Buddha would not have been so unkind to his followers by prohibiting these. He blames the older brother-monks who would have suppressed the original canonical texts permitting wine and women for the monks.

105. *MV*, N.P. Unni edn., Trivandrum, p. 45.
106. Ibid., p. 46.
107. Ibid., p. 50.
108. Ibid., p. 61.
109. *MV*, pp. 48-49.

It would be his life's mission to restore the original texts granting these things.[110] He has a weakness for women. At the sight of Devasomā he remarks, *aho lalitarūpā upāsikā*.[111] Under the pretext of helping Devasomā get up after her fall, he takes hold of her hand, but justifies his action saying, *dharmaḥ khalu asmākam viṣamapatitānukampā*.[112] He wants to avoid an encounter with the drunken Kāpālika but when provoked he knocks out both his opponents at one stroke. He thanks Lord Buddha for prescribing shaven head for monks when Devasomā tries to pull his hair but falls down without getting a hold.[113] When liquor is offered to him he wants to grab it but hesitates since others may see it.[114] He is of course aware of some of the important precepts of his religion.[115]

Babhrukalpa, the Pāśupata

The character of the Pāśupata is the weak link in the play. He has been introduced as a pseudo-religious person just to give variety in the cast. He does not lag behind the Kāpālika in his weakness for wine and women. He is angry with the Kāpālika for usurping his love and he vows to avenge for it.[116] He offers to mediate between the two parties but remains a silent spectator when the Kāpālika and the Buddhist monk fight tooth and nail for the alms bowl. He admits his inability to settle their dispute and suggests that they refer the matter to the court. His reference to those who mete out justice is significant:

110. *MV*, pp. 48-49.
111. Ibid., p. 51.
112. Ibid., p. 55.
113. Ibid.
114. Cf. ibid., p. 53.
115. Ibid., pp. 56-57.
116. Cf. *MV*, p. 56.

अजिह्मैः सारगुरुभिः स्थिरैः श्लक्ष्णैः सुजन्मभिः।
तैर्धर्मो धार्यते स्तम्भैः प्रासाद इव साधुभिः॥

— *śl.* 18

His blessing for the disputants is interesting:

विरोधः पूर्वसम्बद्धो युवयोरस्तु शाश्वतः।
परस्परप्रीतिकरः किरातार्जुनयोरिव॥

— *śl.* 22

He has real interest in the religious rites of his sect, for instance, he observes the *dhūmavelā* strictly.[117]

LITERARY MERITS

The feebleness of the theme in *MV* should not make us ignore the literary merits of the poet. The work reveals the poet's descriptive powers, clever handling of *hāsya*, usage of appropriate *alaṁkāra*s and metres, and deftness in characterisation — in short, all the merits of a good dramatist. His description of the feminine charms is quite beautiful, as in:

उद्भिन्नरोमाञ्चकपोलरेखम् आविर्मयूखस्मितमञ्चितभ्रु।
लब्ध्वा प्रिये दुर्लभमाननं ते भूयोऽपि किं प्रार्थयितव्यमस्ति॥[118]

The Kāpālika's description of his fiancee is noteworthy for its passion.

उद्भिन्नश्रमवारिबिन्दु वदनं सभ्रूलताविभ्रमम्
खेलं यातमकारणानि हसितान्यव्यक्तवर्णा गिरः।
रागाक्रान्तमधीरतारमलसापाङ्गं युगं नेत्रयोर्
अंसोपान्तविलम्बिनश्च विगलन्मालागुणा मूर्धजाः॥[119]

— *śl.* 6

117. Cf. p. 67.

118. *MV*, *śl.* 2.

119. Cf. *Abhijñānaśākuntala*, I.30: *srastāṁsau*, etc.

The description of Kāñcī is pleasant.[120] The scene of the dancing drunkards in the liquor shop brings out the poet's minute observation.

> अहो दर्शनीयानि प्रहतमर्दलकरणानुगतानि विविधाङ्गहारवचनभ्रूविकाराणि उच्छ्रितैकहस्तवलम्बितोत्तरीयाणि विगलितवसनप्रतिसमाधानक्षणविषमित-लयानि व्याकुलितकण्ठगुणानि मत्तविलासनृत्यानि ।[121]

The poet has given a few thought-provoking axioms and some of them reveal his mastery over the Nyāyaśāstra.

(i) न हि प्रतिज्ञामात्रेण हेतुवादिनः सिद्धिरस्ति ।[122]

(ii) प्रत्यक्षे हेतुवचनं निरर्थकम् ।[123]

(iii) कुतश्चिदपि न्यायवृत्तेः भयं नास्ति ।[124]

The poet is adept in the use of *anuprāsa* as revealed in:

(i) भाषावेषवपुःक्रियागुणकृतानाश्रित्य भेदान् गतं
भावावेशवशादनेकरसतां त्रैलोक्ययात्रामयम् ।
— *śl*. 1

(ii) न हि लोकोपकारनिरतो लोकनाथो लोकं विनाशयति ।[125]

The play has *śloka*s composed in well-known metres like *anuṣṭubh, āryā, indravajrā, mālinī, rucirā, vaṁśastha, vasantatilakā, śārdūlavikrīḍita* and *sragdharā*.

ALAṀKĀRAS

Upamā figures prominently among the *alaṁkāra*s. The poet

---

120. *MV*, p. 45.
121. Ibid., p. 46.
122. Ibid., p. 57.
123. Ibid., p. 57.
124. Ibid., p. 63.
125. Ibid., p. 46.

being compared to the Primeval Being,[126] and the absence of bowl saddening the Kāpālika like the loss of a worthy friend,[127] are noteworthy. Some of the similes serve to heighten the comic effect, as in the Pāśupata's words:

तां क्षौरिकस्य दासीं मम दयितां चीवरान्तदर्शितया।
आकर्षति काकण्या बहुशो गां ग्राससमुष्ट्येव॥

— *śl.* 14

We have an instance of *rūpaka* in the following passage:

आ मम नष्टभिक्षाभाजनदर्शनकुतूहलमलयानिलप्रयुक्ताया ध्रुवमस्यनृत्तबुद्धिः प्रीतिलताया विलसितेषु।[128]

A novel idea that Manmatha has not been destroyed by Lord Śiva and that he has taken the form of the liquor inducing passion in the hearts of men, is an instance of *kāvyaliṅga*:

मिथ्या त्रिलोचनविलोचनपावकेन
भस्मीकृतां मदनमूर्तिमुदाहरन्ति।
स्नेहात्मिका तदभितापवशाद् विलीना
सेयं प्रिये! मदयति प्रसभं मनांसि॥[129]

Another passage in praise of the liquor as appearing differently for different persons may be cited as an illustration of *Ullekha*.

एषा भगवती वारुणी चषकेष्वावर्जिता प्रत्यादेशो मण्डनानां, अनुनयः प्रणयकुपितानां, पराक्रमो यौवनस्य, जीवितं विभ्रमाणाम्।[130] etc.

The poet is adept in the usage of puns, of course, with an eye on humour. The Kāpālika accuses the Śākyabhikṣu of

126. See *śl.* 3.

127. Ibid., *śl.* 11.

128. Ibid., p. 58.

129. Cf. *MV*, *śl.* 10.

130. Ibid., p. 46.

"catching hold of the hand" (*pāṇigrahaṇa*) of his beloved,[131] which also means marriage. The Śākyabhikṣu is again charged with the crime of having changed the original colour of the bowl thus, *nanu māyāsantānasambhavāḥ khalu bhavantaḥ*[132] (Indeed you people are descendants of Māyā). Māyā was the name of the mother of the Buddha. It also means illusion.

HĀSYA IN MATTAVILĀSA

Hāsya is aroused here both through characters and situations. The very appearance of the Kāpālika with his fiancee, the crooked looking Buddhist monk, and the lunatic is enough to arouse laughter. The indirect criticism of the degraded life led by the pseudo-religionists of different sects is the chief source of *hāsya*. The bemoaning of the loss of the begging bowl by the Kāpālika and his companion, the announcement of the Buddhist monk about his "life's mission", the fight between the Kāpālika and the Buddhist monk and the incoherent talk of the lunatic are some of the situations that heighten the comic effect of the play.

PRAHASANA ELEMENTS AND VĪTHYAṄGAS IN MATTAVILĀSA

The *prahasana* element *anṛtam* corresponding to the *vīthyaṅga*, *prapañca*, which is based on false praise, figures prominently in this play.

The Kāpālika praises his companion thus:

प्रिये, देवसोमे! सत्यमेवैतत् — तपसा कामरूपता प्राप्यत इति।
यत् त्वया परमव्रतस्य विधिवदनुष्ठानेनान्य एव रूपातिशयः क्षणात प्रतिपन्नः ॥[133]

Another instance of the same element is the famous *śloka*

131. *MV*, N.P. Unni edn., Trivandrum, p. 55.
132. Ibid., p. 60.
133. Ibid., p. 42.

peyā surā . . . etc., where the licentious life of the Kāpālika is mentioned in detail. The comparison of the liquor shop to a sacrificial hall belongs to the same variety.[134]

The opening scene[135] where the Kāpālika and his fiancee talk incoherently due to intoxication is an instance of the *prahasana* element *gadgadavāk* corresponding to the *vīthyaṅga asatpralāpa*.

The prattlings of the lunatic too fall under the same category.

> ग्रामसूकरमारुह्य गगनमुत्पतितेन सागरेण प्रभञ्ज्य रावणं बलाद् गृहीतः शक्रसुतः तिमिङ्गलः। . . . यस्य वा कस्य वा भागिनेयः स्वल्वहं, भीमसेनस्य घटोत्कच इव ॥[136]

Terming a merit a defect, or vice versa is called *mṛdava*. The Kāpālika's criticism of the celibacy observed by the Buddhist monks[137] is an instance of this *vīthyaṅga*. Chance coincidence of reference to something and its actual happening is called *avalagita*. When the Kāpālika knows that his bowl is missing, he says, *priye, tarkayāmi śūlyamāṁsagarbhatvāt śākyabhikṣuṇā śunā vā (gṛhītam) iti*.[138] Enters then the Śākyabhikṣu with a hidden bowl arousing the suspicion of the Kāpālika and his companion. Hence this is an instance of the *vīthyaṅga avalagitam*.

When the *bhikṣu* says that the original texts permitting wine and women for the monks have been deliberately suppressed by the old monks of the order,[139] we have the *prahasana* element, *upapatti*. Other instances of *upapatti* in the

134. *MV*, N.P. Unni edn., Trivandrum, pp. 45-46.

135. Ibid., p. 42.

136. Ibid., pp. 62-63.

137. Ibid., pp. 44-45.

138. Ibid., p. 48.

139. Ibid., pp. 48-49.

play are the Kāpālika's accusation that Buddhists have compiled their scriptures from portions stolen from the Vedāntas and the *Mahābhārata*,[140] and the Śākyabhikṣu's salutation to the Buddha for having prescribed shaven head when he escaped being caught by hair by Devasomā.[141] The *prahasana* element *vyāhāra* refers to the humorous conversation between two or three. An instance of this can be found in conversation between the Kāpālika and Śākyabhikṣu.[142] The same can illustrate the *vīthyaṅga vākkeli* also. Another instance of *vyāhāra* can be found in the conversation between the Śākyabhikṣu, the Kāpālika and the lunatic.[143]

The *prahasana* element *pralāpa* consists in showering praise on an unworthy or trivial object. Devasomā's praise of the begging bowl can be cited as an instance of this.

> हा हतास्मि मन्दभागा। सर्वलक्षणसम्पन्नतया कमलासन-शीर्षकपालानुभावस्य पौर्णमासीसोमदर्शनस्य नित्यसुरागन्धिनः एतस्य मलिनपटसंसर्गेणेयम् ईदृश्यवस्था संवृत्ता।[144]

DRAMATIC TECHNIQUE

MV satisfies all the requisites of a good *prahasana*. On account of its simple theme and decent humour it must be classed under the *śuddha* variety. The number of characters in it is five and the play has only one act. It has no *praveśaka* or *viṣkambhaka*. The *kaiśikī* and the *ārabhaṭī vṛttis* have been avoided. *Bhāratī vṛtti* figures prominently. *Hāsya*, of course, figures as

140. See above, "character study" under "The Mattavilāsa-Prahasana". *MV śl.* 12.

141. *MV*, p. 55.

142. Ibid., pp. 51-52, *bho bhikṣo darśaya tāvat . . . namaḥ kharapaṭāyeti vaktavyam*, etc.

143. Ibid., p. 66.

144. Ibid., p. 59.

the *pradhāna-rasa*. The *vastu* or the plot is *utpādya* (invented). The Kāpālika's notice of the loss of the bowl is the *mukha sandhi* (corresponding to the *ārambha* and the *bīja*), and his joy at its recovery is the *nirvahaṇa sandhi* (which is the same as *phalāgama* and the *kārya* achieved). *MV* does not pose any problem in staging, and it just needs one scene-setting, viz. the streets of Kāñcī.

Nāndī

The *nāndī* in *MV* is unique in several respects. It is recited on the stage by the *sūtradhāra* himself and it occurs after the conventional statement *nāndyante tataḥ praviśati sūtradhāraḥ*. The *nāndī śloka*[145] is in praise of Lord Śiva. One of the titles of the king, *avanibhājana* occurs in it. There are veiled references to some of the characters of the play. The word *kapālī* refers to the Kāpālika and the word *bodha* indirectly suggests the Śākyabhikṣu. The word *nṛtta* in it may be taken as referring to the dance of the drunken people, *mattavilāsanṛtyāni*,[146] which incidentally, has relevance to the title of the play also. It may also be noted here that the name of the play itself contains one of the paradoxical titles of the author, viz. *MV*.

The Prologue

The prologue here is carried out by the *sūtradhāra* and the actress, his wife. She is most probably the actress taking the role of Devasomā in the play. The *sūtradhāra*'s description of

---

145. Vide *MV*:

भाषावेषवपुःक्रियागुणकृतानाश्रित्य भेदान् गतं
भावावेशवशादनेकरसतां त्रैलोक्ययात्रामयम् ।
नृत्तं निष्प्रतिबद्धबोधमहिमा यः प्रेक्षकश्च स्वयं
स व्याप्तावनिभाजनं दिशतु वो दिव्यः कपाली यशः ॥ (śl 1)

146. Ibid., p. 46.

her as *udbhinnaromāñca* . . . etc., (*śl.* 2) fits in with the description of Devasomā by the Kāpālika in the *śloka udbhinnaśramavāribindu* . . . etc. (*śl.* 6). The *naṭī* in the prologue refers to another title of the royal poet, viz. *guṇabhadra*. The author pays glowing tribute to his father Siṁhaviṣṇupallava in the prologue.

> पल्लवकुलधरणिमण्डलकुलपर्वतस्य सर्वनयविजितसमस्तसामन्तमण्डलस्य आखण्डलसमपराक्रमश्रियः श्रीमहिमानुरूपदानविभूतिपरिभूतराज-राजस्य श्रीसिंहविष्णुवर्मणः पुत्रः।[147]
>
> Son of Siṁhaviṣṇuvarman — the principal mountain in supporting the earth in the form of the Pallava race, who has won over all the feudatory princes by his prudence, who in valour and prosperity is an equal to Indra and who has humiliated Kubera by munificence befitting his prosperity.[148]

The poet speaks of his own virtues and poetic talents in the same vein. Of these talents one may note the author's reference to his being the chief repository of wise sayings.[149]

> . . . शत्रुषड्वर्गनिग्रहपरः परहितपरतन्त्रतया महाभूतसधर्मा महाराजः श्रीमहेन्द्रविक्रमवर्मा नाम। अपि च —
>
> प्रज्ञादानदयानुभावधृतयः कान्तिः कलाकौशलं
> सत्यं शौर्यममायता विनय इत्येवम्प्रकारा गुणाः।
> अप्राप्तस्थितयः समेत्य शरणं याता यमेकं कलौ
> कल्पान्ते जगदादिमादिपुरुषं सर्गप्रभेदा इव॥
>
> — *śl.* 5

The word *saṅgītadhanaḥ* in the prologue is suggestive of the author's talent in music. It may be noted that Mahendravarman has a title *saṁkīrṇajāti* probably because he invented the *saṁkīrṇajāti* variety of *tāla*.

---

147. *MV*, N.P. Unni edn., Trivandrum, p. 41

148. Ibid., p. 72.

149. Ibid., *śl.* 3 ff.

The entry of the character in the main play is through the device known as *prayogātiśaya*. It is significant to note that in five of the seven mss. used in Dr Unni's edition of *MV*, the prologue ends with the words *iti sthāpanā* and in the other two we have *iti āmukham*. The word *prastāvanā* is not used anywhere. Though these three terms are loosely employed to denote the prologue, there is subtle difference between them and there is reason to believe that these three terms refer to the three stages of a prologue.[150]

Bharatavākya

Special mention must be made of the Bharatavākya in *MV* since it is here that the real significance of the play is reflected. It extols the Hindu form of worship and thereby hints at the revival of Hinduism during the time of the author. In it is also mentioned another title of the king, Śatrumalla. It may be noted that the deity of the temple built by Mahendravarman at Dalavanur is called Śatrumalleśvara. Another significance of the Bharatavākya is that it seems to be recited from behind the stage after the exit of all the characters from the stage. In most of the available plays, the Bharatavākya verse is recited by one of the characters, before the end of the play.

Time Analysis

The incidents of the play cover a day's time, approximately from 8 a.m. to 6 p.m. It may be presumed that the Kāpālika and his companion start the proceedings in the morning and by the time they reach the liquor shop after roaming in the streets of Kāñcī, it might be around 11 a.m. and the two decide to go for their alms. Buddhists are expected to finish

150. Cf. "Prologue in Sanskrit Drama" — Seminar paper presented by the present writer at Madras University Sanskrit Department, March, 1978.

their lunch before midday and the Śākyabhikṣu in the play has already finished his lunch before he meets the Kāpālika. By the time the quarrel for the bowl and the mad man episode end with the recovery of the bowl, it is evening. Devasomā in her last speech refers to the evening sky with the moon. The Pāśupata too starts for his *dhūmavelā* which usually takes place after the sunset.

THE PRĀKṚT IN MATTAVILĀSA

Though a short play *MV* shows varieties of Prākṛt. Of the five characters only the Kāpālika and the Pāśupata speak in Sanskrit and the rest in Prākṛt. Devasomā and the Śākyabhikṣu speak in the Śaurasenī while the Unmattaka speaks in Māgadhī. Prof. Keith observes[151] that the Prākṛt employed in *MV* is similar to that in Bhāsa's plays. For instance the particle *mā* is used along with the infinitive in Prākṛt in the sense of prohibition, in the style of Bhāsa.[152]

MATTAVILĀSA ON STAGE

In his introduction to the edition of *MV*, Dr Unni has given a detailed account of how the play is staged in the Kerala dramatic style of Kūḍiyāṭṭam. He has also appended to the text, a metrical commentary or *ṭippaṇī* of unknown authorship. The work has 41 stanzas and explains the mode of enactment of the play in the Kūḍiyāṭṭam.

Kūḍiyāṭṭam is an ancient traditional art of the staging of Sanskrit drama in Kerala. King Kulaśekharavarman of tenth century is credited with the popularisation of this art. Kūḍiyāṭṭam is somewhat different from the forms of

---

151. *Sanskrit Drama*, p. 181.

152. Cf. *devasomā: bhāvam, mā, mā mama kāraṇāde vadbhangeṇa tave ave khaḍedum* (p. 44).

dramatic representation prevalent in other parts of the country. In it, Sanskrit dramas are not rendered as they are. They are adapted to suit the local needs. There will be a lot of digression from the original narrative. The performance will thus last for 40 hours or more, spread over 7 or 8 days normally. The vernacular, Malayalam, is used extensively, especially for characters like *vidūṣaka*. There will be more music and dance than normally found in Sanskrit drama. The Kūḍiyāṭṭams are usually staged during the temple festivals in the temple-theatres called "Kūṭṭambalam". The Cākyārs, the Nambiars and their women *nañyar*s enact these plays. A special kind of drum called *mizhavu* is played during the performance.

The adapted version of *MV* for the Kūḍiyāṭṭam stage is given a totally religious colour. The reference to Śiva in the opening stanza affords scope for the narration of the entire story of Śiva-Pārvatī marriage. Verses from Kālidāsa's *Kumārasaṁbhava* are also quoted at appropriate places. The farcical element of the play is almost completely suppressed.

Nevertheless *MV* occupies a unique place in the Kūḍiyāṭṭam tradition. Its popularity is hinted at by Nīlakaṇṭha (tenth century) the author of *Kalyāṇasaugandhika*, thus: *nr̥tyan-mattavilāsajām dhanapateḥ prītim kariṣyāmyaham.*[153]

EPISODES, ALLUSIONS AND OTHER REFERENCES

Though essentially a farce, *MV* makes references to certain episodes and allusions from Purāṇas and other texts, revealing the author's firm grounding in the Hindu traditional lore. The Kāpālika in the play feels that though polluted by the Buddhist monk, his begging bowl can be purified by an expiatory rite. Reference is made here to Lord Śiva's assuming His terrible aspect, Bhairava for removing the pride of Brahmā.

153. Quoted in N.P. Unni's edition of *MV*, p. 32.

He chopped off one of the heads of Brahmā and carried his skull in his hand and thus came to be called "Kapālin". Reference is made to the Vedic legend of Indra's killing Vṛtra in the same context. The poet refers to two *Mahābhārata* characters, Ghaṭotkaca and Bhīmasena in another context,[154] which does not, of course, carry any special significance. Towards the end of the play there is a reference to the Kirāta-Arjuna episode.[155]

The poet also mentions Kharapaṭa,[156] an eponymous author of a treatise on the art of thieving. Kharapaṭa has been mentioned by Kauṭilya[157] and Bhāsa.[158] The Tamil epic *Silappadikāram* refers to one *tandirakaraṇam* which is explained in the commentary as Kharapaṭa's treatise on theft.[159] Kharapaṭa is sometimes identified with Mūladeva (also known as Karṇīsuta) an outstanding figure in Kathā literature.[160]

MATTAVILĀSA AND OTHER RŪPAKAS

MV shows considerable influence of Bhāsa's plays over it. The opening remark of the play with *nāndyante tataḥ praviśati sūtradhāraḥ*, certain similarities in Prākṛt,[161] the lunatic speaking in Māgadhī like his counterpart in the *Pratījñāyaugandharāyaṇa*, and the repeated usage of the expression *aho nu khalu* and *kim nu khalu* — may be taken as proofs in this direction. The

154. Quoted in N.P. Unni's edition of *MV*, p. 63.
155. Ibid., *śl.* 22.
156. Ibid., p. 52.
157. *Arthaśāstra* IV.8.
158. Cārudatta III, *śl*s. 10 f.
159. *Silappadikāram*, book II, story 16, line, 180, Saiva Siddhānta Society, 1970.
160. Introduction to *Avantīsundarīkathā*, Madras: KSR Institute, 1957.
161. See above, p. 128.

Buddhist code of conduct is reproduced almost *verbatim* from the *Bhagavadajjukīya*.

MV has influenced later *prahasanas* to a great extent. Degraded monks belonging to different religious sects are to be found in a number of later *prahasanas*. Kukṣimbhara in the *Kukṣimbharabhaikṣava* and Viṣṇumitra in the *Madanaketucarita*, are prototypes of the Śākyabhikṣu of *MV*. The street scene has become the chief venue in a number of later *prahasanas* like the *Kukṣimbharabhaikṣava* on the model of the *MV*.

The verse *peyā surā* . . . has been attributed to Bhāsa by Somadeva in his *Yaśastilaka*.[162] But nowhere do we find this verse in the available thirteen plays of Bhāsa. The allegorical drama *Prabodhacandrodaya* of Kṛṣṇamiśra also seems to have been influenced by *MV* to a large extent.[163] The whole of its third act where the Jaina, Buddhist, Kāpālika and Digambara monks appear seems to have been modelled on *MV*. All the monks are pseudo-ascetics given to worldly pleasures. The Buddhist monk in the *Prabodhacandrodaya* for instance, is happy about the provision for sensual enjoyment in his religion.

आवासो लयनं मनोहरमभिप्रायानुरूपा वणिङ्-
नार्यो वाञ्छितकालमिष्टमशनं शय्या मृदुप्रस्तराः।
श्रद्धापूर्वमुपासिता युवतिभिः क्लृप्ताङ्गदानोत्सव-
क्रीडानन्दभरैर्व्रजन्ति विलसज्ज्योत्स्नोज्ज्वला रात्रयः॥

— III.9

He openly boasts of his achievement:

रण्डाः पीनपयोधराः कति मया चण्डानुरागाद्भुज-
द्वन्द्वापीडन-पीवरस्तनभरैर्नो गाढमालिङ्गिताः।

162. *Yaśastilaka*, vol. II, p. 251.

163. See article, "Kṛṣṇamiśra's Indebtedness to Mattavilāsa" — *Visvesvaranand Indological Journal*, vol. XII, pp. 119-26.

बुद्धेभ्यः शतशः शपे यदि पुनः कुत्रापि कापालिनी-
पीनोत्तुङ्ग-कुचावगूहनभवः प्राप्तः प्रमोदोदयः ॥
— III.18

STATE OF SOCIETY AS REPRESENTED IN THE MATTAVILĀSA

The social conditions as represented in *MV* give a good account of the Pallava rule during the reign of King Mahendravarman. The prologue mentions about six classes of enemies the king had to face (*śatruṣaḍvarganigrahaparaḥ*).[164] Of course, this usually may be taken as the internal enemies, viz. *kāma, krodha, lobha, moha, mada* and *mātsarya*. But history tells us that after coming to power Mahendravarman conquered the Coḷas, the Pāṇḍyas and halted the advances of the King Pulakeśin II. He conquered the Gaṅgās, Kadambas and Rāṣṭrakūṭas also. Though the state was thus constantly at war, the normal life of the citizens was not much affected. Kāñcī, the capital was an important seat of learning in the south and was a meeting place of scholars from different parts of the country. The city was also famous for its beauty and splendour. Art and architecture flourished well. Artists were rewarded suitably.[165] Qualified judges attended to the legal problems of the city. Cases were enquired into and justice was always upheld.[166] Polygamy was perhaps quite common as evident from the *sūtradhāra*'s statement.[167]

There was complete religious freedom. People were free to switch over from one religion to the other. Ascetics belonging to different religious sects like the Kāpālikas, the Pāśupatas, the Buddhists and the Jainas pursued their religious activities without interference. They often debated fiercely

164. Cf. *MV*, prologue.

165. Ibid.

166. Cf. *MV*, *śl.* 15.

167. Cf. *MV*, Prologue.

with one another on the relative superiority of their own sect over the rest. Ascetics generally lived in their respective temples of worship. The poet refers to the "Ekāmra" Temple of Kāñcī, near which the Kāpālika resided. On one of the pillars of the Ekāmranātha Temple we have an inscription of King Mahendravarman. The poet also makes mention of the Rājavihāra of the Buddhist monks. According to Hieun Tsang, the city of Kāñcī was about 6 miles in circumference. He notes that there were more than 100 Buddhist monasteries with more than 10,000 monks. To the south of the city was a large monastery where scholars used to assemble for discussions. It is perhaps this monastery which is referred to as "Rājavihāra" in the *MV*.[168]

People respected the religious monks and offered them *bhikṣā*. This easy access to food had its side-effects too. Men with no deep religious motive took to asceticism and brought down the prestige of their religion. The Kāpālika and the Śākyabhikṣu depicted in the *MV* belong to this class. Though clad in yellow robes, they carried on unabated, every kind of irreligious act. The Buddhist society as reflected in the play shows corruption at its height, which paved way for its rapid decline in India.

The state of society depicted in *MV* is in general, one of peace and prosperity. But it is difficult to say much about the way of life led by the general public in *MV*'s time since it presents only one side of the picture, viz. the life led by pseudo-religious mendicants of different sects. It may however be noted that *MV* reveals a revival of Hinduism in south India, recovering the lost ground from Buddhism and Jainism. The Bhakti cult spread by the Nāyanmārs and the Āḻvārs was chiefly responsible for the revival of Hinduism in this part of the country. King Mahendravarman who had

168. Cf. *MV*, p. 92.

embraced Jainism in the early part of his life, switched back to Śaivism in later years, probably due to the influence of saints in general and that of the great Nāyanmār, Tirunāvukkarasar in particular.[169] The extolling of the sacred fire in the Bharatavākya reveals the author's firm faith in the Hindu form of worship and his interest in its revival.

Hāsya Cūḍāmaṇi Prahasana

After the *MV*, there is a dark period in the history of *prahasana* literature for nearly five centuries (seventh to twelfth century CE). No *prahasana* belonging to this period has come down to us. Then we have the *Laṭakamelaka* of Śaṅkhadhara Kavi and the *Hāsyacūḍāmaṇi* (*Hā.Cū.*) of Amātya Vatsarāja written during the twelfth century. While the *Laṭakamelaka* is a *vikṛta* type of *prahasana*, the first of its kind preserved, *Hā.Cū.* is a delightful *śuddha* piece. The hero of *Hā.Cū.*, Jñānarāśi by name, is a teacher who claims to possess the knowledge of many things including Astrology but he cannot stand in comparison with the *parivrājaka yogin* of the *Bhagavadajjukīya*. Nevertheless on account of its theme, nature of characters employed and the language which is free from coarseness and vulgarity, *Hā.Cū.* should justly be called a *śuddha* type of *prahasana*.

Vatsarāja was a minister under the Cāḷukyan king Paramārdideva of Kālañjara, who reigned from CE 1163 to 1203.[170] He continued in the same capacity under his son and successor, King Trailokyavarmadeva (CE 1204-41). Vatsarāja wrote 6 dramas each belonging to one variety of *rūpaka*.[171]

169. See *Mahendravarman* by Mylei Sini Venkataswami, Madras: Shaiva Siddhānta Publication, 1 January 1959 (Tamil), p. 33; *History of Tamil Nadu* by N. Subramaniam, Madras: Koodal Publishers, pp. 152-53.

170. See Keith, *Sanskrit Drama*, p. 265.

171. These six plays appeared under the title *Rūpakaṣaṭka* in the G.O.S. VIII, 1918.

They are: (i) *Karpūracarita*, a *bhāṇa*, (ii) *Tripuradāha*, a *ḍima*, (iii) *Rukmiṇīharaṇa*, an *īhāmṛga*, (iv) *Samudramanthana*, a *samavakāra*, (v) *Hāsyacūḍāmaṇi*, a *prahasana*, and (vi) *Kirātārjunīya*, a *vyāyoga*. Of these, the first five were presented before King Paramārdideva and the last one at the bidding of King Trailokyavarman.

The *Karpūracarita bhāṇa* is a one-act monologue. The hero, Karpūraka, a *viṭa*, narrates the experiences of his erratic life and how he won over his beloved by deceitful means. The *ḍima* piece, *Tripuradāha*, is a four-act play, based on the Purāṇic story of the destruction of the three cities of the demon, Māyā by Lord Śiva. The *Rukmiṇīharaṇa* is based on the well-known Purāṇic story from the *Bhāgavata*. The *Samudramanthana* is a *samavakāra* in three acts, dealing with the legend of the churning of the Milky Ocean by the gods and the demons and the consequent emergence of several precious objects including Goddess Lakṣmī. Bhāravi's *mahākāvya*, *Kirātārjunīya*, has provided the theme for the *vyāyoga* piece of its namesake. The *ḍima*, *samavakāra* and *īhāmṛga* pieces are the earliest of their respective types of *rūpaka* that have come down to us. Evidently Vatsarāja, with no model play available for him, has based these plays on the theory found in the dramaturgical works. It may be noted that *Tripuradāha* and *Samudramanthana* are also the names of the plays supposed to have been staged first by Bharata before the gods. The *prahasana* under study, the *Hā.Cū.* is a two-act play with *hāsya* as its predominant sentiment.

Dramatis Personae

Sūtradhāra	:	the stage manager.
Pāripārśvika	:	his assistant.
Kapaṭakeli	:	the mother of *gaṇikā*.

Madanasundarī	:	the heroine.
Kokila and Pārāvata	:	male attendants on Kapaṭakeli.
Kusumikā and others	:	female attendants an Kapaṭakeli's house.
Jñānarāśi	:	the teacher.
Kauṇḍinya	:	his disciple.
Mudgaraka	:	male attendant on Kapaṭakeli.
Kalākaraṇḍaka	:	Madanasundarī's lover.

THE PLOT

In the opening scene, we find Kapaṭakeli, the *gaṇikā*-mother waking up from her slumber and feeling happy that the liquor that she took the previous night had worked well. A maidservant enters now and conveys the bad news relating to the theft of jewels from her house. The shocked Kapaṭakeli surmises that her daughter Madanasundarī herself might have given the jewels to her lover Kalākaraṇḍaka in order to aid him in gambling. Anyhow she wants to approach the monk Jñānarāśi with a view to finding out the actual thief. She wakes up her attendant Mudgaraka who grudgingly remarks that her avariciousness is justly punished. She tempts him with a drink of wine and he promises to accompany her to the *maṭha* of Jñānarāśi.

At the *maṭha* we find Jñānarāśi teaching his pupil Kauṇḍinya. The following interesting discussion takes place between them.

Teacher	:	Have you got by heart the two *śloka*s that I taught?
Student	:	I have got them by my belly, Jñānarāśi.

Teacher : (Angrily) Fool! Why do you call me by my name?

Student : Should I not call you by your name?

Teacher : Fool, you should not address the *guru* (teacher) by name.

Student : Then how to mention the mountain? (which is also *guru* — big)

Teacher : I used the word *guru* in the sense of "teacher" and not in the sense of "big". You must address me as "Sir" or as "Teacher".

Then the student misquotes the *śloka*s he had learnt, which give an entirely different meaning. The teacher scolds him for having changed the *varṇa* (letters) in the original *śloka*. The student takes the word in the sense of "colour" and maintains that he had not changed the colour of what the teacher had written with a white chalk. Again the teacher has to appeal to the common sense of his disciple.

After some more exchanges like this, the student feels that what the teacher had prescribed is difficult to learn and that there is very little use of what he has learnt. He requests the *guru* to teach him the *kevalī vidyā* by which he can gain instant money at the cost of others. The teacher despises him saying that it is wrong to aspire for others' wealth, and as such *kevalī vidyā* would not be imparted to him. The student is quick to remark that perhaps the teacher himself does not know the *kevalī vidyā*.

Meanwhile Kapaṭakeli and Mudgaraka enter and wait outside. Sensing that there is somebody at the doorstep, Jñānarāśi boasts loudly about his talents. He knows the origin and end of all beings in the world. He would even restore the stolen goods at once. On hearing this, Kapaṭakeli is happy that she has approached the right man. She appears before the teacher and after offering her salutations places her problem before him. The teacher asks his student to bring the *kevalī pustaka* and the resourceful student asks Kapaṭakeli to offer worship to the book with gold, and makes her part with her ring. After some tall talks and false pretensions the teacher decides to find out the culprit by some numerological calculation in which he fumbles very badly. Deciding within himself that arithmetic is not his field, he decides to adopt some other procedure. He writes down the names of all the members of the family and wants to pinpoint the thief by fluke. After some time he announces that Kapaṭakeli must have stolen the jewels. (Evidently he has forgotten that Kapaṭakeli is the name of the client.) Mudgaraka laughs loudly and wonders whether she would burgle her own jewels. Jñānarāśi realises his mistake but hushes it up by calling Kapaṭakeli aside and telling her that he purposely utters her name so that others may not know the real thief and caution him before being caught. He also suggests that she must enquire of her servants Kokila and Pārāvata and permits her to leave.

The teacher now remembers that his devotee Kalākaraṇḍaka has sought his blessings for winning the gamble that day. Hence he must perform meditation for the sake of his devotee. With his disciple he resorts to a quiet garden for meditation. Here ends the first act.

In the beginning of the second act, we find Jñānarāśi engaged in meditation and the student standing by his side. Kauṇḍinya asks his teacher to stop his meditation which is definitely going to be futile since Kalākaraṇḍaka is not likely to win. They must rather resort to some other shady place in the garden and escape from the heat of the midday sun. The teacher agrees readily. They now observe Madanasundarī and her *ceṭī* entering the garden. Though attracted by her beauty himself, he reprimands the student for appreciating her beauty. He then complains of high fever and asks the student to bring a birch-leaf and a pen to compose a *mantra* which would treat the fever. He actually writes a *vaśīkaraṇa mantra* in order to captivate the heart of Madanasundarī and asks Kauṇḍinya to powder the leaf, mix it up with sandalpaste which, when applied on his body, would contain the fever. Kauṇḍinya finds to his surprise the name of Madanasundarī and a *vaśīkaraṇa mantra* on the leaf. He knows the intention of the teacher but wants to outwit his own teacher. How can he permit him to acquire Madanasundarī whom he himself loves? He erases the name of Madanasundarī from the leaf and writes instead the name of the old Kapaṭakeli. Unaware of this, the teacher applies the paste all over his body. He orders Kauṇḍinya to go and bring flowers for his worship since he does not want the presence of the student when the *vaśīkaraṇa mantra* starts working. But the clever student climbs a tree nearby and wants to observe the effect of the *mantra* on Kapaṭakeli. Now under the spell of the *vaśīkaraṇa mantra* Kapaṭakeli approaches the monk with flowers and openly solicits him. In order to project her image as still young she calls Madanasundarī her elder sister. She also informs the monk that the stolen jewels have been recovered. She appeals to the teacher to abandon his *kaṣāya vastra* so that she can apply sandalpaste on his body. The angry monk tries to avoid her and even starts beating her up. The old woman calls for her servants Kokila and Pārāvata. The two are already in search of the monk in order to settle an account with him since he has branded them as thieves. On seeing them even from a distance the monk is frightened and falls flat at the feet of the old *gaṇikā* and requests her to save him from the two rogues. Kapaṭakeli suggests that he should sit pretending to be in deep meditation. The two approach the teacher and provoke him. They identify the ring on his finger to be Kapaṭakeli's and take their mistress to task,

> *sādhu amba, sādhu, sarvasvam etasya samarpayasi* ।
> *corikā-kalaṅkam punarasmākam mastake āropayasi* ॥

The two catch hold of the teacher by his hands and feet and swing him right and left. The helpless Jñānarāśi calls for this student Kauṇḍinya. Kauṇḍinya who is atop the tree observing the fun comes down and poses himself as the keeper of the garden. He accuses Jñānarāśi of stealing flowers from his garden and says that he deserves to be beaten up. But Kokila is shrewd enough to identify him to be the disciple of Jñānarāśi. Kokila and Pārāvata tie up both the teacher and student to a nearby tree. The clever Kauṇḍinya shouts loudly,

> Let the hidden treasures remain in their respective places forever. Let the world remain poor forever. The teacher who is the only man who knows where the treasures are hidden, is going to be killed by these people.

Kauṇḍinya's trick works and the two stop beating the teacher and fall flat at his feet begging pardon and requesting him to reveal the places of the hidden treasure. The teacher asks Kauṇḍinya to bring the *lāṅgalī rasa* and applies it to the eyes of the two greedy fellows and also to Kapaṭakeli at her request, and assures them that they would be in a position to see the hidden treasures when the charm begins to work. All the three are rendered temporarily blind and also experience severe irritation in their eyes. Kokila and Pārāvata now realise that they have been deceived. But they catch hold of the teacher and the student and taking out the ointment from their eyes apply it forcibly in their eyes too. These two also now experience a burning sensation in their eyes. The teacher wonders whether Kauṇḍinya had brought the wrong ointment. As all the five stumble over one another in total blindness, Kalākaraṇḍaka and Madanasundarī arrive on the scene by chance. At the request of the teacher they bring water from a nearby pond and help the people wash their eyes. Kokila and Pārāvata accuse the teacher of the mischief but Kalākaraṇḍaka orders them to keep quiet. He praises his teacher in glowing terms and asks everybody to apologise to the teacher. Kalākaraṇḍaka thanks the teacher profusely for his prayers due to which he gained success at the gamble and the play comes to an end with the usual Bharatavākya.

CHARACTER STUDY

Jñānarāśi (lit. Heap of Knowledge)

Jñānarāśi, the teacher-monk in the play is a typical *prahasana* character, a pseudo-religious man of the Bhāgavata school. His is only a paradoxical name since his ignorance is exposed at every instance. He became a Bhāgavata since he failed miserably in his earlier career as an astrologer. He predicted a win for a king who took to battle, but when his prediction failed, the defeated king wanted to kill him. In order to escape the wrath of the king he took to *saṁnyāsa*.

He is a hypocrite of the first order. He has only a superficial knowledge of the scripture but would pose as though he knows everything. When his disciple pesters him to teach the *kevalī vidyā*, he evades him saying that it should not be taught to talkative persons. The student wonders whether the teacher knows the *kevalī vidyā* at all. Jñānarāśi professes to know it but does not want to practise it since such a practice brought about calamity in his own family. Being insisted by his student, the teacher decides to impart the first step in the art of prediction.

किं वाग्भिर्निकषो हि नः फलमिति स्याद्गूढगर्वग्रहः
प्रश्नेष्वाविलमुत्तरं विरचयेन्न व्याहरेन्निर्णयम् ।
सिद्धं कार्यमवेक्ष्य निश्चितमिदं पूर्वं मयासीदिति
स्फारं स्फारमुदीरयेदुपचरेत् किञ्चिन्मृषा साक्षिणाम् ॥
— I.18

You must assume airs and keep saying that you do not attach importance to money. You must give confusing and vague replies for queries. Never should a clear-cut answer be given. Knowing about success in an enterprise, you must say that you predicted it already. You must always indulge in tall talks and keep false witnesses in good humour.

चिन्ताचुम्बितचेतसा न रचितः प्रश्नः प्रशस्तस्त्वया
नूनं सम्यगुपश्रुतिर्न भवता ज्ञाता ग्रहीतुं तदा ।
त्वद्दोषेण फले भ्रामोऽयमभवद्विद्या हि नः केवली
कल्पान्तेऽपि न कम्पते जनमिति प्रत्याययेद् वञ्चितम् ॥
— I.19

In cases of reverse you must sit as though lost in meditation or keep saying that the client has not put a relevant question or that he has not properly reported the *upaśruti* (unseen messages) or that the reverse is due to his (the client's) own sin and that the *kevalī vidyā* as a science is quite infallible. You must keep people at bay by your deceitful means.

One must also boast of his powers as he himself demonstrates.

मद्भ्रूभङ्गि-समादिष्टा कुम्भदासीव भूरियम् ।
निधानकुम्भसम्भारं गेहे कस्य न ढौकयेत् ॥
— II.10

True, the deceitful tricks adopted by Jñānarāśi brought him success and fame. As soon as she comes to know of the theft in her house the first thing that strikes Kapaṭakeli is to approach him. Kalākaraṇḍaka has immense faith in the powers of this cheat. But alas, luck runs out for the monk at a crucial time when he is caught by the two rogues Kokila and Pārāvata. Though a monk, he is not free from the worldly desires. He is deeply attracted by the beauty of Madanasundarī.

उन्मुच्य दूरमपयाति यथा यथेयं छायेव मन्मथतरोस्तरलायताक्षी।
अङ्गानि मे प्रसभमेष तथा तथैव क्रोडीकरोत्यहह दुर्विषयप्रतापः॥

— II.4

Even the stone slab where she sat is enchanting for him. He simply wallows over it. But he advises his student to control the sense organs and be disciplined. Though greedy for money, he poses as though he is the least interested in it. When Kapaṭakeli offers the ring, he behaves likewise.

ज्ञानराशिः — (स्वगतं सहर्षं) स्वीकृतः तावदस्माकम् अनया मनोरथः।
तथापि निरीहतामेव अभिनयामि।
"न जानामि न गृह्णामि मम किं चिन्तयानया।
अनङ्गीकार एवायं दाम्भिकानां महाफलः॥"

— I.21

For all his boasting he is in reality an ignorant fellow. He does not know even simple arithmetical addition. For him, 5 plus 13 is 20. When the mistake is pointed out, he manages the situation by saying that it is a different type of calculation that is adopted in his method. He fares no better in astrological calculations.

यदि पश्यति रविसूनुः विंशस्थानस्थितं व्यतीपातम्।
यदि राहुः शकटभेदी स भवति कटुश्च मेषस्थः॥

— I.23

रविरङ्गारकलग्ने भवति यदा पापवीक्ष्यमाणश्च।
अर्धशरीरभावं प्रश्ने ब्रूयात्तदा नियतम्॥

— I.24

The mention of the 20th house (there are only 12 houses) and the *aṅgāraka lagna* (there is no such *lagna*) are enough to point out his total ignorance in astrology.

Jñānarāśi is, of course, resourceful. When he announces that Kapaṭakeli is the thief, forgetting that it was she who brought the complaint, he manages the situation by calling Kapaṭakeli aside and convincing her that it was just one of the tricks to find out the real culprit. None can beat him in showmanship. When the student offers him Kapaṭakeli's ring he talks philosophy.

जरामृत्युव्याधिव्यसनघटनैकाग्रहृदयो
विपर्यासं यस्याः प्रगुणयति कालः प्रतिकलम्।
तनौ तस्यामस्यामलमलमलङ्कारघटनम्
ज्वलद्वह्नौ गेहे रचयति चतुष्कानि कतमः॥

— I.25

When the student suggests that they go to the *mādhavī maṇḍapa* to have a good look at the harlot who had come there, he declines but resorts to another vantage point from where he can see the girl much better, which evokes the admiration of the student, *ahe upādhyāyaḥ, suṣṭhu khalu eṣā ihasthitena pralokyate* (II. bet. *śl*s 1 and 2). Though he appreciates within himself, the remarks made by Kauṇḍinya on the beauty of Madanasundarī, he scolds the disciple:

> *(svagatam) samyagāha kauṇḍinyaḥ (prakāśam-sakrodhamiva) re re, kim pralapasi, āh, pāpa, śāpodakena nirvāpayāmi tvad-durvinaya-pāvakam.* — II, bet, *śl*s. 3 and 4

He has no firm control over his mind and allows it to waver at its will. Being captivated by the beauty of Madanasundarī he wants to acquire her through the *vaśīkaraṇa mantra* which, of course, misfires due to the mischief of the disciple. The teacher too does not lag behind in mischief-making. He promises to make Kokila and Pārāvata see the hidden treasure by applying the so-called *lāṅgalī rasa* in their eyes. Kokila comes forward first, and the other fellow wants to wait and see whether the teacher's charm works. As suspected the teacher's charm is a mere hoax and Kokila says that he is not able to see anything, leave alone the treasure. Pārāvata becomes suspicious. But the mischievous Jñānarāśi calls Pārāvata aside and tells him.

वत्स, पारावत, सत्येयं जनोक्तिः "अर्थातुराणां न सुहृत् न बन्धुः", यदयं पश्यन्नपि न कथयति तत्त्वम्, अन्यदेव दर्शयामि।

— II. bet. *śl*s. 11-12

Pārāvata is also thus deceived. But the two rogues have the last laugh as they catch hold of the teacher and forcibly apply the ointment to his eyes, thus making the teacher lick his boots. As a result, the teacher is also rendered temporarily blind. For all his foolhardiness the teacher has some luck. Kalākaraṇḍaka, his ardent disciple, not only saves him from the tight corner but pays glorious tributes to him. He calls the teacher a *jagadguru* and says that there is nothing that one cannot achieve by his grace.

नास्त्यसाध्यं किमपि मे भुवने भवदनुकम्पासनाथस्य।

— II. bet. *śl*s. 12-13

Kauṇḍinya

Kauṇḍinya, the disciple of Jñānarāśi, belongs to the same class of such disciples, whom we can come across in works like the *Bhagavadajjukīya* — impertinent, penny-wise and pound-foolish, and fault-finding. When the teacher pulls him up for calling him by his name saying तत्कथं शैलानां नाम गृह्यते। Kauṇḍinya asks, धिङ्मूर्ख, न गृह्यते गुरूणां नाम, taking *guru* to mean "big" instead of "teacher". Again when the teacher refers to his wrong usage of the *varṇa* (letters), he says he has not changed the *varṇa* (colour) of what the teacher had written. In spite of his foolishness, he considers himself to be a *medhāvin* and accuses his teacher of being jealous of him.

किं मां ताडयसि? एते खलु हताशा उपाध्याया न सहन्ते आत्मनः समधिकमेधाविशेषं शिष्यम्।

— I. bet. *śl*s. 12-13

He is not really interested in studies. He cannot recite even a single *śloka* correctly due to his utter lack of concentration while being taught. His only interest is how to get some quick money.

उपाध्याय, सुष्ठु कट्वक्षरं तवैतद् अध्ययनम्। न च एतेन किमपि प्राप्यते। तन्मां केवलीविद्याम् अध्यापय, यया मे जनस्य धनानि स्वाधीनानि भ वन्ति।

— I.15-16

He never misses an opportunity to criticse his own teacher. When the teacher refuses to impart the *kevalī vidyā*, he remarks:

अलभमानः एवं मन्त्रयसि। न च त्वं जानासि केवलीविद्याम्।

— I.16-17

When the teacher narrates the calamities that have befallen his family due to the practice of the *kevalī*, the student remarks:

ज्ञातं तावत् त्रिपौरुषं युष्माकं ज्ञानमाहात्म्यम्।

— I.17-18

When the teacher hesitates to accept the ring presented by Kapaṭakeli, he sarcastically remarks,

उपाध्याय, तवैवाहं शिष्यः। किं मां प्रत्याययसि। गृहाण तावत्।

— I.25-26

He knows pretty well about the limitations of his teacher. When the teacher pretends to perform *mantra-japa* for the welfare of his devotee, he asks him to stop it forthwith.

उपाध्याय, बहुसंख्यया कृतो मन्त्रजपः। जाने जितमेव कलाकरण्डक-द्यूतकरेण। न खलु ते विलम्बितप्रभावो मन्त्रः।

— II. before *śl*. 1

When the teacher vows to curse him by sprinkling water

from the waterpot (*kamaṇḍalu*) for mentioning the name of Madanasundarī, he ridicules him by saying —

> किमकारणं कमण्डलुजलं प्रवाहयसि? क्लमिष्यसि मध्याह्नतृष्णया, जानामि तव प्रभावम्। —
> II.3-4

He is adept in reading the mind of his teacher. When the teacher avoids the *mādhavī maṇḍapa*, and resorts to another place pretending *vairāgya*, he knows fully well that the teacher had only chosen a better place from where he can have a good look at the harlot. He is fickle by nature. He is attracted even by the voice of Madanasundarī and does not like to be disturbed by the teacher.

> ज्ञानराशिः — कौण्डिन्य, किमस्माकमिह निस्सङ्गानाम्। तदेहि। गच्छावः।
> कौण्डिन्य — उपाध्याय, तिष्ठ, तिष्ठ, तव दुरध्ययनदूनौ शीतलायतः कर्णौ एतयोः मधुरालापैः।
>
> — II.3-4

Kauṇḍinya is very shrewd at times. Kapaṭakeli approaches the teacher with the problem of theft in her house and the teacher, bids Kauṇḍinya to bring the *kevalī pustaka*. Without even a hint from the teacher, Kauṇḍinya asks Kapaṭakeli to offer her golden ring as *dakṣiṇā* for the *pūjā*. He has a fine sense of humour and plays a practical joke on his teacher by changing the name in the *vaśīkaraṇa mantra*, as a result of which we have a truly comic situation with the old Kapaṭakeli making amorous advances to the monk. When Kokila and Pārāvata beat up the teacher he simply watches the fun from a tree top. When he faces the danger of being found out, he jumps down from the tree and poses himself as the keeper of the garden. Even when he is recognised to be the student of Jñānarāśi and bound, he does not flinch a little. He shouts aloud that they are going to be killed and that the hidden treasures are going to remain idle forever. The trick works and the two rogues release both the teacher and the disciple and ask for pardon. Kauṇḍinya is responsible for the climax-fun when he brings the wrong ointment instead of the intended *lāṅgalī rasa*.

The other characters in the play, viz. the lovers, Kalākaraṇḍaka and Madanasundarī and the two servants Kokila and Pārāvata have only limited role in the play.

LITERARY MERITS OF THE PLAY

With *BA* and *MV* serving as his model plays, Vatsarāja has structured his play meticulously infusing it with a number of *prahasana* elements. The chief merits of the play are its excellent theme and classic humour arising out of both situations and characters.

HĀSYA IN THE HĀSYACŪḌĀMAṆI

As the title, i.e. Crest-jewel of Humour, suggests, the play abounds in true and good *hāsya*. The hypocritic teacher, the impertinent student and the foolish Mudgaraka are the chief contributors to *hāsya* in the play. The effect of the *vaśīkaraṇa mantra* on the old Kapaṭakeli, the treatment meted out to the teacher by Kokila and Pārāvata and the *lāṅgalī rasa* episode are the most amusing situations in the play. On coming to know of the theft in their house the servant Mudgaraka is surprised,

> *na tathā mām bādhate arthanāśo yathā āryā 'pi iti parābhavaḥ* ।
> *na khalu agniḥ kenāpi dagdhaḥ śrūyate* ॥ — Act I, bet. 7-8

The conversation between the teacher and the student already quoted above[172] is another instance of good humour. Kauṇḍinya has very poor memory and recites even the well-known *śloka*s in a wrong way which give a totally different meaning.

172. See above "The Plot" under "Hāsyacūḍāmaṇi" in this chapter.

आलोक्य सर्वगात्राणि (सर्वशास्त्राणि) विचार्य च पुनः पुनः।
इदमेकं तु निष्पन्नं ध्येयो नारीजनः (नारायणः) सदा॥

— I.11

नमस्ते पुण्डरीकाक्ष नमस्ते विश्वतापन (विश्वभावन)।
नमस्तेऽस्तु मृषाकोष (हृषीकेश) महापुरुषकूर्चक (पूर्वज)॥

— I.12

The teacher's abortive attempts to find out the culprit, his atrocious astrological calculations, the vain boasting of the teacher and his being exposed by the student, the *śṛṅgārābhāsa* figuring in the lovesickness of the teacher, the play on the words *nidhāna* (treasure) and *nidhana* (death)[173] are other instances of *hāsya* in the play.

PRAHASANA ELEMENTS AND THE VĪTHYAṄGAS IN HĀSYACŪḌĀMAṆI

The conversation between the teacher and the disciple already referred to above[174] is an instance of the *prahasana* element *vyāhāra*. The following passage is an instance of the *vīthyaṅga*, *avalagitam*.

कपटकेलिः — (सप्रश्रयम्) भगवन्, अद्य मे रजन्यां मुषितं सर्वस्वम्। अर्पयतु भवान्।

शिष्य — (ससंभ्रमम्) किं मन्त्यते, अद्य रजन्यां मठं मुक्त्वा न कुत्रापि गतः उपाध्यायः।

कपटकेलिः — (कर्णौ पिधाय ससंभ्रमम्) शान्तं पापं, ज्ञानशक्त्या चोरं ज्ञात्वा अर्पयतु इति मया मन्त्रितम्।

— I.20-21

The disciple calling himself a *medhāvin*[175] and the boasting of the teacher[176] are instances of the *vīthyaṅga chalam*. There are

173. Cf. Act II, 10-12.

174. See above, "The Plot" under "Hāsyacūḍāmaṇi" in this chapter.

175. Cf. Act I, 12-13

176. Cf. Act I, 20.

a number of instances of the *vīthyaṅga prapañca* (corresponding to the *prahasana* element *anṛtam*), which is based on false praise. Observing the shallowness of his teacher with respect to astrology, the student says,

> *aho upādhyāyasya māhātmyam! sakalā api śālihotragāthāḥ kaṇṭhe kṛtāḥ* — I. 24-25

which is one such instance of *prapañca*. The lovesickness of the old Kapaṭakeli under the influence of the love-charm (*vaśīkaraṇa mantra*) may be cited as an instance of the *prahasana* element, *vibhrānti*.

DRAMATIC TECHNIQUE

Laṭakamelaka and *Hā.Cū.* are the earliest two-act plays in *prahasana* literature. Curiously Keith (p. 265) calls it (*Hā. Cū*) a one-act piece. The first act may have to be divided into two scenes. The first scene is laid in Kapaṭakeli's house and the next in Jñānarāśi's *maṭha*.

Vatsarāja excels in the effective usage of the *svagata* technique. The "aside", extensively employed in the play, helps shielding the hypocrite teacher from the other characters. Unaware of his weaknesses and limitations all the other characters (excepting Kauṇḍinya) show high regard for him. Kalākaraṇḍaka even goes to the extent of calling him a *jagadguru*. But the audience do very well know about his amorous inner inclinations, greed for wealth, etc. through his *svagata* utterances, which add to the comic effect of the play.

Nāndī and the Prologue

The play opens with two *nāndī ślokas*. In the first *śloka,*[177] the

177. *kalyāṇam vitarantu vaḥ pṛthujaṭājūṭāgra-vistāriṇaste*
cūḍāśaśinaḥ śiraḥsuradhunīdhārānukārāḥ karāḥ ।
yānutprekṣya madoṣmabhāravidhure śuṇḍāladaṇḍam mṛṣā

→

poet invokes the blessings of Lord Śiva who smiles at the sight of Gaṇeśa extending the trunks into the spreading rays of the moon from Śiva's head, thinking them to be the stream of the Ganges. At least three purposes are served by this *śloka*. (i) Invoking the blessings of Lord Śiva, (ii) Reference to the moon in compliance to the rules of dramaturgy, and (iii) Suggestion through the word *ullāsīhāsa* that *hāsya* is going to be the main sentiment in the play.

In the second *śloka*, an imaginary love quarrel between Śiva and Pārvatī is set forth. Pārvatī accuses Śiva by saying,

> You have many arms to embrace (as Naṭarāja), many eyes to look at and many lips to kiss. Indeed you are justified in having many wives. Who am I for you?

At the end of the *nāndī*, the *sūtradhāra* enters and recites a verse describing the sunset. The *pāripārśvika* enters and says that they are to stage a play under orders from King Paramārdideva, in connection with the "Nīlakaṇṭha-yātrā" festival. Since *hāsya* is best suited for the diversified audience, they may stage the *Hā.Cū.*, a *prahasana*. The *sūtradhāra* then eulogises the scholarship of King Paramārdideva.[178] The next verse[179] is modelled on the verse *śrīharṣo nipuṇaḥ kaviḥ* found in the Harṣa plays. The last verse in the prologue which is a *dhruvā* song sung from *nepathya*, refers to the theft in Kapaṭakeli's house and her plan to approach Jñānarāśi for advice.

→ *herambe ghaṭayatyanāratamabhūd ullāsihāso haraḥ* ||

178. *Hā.Cū*, 1.4.

179. Ibid., 1.5.

परिषदियमुदार-ज्ञान-सौजन्यधन्या
रसपरवशवाणीवत्सलो वत्सराजः।
अयमपि नटवर्गो नाट्यमुद्राप्रतिष्ठः
फलति सुकृतराशिः प्राक्तनः कोऽप्ययं मे॥

MERITS OF THE PLAYWRIGHT

The chief merits of the poet lie in his excellent handling of the comic sentiment and masterly character portrayal. But the poet has cleverly interspaced the dialogues with traditional teachings of ethical values and religious codes. Man should employ his sense-organs cautiously and should not allow them to wander at their will. It is a pity that people run after worldly pleasures and bind themselves fast, of their own accord, like the deer falling into the trap.

> मृगः पाशान् प्रायः परिहरति यत्नेन मृगयोः
> प्रमादाद् आविद्धो भवति सहसा शोकविकलः।
> अये मुग्धो लोकः प्रकृतिविषमान् हन्त विषयान्
> स्वयं कण्ठे पाशान् घटयतितरां हृष्यतितराम्॥
> — I.16

Adorning the body with ornaments is as useless as decorating a room blazing with fire.[180] There is nothing wrong in the teacher punishing his erring student. The king too punishes the wicked in order to instil discipline in the state affairs. The heat of the Sun's rays, though unbearable, is conducive to the happiness of the earth.

> नृपतिरखिललोकान् पालयत्यात्तदण्डः
> सुखयति जगदर्कः स्वीकृतोष्णस्वरूपः।
> गुरुरपि कटुचेष्टः शास्ति शास्त्राणि शिष्यं
> परिणतिहितभाजां भङ्गिरेवंविधैव॥[181]

The corrected versions of the two *śloka*s wrongly recited by the student bring out the poet's acquaintance with the traditional texts.

180. See above in this chapter, *Hā.Cū.* I.25.

181. *Hā.Cū.* I.13; Cf. *Abhijñānaśākuntala*, V.8.

THE INFLUENCE OF BA ON HĀ.CŪ.

Vatsarāja is clearly indebted to the author of *BA*. The student teacher dialogues and the presentation of the lovers like Kalākaraṇḍaka and Madanasundarī may be cited as instances. Kalākaraṇḍaka like his counterpart in *BA*, also resorts to the *pānagoṣṭhī*, neglecting his fiancee who languishes in separation. Like the heroine in *BA*, Madanasundarī too is a *gaṇikā* yet devoted to a single lover. The reference to the teacher punishing the student[182] cited above strikingly resembles a similar incident in *BA*. The teacher in *Hā.Cū.* is also addressed as "Bhagavān", though he lacks the merits of his counterpart in *BA*.

THE INFLUENCE OF HĀ.CŪ. ON LATER PRAHASANAS

In spite of the influence of *BA* over it to a certain extent, *Hā.Cū.* is one of the few original pieces in *prahasana* literature. In *BA*, the hero is a true *yogin* and the *MV* has too trivial a theme. Plays like the *Laṭakamelaka* have several *adhamas*. *Hā.Cū.* is unique in the sense that it is the first *prahasana* with a single *adhama* hero and it has a fairly good theme too. Thus it has served as a model for many later *prahasanas* which have themes centring around a single *adhama* hero. Prominent among the *prahasanas* influenced by *Hā.Cū.* are the *Dhūrtanartaka*, the *Muṇḍita Prahasana*, the *Kāleyakautūhala*, *Somavallīyogānanda*, *Kuhanābhaikṣava* and the *Kukṣimbharibhaikṣava*.

PRĀKṚT IN THE HĀ.CŪ.

On the basis of the number of characters speaking in Prākṛt, *Hā.Cū.* may even be called a Prākṛt play. Excepting the teacher Jñānarāśi, all the other characters speak in Prākṛt. The only other character to speak in Sanskrit is the *nāgaraka* Kalākaraṇḍaka, but he has very little role in the play. (He has just eight dialogues to render.) There are quite a few

182. *Hā.Cū.* I.13; Cf. *Abhijñānaśākuntala*, V.8.

Prākṛt *ślokas* too.[183] Only on one occasion do we find a Prākṛt-speaking character resorting to Sanskrit, that is, when Madanasundarī expresses her state of lovesickness.[184] The Prākṛt employed throughout the play is Śaurasenī.

STATE OF SOCIETY AS DEPICTED IN THE HĀ.CŪ.

The reference to King Paramārdideva in the prologue indicates the continuance of the tradition of royal patronage for poets in Vatsarāja's time. The reference to the *vaśīkaraṇa mantra* and the *upaśruti,* etc. and also Kapaṭakeli's blind belief in the powers of the recluse bring out some of the superstitions of the people in medieval India. The society has not changed much from the times of *BA,* with respect to the student-teacher relationship and life of the *nāgarakas* and the *gaṇikās*.

The Madanaketucarita

The *Madanaketucarita* (*MKC*) of Rāmapāṇivāda represents the last stage of Sanskrit drama. *MKC* is unique in several aspects. Though written during the eighteenth century, the society and culture it represents get transposed back by at least ten centuries. The sweet Vaidarbhī style adopted in the play and its remarkable similarity with the *BA* make it appear like a play belonging to the seventh and eighth centuries. It is probably out of modesty that the poet expresses his doubt whether his play can be called a *prahasana* at all, in the epilogue.[185] But *MKC* not only satisfies most of the theoretical rules of the *prahasana,* but also excels many of the earlier *prahasanas* in the choice of the theme and structure. *MKC* is a one-act play with a well-knit plot and delectable blend of *rasas*.

183. *Hā.Cū.* 1-12.

184. Ibid., II.3.

185. Cf. *prahasanalakṣaṇaleśaih spṛṣṭam cet prahasanābhidhām labhatām no cet punaranyadidam vinodanam pāṇivādasya.*

The language is free from coarseness and vulgarity. The main sentiment is, of course, *hāsya* which is evoked mainly through the ridicule of the licentious life led by a Buddhist monk. But unlike the other later *prahasana*s (between twelfth and nineteenth centuries) the play does not just stop with the criticism of the wayward life led by the pseudo-religious man; it also brings out how the monk is reformed at the end. The *hāsya* in *MKC* is not just the cheap slapstick comedy but is aroused by really humorous situations. The *hāsya* in *MKC* is gentle and dignified. Hence it would be reasonable to include *MKC* in the *śuddha* class of *prahasana*.

THE AUTHOR

Rāmapāṇivāda hails from Kerala and belongs to the eighteenth century. He is a prolific writer in both Sanskrit and Prākṛt. The *Uṣāniruddha*[186] and *Kaṁsavadham*[187] are his full-fledged Prākṛt *kāvya*s. Rāmapāṇivāda has shown his mastery over the Prākṛt language by writing a commentary on the Prākṛt *sūtra*s of Vararuci.[188] His contributions to Sanskrit range from *mahākāvya*s to *stotra* literature. He has two *mahākāvya*s to his credit — the *Rāghavīya*[189] in twenty cantos and the *Viṣṇuvilāsa*[190] in eight cantos. In the field of drama, he has contributed the *Sītārāghava*,[191] a *nāṭaka* and two *vīthī*s, *Candrikāvīthī*[192] and

186. Pub. Adyar Library and Research Centre, Madras, 1943.

187. Ed. A.N. Upadhye, Kolhapur, 1940, and Motilal Banarsidass, 1966.

188. Pub. Adyar, 1946.

189. Pub. University Manuscripts Library, Trivandrum, 1942.

190. Ibid., 1951.

191. Govt. Oriental MSS. Lib., Madras. D. No. 12721 and R. No. 5135.

192. *Bulletin of the Ramavarma Research Inst*, no. 3, pp. 1-14, 1934, published.

Līlāvatīvīthī[193] and also a *campū*, the *Bhāgavatacampū*.[194] His mastery over music is revealed by his works, *Gītārāma*, a *nṛtyaprabandha*, *Śivagīti*, a musical lyric on the lines of the *Gīta Govinda* and *Tālaprastara*, a work dealing with musical beats (*tāla*).[195]

It is clear from the references he makes to a number of kings and feudal lords in his works, that Rāmapāṇivāda moved from place to place in search of recognition and patronage. Rāmapāṇivāda was a disciple of one Nārāyaṇa Bhaṭṭatiri whom he refers to with reverence, in his works.[196] The poet also refers to his native village, Maṅgalagrāma[197] in some of his works. There is a bitter controversy among the Kerala scholars on the question of the identification of Rāmapāṇivāda with the well-known Malayalam poet Kuñcan Nambiar. But the arguments against the identification of the two poets seem to carry more weight.[198]

Dramatis Personae

Sūtradhāra	:	the stage manager.
Pāripārśvika	:	his assistant.
King Madanaketu	:	King of the Siṁhala country.
Queen Śṛṅgāramañjarī.		

193. Pub. University Manuscript Library, Trivandrum, No. 14, 1948.

194. Ibid.

195. Ref. in "A Critical study of Sanskrit Dramas by Kerala Authors" by S. Subramanya Iyer, unpublished thesis submitted to Kerala University, 1971.

196. In *MKC* the poet refers to his teacher in *śl*s. 2-4 in the epilogue.

197. *MKC*, p. 2, ed. University MSS. Lib., Trivandrum, 1948. The references to page numbers of the *MKC* in this dissertation are from this edition only.

198. See K.K. Raja, *Contribution of Kerala to Sanskrit Literature*, p. 186.

Candralekhā	:	a *gaṇikā* from the Karṇāṭa country.
Viṣṇumitra	:	a Buddhist monk.
Anaṅgalekhā	:	a *gaṇikā*.
Śivadāsa	:	a *yogin*.

Others in the cast: Female attendants, Candanikā, Jayantikā, messenger Jambhaka, male attendant Kāmbilyaka, a Kāñcukīya, Anaṅgalekhā's mother, and Prince Madanavarman, the younger brother of King Madanaketu.

THE PLOT OF THE MADANAKETUCARITA

Viṣṇumitra, a Buddhist monk is deeply in love with a *gaṇikā* Anaṅgalekhā by name. With a view to testing the will-power of the monk, the queen arranges for a secret meeting between the two in the royal garden. The monk makes amorous advances towards the girl and is caught red-handed by the girl's mother who drags the monk to the royal court under charges of attempted rape. King Madanaketu promises to inquire into the matter.

Meanwhile, a *yogin*, Śivadāsa by name, who has been sent by the king's younger brother Prince Madanavarman, arrives on the scene. Śivadāsa demonstrates his yogic power by procuring for the king his sweetheart Candralekhā, a *gaṇikā* from the distant Karṇāṭa country. The jealous queen is also pacified by him. He then temporarily abandons his body and enters into the body of Anaṅgalekhā, who had died due to serpent-bite. Directed by the soul of Śivadāsa from inside, the *gaṇikā* begins to behave differently. She solicits the Buddhist monk in the open court unmindful of the presence of the king and his consorts. Her amorous advances put everybody to shame. The monk himself retreats and is disgusted with the lust of women. Meanwhile the body of Śivadāsa is brought to the court. As the king and his queens express their shock and as the monk laments over his death, Śivadāsa witnesses all this from inside the body of Anaṅgalekhā. The Buddhist monk resolves to eschew worldly desires and take to religious pilgrimage. Being convinced that he is reformed, Śivadāsa feels that his mission is complete, enters into his own body and revives Anaṅgalekhā too.

CHARACTER STUDY

Śivadāsa

The only true *yogin* other than the one in *BA*, in the whole range of *prahasana* literature is Śivadāsa of *MKC*. He seems to be a Kāpālika by faith and he pronounces his staunch belief in his religion which justifies his name too, i.e. Śivadāsa — servant or devotee of Śiva.

सद्यःकृत्तनृमुण्डकुण्डलधरश्शुक्लास्थिमालावलीं
विभ्राणो धवलश्मशानभसितप्रोद्भासिना वक्षसा।
पूर्णं ब्रह्मशिरःकपालचषकं पाणौ सुराया दधत्
स्वच्छन्दं विहरन्नसौ विजयते देवो महाभैरवः॥

— *śl.* 16

He is a truly detached soul as is evident from his advice to the monk Viṣṇumitra.

क्वासौ संसारसिन्धोस्सुतरणतरणिर्योगिनामाश्रमस्ते
क्वामी निर्वाणचन्द्रोदयबहुलनिशाः केवलं वेशनार्यः।
कल्याणं कामयेथाः परिचिनु च सभामुज्ज्वलां सज्जनानां
तीर्थस्नायी दुराशाकलुषितमधुना मानसं वा पुनीहि॥

— *śl.* 60

Śivadāsa is held in high esteem by all the characters in the play. They are mere pawns in his hands and act according to his will. They all look forward to him for the fulfilment of their aspirations. Prince Madanavarman requests him to reform the Buddhist monk Viṣṇuvarman. King Madanaketu expresses his desire to obtain Candralekhā, the *gaṇikā* from the Karṇāṭa country, and she is immediately brought forth before him by his yogic power. He rescues the monk from the clutches of Anaṅgalekhā's mother. He then helps the king overcome the wrath of the queen for his affair with Karṇāṭa-*gaṇikā*. In short, there is nothing that is impossible for him. The king says, . . .

> *yadasya sarvādbhutanidheḥ śivadāsasya sakāśāt sarvam sambhāvyata eva.*
> —p. 15

The Buddhist monk too expresses his surprise at the all-pervading influence of the *yogin*.

> अहो महानुभावः खलु शिवदासः। अनेन-
> प्रत्यक्ष-दृष्ट-निजवल्लभ-दुर्नयापि
> देवी तथा नयविदा गमिता प्रसादम्।
> नीरन्ध्रसंतमस-संव्रियमाणमूर्तिः
> सन्ध्या यथा शरदि कैरववल्लभेन ॥
> — *śl.* 35

The *yogin* himself proudly asserts that he would produce any desired object in a minute: *asmin brahmāṇḍakhaṇḍa* . . . etc. (*śl.* 120).

Śivadāsa possesses miraculous yogic powers. He can read the thoughts of others. He is skilled in the art of *parakāyapraveśa* and can revive the dead. But he employs his talents with purpose. The Candralekhā-episode which he stages helps to win the confidence of the king. The Buddhist monk too requests him to win the love of the *gaṇikā* Anaṅgalekhā for him. Śivadāsa first advises the monk to shun lustful thoughts which are unbecoming of a religious man. It is only when mere verbal advice does not produce the desired result that the *yogin* decides to infuse his soul into the body of Anaṅgalekhā and make her act in a lustful manner which brings a sense of remorse in the mind of the Buddhist monk. The *parakāyapraveśa* helps the *yogin* assess the opinion of others about his own self when his lifeless body is brought to the court. The Buddhist monk bewails thus,

> *hā mahopakārin, hā mama sanmārgopadeśadeśika, hā nikhilayogavidyānidhe, hā niṣkāraṇavatsala, kvāsi? dehi me prativacanam.* — p. 48

The king too is overcome with grief at the sudden demise of his benefactor and pays glowing tributes to him.

> स्वार्थं सन्त्यजतः परार्थ-घटन-व्यापार-निष्ठस्य ते
> कष्टं निष्ठुरमीदृशं कृतवता दैवेन किं दुष्करम्।
> कल्याणिन् शिवदास वासवपुरे तत्तादृशैरद्भुतैः
> देवानामपि सम्मदं प्रबलयन् किञ्चित् प्रतीक्षस्व नः॥
> — *śl.*103

The Heroine of the Play

We have three young women in *MKC* who stake the claim for heroineship of the play: Queen Śṛṅgāramañjarī, Candralekhā, the harlot from the Karṇāṭa country, and Anaṅgalekhā. The queen has a very little role to play. She raises objections to the king's love for Candralekhā at first but submits to the request of Śivadāsa and accepts Candralekhā as the co-wife. The main motive of introducing the character of Candralekhā is to demonstrate the yogic power of Śivadāsa and she has only a minor role in the play. But Anaṅgalekhā has a much wider role. She is a very beautiful girl. Her bewitching beauty captivates the heart of even religious mendicants. It is only Anaṅgalekhā who is used as an instrument by Śivadāsa to reform the Buddhist monk. Hence it is reasonable to assign the role of the heroine only to Anaṅgalekhā. Even the *yogin* is appreciative of her beauty,

> *api kuśalam asya yogināmapi manovikārajanakasya śarīrasya?* — p. 27

She joins hands with Śivadāsa in exposing the degraded nature of the monk Viṣṇumitra. She even advises the monk not to bring discredit to his religious order.

> मदनविलासविरुद्धं चिरकालोत्पन्नपुण्यपरिपाकम्।
> एतमाश्रमसारं मा मम स्पर्शेन दूषय॥
>
> — *śl.* 50

When the monk makes advances unmindful of her warnings, she bursts out,

> *uttiṣṭha duṣṭavaṭuka, uttiṣṭha kimadyāpi durabhilāṣam na muñcasi?* — p. 29

She later pacifies the monk at the instance of Śivadāsa. She proclaims the trade secret of her profession.

> अनुरागपरीक्षणोचितानि प्रथमं चाटुशतानि दर्शयन्ति।
> अथ बाहुलताभ्यां कण्ठनालं परिगृह्णन्ति यूनामस्मादृश्यः॥
>
> — *śl.* 56

The next time when we meet Anaṅgalekhā, she is infused with the soul of Śivadāsa (after her death by the snake-bite) who directs her speech, action, etc. from inside. Among others it is the Buddhist monk who is elated at her revival.

> निर्वाणाप्यनिलेन दीपकलिका सद्यः स्वयं दीप्यते
> राहोर्वक्त्रमुपेयुषी शशिकला भूयः समुन्मीलति।
> संप्लुष्टापि समुद्भिनत्ति सहसा दावाग्निना मालती
> सर्पेणाहृतजीवितापि सुदती सञ्जीविताभ्येत्यसौ॥
>
> — *śl.* 72

When the revived Anaṅgalekhā directed by the soul of Śivadāsa from inside, makes amorous advances towards the monk, the king enjoys the fun for some time. But when she crosses the limits of modesty, he condemns her,

> *āḥ kulaṭe apehi tāvat* — p. 41

The queen too becomes angry and requests him to take action on her. The Buddhist monk gets disgusted with the lust for women and becomes ashamed of his past actions. When Śivadāsa abandons Anaṅgalekhā's body and again revives her with her own soul, she behaves normally. She is shocked to hear the queen's charge,

> *pūrvam punaḥ strījana-viruddham bahu pralapantyā tvayā ciram kadarthitāsmi* — p. 52

With fear she asks, *atha kayā tathā parlāpitaṁ?* (p. 53). She asserts that she had been fast asleep for a long time. When Śivadāsa explains what had happened, she heaves a long sigh of relief. Being convinced of her innocence, the queen compliments her,

> *anaparāddhā khalu eṣā tapasvinī Anaṅgalekhā* — p. 55

Viṣṇumitra

Viṣṇumitra belongs to the same class of Buddhist monks who figure in the earlier *prahasana*s, having a false outer robe and amorous inner inclinations. His love for the harlot Anaṅgalekhā is revealed in the *prastāvanā* itself. In the *viṣkambhaka*, he appears describing his love-lorn condition. He is fully aware that what he does is against the norms prescribed for monks. He says,

> अहो नु खलु विषमो मम संसारभारः ; कुतः-
> वसानः काषायं वसनमपिधानं रतिपतिः
> दधानस्तां चित्ते चकितहरिणीशावनयनाम्।
> वहन् पाणौ दण्डं विषयशफरीजालवलिशं
> परीरम्भाशंसी कथमपि नयाम्येष दिवसान्॥
> — *śl.* 7

In one of his weaker moments, he goes to the extent of molesting the harlot. For this offence he is dragged to the court of King Madanaketu by the harlot's mother. His guilt being proved he stands condemned in the open court. Still desire lingers in his mind. The Candralekhā episode arouses hope in his mind and he turns to Śivadāsa for the fulfilment of his wish. His hypocrisy is exposed by Śivadāsa as he hesitates to accept the liquor offered to him, *ko 'yam evam parivrājakadharmādhikārī* —

> *anaṅgalekhādhara-śīdhupāne samutsukastvam kila kāmalolaḥ*
>
> — *śl.* 39

As Anaṅgalekhā appears there, at the instance of Śivadāsa, he falls flat at her feet and begs for her love, forgetting his stature as a monk. But he is enraged at her when she despises him. He calls her *puṁścalī* and curses womanhood as a whole.

> निम्नं क्वाप्युन्नतं क्वाप्यतिकृशमपरत्रान्यतोऽत्यन्तपीनं
> सावज्ञं स्त्रीति योगी विधिरकृत यथाप्राप्तमङ्गं यदासाम्।
> मूढास्तन्नाम नाभिस्तनमुदरनितम्बं च चारुत्वपक्षे
> निक्षिप्तं मन्यते चेदिह घुणलिपिषु व्यस्त एवावमानः॥
>
> — *śl.* 54

Even the announcement of the noontime reminds him only of the matutinal love sports of the lovers. Still he feels that he should not abandon the noontime rites. It is only when Anaṅgalekhā, infused with the soul of Śivadāsa, exhibits extreme lust that the monk gets disgusted with the ways of women and decides to mend his way of life and become a true monk. He observes,

> वाराङ्गनाजनविलासपलालजालविप्लोषकर्मणि कृशानुशिखायते या।
> सा योगवृत्तिरतिवृत्तरजस्तमस्का निर्वाणवर्त्मघटनाय ममानुकूला॥
>
> — *śl.* 98

His aim now would be to visit holy places and spend the rest of his life peacefully.

पुण्यानां पुलिनस्थलानि सरितां जुष्टानि वैखानसैः
कान्ताराण्युपशान्तसत्त्वकलहप्रस्तावरम्याणि च।
नित्यावर्तितवेदशास्त्रमुखरब्रह्माणि देवालयान्
आसेवेमहि जीवशेषनिगलच्छेदाय मोदाय च॥

— *śl.* 114

Other Important Characters in the Play

Madanaketu whose name the play bears, is the king of the Simhala country. His role extended beyond the shores, right up to the Kaliṅga country in India where he has installed his younger brother Madanavarman as his representative ruler. He is a hero of the *dhīralalita* type. He has high regard for his wife Śṛṅgāramañjarī, but is also in love with the *gaṇikā* Candralekhā from the Karṇāṭa country. He shows great reverence for the *yogin* Śivadāsa. He scrupulously maintained justice in his country as is evident from the Viṣṇumitra episode.

Queen Śṛṅgāramañjarī is the prototype of the queens we come across in plays like the *Mālavikāgnimitra* and *Ratnāvalī*. She is devoted to her husband and cannot tolerate his love being shared by another lady. She is jealous of Candralekhā and is angry at the king's action but is later reconciled to the situation at the intervention of Śivadāsa and treats Candralekhā as her co-wife. She is totally displeased with the degraded life led by the Buddhist monk and decides to draw the attention of the king to his atrocities. Modest as she is, she becomes enraged at the outrageous behaviour of the *gaṇikā* Anaṅgalekhā (under the influence of Śivadāsa's soul) and resolves to punish the sensuous girl. When the whole plot of Śivadāsa is unfolded, she becomes apologetic and even calls the *gaṇikā* a *tapasvinī*.

Candralekhā the *gaṇikā* from the Karṇāṭa country has only a minor role to play. She is introduced in the play mainly to demonstrate the yogic powers of Śivadāsa. Prince

Madanavarman though not appearing on the stage, has a vital role to play in the proceedings since it is he who sends Śivadāsa to the court of King Madanaketu.

LITERARY MERITS OF THE PLAY

Rāmapāṇivāda shows an amazing command of language — both in Sanskrit and in Prākṛt and high dramatic skills, which are rarely found combined in the poets of his times. His verses are lucid, spontaneous and full of vigour. The narration is straight and free from confusion in spite of the introduction of change of souls. His descriptive powers, power of observation and depiction of human nature and tendencies, delineation of sentiments and the effective use of the *alaṁkāra*s — all combine to make him one of the gifted dramatists in Sanskrit literature. The employment of successive metaphors in the description of the evening is appealing.

> नीरन्ध्रध्वान्तदन्तावलहरिनखरश्रेणयः पद्मवाटी-
> सद्मान्तस्सुप्तमत्तभ्रमरकुलवधूसाधुबोधप्रदीपाः ।
> पूर्वाशावेशनारीमुखलिखितपरिस्पष्टसिन्दूररेखाः
> केकीशोकार्णवौर्वानलविपुलशिखा भान्ति भानोर्मयूखाः ॥
>
> — *śl*. 10

> The sun's rays are beautiful and sharp as the nails of the lion of light pouncing on the black elephant of darkness. The rays are like the waking lamps (*bodhapradīpa*s) for the princesses of female bees sleeping inside the palaces of the closed lotus. They are like the streaks of *tilaka* mark (*sindūra*) on the forehead of the harlots in the forms of Eastern direction. They are again the shooting flames of the fire from the ocean of grief of the *cakravāka* birds.

The poet is an adept in the description of the charms of women. For the lover his sweetheart is the most beautiful girl in the three worlds. With her charms she waters and nourishes the tree of the pride of Madana in the heart of the lover. The aspiration (of love) has drawn her picture on the canvas of the lover's heart. From her body have been created the sandal, the moon, the gentle breeze and the like which pierce the vitals.

सैवेयं भुवनैकसुन्दरितमा कन्दर्पदर्पद्रुमं
सिञ्चन्ती सुषमामृतेन वपुषश्चित्ताङ्कणे मादृशाम्।
यामेवालिखदन्तरङ्गफलके सङ्कल्पशिल्पी यथा
पूर्वं चन्दनचन्द्रमन्दपवना मर्माविधो निर्मिताः॥
— *śl.* 27

Some of the observations of the poet on the nature of women are noteworthy. Afflictions caused by women are to be removed by women only. Submarine fire is to be quenched by the same seawater.

स्त्रीमूलस्योपतापस्य स्त्रिय एव प्रतिक्रिया।
वह्निश्च वह्निमूलस्येत्यामनन्ति मनीषिणः॥
— *śl.* 65

It is impossible to read the mind of women. They never express their love openly.

अपि विशन्ति कृशानुशिखावलीम्
अपि लिहन्ति महासिलतामुखम्।
अपि गरं निगिरन्ति न कामिषु
प्रकटयन्ति मनो वनिताजनाः॥
— *śl.* 66

On the *gaṇikā dharma* the poet says:

भवत्वक्ष्णा काणो भवतु च जराशुष्कवदनः
पदा खञ्जो वास्तु व्रणविचितगात्रो भवतु वा।
जटी वा मुण्डी वा भवतु खुरणा वा किमु गिरा
यतो वित्तापत्तिः स खलु गणिकानां प्रियतमः॥
— *śl.* 45

From any point of view, the nectar from the lips of women is superior to the nectar that was got from the Milky Ocean.

Since the big snake was used as a rope for churning the Milky Ocean, (some) drops of poison would definitely have polluted that nectar and since the Mandara mountain was used as the base it (the nectar) would have been spoiled by the particles of the mountain ores fallen due to friction.

अजिह्मगमुखोद्गलद्गरलबिन्दुसन्दूषितं
तदेतदपयःपयोनिलयफेनसम्मिश्रितम् ।
अमन्दरपरिस्फुरद्विविध-धातु-धूम्रीकृतं
मनोज्ञमधरामृतं विजयते कुरङ्गीदृशाम् ॥

— *śl.* 96

There are still people in the world who go all out to help their friends out of compassion without absolutely any selfish motive.

निर्व्याजनिर्मलधियां विधुरेषु मन्ये
वीताभिसन्धिकणिकः करुणानुषङ्गः ।
किं चातका विदधते हितमम्बुदेभ्यः
सन्तर्पयन्ति किममून्न हि ते पयोभिः ॥

— *śl.* 111

HĀSYA IN MKC

It is mainly the *śṛṅgārābhāsa* arising out of the Buddhist monk's love for the *gaṇikā* that contributes to the comic element of the play. The scene where the monk, caught unawares by the queen's trap, makes amorous advances towards the girl and is dragged to the court by the harlot's mother is quite amusing. Śivadāsa's tricks to infatuate the monk with Anaṅgalekhā showing signs of love and feigned anger alternately in order to expose his weaknesses, and the curious behaviour of Anaṅgalekhā under the influence of Śivadāsa's soul are some of the other comic scenes in the play. There is a sarcasm in the remark of the indignant queen when she sees the king embracing Candralekhā, *mā khalu mā khalu vyālībhayena candanarasān muñca, kaṇṭakabhayena ketakīmadhūlikām vā* — p. 20

PRAHASANA ELEMENTS AND VĪTHYAṄGAS IN THE PLAY

The king's sarcastic proclamation on coming to know of the degraded life led by the Buddhist monk and Śivadāsa's appreciation of the proclamation is an instance of the *prahasana* element *pralāpa*.

ये नाम केचन तपोनिधयो वसन्ति
सँसारधर्ममपहाय मदीयराज्ये ।
ते सर्व एव मदिरामनिशं पिबन्तो
मच्छासनेन गणिकासदनं भजन्तु ॥
— *śl.* 40

अहो महाराज तव प्रभावः प्रजासुखोत्पादनतत्परोऽयम् ।
पूर्वेषु को नाम समानवृत्तिरेवंविधं शासनमुच्चकार ॥
— *śl.* 41

The humorous explanation of the significance of the string of beads, the stick and the yellow robe of the Buddhist monk may be cited as an instance of the *prahasana* element *upapatti*.

अक्षस्रजा गणयतीव गुणांस्त्वदीयान्
दण्डं च पञ्जशरशासनवद् दधाति ।
काषायमावहति रागमिवैष मूर्तं
धूर्ते किमेनमनु ते वलते न चेतः ॥
— *śl.* 47

Another instance of the same element can be found in the angry remark of the monk on the shapely curves of women.[199] The fear of the monk that his secret affairs might have reached the ear of the king, may be cited as an illustration of the

199. *MKC*, *śl.* 54. See above under "Viṣṇumitra" (Character Study) in this chapter.

element *bhayam*.

ममायमर्थः प्रायेण राजगोचरमेष्यति।
नदीनामम्भसामोघः सिन्धुं नाप्राप्य तिष्ठति॥

— *śl.* 12

There are a number of instances of the element *anṛtam*. The *ceṭī* addresses the monk thus,

yogīśvaraiḥ yuṣmābhiḥ kasya na prayojanam bhavati? — p. 4

Śivadāsa's praise of the liquor may be cited as another instance of *anṛtam*.

पीयूषेण समं पुरा विमथिताद् दुग्धाम्बुधेरुत्थितम्
तत्तादृङ्मदिराभिधं मदपदं किञ्चित् पदार्थान्तरम्॥

— *śl.* 38

RASAS OTHER THAN HĀSYA IN THE PLAY

The *rasa* that figures prominently apart from *hāsya* in *MKC* is *śṛṅgāra*, scope for which is afforded in the Candralekhā episode.[200] There is an element of *adbhuta* when the *gaṇikā* from the distant Karṇāṭa country is produced by Śivadāsa by his yogic power[201] and also on two or three occasions when the dead are revived much to the surprise of the onlookers.[202] In the scene where the king and the monk lament over what they think to be the death of Śivadāsa, there is genuine *karuṇā*.[203]

ALAṀKĀRAS

A number of the popular *alaṁkāra*s have been employed in

200. Cf. *MKC, śl.* 27. See above under "Literary Merits of the Play" in this chapter.

201. *MKC, śl.* 26.

202. Ibid., pp. 35-36.

203. Ibid., pp. 48-49.

MKC. *Rūpaka* seems to be the favourite figure of speech of the poet. There are at least 22 instances of *rūpaka* in the play. The verse *saiveyam bhuvanaikasundarītamā*. . . is an outstanding example.[204] The verse on the sunset already referred to[205] is another instance of *rūpaka* in the play. In another verse the two consorts of the king are fancied as two gems set in one and the same golden plaque.

भिन्नाकरप्रभवमन्यतुलाविहीनम्
धन्योत्तरैरपि दुरापमहो महार्घम्।
रत्नद्वयं तदिदमेकसुवर्णपिण्डे
यत्नं विना विनिहितं विहिताभिसन्धि॥
— *śl*. 67

Upamā too figures prominently. The Buddhist monk is surprised to see the queen leave off her anger and smile at once when pacified by Śivadāsa. The twilight sky, though enveloped by darkness for a moment in winter, is again made bright by the lord of lilies (the moon).[206]

We have *nidarśanā* in —

कामं तया खलु बलादवधीरितोऽहं
रागस्तु सुभ्रुवि तथाप्यतिजृम्भते मे।
धिक्कुट्टिनीं यदियमेव हि तां निरुन्धे
दोषो नियन्तुरिह दुष्यति यत्करेणुः॥
— *śl*. 23

The lover has to bear the responsibility for the anger of his

204. Cf. *MKC*, *śl*. 27. See above under "Literary Merits of the Play" in this chapter.

205. Ibid., *śl*. 10. See above under "Literary Merits of the Play" in this chapter.

206. Ibid., *śl*. 35. See above under "Śivadāsa" (Character Study) in this chapter.

beloved in the same way as the mahout becomes responsible for the abnormal behaviour of his female elephant.

Though conscious of infidelity to his wife the king cannot refrain from loving the harlot Candralekhā. A *dṛṣṭānta* is offered in this context.

व्यालीभयेन मलयाचलकन्दरस्थं
को वा प्रतीरतरुसारमपाकरोति।
— *śl.* 31

The Buddhist monk gets disgusted with Anaṅgalekhā and regrets that he had been foolishly trying to elicit her love. He had been thus foolishly trying to pluck out the sharp tooth from the mouth of a lioness.

सिंहीदंष्ट्राशलाकां सपदि करतलेनाजिहीर्षामि मोहात्।
— *śl.* 52

Even stubborn men are rendered soft by the charms of women. Even a stone (the Candrakānta) is made to ooze water by the moon.

पुरुषान् परुषानपि स्वभावान् म्रदिमानं गणयन्ति नार्य एव।
ननु दीधितयस्तुषारभानोः स्वयमेव द्रवयन्ति चन्द्रकान्तान्॥
— *śl.* 55

We have beautiful *svabhāvokti* in the following verse:

केतकीकुसुमगर्भसंभृतां माधुरीजितसुधामधूलिकाम्।
कण्टकावलिपरिक्षतोऽपि सन्नैष मुञ्चति कृती मधुव्रतः॥
— *śl.* 32

An instance of *mālārūpaka* is found in the following verse where the Buddhist monk expresses surprise at the revival of Anaṅgalekhā.

निर्वाणाप्यनिलेन दीपकलिका सद्यः स्वयं दीप्यते
राहोर्वक्त्रमुपेयुषी शशिकला भूयः समुन्मीलति।

संप्लुष्टापि समुद्भिनत्ति सहसा दावाग्निना मालती
सर्पेणाहतजीवितापि सुदती सञ्जीविताभ्येत्यसौ ॥
— *śl.* 72

Though almost put out by the wind, the flame of the lamp flickers. Though devoured by Rāhu for some time the moon emerges with full splendour. Though scorched by fire the jasmine starts sprouting. Though snatched of her life by the serpent, she is now revived!

There are quite a few apt *arthāntara nyāsa*s in the play. Justifying the fact that there is merit even in the works of modern poets, the *sūtradhāra* says, "Do not the stars shine though flooded by the moonlight?"

ये गृह्णन्ति गुणानणूनपि कवेः काव्येषु नव्येष्वपि
प्रायो नो गणयन्ति दोषनिवहं ते नाम सन्तः किल।
बालोऽप्यात्मकृतिप्रकाशनविधौ शक्नोति तेषां पुरो
दीप्तिं विन्दति किन्न चन्द्रमहसा मग्नोऽपि तारागणः ॥
— *śl.* 4

Being informed that he is to meet the queen the monk fears that the news of his illicit love affair might have reached the ears of the king. The gushing waters of the river do never fail to reach the ocean.[207]

METRES

MKC is one of the longest *prahasana*s with 120 *śloka*s. The poet has a flair for longer metres; there are 31 *śloka*s in *śārdūlavikrīḍita* and 9 in *sragdharā* metres contrasted with only 6 in the popular *anuṣṭubh*. Other metres employed by the poet are *vasantatilakā* (14 *śloka*s), *śikhariṇī* (7), *mālinī* (6), *upajāti* (5), *mandakrāntā* (4), *svāgatā* (4), *āryā*, *rathoddhatā*, *śālinī*, *pṛthvī* and *aupacchandaśikā* (3

207. *MKC*, *śl.* 12. See above under "Prahasana Elements and Vīthyaṅgas in the Play" in this chapter.

*śloka*s each). We have two verses each in *hariṇī*, *praharṣiṇī* and *vaṁśastha* and one each in *vaitālīya*, *drutavilambita* and *upendravajrā*.

PRĀKṚT IN MKC

As per convention all the lower characters and women speak in Prākṛt. But the maidservant Candanikā resorts to Sanskrit while describing Candralekhā.[208] The *gaṇikā* Anaṅgalekhā, infused by the soul of Śivadāsa continues to speak in Prākṛt but there are occasional lapses.[209] The Buddhist monks usually speak in Prākṛt (as in the *MV*, *Laṭakamelaka* and other *prahasana*s), but the monk Viṣṇumitra in *MKC* speaks in Sanskrit throughout. The *pāripārśvika* in the prologue, the messenger Jambhaka and the *pratīhāra* Kāmbilyaka speak in Sanskrit only. Being an authority in Prākṛt himself the poet has composed eleven verses in Prākṛt also.[210]

DRAMATIC TECHNIQUE IN MKC

MKC fares well even when compared with an excellent piece like the *Bhagavadajjukīya*. In *BA*, there is simultaneous exchange of souls which may cause some confusion when being staged, and it has necessitated the introduction of another character, viz. the Yamapuruṣa. Rāmapāṇivāda has avoided these difficulties by introducing the change of soul one at a time. The *gaṇikā* is first killed by the snake-bite and her body is brought to the court. Śivadāsa, who had already left the court on some pretext, keeps his body on a tree top and ensouls the body of Anaṅgalekhā. His body is also brought to the court after some time. Later he leaves the body of the *gaṇikā* and enters into his own. The girl drops dead now. But she is

208. Cf. *śl*. 43.

209. For example, *śl*s. 95-97.

210. *Śloka*s 50, 56, 78, 84, 86-88, 90, 92, 101, 108.

revived by the *yogin* at the request of the king and others. In *BA*, the *gaṇikā* is to act like the *yogin* and vice versa but in *MKC* we do not face this problem. The girl remains her own self with the exception that she appears to be more sensuous and gives expression to her feelings. This technique adopted by the poet is definitely an improvement over a similar scene in *BA*.

The *svagata* technique used in many places in the play helps the audience know the thoughts of the different characters on important turn of events. For instance, it is only from the *svagata* speech of Śivadāsa that we come to know of the role of the prince Madanavarman in the play. The *janāntika* is also helpful for Śivadāsa to instruct people on the line of action, as for instance in the place where the *gaṇikā* Anaṅgalekhā infatuates the Buddhist monk with her feigned love and anger.

Nāndī

The *nāndī*[211] in *MKC* not only serves the purpose of benediction, but it also indicates the main *rasa* in the play, i.e. *hāsya* and it has a reference to the moon (in the word *śaśiśekhara*) as per convention. Pārvatī's friend tells her that she is not going to anoint her breasts with *kastūrī* any more since it is going to be polluted by the ashes (due to Śiva's embrace) very often. The embarrassed Pārvatī casts a bashful glance at the moon-crested lord (Śiva).

The Prologue

The prologue is carried out by the *sūtradhāra* and his associate. The very first verse[212] in the prologue suggests the presence of a *gaṇikā* in the play. We are further informed that the play

211. *MKC, śl.* 1.

212. Cf. *MKC, śl.* 2: *yogini vā bhogini vā rogiṇi vā vittade virāgiṇi vā* ।
sādhāraṇapravṛttir vidagdha-gaṇikājano jayati ॥

is staged in connection with the *yātrā* festival of Śrī Raṅganātha, the presiding deity at Maṅgalagrāma. The *pāripārśvika* then expresses doubt whether a new composition would be accepted by the audience. The *sūtradhāra* allays his fears saying that great men would appreciate a play after duly considering its merits and demerits irrespective of its being modern or old.[213] At the end of their conversation, Viṣṇumitra, the Buddhist monk, is introduced through the *prayogātiśaya* method.[214]

Viṣkambhaka

The one point where *MKC* deviates from theory is the *viṣkambhaka*. *Praveśaka* and *viṣkambhaka* are prohibited in a *prahasana*.[215] The *viṣkambhaka* has been introduced for the purpose of bringing out one side of the character of the Buddhist monk, viz. his lustful passion for the *gaṇikā* Anaṅgalekhā. We are also informed through the *viṣkambhaka* that the queen wanted to meet the monk privately in the royal garden, the intention of which the audience and not the monk as informed later, is to test the integrity of the monk. The monk misbehaves towards the girl and is dragged to the court by the harlot's mother seeking justice. By the introduction of the *viṣkambhaka*, it has been possible for the poet to confine himself to just one act.

Prakarī

Another noteworthy feature of *MKC* is that it has a *prakarī* (a secondary narrative), in the Candralekhā episode. *Prahasana*s generally do not have *patākā* or *prakarī* since the main part of the play itself is, usually, very short. The *prakarī* in *MKC* adds

213. *MKC*, *śl.* 4. See above under "Alaṁkāras" in this chapter.

214. Ibid., *śl.* 5, *pariṣadam-ārādhayitum prayatethāḥ sarvathā durārādhām* ।
gaṇikām anaṅgalekhām bhikṣurasau viṣṇumitra ivā ॥

215. See above under "Characteristics of the Prahasana" in chapter 3.

variety to the plot and the *rasa*, which makes the play all the more interesting. It also helps to stage the demonstration of the yogic powers of Śivadāsa. It is by witnessing the Candralekhā-episode that the Buddhist monk begins to take confidence in the *yogin* and looks forward to him for fulfilment of his ambition, and later remembering the advice, resolves to lead a reformed life.

EPILOGUE

Another peculiarity of *MKC* is that it has an epilogue.[216] In the first verse of the epilogue already referred to, the poet expresses his doubt whether his work can be called a *prahasana* at all. In the other three verses the poet offers glowing tributes to his preceptor, Śrī Nārāyaṇa.

THE INFLUENCE OF THE BHAGAVADAJJUKĪYA ON MKC

Even a cursory glance at the plot of the two plays reveals the extent to which the *BA* has influenced the *MKC*. The following similarities may be noted.

(i) Both the plays are fit to be included under the *śuddha* class of *prahasana*.

(ii) The exchange of souls — *parakāyapraveśa*, is employed in both.

(iii) The first *śloka* in both the plays is addressed to Lord Śiva (while the first *śloka* of *MKC* is the conventional *nāndī*, in *BA*, the first *śloka* in the text is preceded by the stage direction *nāndyante tataḥ praviśati sūtradhāraḥ*).

(iv) The introduction of the main character in both the plays is made through the dramatic device known as *prayogātiśaya*.

---

216. See above under "The Madanakatucarita", in this chapter.

(v) The *bīja* in both the plays is identical, that is, the upliftment of the corrupt religious man.

(vi) Supernatural element plays an important role in both the plays.

(vii) In addition to *hāsya* which is the main sentiment, there is scope for *śṛṅgāra* in both the plays.

(viii) Death scene is introduced in both the plays.

(ix) The incidents of both the plays last for a day. Time analysis in *BA* has already been discussed.[217] In the *viṣkambhaka* of *MKC* the *bhikṣu* says, *sāvaśeṣa iva me prābhātiko vidhiḥ* (p. 5). By the time the Candralekhā episode is over, it is midday and the *bhikṣu* feels that he should not ignore the midday bath at any cost, *sarvathā madhyāhna-snānavidhiḥ na laṅghanīyaḥ* (p. 32). Though there is no other reference to the time factor in the play, there is reason to suppose that the further incidents last till the evening.

(x) The turning-point in both the plays is the snake-bite. This is brought about by the Yamapuruṣa and Śivadāsa in *BA* and *MKC* respectively.

(xi) In both the plays the *yogin*s play a prominent role. Both are detached ascetics, skilled in yogic practices. Incidentally these two are the only specimens of *bhāgavata*s in the whole range of the *prahasana* literature. Perhaps the *Nāṭyaśāstra* recommends only such characters in a *śuddha* type of *prahasana*.[218]

(xii) The heroines in both the plays are courtesans.

---

217. See above under "Time Analysis" in this chapter.

218. See above under "Characteristics of the Prahasana" in chapter 3.

Though thus Rāmapāṇivāda is very much indebted to the author of the *Bhagavadajjukīya* for the plot of his work, he shows remarkably original poetic skill and dramatic technique. It is all the more praiseworthy on the part of the author to have given us a refreshingly new type of *prahasana* at a time when obscenity and base religious quarrels came to be identified with the *prahasanas*. Rāmapāṇivāda's *Madanaketucarita* thus occupies a very significant place in the later *prahasana* literature.

5

The Saṁkīrṇa Type of Prahasanas

All the available *prahasanas* other than the four discussed in the previous chapter can be brought under the *saṁkīrṇa* variety. Here they will be discussed under two groups, viz. (A) The well-known *prahasanas* and (B) The minor *prahasanas*. The works in each group are arranged chronologically, as it would be easier to observe the transition that has taken place in the outlook of the *prahasana* writers through the last seven or eight centuries. Some prominent features common to these *saṁkīrṇa prahasanas* are : (i) Most of them have more than one act, (ii) Large number of characters are introduced in them, (iii) Characters are drawn from every stratum of the society, from the king to a barber, and (iv) *Hāsya* introduced in them is rather crude. The comic element is mainly aroused by totally incongruent speech and action the characters exhibit with respect to the profession they hold — foolish kings and ministers, ignorant teachers, impertinent disciples and ill-equipped doctors and astrologers, etc.

The *saṁkīrṇa prahasanas* show a general degradation of taste in the *prahasana* writers. Almost every *prahasana* has a certain amount of obscenity, this feature being most pronounced in the much later *prahasanas* like the *Lambodara* and the *Caṇḍānurañjana*. Among the available *saṁkīrṇa prahasanas*, *Laṭakamelaka* of Śaṅkhadhara occupies an important place.

The Well-Known Prahasanas

THE LAṬAKAMELAKA

Laṭakamelaka (*LM*) is the earliest among the *saṁkīrṇa* type of *prahasanas*. It is also the earliest among the available two-act *prahasanas*. It is evidently one of the most popular *prahasanas* as some of its verses are quoted in the works on Sanskrit dramaturgy.[1] Two of its verses are quoted in the *Śārṅgadhara-paddhati*.[2] Its manuscripts are available in a number of Oriental Libraries in India and abroad. It was first printed in 1889.[3] The present study is based on a more recent edition of the text.[4]

The Author and Date of the Work

The author, Śaṅkhadhara Kavirāja, flourished in the court of King Govindacandra of Kanyakubja during the early part of the twelfth century.[5] The poet eulogises his patron in glorious terms in the prologue of the play. He refers to some of the ancient villages near Kannauj.[6] He also refers to a clan known as "Rāḍhīyas". A class of brāhmaṇas who came from south India and settled in Bengal during the reign of King Lakṣmaṇasena (1180-1206) was called Rāḍhīya.[7] The date of this king may be taken as the upper limit of the date of the poet. The lower limit is *c*. 1330 as *Sāhitya-Darpaṇa* refers to it.[8]

---

1. *SD* III.219-20. *gurorgiraḥ* . . . (*LM*, II.14).
2. Cf. *Sārṅgadharapaddhati*, *eṣa svargataraṅgiṇī* . . . (*LM*, I.38) and *katipayanimeṣavartinī* . . . . (*LM*, I.9) nos. 3632 & 155 respectively.
3. Nirnayasagar Press, Bombay.
4. Chowkhamba, Banaras, 1962.
5. Keith, *Sanskrit Drama*, p. 260.
6. Cf. Intro., *Laṭakamelaka*, Chowkhamba edn., 1962.
7. Ibid.
8. See fn. 1 above.

Dramatis Personae

Sūtradhāra		Mithyārāśi	a brāhmaṇa
Danturā	a bawd	Mithyāśukla	another brāhmaṇa
Madanamañjarī	her daughter	Phuṅkaṭamiśra	a Vedāntin
Sabhāsali	a teacher	Vyasanākara	a Buddhist monk
Kulavyādhi	his disciple	Jaṅgama	a *caturvedin*
Jantuketu	a doctor	Saṅgrāmavisara	the Army General
Jaṭāsura	a *digambara*	Viśvāsaghātaka	his friend
Ajñānarāśi	a Kāpālika	Jhankaṭasāra	a financier

The Plot

The play proper begins with the bawd Danturā boasting of her professional skills in driving her customers out of their wits and extracting maximum benefits from them. Enters now the teacher Sabhāsali with his impertinent disciple Kulavyādhi. Danturā welcomes them and introduces her daughter Madanamañjarī to them. Coming to know that Danturā has a wound in her thigh, Sabhāsali suggests that the doctor Jantuketu must be called forth immediately. The doctor, a real quack, is noted for his horrible prescriptions. When prescribed by him, even nectar becomes poison. Danturā says that a bone has got stuck up in the throat of her daughter. The quack suggests that the bone must be tied to a rope and pulled out and that he had already treated a camel in an identical situation. The girl laughs at the foolishness of the doctor and in this process, the bone is dislodged from her throat. This the doctor claims as his own achievement. When Danturā complains of cataract in her eyes, the doctor suggests that a red hot iron rod be inserted in her anus. Then turning his attention to Madanamañjarī, the doctor decides to induce spells of *vaśīkaraṇa mantra* to win her love and leaves the scene.

Next to enter are a *digambara* by name Jaṭāsura and a Kāpālika, by name Ajñānarāśi. The latter alleges that his goat was killed by the former. The matter is referred to Sabhāsali who delivers the judgements in favour of Ajñānarāśi but a remark made by the former infuriates the Kāpālika and both quarrel bitterly for some time. When he has a glimpse of Madanamañjarī the Kāpālika regrets that he had wasted his time in vain quarrel. But quarrel erupts again as both Sabhāsali and Ajñānarāśi stake a claim over the girl. The announcement of the nightfall saves the situation and all these people are asked to leave. The first act called *lajjāvikraya* (sale of modesty) comes to an end here.

The second act opens with the entry of the Army Chief, Saṅgrāmavisara (battle-scare) accompanied by his friend Viśvāsaghātaka (faith-killer). The army chief has a notorious record of "battle achievements". Many more rogues enter one after the other — the financier Jhankaṭasāra, the brāhmaṇa Mithyāśukla, the Vedāntin Phuṅkaṭmiśra and the Buddhist monk Vyasanākara. The last two quarrel over the relative superiority of their respective faiths. Now the *digambara* becomes interested in the old lady Danturā and wants to get married to her. Danturā too agrees to his proposal. All others have fun at the expenses of the bride and bridegroom. A priest is also summoned to conduct the marriage. The verses recited by the priest portend only *amaṅgala* for the couple. At the conclusion of the marriage, the priest demands *dakṣiṇā* from the bridegroom who gives only some cowries and this enrages the priest. They start fighting over this issue. The play ends with Sabhāsali describing the gentle breeze that is congenial to the secret meeting of lovers, which may be taken as indicating his bright prospects of meeting Madanamañjarī at the appointed place.

Hāsya in Laṭakamelaka

The *hāsya* in *Laṭakamelaka* is evoked mainly through the

characters and their topsy-turvy behaviour. The opening speech of Danturā about her customers and the introduction of characters from the *nepathya* with particular reference to their vices give us an idea, in advance, about the speciality of each character.

Topping the list of the "assemblage of rogues" in Sabhāsali, the teacher belonging to the *vāmācāra* sect of the Tāntric school. His wife, Kalahapriyā, true to her name, is always at war with him. Himself a patient of cataract, he has been frequenting the harlots since he got disgusted with his wife who has lost her charms due to old age. His action elicits sarcastic admiration from Danturā: *yuktamidam yuṣmākam mahāpaṇḍitānām.*[9] He is described as *dāmbhikacakravartin, mahāhavapātin* and *parāpakāra-vyasanaikaniṣṭhaḥ*. Though posing himself as a teacher he exposes his ignorance every now and then. When asked to mediate between the *digambara* and Ajñānarāśi, he proudly accepts the offer. Ajñānarāśi exploits his ignorance and asks whether he would be an offender if he kills a goat thinking it to be a calf. According to Sabhāsali, this is an unintentional killing and hence is not an offence. He delivers the judgement in favour of Ajñānarāśi. But a sarcastic remark made by him about Ajñānarāśi infuriates the latter and the two start throwing slings at each other, which makes Danturā remark, *yuṣmābhiḥ lajjā kutra vikrītā?*[10]

The shameless teacher immediately replies saying, *adyaiva haṭṭe mahājanapurataḥ suśīlādevyā survarṇadāmnā krītā.*[11] Age has not bedimmed his lust and his open expression of love for Madanamañjarī is not liked by the latter who condemns him

9. *LM*, p. 13. The above passage may serve as an instance of the *prahasana* element *anṛtam*.

10. *LM*, p. 23.

11. Ibid.

forcefully, resorting to Sanskrit,

आयास्यति भवतोऽयं विनयमयस्तादृगनुरागः।
वन्ध्यासुतहृदयगता मालेयं गगनकुसुमानाम्॥
— I.17

When the *digambara* wants to get married to the old Danturā, Sabhāsali humorously remarks that the bridegroom exhibits all the symptoms of death. He also suggests that their nuptial bedding should be so arranged that even if they die due to exhaustion, their cremation can be performed there itself.

Danturā is a typical mother harlot. She zealously guards her daugher Madanamañjarī and cashes in on her. She waits for her customers, muttering the *vaśīkaraṇa mantra*. All other characters show great regard for her. But her figure worn out by age is a source of mockery for her visitors. Her eyes have sunk in and are affected by cataract, the cheeks have caved in and the breasts have fallen. Due to the act of biting her lovers during her own lovemaking, her teeth have become protruding and hence she is appropriately called *Danturā*.

अन्तर्निमग्नं नयनद्वयेन क्वचित्प्रयातं नवयौवनेन।
भग्नौ कपोलौ पतितं कुचाभ्यां मन्ये भयान्मन्मथसायकानाम्॥
— I.14

and,

भुजंगदंशव्यसनाकुलाया दन्ता बहिर्गा इव दन्तुरायाः।
बन्धानुसन्धानपरा यदीया पाशोपमा वल्गति कर्णपाली॥
— I.15

She never hesitates to put inconvenient questions to her customers and extract information from them. She very cleverly handles her customers, enquiring about their personal life, cracking jokes now and then at their expense and pitting them against one another. Her marriage with the *digambara* is the climax of the play.

The doctor Jantuketu is a funny character. He himself proudly declares that his presence on earth has rendered even Yama jobless.

व्याधयो मदुपचारलालिता
मत्प्रयुक्तममृतं विषं भवेत्।
किं यमेन सरुजां किमौषधैर्
जीवहर्तरि पुरःस्थिते मयि॥
— I.22

He curses the practice in the village according to which the doctor must carry his dead patients to the cemetery. That is why he has stopped attending to the elephants and has become a child specialist, since it is much easier to carry the dead children. But the doctor is ruthless in collecting fees even from his dead patients.[12] The doctor is notorious for his topsy-turvy prescriptions. For phlegm trouble the throat must be burnt; for fever caused by indigestion, heavy diet with plenty of ghee and milk must be given and for an eye disease, it must be rubbed with caustic substances — these are some of the prescriptions of the doctor.[13]

His prescription for the cataract in the eye is equally funny.

चक्षूरोगे समुत्पन्ने तप्तफालं गुदे न्यसेत्।
तदा नेत्रोद्भवां पीडां मनसापि न संस्मरेत्॥
— I.25

अर्कक्षीरं वटक्षीरं स्नुहीक्षीरं तथैव च।
अञ्जनं तिलमात्रेण पर्वतोऽपि न दृश्यते॥
— I.26

The "learned" doctor maintains that his prescriptions are based on the *Caraka Saṁhitā*. The *Carakamata* according to him is

12. *LM*, I.24.

13. Ibid., I.21.

यस्य कस्य तरोर्मूलं येनं केनापि पोषयेत्।
यस्मै कस्मै प्रदातव्यं यद्वा तद्वा भविष्यति॥

— I.23

When Sabhāsali teases him by asking whether he (the doctor) was responsible for the loud lamentation heard in the village in the morning, the doctor retaliates by saying that probably Sabhāsali had gone there for blessing somebody (which always has an adverse effect). But Sabhāsali denies that he had gone for any *svastyayana*. His disciple has a dig at both of them when he says, "If both of you had not gone there, then how could the merchant's son have died?"[14]

The army general has, indeed, notable military achievements to his credit. When Danturā asks him what he would do if he were to be given a horse by the king, he unhesitantly replies, *saṅgrāme tadeva āruhya palāyanam vidheyam*, which elicits the admiration of Madanamañjarī thus, *etaireva caritaiḥ sakala-yuvati-vallabhā yūyam.*[15] His sources of revenue are equally ridiculous.

वातालीकृतचटकैः सूकरविड्भिश्च मृतकवस्त्रैश्च।
पवनानीतदलैरपि विक्रीतैः किं न धनलाभः॥

— II.6

When he proudly asks his friend Viśvāsaghātaka, to read out the glory of his village, Nissantāna-grāma (childless village), the friend reveals the secret that the village no more belongs to him,

tasya grāmasya varāṭikā dyūtasambandhena mayaiva gṛhītā ।
anyat punarādāya nivedayatu ॥[16]

14. *LM*, p. 18.
15. Ibid., p. 30.
16. Ibid., p. 32.

True to his name, Viśvāsaghātaka tries to strike a deal with Danturā, according to which the two would share a golden *kalaśa* owned by the General and neck him out.

The Paṇḍit Phuṅkaṭamiśra is a learned scholar in his own way

गुरोर्गिरः पञ्चदिनान्युपास्य
  वेदान्तशास्त्राणि दिनत्रयं च।
अमी समाघ्रातवितर्कवादाः
  समागताः फुङ्कटमिश्रपादाः॥

— II.14

Mithyāśukla claims himself to be the follower of the Pūrva-Mīmāṁsā school, and proudly declares that the gods were bodily present in the sacrifice performed by him. It must be noted here that the old school of the Pūrva-Mīmāṁsā does not believe in the existence of gods as such.

The *digambara* Jaina monk shows scant respect for his own religion, by offering the golden image of the Arhan (which is very sacred to the Jainas) as fee for enjoying the harlot. After all he has been changing his religion very often, without any deep convictions,

पुनस्त्रिदण्डः पुनरेकदण्डः
  पुनः पुनर्वञ्चकतामुपेतः।
तपस्वितामेत्य जटासुरोऽयं
  नग्नोऽभवद्वञ्चकचक्रवर्ती॥

— I.36

The *guru-śiṣya* concept has no meaning at all as far as the Jainas are concerned, according to Sabhāsali, since everybody is equally foolish.

उभावप्यश्रुतग्रन्थावुभावपि जडात्मकौ।
  अहो मोहस्य माहात्म्यं यदेकः शिष्यतां गतः॥

— I.37

The religious quarrel between the Buddhist and the Jaina monks is again humorous.[17]

दिगम्बरः — अरे रे, भिक्षुक, दूरं गच्छ, असदृशजातिस्पर्शदूषितोऽसि।

व्यसनाकरः — धिङ्मूर्ख, जातिरेव नास्ति। किञ्च अस्मन्मते क्षणिकाः सर्वे भावाः न हि आत्मा स्थायीति। तन्नः कुत्र रजकीदूषणम्।

दिगम्बरः — तत्किं दत्तो दोषः उपपन्नोऽस्ति न वा ?

व्यसनाकरः — विनाशशीला भावा जायन्ते।

दिगम्बरः — अरे रे भिक्षुक, उत्पत्तिक्षणो, विनाशक्षण इति परस्परविरुद्धम्। तद्भिन्न उत्पत्तिक्षण इति भिन्नो विनाशक्षण इति।

सभासलिः — (सहासम्)

श्रृणोति श्रुतिहीनोऽपि जातिहीनोऽपि जातिना।
स्वीकृतक्षणभङ्गोऽपि जेतुमन्यं समीहते ॥

— II.26

Pronouncement of most inauspicious words on an auspicious occasion is another farcical element in the play. When a newly-born baby is brought to him, Sabhāsali quotes the rules of "pollution" (*āśauca*) arising out of the death of a child.

आदन्तजननात्सद्य आचूडान्नैशिकी क्रिया।
त्रिरात्रमा व्रतादेशाद्दशरात्रमतः परम् ॥[18]

— I.35

When Danturā and the *digambara* get married, the priest blesses the couple thus:

दोषाकरमुखीमेनां दन्तुरां प्राप्य चण्डिकाम्।
भज त्वं शूलिनः कान्तिं श्मशानाश्रमवासिनः ॥

— II.32

Likewise when the bridegroom makes the conventional

17. *LM*, pp. 44-45.

18. Quoted in Commentary, *Medhātithi* on Manu, p. 506, Gurumandalā Granthamālā, Calcutta.

"request" (*yācanā*) for the bride, Sabhāsali quotes the *Mahābhārata śloka* out of context.

वेपथुर्मलिनं वक्त्रं दीना दृग्गद्गदःस्वरः।
मरणे यानि चिह्नानि तानि चिह्नानि याचके।[19]

— II.30

For the "blessing" of the couple (*svastyayana*) the priest chooses the *Gītā ślokas*: *jātasya hi dhruvo mṛtyuḥ* . . . , etc. The time fixed for the marriage itself is *jyeṣṭhā nakṣatra* in *dhanuralagna* which spells widowhood for the bride, as pointed out by Sabhāsali. But the priest is not concerned about it. "What is wrong if widowhood occurs in old age?" he asks. Then Sabhāsali suggests that their nuptial bedding should be so arranged that the crematory rites may also be performed there itself without delay, if the bride or the bridegroom were to die due to exhaustion.

Literary Merits of the Laṭakamelaka

Śaṅkhadhara has shown considerable poetic skill in this short play though his talents do not find scope in a full measure in the play form he has chosen. Nevertheless the poet does express some lofty ideas. In this transitory world where birth, old age and death always pose a threat, the true relative of the poets is their own fame which lasts till the end of the epochs, says the author:

कतिपयनिमेषवर्तिनि जन्मजरामरणविह्वले जगति।
कल्पान्तकोटिबन्धुः स्फुरति कवीनां यशः प्रसारः॥[20]

— I.9

19. Quoted in *Subhāṣitaratnabhāṇḍāgāram*, p. 76, *śl*. 1.

20. This verse reminds us of Daṇḍin's words, *kāvyam kalpāntarasthāyī jāyeta bhuvanatrayam*.

The heroine standing on the terrace, is a source of attraction for both the terrestrial and celestial beings, observes one of the characters. The former lift their eyes upwards and the latter, downwards, to have a glimpse of her.[21] The poet does not lag behind in describing Nature.

मुखकमलं परिचुम्बन्नलिभरदरदलितपद्मिनीनिवहः।
अयमुपसर्पति मन्दश्चन्दनवनपावनः पवनः॥

— I.10

In another beautiful verse, the poet likens the moon rising from the celestial Ganges in the form of the sky, to a silver pot, to a swan, to a white lotus, to a mass of white foam to an earring made of crystal.[22]

The *rūpaka Alaṁkāra* where the lover's heart is identified with a deer is noteworthy.

नेत्रानन्दभुवः प्रमोदवसतेरस्याः कुरङ्गीदृश-
स्तन्वङ्ग्याः स्तनशैलमूलविलसन्मुक्तालतापाशितः।
विस्तीर्णजघनस्थलीपरिसरे व्यामोहलीलाभर-
भ्रान्तस्वान्तकुरङ्ग यास्यसि कुतःपञ्चेषुबाणार्दितः॥

— I.33

The following verse involving the *sandehālaṁkāra* is quite interesting.

किं नेत्रयोरमृतवर्तिरियं विधातु-
राद्या किमद्भुतशरीरविधानलेखा।
संसारसारमहह त्रिजगत्पवित्रं
तद्रत्नमेतदुपसर्पति पङ्कजाक्षी॥

— II.18

There is *atiśayokti* in the statement that when seen by the charming heroine, the Cupid would become a target of his own arrows.

21. *LM*, II.15.

22. Ibid., I.38.

दृष्टश्चेदनया कुपत्रविषमैः संधानबन्धाकुलैः
किं न स्यान्मदनोऽपि पुङ्खितशरैर्व्यावृत्य लक्ष्यीकृतः॥
— I.19

In another verse, the post fancies that the heroine is superior to Lakṣmī who resides in the Milky Ocean all the time (and hence does not know the charms of the earthly pleasure). She is superior to Pārvatī too as the latter cannot even have the pleasure of embracing or kissing her husband (since Gaṅgā is looking at her all the time).

उपहसति पक्ष्मलाक्षी लक्ष्म्या गभीरजलधिजलवासम्।
आलिङ्गनपरिचुम्बनरहितं गौर्याः सौभाग्यम्॥
— (छाया) II.4

The *upamā* in the following verse where a man who does not harm others is compared to the bellows of a blacksmith, is worth noting.

परोपकारशून्यो यः क्षणार्धमपि तिष्ठति।
स लोहकारभस्त्रेव श्वसन्नपि न जीवति॥
— II.12

The poet is fond of *anuprāsa* which comes naturally to him, as in:

आनन्दकारि मदनज्वरदर्पहारि पीयूषपङ्कपरिहासरसानुकारि।
प्रेमप्रसारि परमाभ्युदयानुकारि वामभ्रुवामहह किं न मनोविकारि॥
— I.16

Dramatic Technique

There are three *nāndī śloka*s in the play, all of which deal with the *saṁbhoga-śṛṅgāra* of Lord Śiva and Pārvatī. There is also a reference to the moon, as per convention, in the first *śloka*. We have a pointer to the main *rasa* in the play, viz. *hāsya*, in the second *śloka*.

There is something special about the prologue of *Laṭakamelaka*. It is a full monologue piece spoken by *sūtradhāra*, using *ākāśabhāṣita*, in the *bhāṇa* style.

Mention is made of certain musical instruments like *diṇḍima, gomukha, jhillī, mṛdaṅga,* etc. in the prologue.

Śaṅkhadhara has employed novel methods of dramatic technique in his play. In her opening speech, Danturā introduces all the characters in the play. A verse recited from *nepathya* before the entry of each character on the stage for the first time, brings out some of his chief characteristics. Sabhāsali, for instance, is introduced with the verse, *vāmāgamācāravidām variṣṭhaḥ* . . . , etc. (I.13) There are some undramatic entries of characters too. Sabhāsali requests Kulavyādhi to call forth the doctor, Jantuketu and immediately enters the doctor, without notice. Similarly there is no stage direction preceding the entry of Jhaṅkaṭasāra.

Texts Quoted in the Laṭakamelaka

The brāhmaṇa, Mithyāśukla, laments that he had ignored sage Vyāsa's advice on the transient nature of the charms of women. The *śloka* that is indirectly referred to, is most probably the one quoted by Ānandavardhana, in his *Dhvanyāloka*,

> सत्यं मनोरमा रामाः सत्यं रम्या विभूतयः।
> किन्तु मत्ताङ्गनापाङ्ग भङ्गलोलं हि जीवितम्॥[23]

The poet quotes two other *śloka*s from the *Mahābhārata*. The one *vepathurmalinam*[24] of Vyāsa is found in the *Subhāsitaratna-bhāṇḍāgāra* and the other one *jātasya hi dhruvo mṛtyuḥ* . . . is from the *Bhagavad-Gītā*.[25]

---

23. *Dhvanyāloka*, III.30-31.

24. Quoted. in *Subhāṣitaratnabhāṇḍāgāram*.

25. II.27.

The poet quotes a Prākṛt verse from an anonymous source. (*bhaṇitam ca kenāpi*)

दुट्टभुअङ्गो जो णियगहलज्जयि
दुट्टसिण्षो जो दानविवज्जयि।
स कुरूपो जो हिअये ण रुच्चयि
पत्तरकठिनो जो निद्दुतं वच्चयि॥

— I.12

The Influence of Laṭakamelaka on Later Prahasanas

Laṭakamelaka has influenced a large number of later *prahasana*s, noteworthy among them being, the *Hāsyārṇava* and the *Dhūrtasamāgama*. Bandhurā in *Hāsyārṇava* is modelled on Danturā. The quacks Vyādhisindhu (*Hāsyārṇava*), Yamānuja (of *Adbhutataraṅga*), and Rogarāśi (of *Subhagānanda*) are modelled on Jantuketu. On the model of Kulavyādhi, we have impertinent disciples in Kalahāṅkura (*Hāsyārṇava*) and Durācāra (*Dhūrtasamāgama*). Sabhāsali is the forerunner for his counterparts Viśvabhaṇḍa (*Hāsyārṇava*), Viśvanagara (*Dhūrtasamāgama*) and hosts of such hypocritic teachers in a number of *prahasana*s. The theme and content of latter *prahasana*s dealt with in the following pages will show to what extent *Laṭakamelaka* has inspired and influenced them.

THE NĀṬAVĀṬA PRAHASANA

The date of *Nāṭavāṭa-prahasana* is uncertain. That it must be quite an early work, is indicated by the close similarity of its style with that of the *Laṭakamelaka*. The style of Prākṛt seems to be archaic and certain dialectical differences are shown in the Prākṛt spoken by the characters. A large number of characters representing different religious sects is introduced in this play. A *gosāī saṁnyāsin*, a *śākteya* and a female ascetic are introduced for the first time. The extensive usage of Prākṛt is another noteworthy feature of this play. In any case this work does not seem to be earlier than fourteenth century CE. Probably the play belongs to the early Vijayanagara period. There is no hint of the splendour and pomp of the later Vijayanagara empire. The Vijayanagara empire was still in its early phase of development during the fourteenth century and there were probably many feudal lords like the one we come across in the play, viz. Nidrāluṭhakkura. The mention of *varāha*, the insignia of the Vijayanagara kings and the *hunna*s (gold coins) is significant. The gold coins used as a medium of exchange during the Vijayanagara period were called *hunna*s. (Origin: Kanarese, meaning gold, corresponding to the Tamil word *ponnu*.) Another significant point is the presence of a *tailaṅga* (a Telugu man) in the play.

The author, Yadunandana, belongs to the Sārasvata family and was the son of Vāsudeva Cayanī as known from the prologue. He does not give any other information about himself in the play.

The present study of *Nāṭavāṭa* is based on the only printed edition of the text available.[26] A few words must be said about this edition. There are certain inevitable mistakes in the Sanskrit part but it looks as though no attention has been paid to the Prākṛt portion at all. The case suffixes are separated from the words and are juxtaposed with the next word, with the result that many of the sentences convey little or no sense. Thus *rāmajaṇīe(ye) vālavallaho mam odhīredi* is wrongly rendered as *rāmajaṇī evālavalla homam odhūredi* (*chāya* : *rāmajanyāḥ bālavallabhaḥ mām avadhīrayet*). The play has not attracted the attention of scholars so far and only brief references have been made in the books on Sanskrit drama and dramaturgy.[27] A detailed

26. *Nāṭavāta Prahasana*, N.S. Press edn., Bombay, 1888.

27. (i) *HCSL*, p. 700; (ii) Schüler, *Bibliography of Sanskrit Drama*, p. 74. (iii) D.R. Mankad, *Types of Sanskrit Drama*, pp. 63 ff.

analysis of the play is presented here for the first time.

Dramatis Personae

Vigra	a Kālāmukha	Gatakrama	a Śaivite
Rāvutta	the royal cousin	Nidrāluṭhakkura	a feudal lord
Dhanānanda	a Vaiṣṇava	Mālinī	Vigra's companion
Mithyāsarvasva	a Gosāī	Madanadūtī	a female ascetic
Bhūtipriya	a Śaivite	Rāmajanī	

The Plot

The play has two acts but there is very little connection between the two with regard to the incidents narrated. One or two characters mentioned in the first act make their appearance in the second act.

In the beginning of the first act, Madanadūtī, a female ascetic, refers to the spring festival that is taking place in the town. *Gaṇikā*s and *nāgaraka*s are seen everywhere, engaged in drinking bouts. She is awaiting one Vigra.

Enters now Vigra, the Kālāmukha, and his companion Mālinī. Vigra is so fully drunk that he searches for Mālinī though she is nearby. He blames the royal cousin, Rāvutta, for his bad habits. Enters now Rāvutta and the conversation between him and Vigra is quite amusing.

Now Vigra wants to demonstrate the Kālāmukha form of worshipping the female organ. With the co-operation of Mālinī, the *pūjā* is performed and the *prasāda* in the form of the liquor from the *pūjā-kalaśa* is offered to Rāvutta. Vigra then extols the greatness of Bhairava and suggests that Rāvutta should join their sect.

Meanwhile, Dhanānanda, a Vaiṣṇava and a boyhood friend of Rāvutta enters along with a lady, Rāmajanī by name. Dhanānanda accuses Vigra and Mālīnī of indoctrinising his good friend Rāvutta with their sectarian beliefs. The Kālāmukha and his companion depart without a word. Rāvutta appreciates the beauty of Rāmajanī and wants to win her love but feels that he must take steps in that direction some time later and departs.

Dhanānanda now summons a Gosāī priest, Mithyāsāgara, since he wants to arrange for Rāmajanī's *mantra-dīkṣā*. Before that, he wants to know about the attainments of Mithyāsāgara, who eloquently glorifies his parentage.

अस्माकं जननी वेश्या पितास्माकं द्विजोत्तमः।
अहं पुनर्निजगुणैर्व्यासः सर्वोत्तमः स्मृतः॥

— I.18

His *pravara* is equally praiseworthy.

Nirmūla-nissantāna-nirvaṁśeti triparvara-maṭavaṭagotram. Dhanānanda is satisfied with the credentials of his *ācāra* and asks him to call forth the priests for the function. The priests arrive and perform the *homa* by chanting the following *mantra.*

अकटो विकटश्चैव कुन्तीपुत्रो विनायकः।
उदिते लङ्काद्वारे सर्वलोक नमोऽस्तुते॥
स्वाहा॥ इति।

— I.21A

When the function concludes, poor Mithyāsāgara gets only a few cowries as fee for his services. Dhanānanda wants to compensate it by imprinting the Vaiṣṇava *mudrā*s on his body free of cost. The imprinting of the *mudrā*s with red hot iron emblems is too much to bear for the old man, who falls down unconscious. Bhūtipriya, supposed to be a specialist in herbal medicine, is called forth to attend on him. He comes there along with his friend Gatakrama. Bhūtipriya administers the narcotic drug *vijayā* and praises its effects.

औत्सुक्याय विलोचनाञ्चलगता लौल्याय हस्तस्थिता
खेदच्छेदकृते मुखान्तिकगता शैत्याय वक्षोगता।
किं ब्रूमः परिणामतो जठरगा निर्मृष्टनानाश्रम
ब्रह्मानन्दपदाय सास्तु विजया देवी जगज्जित्वरी॥

— I.31

अपि च,

लज्जा गच्छति दूरतो धृतिरपि प्रायः परिम्लायति
स्वातन्त्र्यं परिहीयते कुलगता कीर्तिः समुत्सादति।
भूम्ना हास उदीहते बहुविधा वाचालता जृम्भते
वैचित्र्यं पुनरेधते तनुभृतामामूलिकासेवनात्॥

— I.32

Gatakrama is enamoured of the beauty of Rāmajanī and tells her that she must abandon the company of Dhanānanda since the sect to which he belongs, viz. the Vaiṣṇava, is a tāntric sect and hence *avaidika*. The application of *vibhūti* alone is sacred and so is the Śaiva cult. Bhūtipriya appreciates his view and sets forth, what he has understood, to be the path sacred to the Śaivites.

रविवारे तु सम्प्राप्ते विद्वांसमपि भोजयेत्।
वेश्यामलङ्कृतां कृत्वा तस्य पुण्यफलं शृणु॥
दिव्यं विमानमारुह्य शिवलोके महीयते॥

— I.37

Then we have a long discussion on the practices and *sampradāya*s of different cults, between Bhūtipriya, Gatakrama and Madanadūtī.

Now Dhanānanda, who had himself tasted the *vijayā*, complains of giddiness. Gatakrama says that the *vrātyabhiṣak* must be summoned. The *vrātyabhiṣak* arrives along with his friend Mithyāsarvasva, who is to help him in astrological calculations. The *vrātyabhiṣak* is happy that he has got a female patient in Rāmajanī, who is still reeling under the effect of *vijayā*. He says,

तरुणीं सरुजं दृष्ट्वा हृष्यति वैद्यः सिराः स्पृशति।
यावन्नो कुचयुगलीं स्पृशति न तावत्कृतोपायः॥

— I.41

He proudly declares that even as he reads the pulse of a patient Yama gets ready to accomplish his own task. (The patient is sure to die.) When just glanced by the doctor, the patient is drawn forcibly by the attendants of Yama.

सिरानेन धृता यस्य शिरस्तस्य च मृत्युना।
यो दृष्टः स समाकृष्टो बलाच्छमनकिङ्करैः॥

— I.42

He then prescribes a mixture of five plants which he calls herbs but which are actually poisonous creepers.

Now it is Mithyāsarvasva's turn to betray his own ignorance. The astrologer has fixed a date for a function at Nidrāluṭhakkura's house. What he considers to be an auspicious day is actually a most inauspicious day with the conjunction of unfavourable planetary position.[28] Mithyāsarvasva is attracted by the charm of Rāmajanī and feels that she will become alright by the mere touch of his hand just as a creeper withered by the sun's heat regains its freshness by the moonlight.[29] . . . . *vīrunnidāghakalitā tuhināṁśukarādiva*. Dhanānanda does not like his idea and warns him of serious consequences since he is a disciple of one Kāntānanda, whose teachings he sets forth thus.

मृदुवासः परिधेयं निद्रातव्यं सुखेन भोक्तव्यम्।
सेवा निधुवनलीला संफुल्लेन्दीवराक्षीणाम्॥

— I.51

अनुदिनसुगन्धितैलाभ्यङ्गो रङ्गावलोकश्च।
करणीया जनचर्चा यस्मात् तस्माद्धनं ग्राह्यम्॥

— I.52

---

28. See *Nāṭavāṭa*, I.46 and 47.

29. Ibid., I.48.

Madanadūtī intervenes and brings about a compromise by saying that Rāmajanī may be honoured by all assembled there since she cannot be satisfied by just one man. All the rogues feel happy at this. But Madanadūtī warns that the police are patrolling the area and that they must disperse at once. The first act ends here.

ACT II

Nidrāluṭhakkura, the feudal lord, wants to perform a *yajña* for the welfare of his people. Kāntānanda is to be the chief priest. Many people attend the function. One of them, Piśunabhaṭṭa, blesses the *yajamāna* in a peculiar fashion.

रहसि ध्रियतां साधुस्तव गेहे च वाणिका।
म्रियतां वसते बुद्धिरस्तु तद्धनलोलुपा॥
(*sic*) — II.3

Nidrālu welcomes the guests and explains why the Agnihotrins are so called.

न लभन्ते गृहे यस्य भोक्तुं यस्य निशागमे।
वह्नौ जुह्वति तद्वेश्म तस्मादेतेऽग्निहोत्रिणः॥
— II.4

Enters now Kṛṣṇānanda and offers 100 *rūpyaka*s to Nidrālu for getting rid of his enemy, a Telugu brāhmaṇa. After his departure, the Telugu man enters and offers 300 *rūpyaka*s as a fee to kill Kṛṣṇānanda. Nidrālu promises both that he would accomplish their task and gets 400 *rūpyaka*s altogether. He proudly declares that he has become successful in life by such deceitful means only. A *Karaṭakaśrotriya* who is among the assemblage, blesses Nidrālu thus:

पितामहस्त्वत्पिता च यत्र यातौ नरेश्वर।
तस्मिन्लोके सहामात्यः सापत्यस्त्वं सुखी भव॥
— II.5A

He then appreciates Nidrālu's way of life and says that a life of lust alone is suitable for the Kali Age. Then Nidrālu visits the *āśrama* of his priest, Kāntānanda and submits that he had not met him for a long time. The priest says that he had been engrossed in gambling for a long time. A few more people arrive on the scene. Two of the visitors, Gatakrama and Unmāda exchange greetings. Unmāda says that he has been busy with studies. Asked what he has learnt so far, he lists out many non-existing texts like *Paurāpavādaśāstra*. Gatakrama then turns to Piśunabhaṭṭa who comes from his native village and enquires about the welfare of his family there. Piśunabhaṭṭa informs him that his wife has passed away due to the grief of sudden demise of her son Kulāṅgāra. The double shock is too unbearable for Gatakrama who laments for a long time remembering the "exemplary" qualities of his wife and son.

को द्यूतकेलीव्यसनी गृहोपस्कारतस्करः।
वाराङ्गना-रसवशो मामहो नन्दयिष्यति॥
— II.9

पादाघातं शिरस्यथ का करिष्यति मेऽधुना।
आघ्रास्यामि मुखं कस्याः पूतिगन्धि मुखं ननु॥
— II.10

Piśunabhaṭṭa then narrates how Gatakrama's son died. In order to repay the debts incurred in gambling, he stole gold coins from the royal treasury, got caught in the process and was sentenced to death. Gatakrama laments that his wife is fortunate since she followed her illustrious son (in death). Unmāda consoles him by saying,

daivamanukūlam te, yato vadanti "ekākī niḥspṛhaḥ śānta iti."

Now Nidrāluṭhakkura calls forth the waiting suitors and orders Prāṁśu and Jālma to enquire into their cases and pronounce a judgement. The judges themselves have dubious background.

Jālma is sad that the illegal son born to his wife and the village chief, is indisposed. The enquiry begins now. A Vaiṣṇava lady reports that she was publicly raped by the *bhujaṅga* in broad daylight. The *bhujaṅga* maintains that there was nothing wrong since the woman is his own daugher-in-law. He says,

फलोद्‌गमे भूरुहाणां वा एकः फलमश्नुते।
अस्माभिर्वर्धिता एते न भोग्याः केन हेतुना॥
— II.13

The judge appreciates his stand, acquits him of the charge and even presents him with some gold coins. Some more cases are brought before the judges and in each case, the guilty justify their stand and get released. A murderer maintains that he has been only helping human souls get rid of the bondages of their bodies.

पञ्जरबन्धे भग्ने तद्‌गतपक्षी विमुच्यते दुःखात्।
भग्ने शरीरबन्धेऽस्माभिर्विहगः सुखं चरति॥
— II.14

Unmāda recommends that each of these people must be honoured with suitable presents and Nidrāluṭhakkura too approves his idea. The suitors receive gifts and depart happily. The play comes to an end with the usual Bharatavākya.

Criticism

The play possesses certain peculiarities. The prologue is completely a one-man show as in the *bhāṇa*, performed by the *sūtradhāra*. In this respect it resembles the *Laṭakamelaka*. Another peculiarity is the *prastāvanā* at the beginning of the second act, which is evidently a violation of the dramaturgical rules since *prastāvanā* should appear only in the beginning of the first act. There are certain undramatic passages in the play. Thus we have the stage direction, *tataḥ praviśati vrātyaḥ samithyāsarvasvaḥ*, but Mithyāsarvasva does not actually appear on the stage along with *vrātya*. He makes his appearance on the stage only when summoned by the *vrātyabhiṣak* later.

THE DHŪRTASAMĀGAMA PRAHASANA

Dhūrtasamāgama of Jyotirīśvara is a popular *prahasana* from the point of view of the number of editions it has gone through. It has been printed at least five times so far[30] and also has been translated into French and Italian.[31] The present study is based on Lassen's edition of the text.[32] *Dhūrtasamāgama* has been analysed by Wilson,[33] Konow,[34] and Keith.[35]

The author, Jyotirīśvara is considered to be the *pitāmaha* of the Maithilā literature. His *Varṇaratnākara* and *Dhūrtasamāgama* are the first works in this vernacular. In addition to the Sanskrit version of *Dhūrtasamāgama* the poet has two other works in Sanskrit to his credit, *Pañcasāyaka* and *Raṅgaśekhara*, both of which deal with Kāmaśāstra.[36] In the prologue of *Dhūrtasamāgama*, the author gives the names of his grandfather and father as Rāmeśvara and Dhīreśvara respectively. He was patronised by King Harasiṁha (CE 1296-1324).[37] This Harasiṁha

30. See S.S. Janaki, "Two Farces from East India", *Saṁskṛta Raṅga Annual*, vol. VII: (i) Lassen, *Anthologia Sanskritica*, 1838; (ii) Chapeller, *Gurupūjākaumudī*, Jena, Germany, 1883; (iii) from Bombay; (iv) from Calcutta; (v) Jayakant Mishra, *Maithilā Sāhitya Samiti Granthamālā*, no. 6, Allahabad, 1960; (vi) Analysed by Sylvain Lévi, pp. 232-33.
31. Schüler, *Bibliography of Sanskrit Drama*.
32. Text with S.S. Janaki, curator, K.S.R. Institute, Madras.
33. *The Theatre of the Hindus*, II.408.
34. *Indian Drama*, pp. 186 ff.
35. *Sanskrit Drama*, p. 261.
36. Jayakant Misra, *History of Maithilā Literature*, Allahabad, 1949, vol. I, p. 119.
37. Ibid., p. 32.

came in the lineage of Nānyadeva, the Karnataka king who conquered and settled in Mithilā. The poet describes his patron as the "crest jewel of the Karnāṭas and a destroyer of the armies of Sultan".[38] The Sultan referred to here has been identified with Ghiyasuddin Tughlak, who in CE 1324 marched from Delhi towards Bengal through Tirhut.[39] It is evident that the *Dhūrtasamāgama* was composed after CE 1324.[40]

In the prologue of the play, the author describes himself as the venerable teacher of King Harasiṁha. The title *Kaviśekhara* was probably conferred on him by his patron. He further says that he was well-versed in music and has mastered several languages and dialects. He was a devotee of Lord Śiva. He was a liberal donor and honoured brāhmaṇa poets and the needy.[41] He states that he could compose, in a day, 400 *śloka*s, full of *rasa* and *alaṁkāra*.

Dramatis Personae

Sūtradhāra		Naṭī	
Viśvanagara	the teacher	Durācāra	Viśvanagara's disciple
Mṛtāṅgāra	the merchant		
Bandhuvañcaka	Asajjāti's disciple	Asajjātimiśra	the mediator
		Mūlanāśaka	the barber
Suratapriyā	a *gaṇikā*	Anaṅgasenā	another *gaṇikā*

The Plot

Viśvanagara, the Vaiṣṇava teacher, is a man of dubious background and sensuous character. In the begining of the play proper, Viśvanagara is seen conversing with his disciple

38. *Dhūrtasamāgama*, I.3.

39. Manmohan Chakravarti, *Journal of Asiatic Society of Bengal*, vol. XI, p. 412.

40. S.S. Janaki, "Two Farces from East India", *Saṁskṛta Raṅga Annual* VII.

41. *Dhūrtasamagāma*, I.6.

Durācāra (bad conduct), who looks rather jaded. On being enquired by his teacher, the student reveals that he has seen a harlot by name Anaṅgasenā in the morning and had been afflicted by love fever since then. The teacher says that he too has been in love with a harlot, Suratapriyā. The two approach the house of a miserly merchant, Mṛtāṅgāra by name, seeking *bhikṣā*. Mṛtāṅgāra evades them giving one reason or other. The two get disgusted and resort to the house of Suratapriyā, who readily offers to prepare a long list of dishes suggested by the teacher. Durācāra does not want to waste his time till the dishes are got ready and wants to meet the harlot Anaṅgasenā. The teacher too approves his idea wholeheartedly. In Anaṅgasenā's house both the teacher and the student claim the hand of the harlot and a bitter quarrel erupts between them. Anaṅgasenā intervenes and suggests that the matter be referred to Asajjātimiśra. The first Act comes to an end here.

In the beginning of the second Act, Asajjātimiśra and his pupil Bandhuvañcaka are seen discussing about the merits of sexual pleasure and stolen wealth. Viśvanagara, Durācāra and Anaṅgasenā enter now and the case is presented before Asajjātimiśra. The clever Asajjāti quashes the claims of both the parties and claims the harlot for himself as he had seen her first in his dream. Meanwhile Bandhuvañcaka drags the girl aside and tells her that he is more qualified than others to be her partner. Finding that they have no chance there, Viśvanagara and Durācāra decide to go back to Suratapriyā's house and depart. After their departure enters the barber, Mūlanāśaka who demands money from Anaṅgasenā for the services he rendered to her earlier. Anaṅgasenā directs him to Asajjāti who asks the barber to cut his nails. The barber demands the fee in advance since he is not sure whether his client would survive after being attended to by him. Asajjāti gives him a narcotic drug *bhaṅg* as fee. Being satisfied, the barber binds the hands and feet of Asajjāti and in the process of cutting his nails, inflicts deep wounds in his body. Asajjāti complains of severe pain and loses his consciousness. Fearing that his client is dead, the barber flees. Bandhuvañcaka unfetters him and Asajjāti proudly declares that he has achieved his objective by fraudulent means and that the beautiful Anaṅgasenā is in his possession now. The play comes to an end with the usual Bharatavākya.

Hāsya in Dhūrtasamāgama

As is usual in a *prahasana* of this type, the *śṛṅgārābhāsa* arising out of the old and so-called religious men indulging in amorous acts is the chief source of *hāsya*. A new type of character introduced in the play, is the miser Mṛtāṅgāra. He makes no secret of his intentions.

व्ययशीलः कुबेरोऽपि कामं याति दरिद्रतां।
अपि प्राणाः प्रदातव्या नार्थिभ्यो धनिकैर्धनम्॥

—I.20

Since philanthropy, a noble quality, is presented here as *doṣa*, this verse may illustrate the *vīthyaṅga*, *mṛdava*. The scene where Mṛtāṅgāra and Viśvanagara try to outwit each other is quite amusing. Having been informed that Viśvanagara would like to dine in his house the miser offers an excuse that he has been polluted by the *āśauca* arising out of the birth of a child to the female attendant related to the brother of the lady living next door. Viśvanagara says that being a monk he will not be affected by the *sūtakadoṣa* and quotes a text;

न वायुः स्पर्शदोषेण नाग्निर्दहनकर्मणा।
नापो मूत्रपुरीषाभ्यां नान्नदोषेण मस्करी॥

— I.22

The undaunted Mṛtāṅgāra offers another excuse now. He has

incurred heavy loss in business due to famine and debts, and so breakfast has been removed from the daily routine.

अनावृष्टया कृषिर्नष्टा राष्ट्रभङ्गादृणादिकम् ।
वाणिज्यमल्पलाभेन प्रातराशस्य का कथा ॥
— I.23

Durācāra gets angry at this and blames the Goddess of Wealth for favouring only the undeserving. Mṛtāṅgāra himself then suggests that they may approach Suratapriyā and puts an end to further argument on this matter. The humorous conversation between these three may serve as an illustration for the *prahasana* element *vyāhāra*.

The glutton that he is, Viśvanagara has no restriction in his diet. For his *bhikṣā*, he just wants meat, beans, gourd, vegetables, chillies, fish and peas — all blended together and cooked tastefully and also pancakes, thick milk, ghee, curd, buttermilk, fresh bananas and sugar! Being enamoured of the *gaṇikā*, Anaṅgasenā, he feels that by the mere glimpse of her he had attained the fruit of all his long penances.[42] When Anaṅgasenā points out the impropriety of his act and says that the harlots are only after money, the hypocrite with pretended *vairāgya*, says,

saṁnyāsīnām asmākam kuto arthasampattiḥ tadasmaccharīreṇa yathāsukham viniyogaḥ kriyatām.[43]

The teacher, Asajjātimiśra, is no less corrupt. By his vast experience in the worldly affairs, he had found out.

त्रैलोक्ये भोजनं श्रेष्ठं ततोऽपि सुरतोत्सवः ।
भोजनं वास्तु वा मास्तु जीवनं सुरतं विना ॥
— II.1

42. *Dhūrtasamāgama*, I.32. This may serve as an illustration of the *vīthyaṅga, prapañca*.

43. Ibid., I. bet. 33 and 34.

He has a fitting disciple in Bandhuvañcaka, who also declares that cheating others of their wealth and gambling are the only pleasant things in life.[44] Asajjāti's praise of the *indrāśana* drug may be cited as an instance of the *prahasana* element *anr̥tam*.

निद्राकरं दोषविनाशहेतुः
क्षुधाकरं बुद्धिविकासकश्च ।
इन्द्राशनं कामबलानुकूलं
लब्धं मया दैववशादिदानीम् ॥
— II.4

Poetic Merits of the Work

Within the framework of the flimsy theme of *Dhūrtasamāgama*, the poet tries to reveal his talents. The second *nāndī śloka* describes that Śiva's eyes blossomed on seeing Pārvatī's lotus face. On seeing her breasts, his glances put forth bunches and falling at her hips, they became enlarged and so on.

वक्त्राम्भोरुहि विस्मिताः स्तबकिता वक्षोरुहिस्फारिताः
क्षोणीसीमनि गुम्फिताश्चरणयोरक्ष्णोः पुनर्विस्तृताः ।
पार्वत्याः प्रतिगात्रचित्रगतयस्तन्वन्तु भद्राणि वः
विद्धस्यान्तिकपुष्पसायकशरैरीशस्य दृग्भक्तयः ॥
— I.2

The *upamā* comparing the poet's fame to the rays of the moon, is quite appealing.

कर्पूरन्ति सुधाद्रवन्ति कमलाहासन्ति हंसन्ति च
प्रालेयन्ति हिमालयन्ति करलासारन्ति हारन्ति च ।
त्रैलोक्याङ्गनरङ्गलङ्घिमगतिप्रागल्भ्यसंभाविताः
शीतांशोः किरणच्छटा इव जयन्त्येतर्हि तत्कीर्तयः ॥
— I.5

For the lover, his lady love appears everywhere, painted in the sky, as it were, engraved in the directions, reflected in the eyes, tied tight in the mind and appearing like a bee for

44. *Dhūrtasamāgama*, II.3.

the lotus-heart. But he does not know where exactly she is.

आकाशे लिखितेव दिक्षु खचितेवाकीर्णरूपेव च
दृक्पक्ष्मप्रतिबिम्बितेव मनसि श्लिष्टेव बद्धेव च।
सा मच्चित्तसरोरुहे मधुकरीवात्यन्तभावोत्तरी
कान्ता कान्तविलासवासवसतिः क्वास्तीति न ज्ञायते॥

— I.17

Another noteworthy feature of *Dhūrtasamāgama* is that the Maithilā version contains 20 beautiful songs in between dialogues.[45] The songs show unmistakable influence of Jayadeva's *Gīta Govinda*. The *rāga* and the *tāla* of the songs have also been fixed by the poet himself. The *mudrā* of the poet, viz. *jotika* is inserted in each of these songs. The songs may very well suit the *lāsya* dance that may be introduced in the course of the play. These songs corroborate the poet's statement in the prologue that he is *sakala-saṅgīta-viśeṣa-vidyotana*. One such song is given below.

चलसरोज सुन्दरनयने
मामनुकम्पय शशिवदने (चल . . .)
राजमरालविहितगमने
रतिपति हुतवहशमने
बिसलतिका-मृदुभुजयुगले
कामकलामयरसकुशले
कामनिधनकलशपयोधरे
सङ्गतमुनिजन-मनमनोहरे
विश्वनगरमिह भजनमिते
कविशेखर जोतिके भणिते॥[46]

THE HĀSYĀRṆAVA PRAHASANA

Hāsyārṇava (*Hās*) of Jagadīśvara is another popular *prahasana*. It has been printed four times so far.[47] The following account

45. See S.S. Janaki, "Two Farces from East India", *Saṁskṛta Raṅga Annual*, VII.

46. 15th song. Viśvanagara describes Anaṅgasenā, in this song.

47. (i) Calcutta, 1835.

→

is based on the latest edition of the text. Wilson,[48] Keith[49] and Dey[50] have analysed this work. Sten Konow[51] and Mankad[52] have also given an account of this play.

The Author

The author of the play, Jagadīśvara Bhaṭṭācārya, seems to have hailed from Bengal. Seven manuscripts of this work are available in the Asiatic Society of Bengal Library and the Sanskrit College Library, Calcutta.[53] The first three editions of this text were also printed at Calcutta. The oldest manuscript of this work dates back to CE 1783.[54]

Dramatis Personae

Sūtradhāra		Mithyārṇava	a brāhmaṇa
Naṭī		Sādhuhiṁsaka	the Police Chief
Anayasindhu	the King	Mahāyātrika	the astrologer
Kumativarmā	his minister	Madanāndhamiśra	another teacher
Viśvabhaṇḍa	a teacher	Kulāla	his disciple
Kalahāṅkura	his disciple	Mahānindakācārya	a *paṇḍit*
Vyādhisindhu	the doctor	Bandhurā	a bawd
Raktakallola	the barber	Mṛgāṅkalekhā	her daughter
Raṇajambūka	the Army Chief		

→ (ii) Calcutta, 1872.

(iii) Calcutta, 1913, ed. Tarkalamkara Bhattacharya.

(iv) Chowkhamba Publications, Benares, 1963.

48. H.H. Wilson, *The Threatre of the Hindus*, vol. II (1836), p. 408.
49. Keith, *Sanskrit Drama*, pp. 261-62. Also Sylvain Lévi, pp. 233-34.
50. S.K. Day, *Poona Orientalist*, vol. VII, 1942-43.
51. Sten Konow, *Indian Drama*, pp. 186 ff.
52. D.R. Mankad, *Types of Sanskrit Drama*.
53. S.S. Janaki, "Two Farces from East India", *Saṁskṛta Raṅga Annual* VII.
54. *Descriptive Catalogue of RASB*, vol. II, no. 5359.

The Plot

The play opens with two *nāndī ślokas*, both of which refer to the *sambhoga śṛṅgāra* of Lord Śiva and Pārvatī. In the prologue, the *sūtradhāra* appears on the stage and makes references to the poet and his talents. Then we have a description of the spring season (*vasanta*) followed by a reference to King Anayasindhu who appears in the beginning of the play proper.

King Anayasindhu (Ocean of Misrule) regrets that he had long forsaken his duties as head of state due to his indulgence in pleasures. Finding that his courthall is not spacious enough to conduct his assembly meet he resorts to the house of Bandhurā, a bawd, under the advice from his minister, Kumati (Evil intellect). He learns that his own preceptor Viśvabhaṇḍa (Hypocrite of the Universe) is to come there shortly for baptising Bandhurā's daughter Mṛgāṅkalekhā into the erotic art. The teacher arrives there promptly followed by his disciple, Kalahāṅkura (Strife-sprouter) and falls in love with Mṛgāṅkalekhā. Being informed that Bandhurā is indisposed, the king calls for his doctor, Vyādhisindhu (Ocean of diseases), who is a quack. His medicine can kill even Mārkaṇḍeya. Next to enter is a barber, Raktakallola (Blood-surge) whose customers hardly survive after being attended to by him. A customer who had been severely wounded by him, brings his case before the assembly. But the minister Kumati pronounces the judgement in favour of the offender. There are some more entrants like Mithyārṇava (Ocean of untruth), the Police Chief Sādhuhiṁsaka (Oppressor of the Good), Raṇa Jambuka, the army Commander (Battle fox), and the astrologer Mahāyātrika, each of whom is a misfit for his profession. Viśvanagara and his disciple clash for Mṛgāṅkalekhā. Bandhurā stops their quarrel saying that the *purohita*, Madanāndhamiśra (Lust-Blind) who is to perform a *homa* in her house the next day would settle their case. The first Act comes to an end at this point.

The second act opens with the entry of Madanāndhamiśra with his disciple Kulāla, into Bandhurā's house. There is a brief quarrel between Madanāndha and Viśvanagara as both try to outwit each other by composing *śloka*s on Śrī Kṛṣṇa. Being informed by Bandhurā that he must perform *kandarpa homa* in her house, the *purohita* tells her that he must first give some instructions to Mṛgāṅkalekhā in private. This conceded, he takes the girl to a room nearby, and enjoys her. This arouses the jealousy of others; the two old rogues agree that both of them may marry the young Mṛgāṅkalekhā. The two young fellows, Kalahāṅkura and Kulāla, in order to overcome their disappointment, propose to marry the old lady, Bandhurā, who is elated at the prospect of having two young husbands. The two young disciples plan to enjoy Mṛgāṅgalekhā during the daytime when their teachers would be out for alms. A priest, Mahānindakācārya is called forth to perform the marriage of Mṛgāṅkalekhā with the two old men first. When the priest demands his fee in advance, the two teachers ask him to wait for four years. Saying that the bride must remain in his custody till then Mahānindaka drags away Mṛgāṅkalekhā. The play comes to an end with the words of Mahānindaka who is elated at his success.

Hāsya in the Play

Hāsya is evoked mainly through the characters in this play. King Anayasindhu is reduced to a state of a comedian on account of his topsy-turvy speeches and action. Dignity and decency are qualities unknown to him. By entering Bandhurā's house he feels he has attained, *tīrthaśata-paryaṭana-puṇyam*.[55] The efforts of his misrule in his country are very well brought out by the introductory verse at the commencement of the play proper.

---

55. This false praise may illustrate the *prahasana* element *anṛtam*.

नीतिर्भीतिमती दिगन्तमभजत् क्षिप्रं समं साधुभि-
धूर्तानां पटुतापरं परधनाकृष्टं न केषां मनः।
कान्ता कस्य बलान्न केन रमिता राज्ये यदीयेऽधुना
तस्य क्षोणिपतेः समागतिरिह स्थातुं न युक्तं प्रिये॥

— I.10

When he starts out for his *pauraparicaryā* people appear with empty vessels (instead of the *pūrṇakumbha*) and throw the husk of paddy on his head (instead of the rice flakes).[56] His chief spy informs him that everything has become topsy-turvy in the state ever since the king stopped attending to his royal duties.

नारीणां नयनेऽञ्जनं न जघने सिन्दूरभामण्डिते
सीमन्ते न च नूपुरौ पदयुगे यावोऽपि नैवेक्षणे।
वक्षोजे मणिमञ्जरी न चरणे काञ्ची कटौ नाधरे
चेत्थं वेषविपर्ययः प्रतिगृहं दृष्टः सकष्टं मया॥

— I.12

Normal acts like men being attached to their own wives, are great offences in the kingdom of this monarch (I.11) and he resolves to punish the offenders. Since just acts are presented as defects in the two verses quoted above (I.10 and 12) they serve as instances of the *vīthyaṅga, mṛdava.*

Fearing that Bandhurā might ask for some favour, he seeks the advice of his minister Kumati who, of course, lets him down very badly, by saying,

nikhile jagati mahāpātakino bhavanta eva, tat sarvān vihāya te śirasi bhaviṣyati vajrapātaḥ[57]

And then suggests that the king must pronouce total submission to the old lady and undergo fasting for three days before her. The king accordingly falls flat at her feet and asks

56. *Hās.* I.9.

57. *Hās,* I. bet. *sls.* 14 and 15 p. 15.

for her blessings. King Anayasindhu is very proud of his palace and the rampart. Since the ceiling has fallen apart in his palace, there is the advantage of seeing the moon and the stars directly at night. The king and the queen have to keep vigil throughout the night since there is the danger of the walls collapsing any moment. Since the whole building is infested with snakes in pursuit of the frogs, one must always keep the snake charm handy.[58] His queen is the most beautiful lady in all the worlds and it needs a thousand mouths to describe her beauty, says the minister.

दर्शेन्दुतुल्यवदनाञ्जनपुञ्जगौरी
मार्जारचारुनयना घटपीनमध्या ।
प्रोत्तुङ्गपीनकुचचुम्बितनाभिदेशा
त्रैलोक्यमोहवसतिः खलु कामिनी सा ॥[59]

The minister, Kumativarmā, gives the following suggestion to the king, when informed that the capital is attacked by enemies,

> *deva, sainyam susajjīkṛtya prathamato mama rakṣaṇam vidheyam tato devyāḥ, tataḥ prāsādasya ca.*[60]

When a citizen complains that the barber used a hook for cutting his nails and that it has got stuck up in his eyes, the minister pronounces the judgement that the citizen must pay the barber the cost of the hook. The police chief of the kingdom is very happy that he is relieved of his responsiblities, when the capital is taken over by the thieves. He feels that he is now free to resort to harlots. Raṇajambūka, the army chief, has an enviable military record. He faints on seeing anything red, thinking it to be blood.

58. *Hās*, I. bet. *sl*s. 14 and 15, I.42.

59. Ibid., I.43.

60. Ibid., p. 44.

सद्यो दत्तमलक्तकं पदयुगे दृष्ट्वाङ्गनाया रतौ
रक्त-भ्रान्तिवशाद्भयेन नितरां ग्लानेन्द्रियो मेदिनीम्।
पश्यन् दर्शनिशा तमिस्रनिकरच्छन्नामिवाशां तथा
मूर्च्छेयं भुविका कथा समरतो रक्तास्य सक्तद्विषाम्॥

— I.44

The chief *purohita*, Viśvabhaṇḍa, is the foremost among the rogues.

दिनोपवासी तु निशामिषाशी
जटाधरः सन् कुलटाभिलाषी।
अयं कषायाम्बर चारुदण्डः
शठाग्रणीः सर्पति विश्वभण्डः॥

— I.17

His "reputation" as teacher is brought out by himself thus, *asmākam mandiram adhyāpanaśūnyam eva vartate.*[61] Fully aware of his lustful acts Bandhurā blesses him thus, *putra, madanasamudra-santaraṇam bhavatu.*[62] Being disgusted with his pesterings, the heroine complains,

> *mātaḥ eṣaḥ vṛddhaśārdūla iva galita-nakha-daṣano jarā-jīrṇa-panjaraḥ atihatavrīḍaḥ aharniśam mām viḍambayati.*[63]

The ardent disciple, with a dig at his own teacher, chides her,

> Wicked girl, how dare you insult my teacher by saying that he does not have *lajjā*. Even today he lies naked on the lap of his mother, full of *lajjā*.[64]

Viśvabhaṇḍa is fully aware of his ageing body and unageing desires.

---

61. *Hās*, p. 25.
62. Ibid., p. 20.
63. Ibid., p. 26.
64. Ibid., p. 26.

शुक्लत्वं जरसा कचेषु दशनाः शीर्णा विशीर्णातनु-
स्तैमिथ्यं नयने श्रुतौ न च वचोलब्धिः श्लथत्वं पले।
अस्माकं तु कथं तथापि विलसद्वाराङ्गनालिङ्गन-
व्यामोहाय मनः सदैव चलते चित्रं चरित्रं विधेः॥
— I.40

Though a *purohita*, he does not perform correctly even the expiation rites. The conversation between him and Mithyāśukla brings out his ignorance in this field.[65]

He stoops down to the level of fighting with his own disciple for the sake of the *gaṇikā*. Then he strikes a compromise with Madanāndhamiśra that they both may get married to Mṛgāṅkalekhā. He justifies his stand by quoting Draupadī's example.[66]

His disciple, Kalahāṅkura, has a peculiar way of pronouncing the *āśīrvacana*. This is how the King Anayasindhu is welcomed.

शत्रोर्वृद्धिर्भियोंवृद्धिर्वृद्धिर्व्याधे ऋणेनसाम्।
दुर्गतेर्दुमतेर्वृद्धिः सन्तु ते सप्तवृद्धयः॥
— I.21

The doctor too gets a similar welcome.[67] It is for the sake of Bandhurā that the doctor is called forth. But Kalahāṅkura attributes the wrong diseases to the wrong person and asks for cure. Then correcting himself he reports that it is Bandhurā who needs treatment but again attributes wrong disease to her,

> *huṁ smṛtam, mahāvaidya, surata-samara-vimardanāt muṇḍa-pīḍāturā bandhurā, tadatra kim karotu?*[68]

---

65. *Hās*, pp. 42-43.
66. Ibid., II.19.
67. Ibid., I.33.
68. Ibid., p. 35.

He vies with his teacher to win the love of Mṛgāṅkalekhā. But he does not lag behind his teacher in choosing a partner. He decides to share the old Bandhurā with Kulāla. The two plan to enjoy Mṛgāṅkalekhā during daytime when their teachers would be out for collecting alms.

The quack doctor, Vyādhisindhu is another comic character in the play. His prescriptions are sure to send a man to cemetery. He prescribes piercing the eye with a red hot iron for stomach upsets, drinking of the boiling oil for rheumatism, chopping of legs for elephantiasis, etc.[69] True to his name, he is an abode of all diseases himself. His legs are swollen and oozing pus and blood. He ia a tuberculosis patient and goes on coughing.[70] He proudly declares that when treated by him even Mārkaṇḍeya will not survive.

वैद्योऽहं व्याधिवर्गाणामाश्रयोप्ययशोनिधिः।
मया चिकित्सितः सद्यो मार्कण्डेयो न जीवति॥

— I.31

सवौषधानि तिष्ठन्तु चिकित्साऽपि च तिष्ठतु।
मम दर्शनतो रोगी किल प्राणैर्विमुच्यते॥

— I.32

The arrangements for the funeral must be got ready before this doctor is called upon to attend on his patient.[71]

The barber Raktakallola too contributes to the humour in the play. He boasts that when he takes up his razor, people lose faith in their lives. When he finishes his job, the entire body of his customer will be besmeared with surging blood.[72] He will tie the hands and feet of his customers if they begin to cry. When he cuts the nails, they never grow again.

---

69. *Hās*, I.28.
70. Ibid., I.30.
71. *Hās*, I.35.
72. Ibid., I.38.

The astrologer is no less comical. He is named "Mahāyātrika" suggesting that the "auspicious" time fixed by him will result in *mahāyātrā,* i.e. death of the persons concerned. He starts his astrological calculations, facing the southern direction which itself is inauspicious. He betrays his ignorance of astrology by his absurd and incorrect planetary calculations.[73] What the astrologer suggests as most auspicious time for the king's departure for the battle, viz. the morning of a Saturday falling on a full moon day with Śrāvaṇa and *vṛścika lagna,* portends only total destruction. When asked to pescribe an auspicious day for marriage, he says,

यत्र कुत्रापि लग्ने च वासरे यस्य कस्यचित्।
यत्र कुत्रापि नक्षत्रे यद्वा तद्वा विधीयताम्॥

— II.28

The priest Mahānindakācārya too contributes to the farcical element of the play by his peculiar *āśīrvacanas*:

श्मशानानलदग्धोऽसि परित्यक्तोऽसि बान्धवैः।
इदं नीरमिदं क्षीरं स्नात्वा पीत्वा सुखी भव॥
(पुनर्दूर्वाक्षतां आदाय)

— II.30

मरणं प्राणिनां नित्यं जीवनं स्वप्नवद् भुवि।
भवद्भिरिति विज्ञाय कर्तव्या नात्र शोचना॥
(पुनरुत्थाय उच्चैः)

— II.31

पितृकाननमेदिन्यां महाशय्यानुशायिभिः।
सुचिरं स्थीयतां नित्यं महानिद्रावलम्बिभिः॥

— II.32

Poetic Merits of the Work

Jagadīśvara has shown considerable poetic skill and originality

73. *Hās,* I.45.

in his small play. Some of his observations are striking, as for instance,

> युक्तं भस्मपुञ्जे सारमेयावस्थानम्
>
> — p. 34
>
> न हि जलौकसां अङ्गे जलौकानां गतिः
>
> — p. 43
>
> जीर्णमार्जारं कञ्चिकया प्रतारयितुं न शक्यते
>
> — p. 70
>
> अन्यस्य पुण्येन किमन्यः पूतो भवति?
>
> — p. 74

There is force of emotion in Kalahāṅkura's statement when he laments that the young *gaṇikā* is to be married to the two old men,

> इदं पुनरेकं परमं दुःखम्, सा त्रिभुवनमोहिनी वृद्धाभ्यां परिणेतव्या, न हि मालतीमाला वानरहस्तगता शोभते, न हि कस्तूरिकागुणग्रामं कुग्रामिनो जानन्ति, न हि गलितयौवनायाः वक्षस्थले मौक्तिकमाला शोभते।
>
> — p. 76

The heroine, Mṛgāṅkalekhā affords scope for the poet's descriptive powers, as for instance,

> अस्या धामसरोवरे भुजविषे वक्त्रारविन्दे भ्रम-
> न्नेत्रभ्रू भ्रमरे सुयौवनजले कस्तूरिकापङ्किले।
> वक्षोज-प्रतिकुम्भिकुम्भदलन-क्रोधादुपेत्य द्रुतं
> मग्नश्चित्तमतङ्गजः कथमसावुत्थाय निर्यास्यति॥
>
> — I.16

> स्वादितं सुदशनच्छदसीधु नामरैर्विधुरबुद्धिभिरस्याः।
> यद्विधुन्तुदमुखादवशिष्टः पीयते प्रमुदितैर्हरिणाङ्कः॥
>
> — I.49

The verse comparing the old lady Bandhurā to the rainy season is charming with pun.

प्रलम्बितपयोधरा क्षतरजा विकारास्पदं
सदा विगतहंसका तिमिरलुप्ततारारुचिः।
तिरस्कृतनिशाकरा गतवया इयं बन्धुरा
सदा सपदि वीक्ष्यतां जलधरागमश्रीरिव॥

— I.23

The *sandehālaṁkāra* in the description of the moonrise is quite interesting.

स्वर्धामामृतपानचारुचषकं किं कामदेवाङ्गना
क्रीडाकन्दुक एष किं सुरनदीहिण्डीरपिण्डः किमु।
किं छत्रं स्मरभूपतेः किमु यशःपुञ्जं पुरस्तादिदं
चेतः संशयकारकं समुदितं शीतद्युतेर्मण्डलम्॥

— I.53

The sunrise kindles the imagination of the poet in different ways. The sun, having deceived his lady love, the lotus pond, at night, has come back in the morning with a reddish countenance indicative of his bashfulness. The lotus pond shows its indignation through fully blown red lotuses (II.1).

The inability of the deer of the mind to escape the arrows of the Cupid on the hazardous and uneven terrain of the lady's body set forth in the following verse is comparable to a similar verse in the *Laṭakamelaka* (I.33).

उत्तुङ्गस्तनशैलदुस्तरमुरो निम्नातिनाभिस्थली
भीमं देहवनं स्फुरद्भुजलतं लोमालिजालाकुलम्।
व्याधः पञ्चशरः किरत्यतितरांस्तीक्ष्णान् कटाक्षाशुगान्
तन्मे ब्रूहि मनः कुरङ्ग शरणं कं साम्प्रतं यास्यसि॥

— II.9

The quarrel between the two teachers and their attempt to outwit the other by composing ślokas in praise of Śrī Kṛṣṇa, affords full scope for the poet to display poetic talents, and relief to the otherwise stereotyped theme.

जिह्वेऽनिशं हरिरिति स्मर लोचनं त्वं
व्याप्तं विलोकय जगद्धरिणा समस्तम्।
आकर्णय श्रवण कीर्तिकथा मुरारे
र्नारायणं शरणमाश्रय चित्तमुच्चैः॥[74]
त्रैलोक्यमौलिमुकुटाञ्चितनीलरत्नं
पद्मालयावदनतामरसद्विरेफम्।
दैत्याङ्गनानयनतोयनिपात धूमं
कृष्णं सदैव मनसा परिचिन्तयामि॥[75]

The Minor Prahasanas

THE DĀMAKA PRAHASANA

The *Dāmaka Prahasana* has aroused a great deal of interest among scholars ever since it was first noticed by M.R. Kavi,[76] who attributed it to Bhāsa. There is no mention of the dramatist's name anywhere in the play. Dr Mankad is of the opinion that it is not a work of Bhāsa. He even doubts if this work can be called a *prahasana* at all.[77] The present estimate of this work is based on the only available printed edition of the text.[78]

The *Dāmaka Prahasana* is a very small piece and may not take more than 15 minutes, when staged. There are large-scale borrowings in it from *Arthaśāstra*, *Svapnavāsavadattā*, *Karṇabhāra* and *Kumārasambhava*. The *nāndī śloka* itself is borrowed from the *Arthaśāstra*. There is a suggestion of *hāsya* in the prologue which is named *sthāpanā*. The *sūtradhāra* confuses between the names of the city and the king, (*brahmadattaṅgare asmin kāmpilyamahārājasadasi . . .*) which can be noticed in *Svapnavāsavadattā*.

74. *Hāsyārṇava*, II.10.
75. Ibid., II.11.
76. Paper read at the AIOC, Madras, 1924.
77. See Mankad, *Types of Sanskrit Drama*, pp. 63 ff.
78. Motilal Banarsidass, Lahore, 1926.

The play has three parts, the first part is a monologue where Dāmaka, a friend of Karṇa, narrates the difficulties experienced by him in adjusting himself to the new surroundings in Karṇa's palace. He has now accompanied Karṇa to Paraśurāma's hermitage. Karṇa is to learn all the *astras* from the great master. Dāmaka could not follow Karṇa who is on a hunting spree. He says:

> नाहमनुगच्छामि महाराजमिति। मृगपक्षिसंकुलं च एतदरण्यं परिभ्रमन्नहं बुभुक्षया ओदनमयमिव जीवलोकं पश्यामि। अस्वस्थशरीरश्चास्मि। . . . अहं खलु शृणोमि गन्धं श्रवणाभ्याम्। अन्धकारपूरिताभ्यां नासापुटाभ्यां पश्यामि। रैभ्यसगोत्रे ब्रह्मबन्धुरहं यस्य कस्य वा भागिनेयः खलु भीमसेनस्य घटोत्कच इव।[79]

He then turns round to find his bark garment being snatched away by a dog. He chases the dog to recover the dress. Here we have a picturesque description of the hermitage. In one place he says,

> *imāśca munikanyakāḥ vṛkṣakān putrakāniva mātaro ghaṭa-stana-prasravaṇaiḥ vardhayanti.*[80]

The second part has a very short dialogue between Karṇa and Paraśurāma (just six lines in all). Karṇa expresses his desire to learn archery from Paraśurāma who accedes to his request after ascertaining from him that he is not a kṣatriya.

The third part is a dialogue between two attendants of Karṇa, Durmukha and Durbuddhi. They discuss about Indra's trick in preventing Karṇa from continuing his studies under his master and the consequent banishment of Karṇa by Paraśurāma.

---

79. Cf. *Mattavilāsa*, pp. 62-63.

80. Cf. *Kumārasambhava*, v. 14.

Criticism

The view that the work is by Bhāsa can be easily dismissed on the ground that the play shows influence of Kālidāsa. The first part where Dāmaka finds himself in a similar state as the *vidūṣaka* in the *Abhijñānaśākuntala*, reveals traces of humour. There is absolutely no *hāsya* in the other two parts. But the brevity of expression in referring to the whole episode of Karṇa's banishment by his master is praiseworthy.

कृत्तो वज्रमुखेन नाम कृमिणा दैवात्तदूरुद्वये
निद्राच्छेदभयादसह्यत गुरोर्धैर्यात्तदा वेदना।
उत्थाय क्षतजाप्लुतः स सहसा रोषानलोद्दीपितः
बुध्वा तं च शशाप कालविफलान्यस्त्राणि ते सन्त्विति॥

THE GAURĪDIGAMBARA PRAHASANA

The *Gaurīdigambara Prahasana* has been printed recently with a Hindi commentary[81] and the present account of the play is based on this edition.

The author, Śaṅkaramiśra, is a versatile scholar. Apart from the *Gaurīdigambara*, he has written two other plays, *Kṛṣṇa-vinoda-nāṭaka* and *Manobhavaparābhava-nāṭaka*. His other works include the *Rasārṇava, Durgāṭīkā, Chandogāhnikoddhāra, Vādivinoda* and commentaries on the *Vaiśeṣika-Sūtras*, the *Kusumāñjali*, and the *Khaṇḍanakhaṇḍakhādya*.[82] Śaṅkaramiśra hails from the famous village Sarisava[83] near Mithilā and lived in the fourteenth century.[84] He was patronised by Puruṣottama Siṁha (son of Bhairava Siṁha), the king of Mithilā, referred to in the *Rasārṇava*.[85] The story

81. Ed. Tarinisa Jha, Chowkhamba, Varanasi, 1969.
82. *Gaurī-Digambara Prahasana*, Introduction, p. 10.
83. Ibid., Introduction, p. 6 (This village has been referred to in a fifteenth-century lyric, *Bhṛṅgadūtam* of Gaṅgānanda).
84. Ibid.
85. Ibid.

goes that his father Bhavanātha Miśra who was a great scholar, prayed to Lord Śiva and got a son, whom he named "Śaṅkaramiśra". It seems that Śaṅkaramiśra composed poems even before he was five years old. Once he surprised the local king with the following *śloka*:

बालोऽहं जगदानन्द न मे बाला सरस्वती ।
अपूर्णे पञ्चमे वर्षे वर्णयामि जगत्त्रयम् ॥

Being pleased, the king asked him to compose a *śloka* mixing both the classical and Vedic styles. The boy immediately recited:

चलितश्चकितश्छन्नः प्रयाणे तव भूपते ।
सहस्रशीर्षा पुरुषः सहस्राक्षः सहस्रपात् ॥

The *nāndī śloka* refers to the cosmic dance of Lord Naṭarāja. In the prologue, the *sūtradhāra* remarks that the poet wrote the play at the instance of his own father (p. 5).

In the opening scene, Nandin and sage Bhṛṅgirīti discuss about the arrangements for the marriage. Himavān's son, Maināka, wants to know the whereabouts of the bridegroom, Śiva. Since the marriage is to take place the next day, he has to take the bridegroom to their house in a ceremonial way. Nandin muses within himself on the incongruence of such formalities with regard to his master,

स्वामी वस्त्रपरिग्रहेऽपि विमुखः क्षौमैः किमस्मादृशा
वृद्धोक्षो यदि वाहनं मम पुनः किं वा फलं डोलया ।
भस्मैवा(र)ङ्गविलोपनं भगवतः श्रीखण्डपङ्कैरलं
श्लाघ्यो हन्त दिगम्बरस्य मिलितः पाणिग्रहाडम्बरः ॥

— *śl.* 11

Covering up all his doubts, he tells Maināka that his master is engaged in serious discussions with Kubera in his inner apartment. But Śiva suddenly appears, fresh from the cemetery, having applied the ash all over his body. Maināka is shocked to find his would-be brother-in-law in such a condition,

> उरसि भुजङ्गपङ्क्तिः स्फारफूत्कारघोरा
> शितिमवति च कण्ठे मुण्डमाला विशाला।
> ज्वलति महति नेत्रे वीतिहात्रः पवित्रः
> क्वचिदपि जगतीदृग्दृष्टपूर्वो न दृष्टः॥
> — *śl.* 13

He accuses Nandin that he had lied to him earlier about the qualifications of the bridegroom and decides to leave. Such an ugly personality as Śiva does not deserve the hand of his beautiful sister, Pārvatī. He remarks that the sugar candy is never offered to an elephant — *na hi sitā karabhāya nivedyate.* Śiva tries to appease him by pointing out to him his attainments, and how Pārvatī will be free from worries, if she marries him.

> गाङ्गं पाथः सुलभमशनं भिक्षया यानमुक्षा
> वस्त्रापेक्षा मम यदि भवेत् स्यात्तदानीममौष्याः।
> मुक्ताहारः स्फुरदहिवरः कण्ठ एवाञ्जनश्रीः
> मामुद्वाह्य क्षितिधरसुता शोचनीया कथं स्यात्॥
> — *śl.* 18

> श्मशाने मत्स्थानं समधिवसतो भङ्गमशनं
> चिताभूतिः सेयं परिलसति सोद्वर्तनविधौ।
> विभूषाहिः कण्ठे विषमनुगतं कज्जलविधौ
> समस्ता सामग्री घटयति भवान्याः परिणये॥
> — *śl.* 19

These braggings infuriate Maināka further more and he departs without a word. But Śiva is adamant that he would follow him wherever he went and follows him persistenly. Nandin hangs his head down in shame saying that he has not seen so far such a farcical *varayātrā*. Enters Nārada after some time reporting that Śiva took Pārvatī away with him even before the marriage rites could be finished. How could such an indiscilpined man punish his own (Nārada's) father, Brahmā? (Nārada here implies the cutting off of one of the heads of Brahmā by Śiva.) Being requested by Nandin, Nārada narrates the whole course of the farcical marriage of Śiva. Even the *pravara* of the bridegroom could not be pronounced since Śiva has neither parents nor grandparents. At the departure of Nārada appear two *piśāca*s holding Sumaṅgalā, Pārvatī's friend. Their contention is that since their master has married Pārvatī, her friend (Sumaṅgalā) must marry one of them. On the arrival of the newly-wed couple, the *piśāca*s disappear. Now Śiva asks Nandin to invite all the gods and arrange for a dance by divine nymphs in connection with his marriage reception. Gaurī is happy now that Śiva is fully clad in appropriate dress. Śiva himself explains the reason for the change in his attitude,

जन्मान्तरप्रणयिनी भवती सती मे
दक्षक्रतौ हुतभुजि स्वतनुं जुहाव।
तेन त्वदीयविरहा परिहत्य वासो
वासो व्यधायि विधुरेण मया चितासु॥

— *śl.* 33

The play comes to a close with Śiva blessing Pārvatī, followed by a Bharatavākya.

The peculiarity of this *prahasana* is that it is the only play in the whole range of *prahasana* literature, that has divine characters on its cast. The author is well within the limits of propriety and is cautious enough not to bring discredit to any deity. There is the inevitable influence of Kālidāsa's *Kumārasaṁbhava* in the play, especially, of the scene in the Vth Canto where the *brahmacārin* sets forth the alleged incongruence of Pārvatī's selection of Śiva as her husband. (Compare *śl.* 14 here and *Ku.* V, *śl*s. 65-73).

THE KUHANĀBHAIKṢAVA

The present account of *Kuhanābhaikṣava* of Ayyālunātha is based on the text published in the *Malayamāruta*[86] by Prof. Raghavan. The play has also been analysed by him in the *Saṁskṛta Raṅga Annual*.[87] The author Ayyālunātha, also known as Tirumalanātha, was the son of Bommaganti Gaṅgadhara and is said to have flourished in the court of Śiṅgabhūpāla[88] (CE 1381-1421), the author of *Rasārṇavasudhākara*.

The *nāndī śloka* invokes the blessings of Lord Nārāyaṇa. In the prologue, the *sūtradhāra* and his wife discuss the fate of their daughter who had been deserted by her husband. They are, however, consoled by a lady soothsayer (*vipraśnikā*) who had assured them that the separated couple would be united soon in the spring season.

The main character of the play is a recluse, Ātmayoni who, ignoring his erstwhile love Śaṅkarakauśikī, loves another dancing girl, Candrarekhā. He engages his pupil Dāmodara for bringing Candrarekhā to his *maṭha* secretly without the knowledge of one Ahmed Khan who has been keeping her under his custody. Śaṅkarakauśikī, who is sore about the teacher's act, decides to put on the appearance of Hammir Khan, a servant of Ahmed Khan, and threaten the monk of grave consequences if he casts his eyes on Candrarekhā.

Enter then, the teacher, who is in a lovelorn condition and his pupil Govinda, into a garden. Candrarekhā and her friend also come to the same garden for collecting flowers. They meet the monk there and offer their salutations to him.

---

86. *Malayamāruta*, part IV, The Rashtriya Sanskrit Sansthan, Delhi, 1978.

87. See "Two More Old Farces", *Saṁskṛta Raṅga Annual*, no. V, Madras, 1967, pp. 55-62.

88. Ibid.

After preliminary enquiries, the teacher expresses his desire to enjoy the company of the girl. The girl simply smiles at the plight of the monk and turns back. But Ātmayoni, under the pretext of helping her, collects flowers from higher branches, lifts her up and enjoys the pleasure of touching her limbs. On seeing a monkey on one of the branches, the girl cries aloud and embraces the monk in fear. The monk's happiness is spoiled by the sudden entry of Jharat Khan, a servant of Ahmed Khan, on hearing the distress cry of Candrarekhā. Ātmayoni hides himself behind a bush and his disciple climbs a tree top. The Musalman volunteers to drive the monkey away and asks the two girls to go to the Kṛṣṇa temple nearby. He then goes about beating every bush in search of the monkey and one such stroke hits the teacher hard on his face. Following an announcement that the monkey has been caught, the Musalman leaves the scene. The teacher and the student come out of their hiding places. The teacher complains that he had been badly stung by the bees that were aroused by Jharat Khan's search and the pupil says that he was bitten by the forest-ants. Even as the two begin to take stock of the situation, Śaṅkarakauśikī enters in the disguise of Hammir Khan and intimidates the monk for coveting Candrarekhā. The teacher and the pupil defy her and attack her with stones, clubs and shoes. Unable to put up with this onslaught, Śaṅkarakauśikī leaves the scene. Her gait arouses the suspicion of the teacher and the disciple.

Govinda then promises to fetch the other student Dāmodara and goes to Candrarekhā's house. Dāmodara informs Govinda of his strategy by which the teacher can have the company of the harlot. Accordingly the teacher comes there in the disguise of Kaumudikā, Candrarekhā's friend. But Ahmed Khan also comes there and he mistakes the monk to be Candrarekhā herself and embraces him tightly. Being demanded by him, the disguised monk has to dance. Now Dāmodara saves the situation by announcing thus from his hiding place: "Well done, Ahmed Khan! You are enjoying the company of Kaumudikā. Our mistress is sore about it and has gone to her inner apartment out of anger!" Realising his fault Ahmed Khan feels that he must approach Candrarekhā after her anger has subsided and leaves the scene. Meanwhile Candrarekhā who is informed about the trick played by the teacher and his disciples comes out of her house to meet the monk. As instructed by the disciples, she proceeds to the garden house where the monk is anxiously waiting for her. The play ends with a description of the monk and the harlot coming out of the garden house with visible signs of love-making.

As seen above, from the summary of the play, there is not much of originality either in the theme or in the manner in which the farcical elements are introduced. The only novelty in the play is the introduction of Musalman characters.

THE SOMAVALLĪYOGĀNANDA

The *Somavallīyogānanda* of Aruṇagirinātha had been printed once in 1895.[89] But since the printed edition could not be procured, a manuscript from Mysore[90] has been used for the present study. The play has been analysed in great detail by Prof. Raghavan in *Saṁskṛta Raṅga Annual*.[91] The author, Aruṇagirinātha, was patronised by the famous Vijayanagara king, Immadi Devaraya (CE 1422-40). The author was well

89. Arsha Library, Vizagapatnam, 1895.

90. Oriental Institute, Mysore, No. 2155. As many as five manuscripts of the work are available, two in Madras, and one each in Tanjore, Mysore and India Office Library, London.

91. V. Raghavan, "Two More Old Farces", *Saṁskṛta Raṅga Annual*, vol. V, Madras, 1967.

known for his forceful poetry and earned the titles, Ḍiṇḍima Kavisārvabhauma and Birudakavipitāmaha. The other works of Aruṇagirinātha are the *Rāmābhyudaya Kāvya* and *Mahānāṭaka-kīrtisudhānidhi*.[92]

The leading characters of the play are Yogānanda, a recluse, and Somavallī, a housewife. The pseudo monk's attempts to win her love forms the main theme of the play.

In the opening scene the monk is seen discussing with his disciple the means of enticing Somavallī. He is not sure whether his love would be reciprocated by her since she is already married to one Mādhavabhaṭṭa. His attention now is drawn to the number of visitors he has. Persons belonging to several walks of life consult Yogānanda for solution to their problems. In the case of the Jaina or the Kāpālika ascetic, it is with regard to their illicit love affair with *gaṇikā*s or housewives. In the case of householders, the main problem they face is the elopement of their wives with somebody else.

At noon, the monk proceeds to a garden along with his disciple. As expected, Somavallī arrives there. There is an interesting conversation between them in which the topics pertaining to Kāmaśāstra are cleverly clothed in indirect language referring to certain technical terms of different Śāstras. Before they depart, they devise a plan to flee the town at the dead of night in disguised forms. But their disguised forms pose problems for themselves in identifying each other. Their attempt to flee the town is finally thwarted by the night police squad who wind them up and produce them before the king. The king simply laughs over the matter and recommends that the monk should give up his ascetic life and marry Somavallī.

---

92. Cf. V. Raghavan, "Two More Old Farces", *Saṁskṛta Raṅga Annual*, vol. V, Madras, 1967.

Though the poet has not handled any novel theme, he has provided some realistic and humorous descriptions in this *prahasana*. This is how an early morning scene is described :

काका मज्जनमाचरन्ति पयसि व्याधूतपक्षाञ्चलाः
श्वानो वर्ष्म धुवन्त्यमी च भसिताकीर्णं प्रसुप्तोत्थिताः, etc.

The play, however, suffers from the usual defect found in the *prahasanas*, viz. vulgarity.

THE KAUTUKA-RATNĀKARA

Kautuka Ratnākara Prahasana belongs to the sixteenth century. The author, Kavitārkika, was the chaplain of Lakṣmaṇa Māṇikyadeva of Bhūluyā (in Naokali district of Bengal). The work does not seem to have been printed yet though it has been noticed by scholars like Sten Konow,[93] Keith[94] and S.K. Dey.[95]

The Plot[96]

King Duritārṇava becomes unconscious on coming to know that the queen had been kidnapped by somebody, in spite of the police chief, Suśīlāntaka, sleeping by her side. Being restored to normalcy, the king intends to hold, in consultation with his minister, Kumatipuñja, the Spring Festival, in which a harlot would represent the queen. The royal priest, Ācārakālakūṭa, too falls in love with the same harlot, but she simply raises him upwards and throws upon the ground which causes the bleeding of his nose. The doctor, Vyādhivardhaka, is called upon to attend on him. The preceptor is now accused of having seduced the queen and is pronounced guilty, but finally all the troubles become resolved

93. *Indian Drama*, pp. 186 ff.
94. *Sanskrit Drama*, pp. 262-63.
95. *Poona Orientalist*, vol. VII, p. 155.
96. Based on Konow's version.

in the celebration of the Spring Festival. Other characters in the cast are Aśubhacintaka, the astrologer; Pracaṇḍaśepha, the overseer of the harem; Samarakātara, the army general; Ajitendriya, a teacher and Kapaṭaveṣadhārin, a brāhmaṇa.

THE KAUTUKA SARVASVA

Kautuka Sarvasva of Gopīnātha Cakravartin is one of the popular *prahasanas*. Not much is known about the author and date of this work. It is likely that this work was modelled on *Kautuka Ratnākara* belonging to the sixteenth century. On the basis of this assumption this work may be assigned to the late sixteenth century or seventeenth century. Keith[97] gives reference to a printed edition of the work but it could not be procured for study. Wilson was the first to analyse *Kautuka Sarvasva*[98] followed by Capeller,[99] Keith[100] and S.K. De.[101] Given below is a brief summary of the play.[102]

The hero of the play is a licentious king, Kalivatsala, who is given to every kind of vice. *Dharma* has no place in his kingdom. The king tortures a pious brāhmaṇa, Satyācāra who finds that everything is wrong in the state, even the people being cowardly, servile and fault-finding. The king has his usual retinue. The army general uses his sword only for cleaving the butter and trembles at the approach of a mosquito. The priest justifies his misconduct by referring to the immoralities recounted in the Purāṇas. Prohibition of

97. Ed. Ramachandra Tarkalamkara, Calcutta, 1828; See Keith, p. 262.
98. Wilson, *The Theatre of the Hindus*, vol. II, p. 410.
99. *Gurupūjākaumudī*, Leipzig, 1896, p. 59.
100. *Sanskrit Drama*, p. 262.
101. *Poona Orientalist*, no. VII, p. 154.
102. Based on Keith's account.

the enjoyment of the worldly pleasures is the result of the old monks' incapacity to enjoy them. The king proclaims free love but gets entangled in an affair with a harlot. He is summoned back to the queen which so annoys the harlot that everybody in the court goes about appeasing her. In order to please her, the king banishes all the brāhmaṇas from his country since they alone are responsible for the framing of impracticable moral codes like fidelity.

THE DHŪRTANARTAKA PRAHASANA

The *Dhūrtanartaka* was first edited in 1828.[103] H.H. Wilson[104] was the first scholar to analyse this work. Sten Konow, Keith and S.K. Dey have given more or less the same account given by Wilson. The present study of the work is based on the photostat copy of a MS. from Bodleian Library, Oxford.[105]

The author, Sāmarāja Dīkṣita is a well-known figure in the field of poetics,[106] his main contribution being *Śṛṅgārāmṛtalaharī.*[107] He belongs to the seventeenth century[108] and was patronised by Ānandarāya the chief administrator of Bundelkhaṇḍ. Sāmarāja has also composed *Tripurasundarī-mānasa-pūjana-stotra*[109] and *Śrīdāmacarita,*[110] a play in five acts. In the prologue of *Dhūrtanartaka*, the author mentions that he is the son of Narahari Bindupurandara and that he has mastered in Tarka and Sāhitya.

103. Ed. Ramachandra Tarkalamkara, Calcutta, 1828.
104. *The Theatre of the Hindus*, II, p. 407.
105. Lent to the present writer by S.S. Janaki, K.S.R. Institute, Madras.
106. *History of Sanskrit Poetics*, Firma KLM Ltd., Calcutta, 1976, p. 311.
107. *Kāvyamālā Gucchak*, xiv.
108. *HCSL*, p. 680, para 757.
109. *Kāvyamālā Gucchak*, ix.
110. CC, II.63 : III.142.

The play opens with a *nāndī śloka* invoking the blessings of Śrī Kṛṣṇa. Śrī Kṛṣṇa poses as an ascetic in the midst of the *gopī*s. One of the girls jokingly remarks that an ascetic need not have a silken garment and drags it and others enjoy the fun.

The hero of the play is a Śaivite monk Mūḍheśvara belonging to the Vāmācāra sect. He is deeply in love with the dancing girl, Vasantavallī. His disciples Jagadvañcaka and Mukhara enquire about his love affair and he obliges them after extracting a promise from them that they would not divulge the secret to anybody.

Enters now Kṛṣṇānanda, a Vaiṣṇava, with his disciples. He boasts of his mastery of different Śāstras and says that a host of disciples always throng at his doorstep for instructions.

यवनशूद्रकुलालकुविन्दकोद्भटकृषीवलगोलकशोण्डिकाः ।
अगणितगणिकाः परिलम्भिताः श्रवणमूलजपान्निजशिष्यताम् ॥

— I.21

A trivial argument rakes up quarrel between Pāpa, the disciple of Kṛṣṇānanda and Mukhara and each tries to establish that his own teacher is the best and in the process proclaim several licentious acts of their teachers. The teacher first scolds his disciple for letting out the secret but himself narrates his experiences at length to Kṛṣṇānanda. Kṛṣṇānanda reveals that he too is in love with a *gaṇikā,* Padmavanitā. After Kṛṣṇānanda's depature, Mūḍheśvara and his disciples proceed to the *maṭha* of Śuṇṭhakācārya and witness a dance performance of Vasantavallī there. Then Śuṇṭhakācārya asks Mūḍheśvara to arrange the articles of worship for his *pūjā*. Several types of food forbidden for religious men, like fish and meat are also asked to be got ready.

The second act opens with a description of the sunset and the advent of night. Mūḍheśvara is woried that his beloved has not turned up yet. The teacher bids his disciples to bring his sweetheart there at any cost since the love fever is unbearable for him. Jagadvañcaka meets Vasantavallī in advance and advises that she must ignore the old teacher and accept himself as her companion. Meanwhile, Mūḍheśvara comes there and both the teacher and student quarrel over the claim for the girl. This brings the police to the scene and all of them are produced before King Pāpācāra. The king himself is attracted by the girl and wants to set her free. A minister, a *purohita* and a *vidūṣaka* are also introduced into the plot without much purpose. Vasantavallī is finally given away in marriage to Mūḍheśvara, who is acknowledged as a rogue among the rogues.

It is quite evident that Dhūrtanartaka follows the beaten track of *prahasana*s, and there is no novelty either in theme or in characterisation. The play is further marred by long and tedious descriptions lacking in literary value.

THE PRAHASANAS OF HARIJĪVANAMIŚRA

The *prahasana*s of Harijīvanamiśra were first brought to light by Prof. Kunhan Raja and Śrī Madhavakrishna Sarma.[111] The *Adbhutataraṅga, Prāsaṅgika, Ghṛtakulyāvalī, Palāṇḍumaṇḍana, Vibudhamohana* and *Sahṛdayānanda* are housed in the Anup Sanskrit Library, Bikaner. These *prahasana*s have been analysed in great detail by George Artola and Prof. Raghavan.[112] In order to avoid repetition, only a brief account of these *prahasana*s is given below, followed by an exposition of the *hāsya-rasa* therein.

Harijīvanamiśra's contribution to the *prahasana* literature is significant. He is the only dramatist to have composed six

111. See *The Adyar Library Bulletin*, no. XV, 1951, pp. 68-71.

112. *Saṁskṛta Raṅga Annual*, vol. IV, Madras, with the exception of acts II and III of *Adbhutataraṅga* and the whole of *Ghṛtakulayāvalī*.

prahasanas. He was patronised by King Rāma Siṁha I (*c*. 1635-89) of Ambar, who was an ally of the Mughal Emperor Aurangzeb.[113]

The present study of two of the six *prahasanas*, the *Palāṇḍumaṇḍana* and the *Vibudhamohana*, is based on the text published by Prof. Raghavan in the *Malayamāruta* (1963 and 1966); a study of the remaining texts is based on transcript copies from the Anup Sanskrit Library, Bikaner.

ADBHUTATARAṄGA

The *Adbhutataraṅga* has three acts which have no common action between them. In fact, the three acts may be considered as three independent *prahasanas*. The only common feature between the three acts is that the scene of action is the same in all of them, viz. the courthall of king.

Act I : There is not much of a novelty in the nature of the characters in this act. We have a foolish king, Madanāṅgavikrama, a hypocritial Vaiṣṇava brāhmaṇa, Gauḍarasamiśra, a *purohita,* Vidhavāvidhvaṁsaka who always creates confusion in explaining the Smṛti texts, the notorious royal physician, Yamānuja and a few more characters of this sort.

In the opening scene the king enters the courthall and is greeted by Gauḍarasamiśra thus, *prārabdhakarmaṇi vighnamastu*. The king becomes angry and announces that he will be punished for his offence. He requests Vidhavāvidhvaṁsaka to suggest a suitable punishment. The latter suggests that the Vaiṣṇava must take the bed with his wife (Vidhavāvidhvaṁsaka's wife) since he himself has become incapable of satisfying her due to his pile complaint. The anger

113. See G. Artola, Harijīvana Miśra and his short Sanskrit plays, *Saṁskṛta Raṅga Annual*, vol. IV.

of the king now turns towards the royal physician Yamānuja who has neglected the royal priest. The king orders that the doctors too must undergo a similar punishment, that he too must satisfy the *purohita*'s wife. Meanwhile the *vidūṣaka* dressed as a woman, impersonates Vidhavāvidhvaṁsaka's wife and enters the bedroom along with Yamānuja. The king knows of *vidūṣaka*'s trick and is satisfied that his incompetent physician is summarily punished.

Act II : The second act has very little action. The scene is again the king's court. It is reported that one Vajrāntaḥkaraṇa is in love with a girl, Pumprāṇaḍhākinī. But she has an affair with her own cousin. Vajrāntaḥkaraṇa has actually seen their love-making and has fainted. One of those assembled, Paraduḥkhāṅkura is asked to help him recover. Many more characters appear. The king finally announces that he would bring Pumprāṇaḍhākinī to his own harem — thus putting an end to the conflicting claims over her by the others.

Act III : An ascetic, Vaiṣṇavāgamanirmūlaka is a licentious man and is always surrounded by harlots. For him, the *āliṅgana* of ladies is the *snāna* and the *cumbana*, the *ācamana*. He spoils young girls under the pretext of *mantra-dīkṣā*. Another brāhmaṇa, Śiṣṭāviṣṭakotpāṭana Bhaṭṭācārya who is jealous of him, reports the matter to the king. The king calls forth the judge Smārtagartabhaṭṭācārya to enquire into the case. Coming to know that Śiṣṭāviṣṭakotpāṭana Bhaṭṭācārya does not have children Smārtagarta offers to raise issues for him through his (Śiṣṭā . . .'s) wife. Śiṣṭā . . . . becomes enraged at this and the two begin to fight. Meanwhile Vaiṣṇavāgamanirmūlaka comes along with his retinue of girls and requests the king that the girls be attached to the harem since he has become impotent. The king is happy at this. Some more farcical scenes like this take place. When Vaiṣṇavāgamanirmūlaka and one of the girls faint due to exhaustion, they are mistaken to be dead and arrangements are made for their funeral. A priest and a barber are called forth. For the ceremony known as *vṛṣotsarga* (branding the bulls and letting them loose) connected with the funeral, the king suggests that the two Bhaṭṭācāryas who are fat like bulls must be branded and paraded in the streets. The Bhaṭṭācāryas suggest that the priest is more qualified than themselves for such a treatment and fighting erupts again and it becomes a free for all. Meanwhile Vaiṣṇavāgamanirmūlaka and the girl regain their consciousness and get up, thus calling off further arguments on the funeral.

Prāsaṅgika

King Pratāpapaṅkti wants to listen to scholarly discussions on the Vedas and the Smṛtis and the scholars are summoned. One of the scholars, Prakṛṣṭadeva and his wife Prakṛtipriyā are very particular about adding the prefix *pra* before each word since it gives the sense of "the best". The other scholar Keralabhaṭṭa is averse to this practice and quarrel erupts between the two. Some more characters are introduced. The husband and a former lover of a lady quarrel over the true parentage of her son. To make matters worse, a monkey enters the court and creates confusion. The only noteworthy feature of the play is the ingenious way the poet has used the prefix *pra* before each word uttered by Prakṛṣṭadeva, resulting in certain roundabout expressions, for instance, *priye pratihatam te apratimaṅgalam khalu*. The *nāndī śloka* itself indicates the predominance of this feature throughout the play.

प्रीतिस्ते प्रभवेत् प्रमोदविधिना प्रोद्यत्प्रजापालने
प्राजापत्यगुरोः प्रयोगचतुरप्रायस्य हि प्राज्ञता।
प्रद्योतप्रकरप्रतापतरणः प्रव्यक्तरङ्गस्य च
प्रमृष्टाः प्रतिपक्षिणः प्रतिदिशं प्रायो भवेयुर्भुवि॥

PALĀṆḌUMAṆḌANA

Palāṇḍumaṇḍana is easily the best among the *prahasana*s of Harijīvanamiśra.[114] The names of the characters in this play indicate the vegetables or eatables they are fond of. The play is named after the main character Palāṇḍumaṇḍana, a brāhmaṇa, who has a craze for onion (*palāṇḍu*), though it is prohibited for a brāhmaṇa[115] The other characters are Laśunapanta (fond of garlic) and Pūrṇapolikā (fond of Poli, a sweetmeat). All these and some more people assemble in the house of Liṅgojibhaṭṭa who is celebrating his nuptial ceremony with his second wife Ciñcā. The Beṅgālī brāhmaṇas criticse the south Indian brāhmaṇas for their preference to the prohibited vegetables like onion and garlic. The south Indians in turn find fault with the Beṅgālī's fondness for fish- eating. The dispute turns violent and the police arrive in time to restore peace. The south Indians cleverly put the whole blame on the Beṅgālīs who are taken into custody by the police. The disturbed Liṅgojibhaṭṭa postpones the *garbhādhāna* ceremony and the guests leave the house disappointed. In addition to this main theme, there is also a funny account of the love affair of the old Laśunapanta with a young girl.

VIBUDHAMOHANA

Vibudhamohana is written by the poet more for demonstrating his knowledge of the different Śāstras than for the sake of humour. The names of the characters themselves indicate the branch of Śāstra they have specialised in (e.g. Tarkakarkaśa, Sāṅkhyānanda, Pātañjalanātha and Vaiśeṣikabhaṭṭācārya). The

---

114. Adapted for the stage by Raghavan, put on boards by the Saṁskṛta Raṅga, Madras.

115. Cf. *Manu* v. 5;

लशुनं गृञ्जनं चैव पलाण्डुं कवकानि च।
अभक्ष्याणि द्विजातीनां . . . . . . ॥

story is about the difficulties experienced by a scholar, Sakalāgamācārya in meeting the expenses of the marriage of his daughter, Sāhityamālā. Her six brothers headed by Tarkakarkaśa try to impress the king by the display of their scholarship and win rewards so that they can arrange for the marriage of their sister. But it is the prospective bridegroom, Akhaṇḍānanda who impresses the king most by his knowledge of the Alaṁkāraśāstra. The king promises to meet the entire expenditure of his marriage with Sāhityamālā. A noteworthy feature of this play is that a number of *subhāṣitas* drawn from various sources like the *Mahābhārata*, the *Hitopadeśa*, *Ratnāvalī*, *Mālatīmādhava* and the *Nalacampū*, are quoted in the prologue and elsewhere in the play.

THE SAHṚDAYĀNANDA

The Sahṛdayānanda is replete with concepts of Alaṁkāraśāstra which seems to be the favourite subject of the poet. The names of the characters themselves are significant — Ālaṁkārika, Abhidhā, Lakṣaṇā, Vyañjanā, Rasapratibandhaka, etc. There is neither story value nor any worthwhile farcical element in the play. The later part of the play is marred by obscene passages and action.

THE GHṚTAKULYĀVALĪ

The manuscript of this work is incomplete and badly damaged and hence we are not in a position to know even the full summary of the play. From the available portion it is known that the scene is laid in the house of a brāhmaṇa, Ghṛtakulāyākuśala who, along with his wife, Patiśīlā, is performing a *prāyaścitta*. Many people are invited for the function. Finding that the available money may not be sufficient to cover the *dakṣiṇā* expenses, the householder decides to distribute cowries instead. When even the cowries are in short supply, it is decided that one cowrie should be shared by four people and this angers the invitees which results in bitter quarrel.

HĀSYA IN HARIJĪVANAMIŚRA'S PLAYS

There is a stamp of originality in the *hāsya* depicted by Harijīvanamiśra. It is not the stereotype comedy of a monk's love affairs that we come across in his plays. There is variety and freshness in his approach. There is, for instance, a parody on the Upaniṣadic style, in the *Palāṇḍumaṇḍana*.

> मूषको वै प्रजापतिरासीत्। तस्य द्वौ दन्तावास्ताम्। दन्तेन दन्तेन बिलं करोति, भाण्डं स्फोटयति, हवींषि भक्षयति, यजमानः प्रहरति, चूञ्चूशब्दं करोति, यजमानं स्वर्गं लोकं गमयति।

According to one of the characters, Lāśunapanta (in *Palāṇḍumaṇḍana*), even gods and demons add garlic to their food in order to make it palatable. The gods draw nectar from the moon only because it resembles the garlic in colour. The tamarind soup is not the relishable at all without the garlic. If there is no sun where is the merit for the moon?

> तिमिरवधधुरीण उष्णरश्मिः यदि न भवेदिह कोऽस्ति शीतरश्मिः।

The merits of the garlic are nicely summed up in the verse:

> अये लशुनपेटिके सकलदुःखसन्त्रोटिके
> महापथसुघोटिके परमापापसम्मोटिके।
> सुगन्धहततोटिके परमसिद्धसच्छोटिके
> प्रसीद परमेश्वरि क्षुधिततृप्तिसद्रोटिके॥

The doctor Yamānuja in *Adbhutataraṅga* always appears with a blazing log of wood in his hand (suggesting that his treatment would assure the cremation of his patients). He finds fault with the doctors who attempt to cure their patients. He, being a practial man, would rather help his patients attain salvation.

> लोका मूढधियो विमूढवचसि प्रामाण्यमेवंविधं
> कृत्वा दीनजनं गतार्थमपि तं सञ्जीवयन्त्येव हि।

अस्माकं तु परम्परार्जितमिदं सर्वस्वरूपं फलं
दृङ्मात्रेण विमुक्तिमेव करवाण्येवंविधं निश्चितम्॥

Some of Harijīvanamiśra's observations are noteworthy.

हर्म्योपरि स्थितानां काकानां कथं हर्म्यं भवति?

— *प्रासङ्गिकप्रहसन*

न अनृतात् परं पातकं, परन्तु अनृतं विना न सांसारिकं कञ्चिदपि।

— *सहृदयानन्द* - Act II

The *rūpaka* in the following verse is interesting:

साहित्यमपि कान्तायाः कान्तदृष्टेः महाञ्जनम्।
रसराशौ निमग्नानां व्यञ्जना जीवनायते॥

— *सहृदयानन्द* - Act II

Taken as a whole, the six plays do not contain much of literary value but the variety in the farcical style is refreshing. Thus we have a farce in the royal court (*Adbhutataraṅga*), in the house of an ordinary householder (*Palāṇḍumaṇḍana*) and an allegorical one (*Sahṛdayānanda*). The author seems to be well informed in different branches of Śāstras, though *Alaṁkāra* appears to be his favourite. Another feature of his plays is the apt names given for the characters though sometimes there are long names like Vākyārthaparibhraṣṭa, Śiṣṭāviṣṭakotpāṭana Bhaṭṭācārya, Vaiṣṇavāgamanirmūlaka and Jagaccarmadaṇḍa-muṇḍamuṇḍasphoṭikā. It is painful to note that for all his scholarship and fine sense of humour, Harijīvanamiśra has not raised his *prahasana*s above the tendency of vulgarity which became a regular feature of medieval *prahasana* literature.

VEṄKATEŚVARA KAVI AND HIS TWO PRAHASANAS

A number of works have been preserved under the names Veṅkaṭeśa and Veṅkaṭeśvara. The *Lambodara* and *Unmattakavikalaśa prahasana*s seem to have been composed by one and the same author, as there is much similarity with respect to the style and subject matter. The author of these two *prahasana*s will henceforth be referred to as Veṅkaṭeśvara for the sake of uniformity. Veṅkaṭeśvara seems to have earned the title "Kālidāsa" from his admirers. The Mysore edition of *Lambodaraprahasana* gives the title of the poet on its title page, *śrīveṅkaṭeśvarāparanāmadheya kālidāsamahākavikṛtam. . . .*[116] In the manuscript libraries in Madras, Mysore and Tanjore, this *prahasana* is preserved under several names — *Lambodaraprahasana,*[117] *Veṅkaṭeśaprahasana,*[118] *Kālidāsaprahasana,*[119] and *Bhānuprabandha,*[120] which has led to some confusion among scholars regarding the exact number of *prahasana*s written by Veṅkaṭeśvara.[121] There is a clue to the date of the author in the colophon of two manuscripts of this work[122] (preserved under the name *Bhānuprabandha*). It says,

आनन्दवल्लीदेव्याः करुणारसेन दुराकटाक्षोर्मिः ।
भोसलकुलमणिदीपं सुखयतु शाहाधिपं नित्यम् ॥

— *sic*

It is quite probable that Veṅkaṭeśvara was a court-poet of

116. *Lambodaraprahasana*, Vidyatarangini Press, Mysore, 1890.

117. The manuscript on which the Mysore edition is based, see also Aufrecht's *Catalogus Catalogorum*, vol. I. p. 542.

118. See *Descriptive Catalogue of Madras Govt. Oriental Manuscript Library*, vol. XXI, no. 8525.

119. See Aufrecht, vol. I, pp. 99 and 104, under the name *Kāśīdāsaprahasana*.

120. Saraswathi Mahal Library, Tanjore, nos. B5304, B5305, B5308 and B10660.

121. For instance Artola says, "Veṅkaṭeśvara has contributed three Prahasanas." See the article of Artola, *Saṁskṛta Raṅga Annual*, vol. IV. M. Krishanamachariar identifies *Lambodaraprahasana* with *Unmatta Kavikalaśa*, which is incorrect. See *HCSL*, p. 661.

122. Tanjore Saraswathi Mahal Library, Nos. B5304 and B5305.

King Shahaji of Tanjore (1684-1710). The historical *campū*, *Bhosalāvaṁśāvalī*,[123] was probably written by him in order to honour his patron. Three dramas, *Rāghavānanda*, *Nīlāpariṇaya* and *Sabhāpativilāsa* are also attributed to Veṅkaṭeśvara.[124] The present study of *Lambodaraprahasana* is based on the Mysore edition of the text and the four manuscripts from Tanjore.

The Lambodaraprahasana

This play owes its popularity to its pornographic value. Obscenity is noticed in almost all the *prahasanas* right from *Laṭakamelaka* in some degree or other. But *Lambodaraprahasana* surpasses them all in vulgarity.

Vakranāsa, a monk, is deeply in love with a dancing girl, Gṛdhrī. He has fitting disciples in Jambūka and Kāsara. From the conversation between them in the opening scene, it is learnt that Kāsara's wife has eloped with one Dīrghadanta, a friend of Vakranāsa. Kāsara is not worried about this since he is after another girl, Alābūstanī.

Coming to know that Gṛdhrī is likely to come to a garden after her dance performance in the royal court, Vakranāsa proceeds there. But the king who is also in love with the girl comes to the same garden and becomes enraged at the monk's illicit love affair. The punishment is that the monk should be dressed as a monkey and paraded in the streets of the city.

When brought to his own house, in the monkey dress, Vakranāsa finds that his wife, Nipuṇikā has an affair with his own disciple Jambūka. When his mask is removed, Nipuṇika exclaims,

---

123. *Descriptive Catalogue of the Tanjore Saraswathi Mahal Library*, vol. VII, no. 3287.

124. See *HCSL*, p. 61.

कर्मणा वानर एष वेषेणापि कृतस्तथा।
मामुज्झित्वा गतो गृध्रीं यद्राज्ञा बहुमानितः॥

The disgusted Vakranāsa resolves to leave the kingdom and proceed to some other place where he hopes to win the favour of the ruler of that area by the display of his scholarship. With that money he hopes to get Gṛdhrī and thereby achieves his life's ambition. For the time being he decides to share his wife with his disciple, Jambūka. He would not condemn him for his offence since *yo hi bhuktavantam prati brūyāt mā bhuṅkthā iti kim tena kṛtam syāt*. The play has the usual Bharatavākya, at the end.

The Unmattakavikalaśa

The poet gives some more information about himself in the prologue of this play. He was the son of one Dharmarāja and belonged to the Maṇalur village on the banks of the Kāverī. He was an authority in the six *darśana*s and was proficient in six languages. *Unmattakavikalaśa* was probably his first work and is less vulgar. Encouraged by the reception it had, he would have written the *Lambodara*. The present account of the *Unmattakavikalaśa* is based on the transcript copies of the manuscripts preserved in the Tanjore Saraswathi Mahal Library.[125]

The *adhama* hero of the play is Kavikalaśa, a poet-cum-teacher.

दौर्जन्यस्य तपःफलं सुचरितस्योत्पातकेतुः कले-
रावृत्तिर्दुरितस्य गर्भसदनं मोहस्य काष्ठा परा।
तृष्णायाः परदेवतानृतगिरां सीमा खलश्रेयसां
आस्थानं कलशास्स एष कविरित्यायाति मायानिधिः॥

125. D4627-28.

In the opening scene Kavikalaśa expresses his fear to his disciple, that he might be in for some trouble since he had seen some bad omens. The disciple asserts that these omens signify nothing but death, and that he need not worry. The teacher then asks him to find out whether he can get some money from sombody to meet the expenses for the day. The student tells him that there is none who is likely to advance him money since he has not cleared the previous loans to them. After all it is his motto that the borrowed money should never be returned.

> ऋणं गृह्णाति निःशङ्कं न भूयस्तत् प्रयच्छति ।
> कलशस्य कवेरेतत् व्रतमारभ्य जन्मनः ॥

Then the teacher and the disciple take an early morning walk and describe the scenes witnessed by them — the merchant and the customers negotiating the price of articles, the *paurāṇika*s discoursing for an audience of widows, the luxurious life led by the *mādhava saṁnyāsin*s, a fight between two heads of *maṭhas*, a *bhāgavata* being dragged to the court by the police for molesting a widow in the temple *maṇḍapa* under the pretext of giving her *mantra-dīkṣā* and a few more scenes like this.

Kavikalaśa is then caught by some moneylenders. With a smiling face he informs them that there is good news for them and presents each one of them with a string of beads. The king has presented him with a village and he would clear their loans soon. Being pleased, the moneylenders depart. The next to appear is a brāhmaṇa asking Kavikalaśa whether he saw his wife going that way. It seems that his wife has eloped with his tenant. Kavikalaśa promises to restore her to him by the power of his *kāmakalā-vidyā* and extracts a handsome amount from him. Then the teacher and the student enter the house of a harlot and Kavikalaśa enjoys her under the pretext of curing her of some ailment.

The teacher and the student then proceed to a merchant's house for *bhikṣā*. But the merchant wants to evade him and so hides himself at the backyard. The unsuspecting Kavikalaśa enters the house and immediately the merchant comes out shouting "Thief! Thief!" One of the persons who rush to his help is a Paṭhān who has lent money to Kavikalaśa. The Paṭhān catches hold of his client and demands money from him. As the two begin to fight, the police arrive on the scence and take both of them to the king. The king who is already aware of the licentious life led by the teacher simply laughs at the sorry figure cut by him. He clears Kavikalaśa's debts to the Paṭhān perhaps with the idea that his act of generosity might bring in good sense in him and help him improve his conduct.

THE SĀNDRAKUTŪHALA OF KṚṢṆADATTA

The *Sāndrakutūhala* is a four-act play and though the poet calls it a *prahasana* it is doubtful whether it deserves to be called so. Only the fouth act shows some signs of *prahasana* elements and the other acts have little or no dramatic action. The play has been noticed by Peterson,[126] Aufrecht[127] and Sten Konow.[128] The present account of the play is based on the transcript of a manuscript available in the Bhandarkar Oriental Research Institute Library.[129]

The author has given a detailed account of himself in the colophon of the work. He was the son of Sadārāma and Ānandadevī. He belonged to the village of Tramatiya in the Vajjada district in Mithilā. Schuyler assigns him to the first part of seventeenth century.[130] The other works of the author

126. Peterson, III, 359, 397.

127. *CC*, I.707.

128. *Indian Drama*, pp. 186 ff.

129. *Descriptive Catalogue of BORI*, D, XIV.238, no. 365 of 1884-86.

130. *Bibliography of Sanskrit Drama*, p. 63.

are *Purañjanacarita*,[131] a drama in five acts based on the Bhāgavata and a *prakaraṇa*, *Kuvalayāśvīya*[132] in seven acts. In his *Rādhārahasyakāvya*, he deals with the love story of Śrī Kṛṣṇa and Rādhā in 22 cantos and it is accompanied by his own commentary. His *Gītagaṇapati* is styled on the model of *Gīta Govinda*. He has also written a commentary[133] on the *Gīta Govinda*.

The author seems to be an ardent devotee of Śrī Kṛṣṇa as is evident from the nature of the works mentioned above. Even in the *prahasana* the poet has sung in praise of Śrī Kṛṣṇa in the whole of the first act and part of the second act too. *Sāndrakutūhala* shows an interesting account of the transition of values of human life represented by four sets of fathers and sons. Thus the first act stresses the value of the *bhakti* cult, the second act, that of literary pleasure and the third act speaks of the value of a closely knit family life and conjugal love. The fourth act touches on the weaknesses of human beings and the degraded nature of certain sections of the society.

The play opens with three *nāndī śloka*s, all dedicated to Śrī Kṛṣṇa. In the course of the conversation between the *sūtradhāra* and the *naṭī*, mention is made of the poet's patron, Dharmavarman, who was probably the ruler of a petty kingdom.

In the first act the poet brings out the efficacy of Kṛṣṇa-bhakti through a conversation between two characters, Padmākara and his son Sukhākara. The father answers to the queries of his son stressing the importance of the *bhakti-mārga*, the means of obtaining Śrī Kṛṣṇa's grace, the path that leads

131. Cf. *HCSL*, pp. 661-62 : *CC*, I.339. The date of the poet is given as early eighteenth century in *HCSL*.

132. Ibid. and *CC*, I.113.

133. Ibid.

to his proximity, of the guildelines for *dhyāna* and on how one should employ the limbs of his body in the service of the Lord. In between there are beautiful descriptions of Vṛndāvana, Govardhanagiri, Gokulagrāma and the banks of the Yamunā where the Lord sports. The poet also recounts the playful acts of the child Kṛṣṇa in the house of Yaśodā. The poet laments that people foolishly bring about their own downfall by engaging themselves in *nara-stuti* and by running after the mundane pleasures without realising that devotion to Śrī Kṛṣṇa alone can save them from the ills of the worldly life.

The second act is mainly devoted to the display of talents of the poet in different poetic gymnastics like the *anuloma-pratiloma* technique, verse with just two letters, verse with a single letter, *pādādi-yamaka, pratipada-yamaka, pratipādānta-yamaka,* the *chatra-bandha,* the *vyajana-bandha,* etc. Kṣapākara asks his father Prabhākara to compose verses in praise of different deities like Lord Śiva, Pārvatī, Gaṇeśa, Śrī Kṛṣṇa, Nṛsiṁha, Śrī Rāma and the holy Ganges and the father obliges with an array of *śloka*s in different styles mentioned above.

The third act is in the form of a conversation between Divākara and his son Guhākara. The main point of discussion is about feminine charm. Divākara recounts the happy youthful days he spent in the company of his wife and upholds the superiority of the bliss of conjugal love over other walks of life.

It is actually in the fourth act that the *prahasana* begins. In the opening scene, Doṣākara and his son Sudhākara enter discussing the means of earning a livelihood. The father bids his son to go to the king's court and win his favour by the show of his scholarship. The son complains that only *naṭa*s and *viṭa*s are favoured by the kings but not real scholars. Doṣākara is sad at the state of affairs. Then follows an intermediary scene wherein Sudhākara's brother Sūcīvaktra appears and narrates how he won the favour of a king by flattering him.

The next scene is laid in the courthall of King Śyāmamukha. His chief priest Kuṭumbakuṭhāra enters and greets the king in a peculiar fashion. He also blesses the king that he may live long with his son Nīlapāda,

सर्वदाटनसञ्जल्पं शयनाशनकर्मसु।
युवयोः साहचर्यं स्याद्यथा मूत्रपुरीषयोः॥

After some discussion on the propriety of this simile, the king announces that his son is going to be married to the daughter of Gotraghātin, Karkaśā by name. The attainments of the bridegroom and the bride are described by the king himself thus:

अहमपि बरुडोऽस्मि स्त्री च चाण्डालपुत्री
यवनयभनजातो बालको नीलपादः।
रजकसदनपुष्टो भिल्लकैवर्ततेऽदः
प्रकृतिरिह कुले मे निर्मले का परीक्षा॥

— *sic*

माता यस्याः पुलिन्दी नट इति जनकः कथ्यते नाममात्रं
जाता या चर्मका यत् स्वजनविरहिता वेश्यया पालिता या।
क्रीतां दुर्भिक्षकाले सदसि च जगृहे गोत्रघाती ततो यां
तस्यां का वा परीक्षा ह्युभयकुलमहाशुद्धियुक्ताऽस्ति कन्या॥

Kuṭumbakuṭhāra laughs and remarks, *aho ratnam kāñcanena saṅgatam*. He then informs the king that a scholar by name Kulakalaṅka is waiting outside. The king calls forth Doṣākara and requests him to test the scholarship of the *paṇḍit*. Doṣākara puts forth certain knotty arithmetical problems in the form of *prahelikā*s and says that the problems can be solved if one is proficient in the Līlāvatī *siddhānta*. The foolish Kulakalaṅka makes no attempt to solve the problems but says he is acquainted with one Līlāvatī whom he has enjoyed previously.

The king then says that the horoscopes of the bridegroom and bride must be placed before the elders. Kulakalaṅka suggests a suitable time thus,

आयातु द्राक भर्तृहीनाऽनपत्या नारी धृत्वा भस्मपूर्णमञ्जलिभ्याम्।
सन्ध्याकाले जन्मपत्रो सभाया संशोधार्थं कन्यकाया वरस्य॥

— *sic*

The king then expresses his wish that his son should get five sons in course of time and the learned scholar says that he would definitely get *pañcatva,* which means death.

सूनुरुद्वाह्य कन्यकामिमाम्।
पञ्चत्वं प्राप्स्यते नूनं नात्र कार्या विचारणा॥

The king then asks Kulakalaṅka to fix a date for the marriage and he chooses an *amāvasyā* day falling on a Saturday with Jyeṣṭhā *nakṣatra* which is most inauspicious for marriage. The king then asks about the things to be got ready for the marriage and the priest starts the list with sesamum seeds which have no place in a marriage but are used only for a funeral ceremony. In the meantime the bride's party arrives. Just before the marriage it is decided to test the potency of the bride and the bridegroom. When the test is conducted it is found that both have defects in their genital organs and so it is decided that there is no disparity between them. The marriage is conducted duly. The *pravara* of both the families as proclaimed by the priests at the time of the marriage is quite amusing. Then comes the *svastivācana* which is equally funny.

मृत्युर्जन्मवतां वीर देहेन सह जायते।
अद्य वा श्वो शतान्ते वा मृत्युर्वै प्राणिनां ध्रुवः॥

At the conclusion of the marriage the priests ask the king for *dakṣiṇā*, but the king says that the opportunity they had in witnessing the "potency" test of the bride and bridegroom must be regarded as their *dakṣiṇā*. Doṣākara gets disgusted with the proceedings and departs saying that being in the company of the rogues itself is a sin and with this the play ends.

THE DHŪRTAVIḌAMBANA OF AMAREŚVARA

A good *prahasana* as *Dhūrtaviḍambana* has somehow eluded the attention of scholars and it has not been printed so far. The work has not been analysed so far in any book on Sanskrit drama. It has been referred to be Aufrecht,[134] Schuyler,[135] Sten Konow,[136] and Krishnamachariar.[137] Only two manuscripts of this work are available, one in Bhandarkar Oriental Research Institute.[138] and the other in Royal Asiatic Society of Bengal.[139] The present account of the play, which is attempted here for the first time, is based on the former one, which is dated CE 1832.

In the prologue of the work the author traces the genealogy of his family. He was the king of Brahmapura and belonged to Kaśyapa *gotra*. He was a descendant of Gajeśvara. Gajeśvara's son Dharmeśvara conquered the Utkala king Nṛsiṁhadeva. His son Dhyāneśvara was also a poet and wrote *nāṭakas*, *prakaraṇas* and a *vyāyoga*. His son, Amareśvara, the

134. CC, I.272.

135. See *Bibliography of Sanskrit Drama*, p. 69 : the author's name is given here is "Maheśvara".

136. *Indian Drama* pp. 186-88.

137. *HCSL*, p. 699.

138. *Descriptive Catalogue of BORI*, no. D XIV, 86, no. 510 of 1891-95.

139. *Descriptive Catalogue of RASB*, VII.5339.

author of *Dhūrtaviḍambana*, was well versed in archery and other martial arts, besides being a poet. The date of the author is uncertain. If anything can be conjectured from the style of the work, the author may be assigned to the eighteenth century.

The plot revolves around a poverty-stricken foolish king, Prajñāneśvara and his equally foolish queen, ministers and other retinue. The king keeps postponing the marriage of his only daughter Muktāvatī, since his treasury is completely empty and he is not in a position to offer even the minimum dowry for the bridegroom. In order to hush up his bankruptcy, he sets an impossible task for prospective bridegrooms that this daughter would be given in marriage only to a man who retrieves the princess's pearl necklace lost in the ocean.

In the opening scene, the king enters his courtroom and appreciates its beautiful structure. His chief priest, Jihvāsaṁvalana, who is, true to his name, a glutton, intervenes and says that there is no use in the courtroom unless it is made up of jaggery. He complains that he has been virtually starving for the past two days since his maidservant has not been bringing the leftover food from the palace. He also justifies the act of partaking the food brought by the maid-servant, which according to him, has been sanctioned by Manu himself.

उच्छिष्टं श्वपचस्पृष्टमन्नं शुनकदूषितम्।
दासीसंपर्कमात्रेण शुद्ध्यतीत्यब्रवीन्मनु ॥

According to him *parānna-bhojana* has nothing equal to it.

न तादृग्राज्यसम्पत्तौ न तादक् पुत्रसम्भवे।
परान्नभोजने यादक् सुखं विप्रस्य जायते ॥
प्रभाते भोजनं स्नानं मध्याह्ने भोजनं जपः।
सायाह्ने भोजनं सन्ध्या निशीथे भोजनं तपः ॥

He also complains that the consumer articles are in short supply and the shops have been closed down for want of commodities. The king is worried that he may not get enough foodstuff for his own family. The minister, Premakaṇṭhaka allays his fears by saying that such a situation may not arise since there has been a mass exodus of people from the town due to the non-availability of essential commodities.

The minister then informs the king that Prince Ratitilaka from the neighbouring kingdom has come to their town along with his friend Lohajaṅghama. He has seen Muktāvatī and has fallen in love with her. He has also retrieved the pearl necklace from the sea and has sent it to the king through his friend Lohajaṅghama. The king wants to dissuade the prince under some pretext or other. He employs a jeweller, Pūñjīcoraka to verify the weight of the recovered necklace. The jeweller has instructions to steal a few pearls from the necklace and show that it falls short of the expected weight, upon which the king will reject the marriage proposal of his daughter. But his plan fails as Lohajaṅghama finds out the truth and takes the jeweller to task. Others too join in the quarrel and it becomes a free for all. The minister, the *purohita* and the jeweller are all after the pearls and the angry Lohajaṅghama snatches away the necklace. Now the *purohita* resorts to a different tactic. He says that the princess is not fit for marriage since there is some defect in her horoscope. He would rather offer his own daughter (to Prince Ratitilaka) whose accomplishments are far superior to those of the princess

बहुलपञ्चदशीन्दुनिभं मुखं शिशिरपद्मदलोपममीक्षणम्, etc.

After Lohajaṅghama's departure, the king feels sorry that if the marriage were to be celebrated with the available resources, he would become a total bankrupt. The only hope in the form of the pearl necklace is also lost. He is consoled by the minister who assures him that he would take steps to stop the marriage at any cost and even if it is celebrated, he would separate the couple. He is after all "Premakaṇṭhaka" and he has the assistance of the royal priest and Pūñjīcoraka.

The second act opens with Prince Ratitilaka and his friend Lohajaṅghama on the scene. The prince laments that he has forgotten everything about his own kingdom ever since he entertained love for Princess Muktāvatī. The king and his company are utterly foolish and it is very difficult to satisfy them. But he is prepared to make any sacrifice for the sake of his sweetheart.

Now the king and his company arrive along with Muktāvātī. The king asks the *purohita* to fix a suitable time for the marriage. The *purohita,* as per the eariler arrangement, purposely chooses that very same day which happens to be inauspicious. Then the minister and the priest clamour for the cotton cloth to be presented by the king and there is a brief quarrel between them. The king intervenes and orders them to stop their quarrel, and make arrangements for the marriage. The priest reads the funeral *mantra*s and the bridegroom denounces him as a *brāhmaṇāpasada*. The prince is appalled at the foolishness of the people around him and feels that Princess Muktāvatī is the only exception.

> दुग्धपयोधौ जातं यद्वत्सुधया समं विषं घोरम्।
> अन्याऽमृतलतिकेयं तद्वज्जाता विषक्षेत्रे ॥

Now it is evident that the king wants to postpone the nuptials as long as possible since he does not have anything to present to his daughter as she goes away with her husband.

Knowing this fully well, Prince Ratitilaka devises a plan in consultation with his beloved and friends. Meanwhile at the palace, the king asks the minister to break the marriage. The minister accuses the princess of spoiling the name of her family by her illicit love affairs, and makes sure that her husband also hears this news. The minister then says that he is prepared to perform any *prāyaścitta* for the blemish that has befallen the royal family. The royal priest suggests death as the *prāyaścitta*. After some humorous exchanges it is agreed that the sin arising out of the princess's act must be divided equally among the four, the king, the queen, the minister and the priest. Meanwhile it is reported that Prince Ratitilaka is dead. The king and his company feel happy that their false propaganda has produced the desired effect and each one takes credit for the success of the plan. Jihvāsaṁvalana is happy that he has got an opportunity of taking the *śrāddha bhojana,* and demands that the princess should perform the *śrāddha* at once. Prince Ratitilaka, who is not actually dead, comes now in the disguise of the brāhmaṇa *śrāddhabhoktā,* and the princess appears in the guise of Lohajaṅghama. The priest is enraged at the appearance of a rival *bhoktā* and after a brief quarrel the prince and the princess make good their escape. Lohajaṅghama appears in the disguise of Muktāvatī. After a small incident which is rather obscene the king hears a tumult in the harem. Lohajaṅghama has dropped the princess's dress and has escaped. But the foolish people in the harem think that the princess had been killed by some unknown demon and go about weeping. Lohajaṅghama then joins his friend who is waiting elsewhere along with Muktāvatī. The prince thanks his friend profusely for his great help and expresses his joy at the success of his plan. The play comes to an end with the usual Bharatavākya.

With most of the later *prahasana*s dealing with the degraded life led by pseudo-religious men, the *Dhūrtaviḍambana* presents a refreshing contrast with a new theme. The *hāsya* in the play is evoked mainly through the characters, viz. the foolish king and his counsel. *Dhūrtaviḍambana* is probably one of the very few *prahasana*s which are fit to be staged. Unlike most of the later *prahasanas*, the farcical element is presented with a fairly good story value. The style is simple and lucid.

THE KUKṢIMBHARABHAIKṢAVA PRAHASANA

Three manuscripts of *Kukṣimbharabhaikṣava Prahasana* are available in the Oriental Research Institute, Mysore.[140] Among them the one in the Grantha script is well preserved and is largely depended on for the present write-up of the play; the other two have also been useful in fixing the correct reading.

The author, Venkappiah,[141] was a well-known figure during the days of Haider Ali in Mysore. He started his life in a small way as a clerk in the Mysore Administration. After Krishnaraja Wodayar came to power in 1734, Venkappiah gained prominence and became the *pradhāna* of the Mysore State. Under the next king Nañjarāja Wodayar too, he held various posts. His sphere of influence extended to almost every field. He even fought a war against the Marāṭhās in 1771 and successfully negotiated for a peaceful settlement. When Haider Ali came to power, Venkappiah suffered a set-back in his life. He was stripped of the titles and was transferred to a distant corner of the state on demotion. He died a sad man.

In spite of his hectic political activity, Venkappiah sparkles as a prolific writer of merit. He has contributed to every branch of *rūpaka* excepting the *nāṭaka* and the *prakaraṇa*. His other works include *Sudhājharī*, a prose work, *Kuśalavacampū*, *Alaṁkāra-Maṇidarpaṇa*, *Jagannātha-Vijayakāvya*, and *Hanumat Śatakam*, besides

140. (i) No. P2773 — Palm leaf — Grantha, (ii) No. SB 192 — Paper — Devanagari, (iii) No. SB 342 — Paper — Kannada. For a detailed account of the play, refer "An eighteenth century farce from Karnataka" *The Mysore Orientalist*, vol. XI, 1978, by the present writer.

141. On Venkappiah's life and works, see M.P. Sastry, *Quarterly Journal of the Mythic Society*, vol. XXXI, Bangalore, July, 1940.

a number of works in Kannada.

Opening his work with an interesting *śloka* on Śrī Kṛṣṇa's role in the Arjuna-Subhadrā episode, the author traces the origin of *hāsya* to three Purāṇic episodes. The play has a *viṣkambha* which is generally prohibited in a *prahasana* according to Viśvanātha.[142]

Kukṣimbhara, a Buddhist monk, is deeply in love with a harlot, Kāmakalikā, who is zealously guarded by a foreigner, Śṛgālakapidhāna. The monk's erstwhile love, Kurkurī, comes to know of this and wants to wreak vengeance on him. She disguises herself as the foreigner, suddenly appears before the monk and takes him to task for coveting Kāmakalikā. Meanwhile the real Śṛgālakapidhāna arrives on the scene and seeing that he is impersonated by somebody, becomes angry and beats up the disguised Kurkurī. Recognising her from her voice, Kukṣimbhara goes for her help. Knowing from Kurkurī that the *bhikṣu* is aspiring for Kāmakalikā, the foreigner severely thrashes Kukṣimbhara and departs. Meanwhile one of his disciples who had been sent earlier to fetch Kāmakalikā, succeeds in bringing her there. The girl is surprised that even a monk is enamoured of her and so, readily offers herself to him. The teacher is happy at the obtainment of *guru-dakṣiṇā* from his disciple and confers the lordship of his *maṭha* on him.

Within the framework of this main theme are included a number of incidents to enhance the comic effect of the play. The way the Buddhist monk solves the disputes between men of different religious sects is amusing. A Liṅgāyata, a Kāpālika, a Kālāmukha, a Jaina, and a Cārvāka are all swamped by the Buddhist monk summarily. His disciples Jambūka and Bhallūka prove a fitting second fiddle. One such situation may be given here as a sample case.

---

142. See *SD*, VI. 264-65.

Two foreigners enter quarrelling with each other over the relative superiority of the enjoyment of another's wife and that of a harlot. The first one says that the *para-strī-gamana* is free from the worry of venereal diseases. The other one argues that in *para-strī-gamana*, there is constant worry about the arrival of the lawful husband. The first one retorts by saying that in resorting to the harlots, there is loss of money and health. Kukṣimbhara intervenes and brings about a compromise by saying that there is merit in both *para-strī-gamana* and *paṇya-strī-gamana*. They are the two ways of knowing the Ultimate (*paramārtha*).

पण्यस्त्रीति परस्त्रीति पन्था एव परं द्विधा।
परमार्थविदां तत्र परानन्दः प्रयोजनम्॥

Bhallūka finds fault with the teaching of his master. According to him both *paṇya-strī-gamana* and *para-strī-gamana* are defective. Enjoyment of the maid-servant is the best way since it does not involve any expenditure and is free from the worry of the diseases and the lawful husband or the mistress of the harlot-house. The foreigners appreciate his stand and depart.

The play is replete with good similes, as in,

यथा सुगन्धैः पिहितेऽपि तूर्णं पलाण्डुगन्धः प्रसरींसरीति।
तथा बहिर्गच्छति गूढवार्ता विरुद्धधर्माश्रयिणां जनानाम्॥

There is novelty in the nature of characters introduced. For instance the Europeans referred to as *pāścātya*s or *hūṇa*s in the play are introduced as characters probably for the first time in a Sanskrit play. The play is fairly long and employs almost all the well-known methods of evoking *hāsya*. The play can be made suitable for stage by removing certain unnecessary scenes.

THE CAṆḌĀNURAÑJANA

Caṇḍānurañjana of Ghanaśyāma is another *prahasana* abounding in vulgarity. Ghanaśyāma was the son of Kamalā and Kāśī

Maheśvara of Mauna Bhārgava family. He had two wives, Sundarī and Kamalā, both of whom were scholars in Sanskrit and composed a Commentary on *Viddhaśālabhañjikā* in emulation of their husband. Besides being a poet, Ghanaśyāma was a skilled politician too. He was the minister of King Tukhoji of Tanjore (1728-35). Ghanaśyāma was a prolific writer. He wrote 64 works in Sanskrit, 20 in Prākṛt and 25 in other dialects.[143] His works include commentaries on *Śākuntala, Uttararāmacarita, Veṇīsaṁhāra, Bhojacampū, Kādambarī* and *Viddhaśālabhañjikā*. The present work, *Caṇḍānurañjana*, of course, does not bring him much credit.

The Plot[144]

After the formal *nāndī*, three libertines, Mārjāra, Barkara and Karṇaka go on narrating their own experiences with women. A Digambara also enters and joins them in criticising the people they come across, in a vulgar language. Granthaśiśna, another libertine, joins the lot. Mārjāra and others then see the followers of Madhva and Rāmānuja coming to a tank for bath and resort to vulgar descriptions. So is the case with a Gosvāmin who is charged with lecturing to widows only on the glory of God. Two others by name Vakraśiśna Bhaṭṭa and Takracorāvadhānin come there, reading extracts from a profane text called *Mehanaprayoga*.

Enter then a grammarian, Nijastrīyāgīn and a logician, Parastrīgāmin using vulgar language in the guise of Śāstric terminology. Then enter a doctor, Vakradanta and a Śrotriya

143. For further details on Ghanaśyāma, See *HCSL*, 248. About *Damaruka*, another interesting work of Ghanaśyāma, see General Introduction.

144. The present account of the play is based on the transcript copy of a MS. of the work from Tanjore (No. 4629. See Tanjore VIII. 3620).

Bhagnadanta with their topsy-turvy professional jargon. A poet Tātajātakavi is also introduced to fill the bill.

Mārjāra now recollects that he has to send a girl to an old man by name, Dīrghaśephas whose wife is fond of other men. He plans to send Barkara, his friend, dressed as a woman to the old man. The old man really thinks Barkara to be a woman. Then follows a description of the evening. The play ends here abruptly.

On the whole, it has to be pointed out that there is nothing significant in this play, excepting that the author has a knack of introducing vulgarity in almost all passages and even in the names of the characters.

THE MUṆḌITA PRAHASANA

The *Muṇḍita Prahasana* of Śivajyotirvid belongs to the nineteenth century. The present account of the work is based on a manuscript preserved in the Bhandarkar Oriental Research Institute Library, Poona.[145]

Plot

Gaṇḍakīdāsa, a pseudo Vaiṣṇava ascetic, is deeply in love with Līlāvatī, a lady belonging to the Jaina merchant community. His daily prayer consists of nothing but an appeal to Śrī Kṛṣṇa to fulfil his wish, namely to have Līlāvatī.

कृष्णावतारे किल गोपकन्याः सहस्रशः कामितवानसि त्वम्।
स्वेच्छामयत्वान्मम तामथैकां त्वद्भक्तियुक्तस्य न किं ददासि॥

— I.8

He would rather stop praying to Kṛṣṇa who gives only *mukti*. Who wants *mukti* which is bereft of both pleasure and pain and which may have to be compared to the *ajāgalastana*?

---

145. No. 83 of A 1883-84, BORI library.

अविदितसुखदुःखं निर्गुणं वस्तु किञ्चिज्जडमतिरिह कश्चिन्मोक्ष इत्याचचक्षे ।
मम तु मतमनङ्गस्मेरतारुण्यघूर्णन्मदकलमदिराक्षीनीविमोक्षो हि मोक्षः ॥

— I.11 (See *Śṛṅgārarasaṣṭaka, śl.* 1 and *Mahāsubhāṣitasaṁgraha, śl.* 3343)

Sages of yore, themselves enjoying pleasure of life, prescribed stringent rules for fellow ascetics. A virulent ascetic like Gaṇḍakīdāsa need not follow them. He then decides to seek the help of Viṭṭhalī, his erstwhile sweetheart and a female ascetic, in winning the love of Līlāvatī.

In the beginning of the second act, the ascetic is seen anxiously waiting for Viṭṭhalī. She brings the happy news that she would get Līlāvatī there, under some pretext or other. Gaṇḍakīdāsa's happiness is marred by the unwarranted entry of his elder brother Haridāsa, another degraded monk living at Benares. With great difficulty he disposes of Haridāsa. But the latter grows suspicious and hides himself in the garden at the backyard of the *maṭha* to watch the movement of his brother. Viṭṭhalī and Līlāvatī arrive after some time and offer their salutations to the teacher. Viṭṭhalī requests Gaṇḍakīdādsa to initiate Līlāvatī by which she would become spiritually strong. The teacher sends Līlāvatī to the *maṭha*-pond for an ablution preparatory to the *mantra-dīkṣā* ceremony, and enjoys the bathing scene from a vantage point. When the girl is ready for the *mantra-dīkṣā,* he convinces her that he must first worship the deity presiding over each limb of her body. The girl is slowly stripped of her dress. The hesitant Līlavatī is deceived by the cunning talks of Gaṇḍakīdāsa, who misquotes some texts to vindicate his stand. He then takes her to his private garden resort for a fuller course of *dīkṣā.*

The third act opens with the appearance of a Jaina monk, Bhadanta, who is the family priest of Līlāvatī. He is worried about the absence of Līlāvatī at the congregation that day and suspects some foul play. He straightaway comes to Gaṇḍakīdāsa's *maṭha* and surmises that the rogue had already spoiled the innocent girl. Finding that he cannot outwit Bhadanta who exposes all his weaknesses, Gaṇḍakīdāsa surrenders to him and requests him to prescribe a suitable time for his departure from the town. The clever monk who suspects that he might elope with the girl, suggests the third part of the night for the purpose, hoping that they would be wound up by the night police squad.

Just as Gaṇḍakīdāsa heaves a long sigh of relief at the departure of the Jaina monk, enters Haridāsa professing to know every act of his brother. He wants to blackmail Gaṇḍakīdāsa that he would report the matter to the king if he is not allowed to enjoy Līlāvatī. The clever Gaṇḍakīdāsa pacifies him offering some other obscene concessions, and sends him away. Līlāvatī is sent home now and is asked to be ready to elope with him at the dead of night. The two prepare to escape as planned but are caught by the police who had been alerted by the Jaina monk. The king too arrives there and enquires into the matter. The king's aide suggests that Gaṇḍakīdāsa and Līlāvatī be made to sit on a donkey and paraded in the streets of the city. The undaunted Gaṇḍakīdāsa pleads guilty and cuts some obscene joke. According to him, it is a man's bounden duty to give sexual pleasure to a woman and that it is equivalent to *Īśvara-pūjā*.

येन केन प्रकारेण यस्य कस्यापि देहिनः।
सन्तोषं जनयेत्प्राज्ञस्तदेवेश्वरपूजनम्॥
— III.19

He further says,

स्मरार्तां विह्वलां दीनां यो न कामयते स्त्रियम्।
भ्रूणहा स तु विज्ञेय इति मनुनाप्ययं धर्मोऽङ्गीकृतः॥
— *sic* III.20

The king now asks Līlāvatī what she would like to do now. She says that she would rather live with the monk since she would not be accepted by her community anymore. In a lighter vein, the king orders that the monk should carry the girl on his shoulders and dance and the latter gladly agrees to undergo this punishment. As he dances, he sings in praise of the king in *daṇḍaka* metre. The play comes to an end with the usual Bharatavākya.

Now for the literary merits of the play, there are quite a few verses which are appealing for their poetic fancy. When Brahmā created Lilāvatī's face, his lotus seat began to shrink and he was in a fix. A lump of charming material intended originally for the thin waist was left behind and in utter confusion he made it into two balls and fixed on her chest.

> जानीमो वयमेणशावनयनामध्यं कृशं वीक्ष्य तं
> पुष्टिं कर्तुमथो धृतं करयुगे गोलद्वयं वेधसा।
> एतस्या मुखचन्द्रकान्तिनिवहात संकोचिते स्वासने
> पद्मे तच्चलचित्तवृत्तिवशतो भ्रान्त्या हृदि स्थापितम्॥
> — II.12

The limbs of the heroine are fancied as the nine planets in the following verse:

> भास्वन्मुखेन्दुकृतमङ्गलमादधाना सौम्याकृतिर्गुरुपयोधरभारनम्रा।
> काव्यं धिया मृदु शनैश्चरपादपद्मा वेणी तमश्चयवती स्मरकेतुयष्टिः॥
> — II.13

Some of the observations of the poet are noteworthy for their humour, for instance,

> अप्राप्तशाल्योदनस्य कोद्रवा अपि बहुमता भवन्ति
> — I. bet 25 and 26

and

> अपमानं पुरस्कृत्य मानं कृत्वा तु पृष्ठतः।
> स्वकार्यं साधयेत्प्राज्ञः कार्यध्वंसो हि मूर्खता॥ — III.6

The *ślokas* in the *daṇḍaka* metre towards the end of the play are quite pleasing for their sound and sense. To quote just one instance,

जय श्रीमहाराज विख्यातकीर्तिंप्रतापैः परिक्षिप्तरात्रीशभानो ।
विभूषामणीनां रुचा भासितान्तदिशामण्डल श्रीशभक्ताग्रवर्तिन् ॥
— III.23

THE KĀLEYAKUTŪHALA OF BHARADVĀJA

The *Kāleyakautūhala* probably belongs to the nineteenth century. Not much is known about the author. The work was first edited in 1882, in the *Kāvyetihāsa-Saṁgraha*, vol. 5, from Poona. It was again edited in 1960, from Japan[146] (ed. Y. Ojihara, Kyoto, 1960). The present account, however, is based on the transcript copy of a manuscript[147] from the Bhandarkar Oriental Research Institute Library, Poona.

The play opens with *nāndī śloka* dedicated to Goddess Pārvatī. After a conventional prologue, the main character of the play, Viratisāgara enters the scene. The pseudo monk boasts of his powers to hold sway over his disciples and devotees alike. He now awaits his devotees, largely the womenfolk, who are discussing among themselves how they have cheated people in their household and brought valuable presents for their preceptor. Enter now the ladies and offer their salutations to Viratisāgara. He correctly diagnoses the problem of one of them, Hemalatā, whose husband has, of late, become indifferent towards her since she has not borne him a child yet. The teacher asks the girl to enter his private room for *mantra-upadeśa* which alone can solve her problem. Obviously Viratisāgara has planned to enjoy the girl under the pretext of *mantra-dīkṣā* but the presence of other waiting devotees for

146. Cf. *NCC*, vol. IV, p. 81.

147. Cf. D.XIV, 58, *BORI Descriptive Catalogue*, no. 116 of 1875-76.

the *tīrtha-prasāda* upsets his plan. The teacher says that she may have to wait and Hemalatā takes leave of him.

Enters now Anaṅgasenā, the regular female companion of Viratisāgara. She entertains the monk with a *vīṇā* recital. A Bauddha *bhikṣu*, who is equally corrupt as Viratisāgara, and a boyhood friend of his, arrives now and reports that he had seen a girl in the house of a merchant the previous day and fell in love with her. He seeks Viratisāgara's advice on how to get her. Viratisāgara asks him to reveal his *kula-dharma* first and the *bhikṣu* too obliges him by saying,

मन्त्रो न तन्त्रं न च किमपि ज्ञानं ध्यानं च नो कोऽपि गुरुप्रसादः।
मद्यं पिबामो महिलां रमयामो मोक्षं च यामः कुलमार्गलाभः॥

He also quotes the famous *Karpūramañjarī* verse, *raṇḍā caṇḍā* . . . , etc., and futher says,

मुक्तिं भणन्ति हरिब्रह्ममुखा हि देवाः ध्यानेन वेदपठनेन क्रतुक्रियाभिः।
एकेन केवलमुमादयितेन दृष्टो मोक्षं समं सुरतकेलिसुरारसाभ्याम्॥

Viratisāgara then requests Anaṅgasenā to act on behalf of the monk and carry his love message to his beloved. She refuses but the *bhikṣu* persuades her. The angry girl slaps him on his face. Reeling under the blow, the *bhikṣu* catches hold of Sadānanda, Viratisāgara's disciple, and embraces him tightly mistaking him to be his beloved. Anaṅgasenā punches some more blows on him and brings him back to his senses. The monk feels ashamed of his acts. Being then advised by Viratisāgara not to get involved in love affairs but to pursue his religious life sincerely, the Buddhist monk departs.

Next to enter is a merchant by name Kinnaradāsa who is worried about his childlessness. Viratisāgara advises him to send his wife to the *maṭha* for *mantra-dīkṣā* and asks him to pay a fee of 10,000 gold coins. The merchant agrees and departs.

Enter now Tāṇḍyāyana and his impertinent son. The son

complains to Viratisāgara that his father always beats him up for some trivial reason and asks him whether his (Viratisāgara's) devotees receive only such instructions at the *maṭha*. The father reports that the boy is negligent in studies. The boy, on the other hand, feels that he has already completed his course of study and is now ready for marriage. The father complains that the boy coughs throughout the night and disturbs him while making love to his wife. Viratisāgara advises the father to be more considerate towards his son. He advises the boy to be more obedient towards his father and then sends them away.

Following an announcement from the *nepathya*, the king and his retinue arrive at the *maṭha*. The king offers some gold coins at the feet of the teacher. The monk then blesses the king and asks him the purpose of his visit. The minister reports that the king has been pining for a son for a long time. Viratisāgara, as before, asks the king to send his queen to the *Maṭha* for *mantra-dīkṣā*. As the bards announce the advent of *sandhyā*, the king and his company take leave of the teacher and Viratisāgara himself rises for the evening worship. The play comes to an end with the usual Bharatavākya.

THE SUBHAGĀNANDA

The *Subhagānanda*[148] seems to be a very late work, probably belonging to the nineteenth century. The author, Govinda Śrīvatasāṅka of the Gautama *gotra* was a native of Kashmir and was the son of Vāsudeva and Mahāmbikā.

The main character of the play is as usual a *yati*, Kāmāraṇya (Forest of Lust) by name. His illicit love affair with a mendicant lady, Kaṇḍūlakacchā has resulted in the latter's pregnancy. But what worries Kāmāraṇya is that he is not in a position to

148. The present account of the work is based on a single manuscript available in the Tanjore Saraswathi Mahal Library, no. D.4641.

arrange for the *Puṁsavana Sīmanta* function. In his confused state, he goes to a garden and mistakes a she-bear sitting on a tree, to be his beloved and goes to embrace it. The bear pounces on him, badly mauls him and runs away leaving Kāmāraṇya unconscious. His disciple who happens to come there brings him back to his consciousness.

On the way to a temple nearby, they meet many people, — a Jaina monk, a *paurāṇika* by name Bhaṭṭaśṛgāla, a doctor by name Rogarāśi, and finally Kaṇḍūlakacchā herself. One Bhaṭṭarudra enters and narrates how he was duped by a monk who ran away with his wife. On a closer examination, he identifles Kāmāraṇya as that monk and Kaṇḍūlakacchā as his own wife. As they quarrel, a police officer comes there and orders all of them to proceed to the king's court. Bhaṭṭarudra complains to the king that Kāmāraṇya has abducted his wife. The chief judge, Uṣṭrāsya, is called upon to deliver the judgement. Uṣṭrāsya quotes some unknown texts like the *Ulūkasmṛti* and announces that since the lady has already entered the *saṁnyāsāśrama* she cannot go back to the *gṛhasthāśrama* once again and live with Bhaṭṭarudra. The disappointed Bhaṭṭarudra leaves the scene.

Bhaṭṭaśṛgālaka then advises the king that he must arrange for the *sīmanta* function of the two ascetics since otherwise the king will incur sin. Then Kāmāraṇya requests that since he is a *yati* the *sīmanta* must be performed in strict secrecy. The king agrees and orders his minister that the following announcement must be made in the city:

अस्यां कण्डूलकच्छायां कामारण्येन योगिना।
स्वयमुत्पादितो गर्भः निजाश्रमविभूतये॥
अयं रहस्यव्यापारो न प्रकाश्यः कथञ्चन।
अन्यथा मृतिदण्डे वः स्यातां भूपालशासनात्॥

Kāmāraṇya is satisfied and the king orders the minister to

expedite the arrangements of the *sīmanta* function. An astrologer is called forth who, as usual, fixes an inauspicious time for the function. A priest arrives and pronounces peculiar *āśīṣa*. Now one of the invitees, a lady by name Varṇagāminī, is afflicted by hunger and feels that she cannot wait till the function is over. She acts as though she is possessed by a spirit and shouts at the top of her voice. Kāmāraṇya, out of fear, asks what *aparādha* has been committed by him. The lady says that the presiding deity of the town has not been propitiated by the offer of food articles. She then exhausts all the sweetmeats got ready for the function and departs. With the pronouncement of a farcical blessing, the priest concludes the function:

sarve grahāḥ samavagrahāḥ tadaśubhasthānaphaladāḥ nāśakāriṇo bhavantu.

All the invitees say *tathāstu* and bless the couple by throwing *akṣata*s.

There is a good number of humorous situations and verses in the play. The bear-episode, the conversation between Kaṇḍūlakacchā and her friend in the course of which the latter extracts the truth from the former that she is pregnant, the peculiar descriptions of the doctor, the way Bhaṭṭarudra is deceived by the antics of the police officer, the farcical *sīmanta* function — contribute to the comic effect of the play. This is how the doctor, Rogarāśi is ridiculed:

यत्र यत्र जनता विरला स्यात्, यत्र यत्र कुपिता अपि रोगाः।
यत्र यत्र मृतयो बहुसंख्यास्तत्र तत्र हि तवैव चिकित्सा॥

The king is no less comical. He is described thus:

निर्यद्दूषिकनेत्रलीनमशकामुत्सारयन्नादिनो
अत्यस्तेन करद्वयेन वपुषा ग्राम्यं हसन् सूकरम्।
आशागर्दभनिः स्वनैर्मुखरयन् भल्लूकवक्त्रः सभा —
वेद्यामुल्लसति प्रजापतिरसौ युक्तैर्जनैः सेवितः॥

— *sic*

He addresses his minister thus:

अयि स्वर्गाङ्गभरो मे त्वयि विन्यस्त एव हि।
वध्वां मे जनयापत्यमवशोऽहमितः परम्॥

The minister replies:

यद्येवं हन्त यन्त्राधः पतितोमूषकोऽस्म्यहं
ततः पक्षोऽस्तु पर्यङ्के पूर्वस्ते मयि तूत्तरः।

The union of Kāmāraṇya and Kaṇḍūlakacchā is extolled thus —

मासोपवासिनी श्रेष्ठा विश्वस्तानां व्रतित्वतः।
यतिनस्तत्र गर्भश्चेत इक्षोः फलमुदीरितम्॥

This is how Kaṇḍūlakacchā is decorated for her *sīmanta* function,

गर्भभाजनसंवीतां एकनेत्रार्पिताञ्जनाम्।
लाक्षारससमालिप्तश्यामाननपयोधराम्॥
सुधामक्षीगैरिकादिबिन्दुभिश्चित्रिताननाम्।
नासावसरसूत्राग्रलम्बमानवराटिकाम्॥

The description of Kāmāraṇya when he gets ready for the function is equally funny:

नीलाम्बरपरीधानः कण्ठे बद्धकपर्दिकः।
सारमेयसिरातन्तुनिर्मितब्रह्मसूत्रभृत्॥

THE VINODARAṄGA

The present account of the *Vinodaraṅga* of Sundaradeva is based on the microfilm copy of a manuscript available in the India Office Library, London.[149] The date of the work is unknown.

The main character is a priest, Dhūrtāvataṁśa, who is in love with Rāgamañjarī, the daughter of Luṇṭhakopādhyāya. In the opening scene, Dhūrtāvataṁśa expresses to his disciple, his wish to meet her. Enters now Kalahavratā,

149. Skt. MSS. no. K.7424. See also Aufrecht I, p. 577.

Dhūrtāvataṁśa's wife. Being provoked by the student, the irate lady beats up both the teacher and the disciple and drives them away. On their way they meet Rāgamañjarī who sympathises with the teacher for the blows he received from his wife and offers to serve him a sumptuous dinner with meat, fish, onions, garlic and all other prohibited stuff. Enters now a doctor, Vaidyapāśa who boasts that when treated by him, his patients would become guests of Vaivasvatapurī (of Yama). Many characters appear now, a Śaivite, a Vaiṣṇavite, a Mādhva and others. All these people proceed to the house of one Vinodaraṅga, who is celebrating her *prathama ṛtu* (puberty). Many people are assembled there and quarrels erupt. The first act ends here.

The scene of the second act is laid in the court of a local king who is celebrating the *garbhādhāna* (nuptials) ceremony of one of his *gaṇikā*s. Scholars in Vyākaraṇa, Vedānta, Mīmāṁsā and Nyāya discuss the epistemology of their respective faiths (*pramāṇa* and *prameya*). As is usual in a *prahasana* an astrologer fixes the most inauspicious time for the function. A Digambara *saṁnyāsin* is given the first chance to share the bed with the harlot. Dhūrtāvataṁśa who acts as the chief priest demands a fitting *dakṣiṇā* for his services and takes Rāgamañjarī as the fee and departs happily.

THE HĀSYAKAUTŪHALA PRAHASANA

A manuscript of the *Hāsyakautūhala Prahasana* is housed in the Anup Sanskrit Library, Bikaner.[150] The author Viṭṭhalakṛṣṇa hails from Gokula of the Telugu country, according to the prologue of the play. He seems to have earned the title Vidyāvāgīśa. He was patronised by King Sujānasiṁha, son of Paharsiṁha and probably was a ruler of a petty state in Rajasthan during the eighteenth or nineteenth century.

150. No. 3183. A transcript copy of this manuscipt is used for the present account.

The two-act play deals with a funny account of several rogues and the presentation of their cases before a foolish king, Dhr̥tarāṣṭra who has an equally foolish minister in Andhabuddhi. The silly nature of the complaints brought before the king and the peculiar punishments meted out to the offenders by the king and the minister contribute to the comic effect of the play. Sometimes men found guilty turn out to be innocent people. One novelty in the play is that the *sūtradhāra* has a role in the main play itself and the Bharatavākya is also pronounced by him.

THE MITHYĀCĀRA PRAHASANA

The *Mithyācāra Prahasana*[151] of Vaidyanātha follows the beaten track of the earlier *prahasanas*. We have a corrupt monk Mithyācāra[152] who is in love with a young widow, a foolish doctor Prāṇahara, a pseudo philosopher Prajñāndha Daṇḍī, an ill-equipped astrologer Nakṣatrasūcī, and ignorant teacher Kuṭhārabhaṭṭa, and a few more people of this sort.[153] A farcical marriage

---

151. The present account is based on the Xerox copy of the MS of this *prahasana* obtained from Bombay University Library. (See also Aufrecht I, 455.)

152. His philosophy is set forth thus.

    मिष्टान्नभोजनमनुक्रमलभ्यवामाडिण्डीरपुञ्जविशदश्च विशालतत्यः।
    सौधाः सुधाकरकर्णकलिता वलक्षाः पुष्पैरिदं गुरुपदं भुवि नागरीणाम्॥ — *sic*

153. The doctor boasts thus:

    रोगाभिभूते ममौषधस्य प्रभावतः प्राणिति नैव कश्चित्।
    उपक्षते चेच्छमनः कदाचित् परन्त्वहं प्राणहरो हि तस्य॥

    The philosopher says:

    शास्त्रं कणादमुनिनिर्मितमस्ति किञ्चित् प्राभाकरश्च मम कर्णपुटे कदापि।
    नैवागतः श्रुतिपथं प्रति शास्त्रमल्पं कल्यं करोति किल दीक्षितकौमुदीयम्॥

    Ths astrologer prescribes the day of an eclipse as suitable for marriage.

    According to the teacher, taking the narcotic drugs, taking liquor, eating meat and deceiving others by uttering falsehood are the four Vedas.

between one Paṇḍitammanya and his widowed cousin also finds place in the play. All the ingredients of a farcical marriage like the choice of an inauspicious time for marriage (it happens to be an eclipse-day), a peculiar presentation (*asmin kanyāpradhānasamaye sahasragrāma-bhikṣāṭanāya tubhyamaham sampradade*), the inauspicious *svastivacana* (*acrireṇaiya raṇḍā bhavatu iyam*), the arrangement of the crematory bed alongside the nuptial bed, the quarrel for *dakṣiṇā* and the priest eventually taking away the bride as fee — are inevitably found in this two-act play. The literary value of this *prahasana* is almost nil.

THE LOKARAÑJANA PRAHASANA

The following summary of the *Lokarañjana Prahasana* of Śrīnivāsācārya is based on two incomplete manuscripts available in the Oriental Research Institute, Mysore.[154]

Two Liṅgāyata *saṁnyāsins*, Siddhaliṅgadeva and Kuhanācāra enter the house of a lady Śivadattā for *bhikṣā* and begin to quarrel since each one of them suspects that the other might forcibly enjoy her in his absence. Siddhaliṅga finally suggests that they both may share her. Meanwhile Śivadattā's husband Gaurīpāda enters the house suddenly and Siddhaliṅga alone succeeds in finding a hiding place. Kuhanācāra is caught and produced in the court by Gaurīpāda. At his departure, Siddhaliṅga comes out of the hiding place and persuades Śivadattā to elope with him. In order to avoid the suspicion of the neighbours, he dresess himself as a woman and both of them leave the house.

Danger comes now in the form of a drunken Musalman, Hammīr Khan, who mistakes Siddhaliṅga to be a lady and wants to enjoy him forcibly. Being not satisfied he demands

---

154. (i) No. SP 946, (ii) P. 1196.

that the younger girl who accompanied him (Śivadattā) must be produced before him at once. Since she had already run to a safer place as advised by Siddhaliṅga, he appeases the Musalman by pointing out to a harlot, Durbhagā, who comes that way. Hammīr Khan forcibly enjoys her and leaves the scene. The lady then takes Siddhaliṅga to task and beats him up heavily. Meanwhile the police come there searching for a thief who robbed a merchant. Observing Siddhaliṅga's disguised form they mistake him to be the thief and take him to the court. Kuhanācāra who is already there greets Siddhaliṅga with obvious glee. The play breaks off here.

6

Theory and Practice of the Vīthī

Vīthī and the Open Air Theatre

THE *vīthī* was probably the firstever attempt as an open air theatrical device. The theory says that the playform has a minimum number of characters and is confined to just one act. *Vīthī* perhaps died early lending its characteristics to the *prahasana*. But the features of *vīthī* perhaps to inspire the Indian theatre in many ways. Prominent features of the *vīthī* are:

i. simple theme
ii. fewer characters
iii. absence of a regular stage
iv. question and answer technique
v. folk elements
vi. a mixture of all the *rasa*s
vii. witty dialogues
viii. riddles to sustain the interest of the audience
ix. unexpected twists and turns
x. characters trying to outwit each other
xi. re-interpretation of speeches
xii. euphemism

We may observe that many of these features were slowly adopted by the various theatre forms of the different regions of India. The common feature of all these forms is that most of them are performed not in regular theatres but only in open grounds or street corners.

Rāmlīlā is performed during the Daśahrā festival (Dussehra) in Uttar Pradesh. In Delhi it is performed in the Rāmlīlā grounds. The main theme is the ultimate victory of the good over the evil; the former represented by Rāma and latter by Rāvaṇa. It is an interesting mixture of music, mime and narration. The *Rāmlīlā* performance, apart from being rich in the dancing steps, is also rich in its costumes, jewellery, masks, headgear, make-up and decoration.

Rasa dance of Manipur is replete with both *nṛtta* and *abhinaya* in the Manipuri style. The love ballads of Sri Caitanya, Sūrdās, Jayadeva and other Kṛṣṇa devotees figure prominently in *rasa*. It is generally performed in the open area of the temples. Lilting music and enchanting dances are the special features of *rasa*. Through each sequence the dancers present several *vyabhicāri bhāvas*. The various rhythms of the *bhaṅgī*s give full scope to the dancer to present variations on a given theme. It may consist of both *daṇḍa rasaka* (dancing with sticks in the hands) and the *maṇḍala rasaka* (dancing in circles). We will see that *lāsya* dance may form part of the *vīthī*.

Bharat Līlā is the most colourful presentation of the folk-dance prevalent in Gañjam area in Orissa. The leading story is based upon Subhadrā Pariṇaya, a beautiful part of the epic *Mahābhārata*. Subhadrā is the sister of Lord Kṛṣṇa. Kṛṣṇa himself, plays the role of mediator between the two sweethearts, i.e. Arjuna and Subhadrā in the guise of a *dvārī* (sentry) and makes the lovers unite. Arjuna, at first, hesitates to accept the love of Subhadrā since she, being the sister of Kṛṣṇa, is like his own sister. But the *dvārī* convinces him by quoting incidents from various epics and religious texts.

Bhramyaman Mancha or mobile theatre is a phenomenon in the modern-day Assamese theatre. Touring repertories with a difference, they visit towns and remote villages and present their plays. They have makeshift stages which can be easily assembled. The themes vary from mythological stories to episodes of contemporary nature. Fast adaptation of ever-new themes with an eye on changing interests have ensured that the mobile theatre genre does not lose its appeal to the young audience either.

Kabigan was a very popular form of dramatized singing in the rural Bengali theatre. Its merit lies in simplicity of content and delivery, and its theatrical distinctiveness in the extempore debates that the singers initiate and develop. This was originally characterized by Vaiṣṇava devotion since its inception in the mid-eighteenth century. Its central themes usually related to Rādhā and Kṛṣṇa. More than their love, however, the focus gradually shifted to the elements of *kalaṅka* (taint) and *chalana* (deception) in the myths.

Gondhal, the literal meaning of which is "commotion", is the dramatic narration of mythical stories, praise of heroes or narration of folk legends. All these form part of a ritual dedicated to different divinities. This Marathi folk theatre in the form of worship is performed exclusively by a group of men as part of rituals after ceremonies like marriage etc.

Galihyun is a narrative verse glorifying the legendary heroic deeds and romances of rulers and chieftains. This is the oldest Sindhi theatrical form; its origin is traced to the Sumra period during the eleventh century. This theatre was under the native kings who were great patrons of culture. The earlier Sumra Galihyun was in *campū* format, where prose narration was interspersed with poetry. These poems were not composed in any particular metre; their main features were rhyming and rhythm which aided melody in singing. The subject matter in the Samma Age gave place to the romances of common people rather than the heroic exploits of rulers.

Kurattiaṭṭam: *Kuratti* means a gypsy and *aṭṭam* means dance in Tamil. It is again an unconventional form of folk presentation. The instrumentalists and vocalists who support the actors sit at the rear with *mr̥daṅgam* drums and *kaimaṇi,* i.e. small cymbals. They commence by singing in praise of the God Gaṇeśa and Goddess Sarasvatī, followed by the entrance of two Kurattis who assume the characters of the spouses of Lord Viṣṇu and Lord Śiva. They engage in a wordy duel, dramatized through singing and dancing. In their quarrel they find fault with each other's husbands. In the end, a third Kuratti impersonating Sarasvatī comes to the rescue and strikes a compromise. Then the Kuravan exhibits many acrobatic feats including rope dancing to musical accompaniment. Finally his old mother dances, which provides a lot of fun to the audience.

Mutiyettu is a ritualistic prototype of theatre, one of the earliest known and representing the fertility cult in Kerala. Kālī or the Goddess Śakti is the protagonist, and Darika the demon antagonist. The slaying of evil forces, represented by Darika and his elder brother Danava, by Kālī and her retinue, the Kulis and Koimpidar form the storyline. Koimpidar also calls the Koimpida Nayar, i.e. a warrior who interjects with comical comments and dance. The musical prelude, called *kalampattu* or ***kalamezhutupattan,*** sometimes takes place by itself, not followed by the play. It occurs within the building in front of a temple sanctum. When organized at people's residences, a special *paṇḍal* or thatched shed is erected in an open space in front of the house. Usually, this is decorated with fresh coconut leaves, flower garlands, and so on. The figure of Kālī is drawn on the floor with five colours. This is known as *kalam*. The five colours are white, i.e. rice powder, black, i.e. charred rice husk, yellow, i.e. turmeric, green, i.e. leaves, and red, i.e. mixed lime and turmeric. This is drawn by two or three members of the community of temple artists known as Kurup.

Nondī Nāṭakam is a popular Tamil form of dance theatre known for its simple language and engaging music. In Nondī Nāṭakam the dancers tie up one leg during the performance; that is why it is called "lame drama". It is closely associated with Terukkūttu and Kuravanji Nāṭakam, and was in vogue during the seventeenth and eighteenth century CE. Traditionally, it was presented as an offering to the ruling deity of a village at the temple. The story deals with a lame thief, his love life, devotion and conviction.

Palagān belongs to Bengal. It has been derived from *pala*, i.e. a part, phase, chapter or episode of a longer narrative and *gāna*, i.e. "song". Palagan is a Bengali term that covers a range of oral narrative besides musical and theatrical traditions. *Pala* was added to titles describing particular episodes from myths narrated or performed in various traditional modes. The Vaiṣṇava *līlā-kīrtan*, celebrating Kr̥ṣṇa's activities, actions and exploits of *līlā* in elaborate suites of songs, is known as Palagān since it breaks up Kr̥ṣṇa's life into separate *līlā*s. This became popular after the great Kheturi festival.

Paṇḍavānī is a narrative ballad form of Chhattisgarh, sung primarily by the Pardhan and Devar castes. This is based essentially on stories from the *Mahābhārata*. Since the epic was read by and accessible only to upper castes, a body of folk poetry developed around it that became popular in villages and among lower castes. This literature is the source for Paṇḍavānī.

Shumang Līlā is a Manipuri courtyard theatre by the elite. It evolved earlier through various stages from the Phagi, i.e. clown plays of the nineteenth century. The genre denotes the contemporary popular and itinerant dramatic performances held in open spaces. It is performed especially in the courtyards of extended households, playgrounds in front of public schools, precincts of native spirit deities or riversides with embankments designed for all-round viewing.

Tālamaddale is derived from *tāla* meaning cymbal and *maddale,* i.e. the *yakṣagāna* drum. This is a variant of the Kannaḍa theatre form of *yakṣagāna*. This is quite popular in the western districts of Karnataka. It essentially presents *yakṣagāna* with songs and dialogue but without dances and stagecraft. Historically, it seems to have originated before *yakṣagāna* but continued to retain a separate identity and stronghold even after the latter gained popularity.

Āṅganamañca actually means the courtyard theatre. It was meant to extend the horizon of Bengali theatre. It was also expected to rescue it from its staleness and rusted practices and preoccupations. It is a combination of urban and rural styles, with socially committed themes, performed informally in round spaces, taking theatre to people everywhere.

— Indianetzone.com

Characteristics of the Vīthī

The earliest dramaturgical text dealing with the theory of the *vīthī* (as also the other *rūpaka* varieties) is, of course, Bharata's *Nāṭyaśāstra*. Given below are the stanzas dealing with the *vīthī* features as found in the G.O.S. edition of *Nāṭyaśāstra*, which is by far the most authentic among the editions of Bharata's text. Variant readings found in the other editions are also given below for reference.

वीथ्याः सम्प्रति निखिलं कथयामि यथाक्रमं विप्राः
सर्वरसलक्षणाढ्या युक्ता ह्यङ्गैस्त्रयोदशभिः
वीथी स्यादेकाङ्का तथैकाहार्या द्विहार्या वा।
अधमोत्तममध्याभियुक्ता स्यात्प्रकृतिभिस्तिसृभिः।
उद्धात्याकावलगितावस्यन्दितनाल्यसत्प्रलापश्च
वाक्केल्यथ प्रपञ्चो मृदवाधिबलं छलं त्रिगतम्।
व्याहारो गणडश्च त्रयोदशाङ्गान्युद्दृतान्यस्याः॥

— *NŚ*, vol. II, ch. XVIII, *śl.* 111-14

The reading according to the Kāvyamālā edition is given below:

वीथी स्यादेकाङ्का[1] तथैकहार्या द्विहार्या वा।
अधमोत्तममध्याभियुक्ता स्यात् प्रकृतिभिस्तिसृभिः॥
सर्वरसलक्षणाढ्या युक्ताह्यङ्गैस्त्रयोदशभिः॥
[2]उद्धात्यकावलगितावस्यन्दितनाल्यसत्प्रलापश्च।
वाक्केल्यथ प्रपञ्चो मृदवाधिबलं छलं त्रिगतम्।
व्याहारो गणडश्च त्रयोदशाङ्गान्युदाहृतान्यस्याः॥
अङ्गानां वक्ष्येहं लक्षणमधुना यथोद्देशम्।

1. KSS द्विपात्रहार्या वा
2. KSS varies absolutely.

The KSS edition carries two more verses.

एतान्याङ्गानि यत्रस्युः स्पष्टार्थानि त्रयोदश॥
तथागमसमुद्दिष्टैर्युक्ता प्रकृतिभिस्तथा॥
रसैर्भावैश्च निखिलैर्युक्ता वीथी प्रकीर्तिता॥
एकहार्या द्विहार्या वा कर्तव्या कविभिः सदा। — XX, 134-35

Consolidating the features of the *vīthī* as given in the variant readings we can arrive at the following characteristics, in general.

1. The *vīthī* may have a single act.
2. It may have just one or two characters.
3. It may have either noble, middle level or low level characters.

4. It should have all the *rasa*s.

5. It may have all the *lakṣaṇa*s (36 of them)

6. It may have 13 limbs, namely *udghātyaka, avalagita, avasyandita, nālikā, asatpralāpa, vākkeli, prapañca, mṛdava, adhibala, chala, trigata, vyāhāra* and *gaṇḍa*.

Abhinavagupta clarifies some more points:

1. Since it can have a single character, there is provision for use of the *ākāśabhāṣita* as in *bhāṇa*.

2. The *vīthyaṅga*s, having the scope for all *rasa*s, may be employed in other play-forms as well.

The nature of *vīthī* is such that its theme is worked out afresh by the imagination of the poet like that of the *prakaraṇa*, *bhāṇa* and *prahasana*.

There are several references to *vīthī* in the *Nāṭyaśāstra* itself apart from the chapter on *Daśarūpaka*.

(i) वीथी . . . प्रहसनं डिमः ।
कैशिकीवृत्तिहीनानि रूपाण्येतानि कारयेत् ॥

— *NŚ*, ch. XVIII, *śl.* 7, Kāvyamālā edition

Kaiśikī, ārabhaṭī, bhāratī and *sātvatī* are the four styles of expression. *Kaiśikī* is soft and gentle and is suited for *śṛṅgāra*. *Ārabhaṭī* which is the opposite of it is used for representing conflict, rage, frenzy and the like. Virtue, courage, self-sacrifice and the like are best expressed through the *sātvatī* style. *Bhāratī* is the eloquent style which can be used in any situation. Of all the *rūpaka*s, the *nāṭaka*, and the *prakaraṇa* are called the *pūrṇa vṛttirūpaka*s since they can accommodate all the four *vṛtti*s.

Vīthī along with *prahasana, ḍima*, etc. is deviod of the *kaiśikī vṛtti* since it has very little scope for *śṛṅgāra* and its outward expression through song, dance, coquetry and the like.

(ii) द्विसन्धि तु प्रहसनं वीथ्यङ्कौ भाण एव च
मुखनिर्वहणे स्यातां तेषां वृत्तिश्च भारती ॥

— *NŚ*, ch. XXI, *śl.* 47, Kāśī edition

Bharata points out that the Bhāratī *vṛtti* shall be mainly employed in *vīthī, prahasana* and *bhāṇa*. They may have only two *sandhis*, namely *mukha* and *nirvahaṇa* (the opening and the denouement). This is evidently due to the simplicity of the plot and structure of these play-forms.

(iii) भेदास्तस्यास्तु विज्ञेयाश्चत्वारो अङ्गत्वमागतः।
प्ररोचना आमुखं चैव वीथी प्रहसनं तथा।

— *NŚ*, ch. XX, *śl.* 26, GOS, edn.

What Bharata means here, is that the Bhāratī style shall be employed in the *prahasana* and the *vīthī* and in parts of the prologue, "*nāndī, prarocanā* and *āmukha*". Many later writers on dramaturgy including Dhanañjaya have confused the issue by taking all these four names as constituting the *aṅgas* of the Bhāratī *vṛtti* which shall be employed in the prologue. Prof V. Raghavan has clarified this point in his Bhoja's *Śṛngāraprakāśa* and also in his papers on *vṛttis* (*JOR*, vols. VI and VII). By the expression *aṅgatvamāgataḥ*, Bharata just means "find expression in". Bhāratī is a style of expression and it finds use in *vīthī* and *prahasana*, etc. is the proper way of construing Bharata's statement in this context.

Now let us look at the Daśarūpaka definition of *vīthī*:

वीथी तु कैशिकीवृत्तौ सन्ध्यङ्गाद्यैस्तु भाणवत् ।
रसः सूच्यस्तु शृङ्गारः स्पृशेदपि रसान्तरम् ॥ — III.68

The additional information that we get from *DR* is that the *kaiśikī vṛtti* may be employed in *vīthī*. This is understandable since the *śṛṅgāra rasa* has a scope for it. The other *rasas* may also be touched upon. As for the *sandhis* and the *sandhyaṅgas*, *vīthī* follows the *bhāṇa*. In other words, the *mukha* and the *nirvahaṇa sandhi*s and the links belonging to them may be employed in a *vīthī.*

Sāhitya-Darpaṇa (6.253-5) gives some more information on the *vīthī.*

वीथ्यामेको भवेदङ्कः कश्चिदेकोऽत्र कल्प्यते।
आकाशभाषितैरुक्तैश्चित्रां प्रत्युक्तिमाश्रितः॥

सूचयेद् भूरिशृङ्गारं किंचिदन्यान् रसान्प्रति।
मुखनिर्वहणे संधी अर्थप्रकृतयोऽखिलाः॥

कश्चिदुत्तमो मध्यमोऽधमो वा।
शृङ्गारबहुलत्वाच्चास्याः कैशिकीवृत्तिबहुलत्वम्॥

We may notice that, according to *SD*, the technique of *ākāśabhāṣita* may be empoyed in a *vīthī. DR* has given a clue that *vīthī* shares some common features with *bhāṇa. SD* goes one step further and prescribes the *ākāśabhāṣita,* which is a special feature of *bhāṇa*. Probably Viśvanātha has seen some *vīthī* specimens employing the said technique. *SD* states explicitly what *DR* has suggested. That is, on account of the prevalance of *śṛṅgāra* in it, *vīthī* has a large scope for *kaiśikī vṛtti. SD* also says that all the *arthaprakṛti*s may be employed in a *vīthī.*

Pratāparudrīya does not differ much from *SD.*

यत्र भाणवदङ्गानां क्लृप्तिर्वृत्तिस्तु कैशिकी।
शृङ्गारः परिपूर्णत्वात् सूचनीयोऽतिभूयसा॥

— *Nāṭakaprakaraṇa*, 53-54

Bhāvaprakāśana has some interesting infomation to convey:

मुखनिर्वहणे संधी वीथ्यां वृत्तिस्तु कैशिकी।
द्वाभ्यां प्रयोज्या पात्राभ्यां क्वचिदेकेन वा भवेत्॥

अङ्गी सर्वरसस्पर्शी शृङ्गारोऽस्याः प्रधानतः।
युक्ता लास्यङ्गवीथ्यङ्गैः सम्यगुद्घात्यकादिभिः॥

भवेयुर्वा न वेत्यस्यां लास्याङ्गान्याह कोहलः।

वीथ्यां शृङ्गाररूपत्वात् विधेयानीति भोजराट् ॥

एकाङ्केव भवेत्वीथी रससूच्योऽत्रसंभृतः ।
यथा बकुलवीथी स्यादिन्दुलेखादयो यथा ॥ — Ch. 8; sec. 192

There is a controversy regarding the employment of *lāsyāṅgas* in the *vīthī*. Kohala was of the opinion that they may or may not be employed in the *vīthī*. But Bhoja categorically states that they can be employed, since the *vīthī* has a wide scope for *śṛṅgāra*. *BP* follows *SP* totally. *BP* also prescribes only one act in a *vīthī*, though some of the earlier writers have given the option of having two acts as well. The most interesting point *BP* makes is with respect to the mention of *vīthī* specimens. Bhoja has already mentioned two works of this class, namely Mālatikā Vīthī and Indulekhā. *BP* mentions one more, namely Bakula Vīthī, though nothing else is known about this work.

The *Rasārṇavasudhākara* (*RS*) refers to one Mādhavī Vīthī. The account of this *vīthī* runs thus:

सूच्यप्रधानशृङ्गारा मुखनिर्वहणान्विता ।
एकयोज्या द्वियोज्या वा कैशिकीवृत्तिनिर्भरा ॥

वीथ्यङ्गसहितैकाङ्का वीथीति कथिता बुधैः ।
अस्यां प्रायेण लास्याङ्गदशकं योजयेन्नवा ॥

सामान्या परकीया वा नायिकात्रानुरागिनी ।
वीथ्यङ्गप्रायवस्तुत्वान्नोचिता कुलपालिता ॥

लक्ष्यमस्यास्तु विज्ञेयं माधवीवीथिकादिकम् । — III, 265-267

RS reverts back to the old position with respect to the use of *lāsyāṅgas* in the *vīthī*. It states that they may or may not be employed. For the first time, *RS* mentions about the heroine of the *vīthī*. She may be a "common woman" or a "public woman". She is "dependent" in the sense that she makes a living on the money paid by her customers. *RS* further says that a chaste woman may not figure as a character in a *vīthī*. The reason given is rather unconvincing. *RS* says that a noble woman character has no role in *vīthī* since it employs the *vīthyaṅgas*. Even the view that a chaste woman has no role in a *vīthī*, is questionable. Probably, *RS* is influenced by the nature of heroines that are found in *prahasanas* and *bhāṇas*. Though *vīthī* bears resemblance to *prahasana* and *bhāṇa* in many respects, there is no hard and fast rule that a chaste woman should not be a heroine in a *vīthī*. In fact, in one of the available specimens, *Sītākalyāṇa vīthī*, Sītā is the heroine. *RS* should have stopped by saying that the *gaṇikās* are generally employed as heroines in a *vīthī* instead of barring the role of chaste women in it. The reason given is all the more puzzling. There is no rule that the employment of *vīthyaṅgas* excludes noble women. In many of the illustrations of the *vīthyaṅgas*, given by the dramaturgical texts, noble heroines do figure as characters. *Śṛ.Pra* cites an example for *avalagita* from the famous *citraphalaka* scene of *Ratnāvalī* where Sāgarikā, the heroine is involved. For the element *gaṇḍa*, Avaloka quotes a passage from *Uttararāmacarita*. For *avasyandita* again, Avaloka cites an illustration from Chalitarāma where Sītā appears in a conversation with Lava. For the *vīthyaṅga*, *vyāhāra*, *DR* cites the *lāsyaprayoga* scene of *Mālavikāgnimitra* where the heroine, Mālavikā, smiles at a witty remark made by the *vidūṣaka*. It is, therefore, unreasonable to say that the *vīthyaṅgas* stand in the way of noble heroines appearing in a *vīthī*. The *RS* view has, therefore, to be re-interpreted in the following way:

i. As in *prahasanas*, the *gaṇikās* appear as heroines in a *vīthī*. Chaste women make only a rare appearance.

ii. The *vīthyaṅgas* may be employed for ridiculing the licentious life led by immoral men and women.

The Vṛttyaṅgas and the Vīthyaṅgas

The four *vṛttis*, namely *kaiśikī, ārabhaṭī, bhāratī* and *sātvatī* are subdivided into minor classification by writers on dramaturgical texts. Bhoja speaks of four varieties of each of these four *vṛttis*. As we have seen earlier, Bharata speaks of four *aṅgas* of *bhāratī vṛtti*, namely *prarocanā, āmukha, vīthī* and *prahasana*. Of these, *āmukha* consists of five elements, namely *udghātyaka, prayogātiśaya, pravṛttaka* and *avalagita*. Of them, *udghātyaka* and *avalagita* are forms of the thirteen *vīthyaṅgas*. Later writers have not understood the intention of Bharata and have given a confused accound of *vṛttyaṅgas* mixing the *vīthyaṅgas* in between. Bhoja, for example, adds *kaṭhodghāta, pravṛttaka* and *prayogātiśaya* to the list of thirteen *vīthyaṅgas* making them sixteen in all. It is unwarranted. *Kaṭhodghāta pravṛttaka* and *prayogātiśaya* are clearly part of *āmukha* or prologue. The *vīthyaṅgas* are different and they can be employed not only in the prologue but also in the main part of the play as well.

Some of the *vīthī* writers also have tried to define the play-form. For example, Rāmapāṇivāda says in his *Candrikāvīthī*,

> *pātradvayaprayojyā bhāṇvadekāṅkikā dvisandhiśca* ।
> *ākāśabhāṣitavatī kṛtrimamitivṛttamāśritā vīthī* ॥

Thus *ākāśabhāṣita* is recognized as a characterstic of *vīthī*.

Veṅkāmātya, the author of *Sītākalyāṇavīthī*, says that it is a rare feature of the goddess of learning as she has done the *vīthī* garb of beauty to move about. He also says that it is a garland of sentiment of love. Śāradātanaya says that *vīthī* is comparable to an avenue of *bakula* trees or to a streak of moonbeam.

The Relation between the Vīthī and Other Rūpakas

It has already been pointed out that the *nāṭaka* and the *prakaraṇa* are the most perfected forms of the *rūpaka*s and they contain all the features of the rest of the *rūpaka*s. Thus, the prologue of the most of the plays contain the elements of *vīthī*. *Vīthī* bears close resemblance to the *prahasana* in many respects including their respective elements. The main feature of the *bhāṇa*, namely *ākāśabhāṣita* may be employed in the *vīthī* also. The *vīthī*, the *prahasana* and the *bhāṇa* are all short plays containing not more than two acts. All the three generally have the *utpādya* theme. The *aṅka* is totally different from the *vīthī* since the former is full of tragic elements. The *īhāmṛga* is similar to the *vīthī* in several respects. The heroic play-forms like *ḍima*, *vyāyoga* and *samavakāra* are different in their nature but they may also contain the *vīthyaṅga* in their prologues. Thus the *vīthī* has something in common with the other *rūpaka*s.

Characters Appearing in the Vīthī

According to the definition of Bharata, the *vīthī* may have all types of characters: *uttama*, *madhyama* or *adhama*. The dramaturgical texts are silent about the theme of *vīthī*. It is understood, therefore, that the *vīthī* may have either *prakhyāta* or *utpādya*. As it started as a street play, the *vīthī* perhaps had the freedom of choice with respect to the theme. That led to the choice of characters as well. Thus, in the *vīthī* specimens, we have both Pūraṇic/historical as well as social characters. The *Dūtavākya* of Bhāsa, if it can be considered as a *vīthī*, contains Purāṇic characters as also a later specimen, *Sītākalyāṇavīthī*. Two of the early specimens, *Mālatikā* and *Indulekhā* and later specimens like *Līlāvatīvīthī* have social characters. Judging from them, the *vīthī* can be called as a light love-comedy with fewer characters than the popular play-forms. It can also be called as a miniature *nāṭikā* which itself is a shorter version of *nāṭaka*. We have in the *vīthī*, kings, queens and heroines on the lines of *Ratnāvalī*. *Vidūṣaka*s also appear in the *vīthī*s, though their role is rather limited. They have twofold activities, primarily to serve as a companion of the hero and secondarily to provide comic relief to the audience.

Rasas in the Vīthī

According to the definition of the *vīthī*, it may have scope for all *rasa*s. In general, they have *śṛṅgāra* as the main sentiment with a sprinkling of others *rasa*s here and there. The *hāsya* and the *adbhuta* serve as supporting *rasa*s as in a *nāṭikā*. With just one or two acts and with just *mukha* and *nirvahaṇa sandhi*s provided, the *vīthī* does not have any scope for the elaboration of any *rasa*, but a few scenes are enough to assess the main sentiment in the play. The two lost specimens *Mālatikā* and *Indulekhā*, as also the *Līlāvatīvīthī*, have unmistakably *śṛṅgāra* as the main sentiment. The latter one fashioned on the lines of *Mālavikāgnimitra* and *Ratnāvalī* have an element of *adbhuta* also contributing to the development of the main sentiment.

Lāsyāṅgas in the Vīthī

Lāsya is a gentle type of dance suited to *śṛṅgāra* performed by female dancers on the stage. It has ten *aṅga*s or limbs. *Nāṭyaśāstra* (XX.136) defines them and states that they are *ekapātrahārya*, that is, performed by a single character on the stage. It can appear in a *nāṭaka*, *prakaraṇa* or a *nāṭikā*. The dance sequence scene in *Mālavikāgnimitra* can be quoted as an example. In *Ratnāvalī* also we have a dance scene performed by many dancers but it can also be called a *lāsya*. The *vīthī* being similar to the *nāṭikā* in several respects, may also have scope for *lāsya* dance and the play *Sītākalyāṇavīthī* does seem to have one. It adds charm to the *śṛṅgāra rasa* which is the main sentiment in a *vīthī*.

Theatrical Aspects of the Vīthī

Bharata (ch.II) gives threefold classification of the theatre, based on its size: *jyeṣṭha* (big), *madhyama* (medium) and *kanīyas* (small). Commenting on this passage, Abhinavagupta says that the *ḍima* with divine characters shall be performed in a *jyeṣṭha* type of theatre. *Nāṭaka* with royal characters in it, requires a medium type of theatre and for the rest of the play-forms, a small theatre would suffice. Thus a *vīthī* can be staged in a small theatre since it does not require much of theatrical sophistication or large scene settings. It may require just one or two scene settings. But if a *vīthī* has a Purāṇic theme like *Sītākalyāṇavīthī*, elaborate scene settings are required. There is reason to believe that the *vīthī*s were perhaps staged in the street corners without any theatrical devices like stage or scene settings in its early form.

Nāndī, Prologue and the Bharatavākya

In addition to serving the usual purpose of benediction, the *nāndī* in a *vīthī* may indicate the main *rasa*, the nature of the theme and a main character of the play. The *nāndī* generally deals with the Śiva-Pārvatī theme in most of the plays.

The prologue in a *vīthī* is carried out in the usual style with the *sūtradhāra* and his associate(s) discussing the merits of the play. It may contain a reference to the author, his works and his attainments. It can also be in the form of a monologue with the *ākāśabhāṣita*, but we have no evidence to this since most of the early *vīthī*s have died out.

The *vīthī* generally ends with a *bharatavākya* in the conventional way. Non-availability of the early specimens prevents any comparison but being styled like a *nāṭikā,* they might have had the *bharatavākya* in the usual pattern. The *Līlāvatīvīthī* ends with one such *bharatavākya.*

With this background we will now be in a position to review some of the available specimens of *vīthī* which is taken up in the next chapter.

7

The Vīthī Specimens

Dūtavākya

THE PLAYS OF BHĀSA

Dūtavākya is one of the thirteen Trivandrum plays attributed to Bhāsa and published by Mahāmahopādhyāya T. Ganapati Shastri, who first identified the manuscripts in Trivandrum Manuscript Library. The problem of authorship of the thirteen plays has been discussed by various scholars for over a century and is not yet settled, perhaps it will never be. Bhāsa as also Kaviputra and Saumilla have been mentioned by Kālidāsa in his prologue to *Mālavikāgnimitra*. The plays of these dramatists were known only through references in other works. Kaviputra and Saumilla are said to have written dramas called *Śūdrakakathā* and *Maṇiprabhā* respectively. That Bhāsa wrote *Svapnavāsavadattā* is known from Rājaśekhara who says:

bhāsanāṭakacakre 'smin cekaiḥ kṣipte parīkṣitum ।
svapnavāsavadattasya dāhako 'bhūnna pāvakaḥ ॥

Bāṇa refers to Bhāsa in glorious terms in his *Harṣacarita*:

sūtradhārakṛtārambhaiḥ nāṭakairbahubhūmikaiḥ ।
sapatākairyaśo lebhe bhāso devakūlairiva ॥

This reference gives the idea that Bhāsa wrote many plays with a variety of characters and incidents. Abhinavagupta, Rāmacandra and Guṇacandra and several other writers quote verses from his works and also make a mention of his best known work, namely, *Svapnavāsavadattā*. The thirteen plays may be classified as follows:

(i) Long plays with Rāma themes:

Pratimānāṭaka and *Abhiṣekanāṭaka*

(ii) Long play with Kṛṣṇa theme:

Bālacaritam

(iii) Long plays with other themes:

Svapnavāsavadattā

Pratijñāyaugandharāyaṇa

Avimārakam

Cārudattam

(iv) Short plays with the *Mahābhārata* themes:

Madhyamavyāyoga

Pāñcarātram

Dūtavākyam

Dūtaghaṭotkaca

Karṇabhāram

Ūrūbhaṅgam

The first two are *nāṭaka*s as mentioned in the titles of the plays themselves. *Bālacarita* is also a *nāṭaka* but with Kṛṣṇa theme. The next four can be grouped under the *prakaraṇa* or social plays. Among the short plays, *Madhyamavyāyoga* clearly belongs to the type known as *vyāyoga* as seen from the title itself. *Karṇabhāra* may be brought under the *aṅka* type since it is a tragedy. *Dūtaghaṭotkaca* may be called a *ḍima* on account of the mixture of divine and semi-divine beings appearing as characters in it. *Ūrūbhaṅga* may belong to the *samavakāra* type. Bhāsa perhaps wrote sample plays for each one of the ten *rūpakas*, some of which might have been lost. There is a difference of opinion among scholars whether *Dūtavākya* can be classified under the class *vīthī* or not. Some say that it can be brought under *vyāyoga*. But a *vyāyoga* hero is of an *uddhata* type. The hero of *Dūtavākya*, Kṛṣṇa, is not an *uddhata* type of hero. Moreover, having already contributed a *vyāyoga* in *Madhyamavyāyoga*, Bhāsa would not have intended another play of the same type. Hence it is reasonable to suppose that he intended *Dūtavākya* to be a *vīthī*. An analysis of the play in the following pages will make this point clear.

THE PLOT

Dramatis Personae

Sūtradhāra

Kāñcukīya (Chamberlain)

Duryodhana

Vāsudeva-Kṛṣṇa

Sudarśana

Dhṛtarāṣṭra

Dūtavākya draws its theme from the Udyoga Parva of the *Mahābhārata* (Chapters 72 to 150). The main theme relates to Kṛṣṇa's role as an ambassador on behalf of the Pāṇḍavas, his attempt to meet Duryodhana and bring about a compromise between the two parties. He has his task cut out since it is the last chance to avert the war which will definitely bring about a great calamity on either side. This important scene from the *Mahābhārata* is taken up and presented as a short play by Bhāsa. The dramatist has introduced certain significant changes in the original plot in order to enhance the dramatic effect and also to make it lively and interesting for the audience.

Duryodhana does not pay heed to the words of elders for peace. He does not want to give an inch of space to the Pāṇḍavas. He is bent upon war and has made elaborate arrangements for it. He has amassed eleven divisions (*akṣauhiṇī*) of army and has put up camps near the battlefield. He calls for a crucial meeting to select the commander-in-chief of the army. Śakuni proposes the name of Bhīṣma and it is immediately accepted by Duryodhana. At this stage, the chamberlain enters and announces the arrival of Kṛṣṇa as a messenger of peace from the Pāṇḍavas. But Duryodhana thinks of humiliating Kṛṣṇa as he enters and also of arresting him. Without him the Pāṇḍavas would become powerless and would get defeated in the war. He asks all the people in the assembly not to stand up or show any respect to Kṛṣṇa. He does not want to recognise the entry of Kṛṣṇa at all and so he pretends to look at the picture of Draupadī being molested by Duḥśāsana in the open court. But as soon as Kṛṣṇa enters the assembly, all the people rise from their seats as though under a spell and greet him. Duryodhana finds that he himself had risen up from his seat without his own knowledge. Has Kṛṣṇa cast any magic spell, he wonders. Kṛṣṇa, soon after entering the assembly, orders for the removal of the picture immediately. Duryodhana enquires about the welfare of the Pāṇḍavas which surprises even Kṛṣṇa who appreciates his gesture and says that the Pāṇḍavas had also enquired about his health and happiness. Kṛṣṇa then conveys the message which runs thus: "We have experienced untold misery. The thirteen-year period of exile is also over. Please give back our rightful share of the kingdom." Duryodhana says that Yudhiṣṭhira and his brothers were not actually born to Pāṇḍu and therefore they have no right to the ancestral kingdom. Kṛṣṇa points out that even the Kauravas cannot stake any claim to the kingdom since their father was not born of Vicitravīrya but of Vyāsa. Kṛṣṇa therefore asks Duryodhana to stop this vain argument and restore the kingdom to the Pāṇḍavas failing which he will face total annihilation of the Kuru dynasty. Duryodhana continues to insult the Pāṇḍavas by saying that kingdoms are not got by begging these from others but by fighting a war and winning it. If they wanted peace they should retire to the forest and live in hermitages. He then turns to Kṛṣṇa and finds fault with him for killing his own maternal uncle Kaṁsa. Kṛṣṇa advises Duryodhana not to resort to fault finding but accede to the request of the Pāṇḍavas. Duryodhana brushes aside Kṛṣṇa's well-meaning words and refuses to part with even a blade of grass from the kingdom for the Pāṇḍavas. He insults Kṛṣṇa again quoting some past incidents. Kṛṣṇa issues a final warning and leaves the hall. Duryodhana asks his associates to follow him and bind him. Finding that others were not obliging immediately, he himself runs after Kṛṣṇa and tries to bind him. But to his utter dismay he finds not one Kṛṣṇa but several Kṛṣṇas all over the place. Whom to bind and whom to leave? Next moment he does not find Kṛṣṇa anywhere in the vicinity. Now Duryodhana tells that it was just a magic and he dares to fight with Kṛṣṇa and asks for his bow and arrow. Kṛṣṇa becomes very angry, calls for his *sudarśana cakra* and orders it to kill Duryodhana. With all humility, *sudarśana* reminds Kṛṣṇa of the purpose of his incarnation. If Duryodhana alone is killed in this way the other Kauravas would escape under some pretext. Accordingly, Kṛṣṇa controls his anger and sends back *sudarśana*. When Kṛṣṇa is about to leave, Dhṛtarāṣṭra comes and requests Kṛṣṇa to accept his worship (and spare his son). Kṛṣṇa obliges him and sends him back, and with this the play ends.

INNOVATIONS IN THE PLOT

According to the *Mahābhārata*, Kṛṣṇa's role as a messenger unfolds in the capital city, Hastināpurī before the arrangements for the war take place. But in the *Dūtavākya*, the scene is laid in the camp at the battlefield and we also understand that Duryodhana is ready for the war. He has also chosen the commander-in-chief before Kṛṣṇa's arrival. This sounds as a dramatic irony since the audience get the clue that the peace efforts are not likely to succeed. In a short play, it is difficult to sketch a character in detail. The dramatist has to give a glimpse of the character through a few incidents and fewer dialogues. Bhāsa succeeds in bringing forth the evil nature of Duryodhana during his conversation with Kṛṣṇa. His decision to dishonour Kṛṣṇa, his glancing at the picture of Draupadī's molestation, his disrespectful words towards Kṛṣṇa, his intentions to arrest him — all bring out his sinister motives. The scene of confusion, caused in the assembly at the entry of Kṛṣṇa, is an innovation of the poet. It also evokes gentle humour in the midst of the audience. Similarly, in the scene where Duryodhana and his associates try to bind Kṛṣṇa is an imagination of the dramatist. The scene of the appearance of *sudarśana* and other weapons, is purposely introduced by the poet to evoke the *adbhuta rasa*. In the *Mahābhārata*, Dhṛtarāṣṭra and Gāndhārī advise Duryodhana to listen to the words of Kṛṣṇa. This scene is avoided by the poet, but the last scene where Dhṛtarāṣṭra tries to appease Kṛṣṇa is enough to represent the feelings of the blind king.

CHARACTERS APPEARING IN THE PLAY

Kṛṣṇa is obviously the hero of the play. The dramatist brings out all the glorious traits of the hero through significant scenes and dialogues. Kṛṣṇa comes as a simple messenger in human form but his divine qualities are revealed at the appropriate time. When his plans to disrespect Kṛṣṇa fail, Duryodhana wonders whether it is some magic. The first thing that Kṛṣṇa does as soon as he enters the assembly, is to ask Duryodana to remove the picture of Draupadī's molestation from the hall. This act of Kṛṣṇa brings out his "dhārmic" sense as brought out in the definition *mahāsattvo 'tigambhīraḥ kṛpāvānavikattanaḥ*. As a true messenger, he observes patience even when provoked by Duryodhana again and again. He rather appreciates Duryodhana when the latter asks about the welfare of the Pāṇḍavas. Without ever getting perturbed, he explains the purpose of his mission, that is, to bring about peace between the two camps. When Duryodhana abuses the Pāṇḍavas about their birth, Kṛṣṇa advises him by saying, *bho duryodhana, alam bandhujane paruṣam abhidhātum*, "Enough of harsh words towards the kinsmen". For all the abuses hurled at him, Kṛṣṇa replies calmly. Only when he is convinced that Duryodhana was not going to listen to his words, Kṛṣṇa reminds him of the valour of Arjuna and the impending doom of the Kauravas. When Duryodhana crosses the limits by saying that it is beneath his dignity to speak to a cowherd (referring to Kṛṣṇa), Kṛṣṇa scolds him and leaves the scene. Duryodhana and his associates try to bind him, but who can bind the Lord? The only blemish we find in Kṛṣṇa is his decision to kill Duryodhana by employing *sudarśana*. But the latter reminds him of the purpose of his incarnation. Though the advice comes from his subordinate, Kṛṣṇa respects it and withdraws his weapon. Here lies the true mark of a hero. Some of the statements made by Kṛṣṇa bring out his all round knowledge and nobility. When Duryodhana taunts him for his maternal uncle, Kaṁsa, Kṛṣṇa replies calmly by saying, *deśakāla-avasthāpekṣi khalu śauryam nayānumāninām*, "the bravery of those who are involved in politics is designed depending upon place and time". His advice to Duryodhana is relevant to all people at all times.

कर्तव्यो भ्रातृषु स्नेहो विस्मर्तव्या गुणेतराः।
सम्बन्धो बन्धुभिः श्रेयान् लोकयोरुभयोरपि ॥२९॥

One must maintain good relationship towards brothers. Faults (in them) are to be forgotten. Association with relatives is good for both this world as well as the other world.

Duryodhana, in contrast to Kṛṣṇa, is presented as a proud and angry man, bent upon crushing the Pāṇḍavas in the war. He will not budge an inch towards peace efforts. Duryodhana's original name was Suyodhana and that is the name employed throughout the play. He did have certain good traits in tune with his original name, but he succumbed to the ill advice of Karṇa, Śakuni and others and consequently his acts turned out to be wicked in nature. In the play, there is no scope for bringing out all these aspects of his character. The audience are aware of his character and so the poet straightaway presents him as a violent and revengeful man. In *Ūrūbhaṅga* and *Pāñcarātra*, the poet has presented some of the noble traits of Duryodhana, but in *Dūtavākya*, he behaves as a true villain. This is because the poet has to contrast him from Kṛṣṇa who is nobility personified. In his very first speech, Duryodhana reveals his true colours. For him war is a festival and peace is scornful. He wants to destroy the Pāṇḍavas completely. He is enraged when the chamberlain introduces Kṛṣṇa as Puruṣottama, (the best among men). He chides the chamberlain and doubts his loyalty. He decides to disrespect Kṛṣṇa and take him as a prisoner much against the rules of *rājadharma*. He warns the councillors of punishment if they showed respect to Kṛṣṇa. He shows cheap taste when he keeps looking at the portrait of Draupadī, as he does not want to take cognizance of Kṛṣṇa's arrival. He could not but get up from his seat on seeing Kṛṣṇa. Being haughty that he is, he hides his action by saying that it was some magic that prompted him to get up. Forgetting that his own royal descendancy is questionable, he casts doubt on the parentage of the Pāṇḍavas. When Kṛṣṇa advises him to give away their share of the kingdom to the Pāṇḍavas, he breathes fire by saying,

> राज्यं नाम नृपात्मजैः सहृदयैर्जित्वा रिपून् भुज्यते
> तल्लोके न तु याच्यते न तु पुनर्दीनाय वा दीयते।
> काङ्क्षा चेन्नृपतित्वमाप्तुमचिरात् कुर्वन्तु ते साहसं
> स्वैरं वा प्रविशन्तु शान्तमतिभिर्जुष्ट शमायाश्रमम् ॥२४॥

> Kingship is enjoyed by princes by defeating the enemies. It is neither begged nor given away as a gift to the suppliants. If they are interested in the kingdom, let them show their valour. Or, if they want peace, let them resort to the hermitages following the sages.

He goes to the extent of abusing Kṛṣṇa, casting aspersions on his killing of Kaṁsa, his maternal uncle. When asked by Kṛṣṇa whether he knows the might of Arjuna, he haughtily says that he does not know. He insults Kṛṣṇa very badly by saying,

> You go to the cowpen with your body smeared with the dust raised by the hoofs of cows. You have wasted my time. I will not speak to men like you who are servants of my vassal kings.

His atrocity reaches its peak when he unsuccessfully tries to bind Kṛṣṇa. He would have been killed on the spot but for the timely intervention of *sudarśana*.

Dhṛtarāṣṭra, the blind king, appears towards the end of the play and offers respects to Kṛṣṇa. Obviously, he is trying to make amends for the audacious act of his son. But the dramatist leaves it to the imagination of the audience. In the *Mahābhārata*, Dhṛtarāṣṭra openly advises his son not to incur the wrath of Kṛṣṇa. But, in the play, the same idea is suggested through the act of Dhṛtarāṣṭra.

The dramatist introduces the novel idea of personifying the weapons of Kṛṣṇa in order to enhance the dramatic effect. Thus the disc, namely, *sudarśana* appears when summoned by Kṛṣṇa and is ordered to kill Duryodhana. But *sudarśana* politely reminds the Lord of his mission and suggests that it would be improper to kill Duryodhana at that time. The other culprits would go unpunished and would continue to cause havoc.

We also have in the play a chamberlain, who announces the arrival of Kṛṣṇa and mentions him as the best among men. Duryodhana is enraged at this and warns him severely. The chamberlain submits that he was confused and hence the mistake. This is a sequel to further confusion that is going to take place in the assembly. Duryodhana pardons him and allows him to leave.

A few other characters are mentioned in the play but they remain incognito. The audience have to imagine that they are present in the assembly as Duryodhana converses with them in the *ākāśabhāṣita* style. By this the dramatist has minimized the number of characters appearing on the stage and after all they have very little role to play. But the mention of the characters helps to produce an impact on the audience. This is a very clever device adopted by the dramatist.

THE RASAS IN THE PLAY

The *vīra* is the main *rasa* in the play which goes well with the hero Kṛṣṇa as well. But the poet delineates it in a suggestive fashion. Strictly speaking, it is *dharmavīra* since Kṛṣṇa observes all the *dharma* of an ambassador. (In *Karṇabhāra*, Karṇa is presented as a *dānavīra*.) As we have seen in the characterisation of Kṛṣṇa, the hero is a *dhīrodātta* and consequently the *rasa* selected is also in line with it (*dharmavīra*). This can be illustrated by a verse occurring in the play.

पुण्यसञ्चयसम्प्राप्तामधिगम्य नृपश्रियम्।
वञ्चयेद् यः सुहृद्बन्धून् स भवेद् विफलश्रमः ॥२५॥

> Having attained the throne which is obtainable only through the merits of the past, if one were to deceive one's own relatives, then such a prosperity becomes a waste.

Kṛṣṇa's stern warning to Duryodhana about the impending calamity, his summoning of *sudarśana* and the words of the latter — all contribute to the development of *vīra rasa* in the play.

We also have scope for *adbhuta rasa;* Kṛṣṇa's appearance in several forms in the council hall and the entry of *sudarśana* and other weapons. Being related to Kṛṣṇa, all these scenes serve as supportive elements to the main *rasa*, the *vīra rasa.* The *hāsya*, though presented in a mild fashion, is also depicted in the play through the scene where the councillors struggle in their attempt to bind Kṛṣṇa. This again contributes to enhance the power of Kṛṣṇa.

THE STYLE OF THE DRAMATIST

The dramatist has employed a simple style which is his forte. A simple style is more difficult to be adopted in comparison to a bombastic style especially in a drama. The general tendency of a writer is to pack all his scholarship in his work. It is difficult to curb this tendency and present a play keeping the interests of the audience in mind. Thus Bhāsa's plays shine in contrast to those of the later dramatists which appear more like plays meant for reading rather than acting. In the present play also, Bhāsa adopts the same technique. His dialogues are short and crisp and the verses are free from long compounds. The verses are introduced only when necessary and most of them are composed in the simple *anuṣṭubh* style. The characters also speak in a style that is suited to their nature. Duryodhana's words bring out his haughtiness, while those of Kṛṣṇa are serene and gentle.

DRAMATIC ELEMENTS IN DŪTAVĀKYA

The dramas of Bhāsa are known for their peculiar characteristics. The *nāndī*, for example, is a benedictory stanza sung at the beginning of a play, after which the stage manager appears on the stage and introduces the play to the audience. But in Bhāsa's plays, *nāndī* is not provided in the text. But we have the statement: *nāndyante tataḥ praviśati sūtradhāraḥ*, meaning that the stage manager enters at the end of *nāndī*. The *nāndī* is probably recited off the stage. Or, perhaps some traditional benedictory song was sung by the background artistes. But the first verse recited serves the purpose of benediction. It runs thus:

> पादः पायादुपेन्द्रस्य सर्वलोकोत्सवः स वः ।
> व्याविद्धो नमुचिर्येन तनुताम्रनखेन खे ॥१॥

> May the foot of Kṛṣṇa, the cause of celebration for the entire world protect us — the foot which with its tender red nails kicked away Namuci into the sky.

The benedictory stanza goes well with the definition of *nāndī* given by Bharata:

> आशीर्वचनसंयुक्ता नित्यं यस्मात् प्रयुज्यते ।
> देवद्विजनृपादीनां तस्मान्नान्दीति कीर्तिता ॥
>
> — *NS*, V.24

The following points become clear from the definition:

i. The *nāndī* is recited by the stage manager.

ii. It is in the form of words of blessings from gods, brāhmaṇas or kings.

iii. It is mandatory to provide *nāndī*.

Dramaturgical writers derive the word from the root *nand* — to please. The *nāndī* is meant to please the gods and thereby ward off the possible impediments to the play.

The opening verse of Bhāsa's plays differs from those of other dramatists though, contentwise, they serve the purpose of benediction. It is possible that Bhāsa followed a pre-Bharata or a non-Bharata school of dramatic tradition in this respect.

The prologues of Bhāsa's plays are characteristically very brief. It is called *sthāpanā* as contrasted with the term *prastāvanā* used by majority of the dramatists. In other plays, the *sūtradhāra* mentions the name of the poet and the play to be staged. But this tradition is conspicuous by its absence in Bhāsa's plays. In *Dūtavākya*, the stage manager is the only character appearing in the prologue. Usually he comes in the company of an actress or an assistant. After reciting the benediction, he wants to make an announcement but he stops on hearing some sound behind the curtain. He listens to it and announces to the audience that the servants are busy organizing the council hall for an urgent meeting on orders from Duryodhana in view of the impending war between the Kauravas and the Pāṇḍavas. After this announcement the *sūtradhāra* leaves the stage and the main play begins with the entry of the chamberlain.

The Bharatavākya of Bhāsa's plays are different from that of the other dramatists. Generally it is recited by one of the characters in the play. But in Bhāsa's plays, it is sung in a general way. In *Dūtavākya* also, we have a similar Bharatavākya,

इमां सागरपर्यन्तां हिमवद्विन्ध्यकुण्डलाम् ।
महीमेकातपत्राङ्कां राजसिंहः प्रशास्तु नः ॥

— verse 56

> May our King Rājasiṁha with undivided sovereignty, rule over this earth surrounded by the seas and adorned by the Himalayas and the Vindhyas serving as a pair of ear rings.

After this song we have the statement *niṣkrāntāḥ sarve* (all leave the stage). Probably all the characters would have assembled back on the stage for the recitation of the Bharatavākya and left after its completion.

King Rājasiṁha, mentioned in the Bharatavākya, was evidently the patron of the poet. With no other details available, it is difficult to identify this particular king.

POETIC MERITS OF THE PLAY

Though being a short play *Dūtavākya* exhibits considerable poetic elements. The very first verse is full of alliterations that make an interesting reading. The first two words begin with the letter *pa*, that is, *pādaḥ pāyāt*. In the expression *utsavaḥ sa vaḥ*, there is alliteration. Similarly, there is a verbal charm in the last two words, *nakhena khe* which when split differently becomes *nakhe nakhe*. It is usual for dramatists, to pack the first verse with such verbal charms or a humorous expression in order to attract the attention of the audience. In the opening verse there is an allusion to the "Vāmana" incarnation of Lord Viṣṇu. The Lord took the form of a dwarf and begged for three steps of space from Mahābali, who unwittingly granted it. The Lord then took a huge form and measured out the heaven and the earth with two steps. For the third step, promised already, Mahābali had to offer his own head. The Lord planted his foot on his head and pushed him to the netherworld.

There is also a reference in the verse to a demon called Namuci. Namuci is mentioned in the Vedas. As the Lord raised his foot covering the heavenly region, his nails pierced Namuci.

By referring to Namuci in the verse, the poet hints at Duryodhana who also possessed demon-like qualities. The piercing of Namuci has a veiled reference to the subjugation of Duryodhana in the play. The *viśvarūpa* of the Lord has indirect reference to the scene where Kṛṣṇa appears in many forms to thwart the attempts of Duryodhana in binding him, both showing the divine aspects of the Lord.

Duryodhana uses the term "Dāmodara" while referring to Kṛṣṇa; he actually uses the term in a derogatory sense. It refers to Kṛṣṇa being tied with a rope around his waist by Yaśodā. It also refers to the act of tying the cows with one end of the rope and tying the other end to one's waist so that the cows do not go astray. Duryodhana indicates that Kṛṣṇa is after all a cowherd. There is also an indirect reference to the rope with which Duryodhana would try to bind Kṛṣṇa in the later part of the play. Bhāsa uses such suggestive expressions in many places of the drama.

The dramatist employs a number appropriate figures of speech. For example, in verse 3, when he says, *nakṣatramadhya iva parvagataḥ śaśāṅkaḥ*, we have a simile, that is, Duryodhana, surrounded by royal umbrella is shining like the moon among stars.

Draupadī caught by Duḥśāsana is like the digit of the moon caught between the jaws of Rāhu — *rāhuvaktrāntargatā candralekheva śobhate* (v. 7). The two young Pāṇḍavas, Nakula and Sahadeva attempting to overcome Duḥśāsana are compared to two young deer trying to pounce on a lion — *harimiva mṛgapotau tejāsabhiprayātau* (v. 10). There are many metaphors as in *kuruvaṁsavana* (v. 14). We have an *arthāntaranyāsa* in verse 18, where it is said "which decent man on earth, with no sense of shame, can express his own crime in a public assembly?"

There is a great charm in the description of the weapons appearing and then departing.

The dramatist has employed *anuṣṭubh* metre extensively throughout the play. The other metres that find a place are — *vaṁśastha, puṣpitāgrā, vasantatilakā, mālinī, śārdūlavikrīḍita* and *sragdharā*.

VĪTHYAṄGAS IN THE PLAY

The *vīthyaṅga*s can be present in any type of play. We have quite a few of them in *Dūtavākya*.

Udghātyaka is a series of successive words with a hidden meaning. The first verse of the play can serve as an illustration of this type. It describes Kṛṣṇa's act of kicking up the demon Namuci in the sky during hid Viśvarūpa posture with which he suppressed Bali. The words of the verse have a hidden meaning in referring to the outwitting of Duryodhana by Kṛṣṇa in the play. Duryodhana is comparable to Namuci on account of his evil designs.

Avalagita consists of an unexpected turn in the events. The following scene may be quoted as an example:

काञ्चुकीयः - प्रसीदतु महाराजः। संभ्रमेण समुदाचारो विस्मृतः।

(पादयोः पतति)

दुर्योधनः - संभ्रम इति। आ मनुष्याणामस्त्येव संभ्रमः। उत्तिष्ठोत्तिष्ठ।

The chamberlain had already been instructed not to give any respect to Kṛṣṇa. But he forgets it and introduces Kṛṣṇa as the best among men. Duryodhana gets enraged and wants to punish him. The chamberlain begs for pardon and says that it was due to confusion. Duryodhana cools down and pardons him, for as he himself says, men are liable to confusion. These twists and turns point to the *vīthyaṅga avalagita*.

Prapañca is unworthy praise. When Duryodhana abuses Pāṇḍavas, Kṛṣṇa ridicules him by saying "You seem to be well versed in the history of the family". This can be taken as an example of *prapañca.*

Mṛdava or euphemism is presenting merits as demerits and vice versa. We have an instance of this in the scene where Duryodhana sees a painting of Draupadī's molestation and appreciates Duḥśāsana for his act.

> दुर्योधनः - अहो दर्शनीयोऽयं चित्रपटः। एष दुश्शासनो
> द्रौपदीं केशहस्ते गृहीतवान्। एषा खलु द्रौपदी,
> दुःशासनपरामृष्टा सम्भ्रमोत्फुल्ललोचना।
> राहुवक्त्रान्तरगता चन्द्रलेखेव शोभते ॥७॥

Similarly, in the scene where he praises Śakuni, there is euphemism.

> अक्षान् क्षिपन् स कितवः प्रहसन् सगर्वं सङ्कोचयन्निव मुदं द्विषतां स्वकीर्त्या।
> स्वैरासनो द्रुपदराजसुतां रुदन्तीं काक्षेण पश्यति लिखत्यपि गां नयज्ञः॥१२॥

Adhibala is a dialogue involving a battle of wits between two parties, each one trying to outsmart the other. In the initial conversation between Kṛṣṇa and Duryodhana where there is reference to family heritage, we have an instance of *adhibala.*

Asatpralāpa is incoherent talk. In the scene where Duryodhana tries to bind Kṛṣṇa, this *vīthyaṅga* is present.

> आः तिष्ठेदानीम्। कथं न दृष्टः केशवः। अयं केशवः।
> अहो ह्रस्वत्वं केशवस्य। आः तिष्ठेदानीम्। कथं न दृष्टः
> केशवः। अयं केशवः। अहो दीर्घत्वं केशवस्य।
> कथं न दृष्टः केशवः। अयं केशवः। सर्वत्र मन्त्रशालायां केशवा भवन्ति।
> किमिदानीं करिष्ये। भवतु, दृष्टम्। भो भो
> राजानः। एकैकः केशवो बध्यताम्। कथं स्वयमेव
> पाशैर्बद्धाः पतन्ति राजानः। साधु भो जम्भक! साधु। — p. 48

Thus we have a fair sprinkling of *vīthyaṅgas* in *Dūtavākya* which make the play interesting and lively.

IS DŪTAVĀKYA A VĪTHĪ?

Now we come to an important question whether *Dūtavākya* can be called as a *vīthī* at all. As we have seen in the definition of *vīthī*, it should have a variety of *rasas*. Though *vīra* figures as the main *rasa* of *Dūtavākya*, there are also other *rasas* like *adbhuta* and *hāsya* to a lesser extent. In the description of Draupadī's molestation there is *bībhatsa*. The number of acts in a *vīthī* is just one or two and *Dūtavākya* fulfills this condition also. The number of characters in a *vīthī* is limited. In *Dūtavākya*, the major characters are just two — Kṛṣṇa and Duryodhana. The other characters like Dhṛtarāṣṭra and the chamberlain just come and go. Sudarśana has a slightly larger role. In order to limit the number of characters the poet has made Duryodhana speak to the councillors in an indirect way. They are not shown to the audience. The play has only the *mukha* and the *nirvahaṇa sandhis*, as per the definition of the *vīthī*. The entry of Kṛṣṇa and the conversation form the *mukha sandhi* while the scene of *māyā kṛṣṇa* is the *nirvahaṇa sandhi*. *Kaiśikī vṛtti* is prescribed for a *vīthī* and the *Dūtavākya* seems to follow it steadfastly.

Another important feature of a *vīthī* is the employment of *ākāśabhāṣita*. The *ākāśabhāṣita* is a technique by which a single character appears and indulges in a conversation with somebody who is not present on the stage. This technique is special to the Bhāṇa, a monologue play in which a single character presents himself before the audience and narrates his experiences in an interesting way. He converses with some other characters who are off the stage. Their voice is not heard but the audience will have to imagine that they are present somewhere and are visible to the character on the stage only. He will ask, for example, "friend, do you ask where I went yesterday? Let me tell you. . . . What what what? you ask why I followed that man ? Let me tell you." In this fashion, the entire story is narrated.

In *Dūtavākya*, the *ākāśabhāṣita* is employed in the opening scene with a telling effect. Actually there is only one character on the stage, namely Duryodhana. But he converses with Śakuni and others as though they are present before him. For the audience they are not actually present.

He first asks Vikarṇa and Varṣadeva as to who should be the commander-in-chief of the army. Then he continues by saying "What? Do the honourable members say that the matter has to be discussed in the council? Let us then enter the hall." Then there is an imaginary discussion on the choice of the commander-in-chief. Turning as it were to Śakuni, he asks "What do you say uncle? Bhīṣma is to be the chief? Well said uncle, let it be." By this technique the audience is made to imagine that Bhīṣma, Droṇa, Karṇa, Śakuni, Vikarṇa, Varṣadeva, Duḥśāsana, Durmukha, Durbuddhi and others are present in the council hall and that Duryodhana is conversing with them.

There is another scene towards the end of the play where the *ākāśabhāṣita* technique is adopted. *Sudarśana* and the other weapons are summoned by the Lord, with a view to kill Duryodhana. But *sudarśana* advises the Lord to be patient. After the Lord gets pacified, *sudarśana* addresses the other weapons in the *ākāśabhāṣita* style. Each one of them is called, its features are described and then it is asked to return since the Lord is pacified. Thus we have descriptions of the *śārṅga* bow, *kaumodakī*, *pāñcajanya*, *nandaka* and ultimately *garuḍa* but none of them will be present before the audience. The idea is to evoke the *adbhuta rasa* through the description.

Thus all the features of a *vīthī*, including the *ākāśabhāṣita* are present in *Dūtavākya* and it is reasonable to accept that it is the earliest specimen of the *vīthī*.

Even if it were not to be a *vīthī*, *Dūtavākya* is a notable play for the moral and ethical values that are imparted in a suggestive way through the incidents. Divine will is supreme and nobody can act against it. One should respect the guests in a most suitable way. One should respect the views of others though one may not agree with them. One should not quarrel with one's own kinsmen. Sharing and caring should be the motto of one's life. One should not revel in the misery of others. There are many such ideas that are enshrined in the play. They are very important especially for the present-day world where intolerance and violence have assumed alarming proportions. A play like this will definitely bring solace to the troubled minds and put them on the right track. This is the very purpose of a drama and literature as a whole and it is very well demonstrated by the play *Dūtavākya*.

Mālatikā Vīthī

Mālatikā Vīthī is known only from references and a few passages quoted from it in the Alaṁkāra texts. *Śṛṅgāraprakāśa* and *Nāṭyadarpaṇa* refer to it. Bahurūpamiśra, a commentator on *Daśarūpaka* also has quoted from it. It is very difficult to assess the full story of the play from the fragments available to us. Bud judging from the trend of the dialogues and the nature of such plays, we may conjecture that it probably had a theme similar to *Mālavikāgnimitra* or *Ratnāvalī*. The hero is a king and he is in love with Mālatikā. He is helped by the *vidūṣaka* in his love affair. Probably there is another character, namely the queen who might have objected to their love affair initially but must have reconciled to the inevitable at the end. The play probably ends with the wedding of the king and Mālatikā.

Bhoja quotes the following passage from the play to illustrate the *vīthyaṅga*, *udghātyaka* (vol. II, Ch. XII, pp. 470 of

Śṛṅgāraprakāśa manuscript deposited in Madras Government Oriental Manuscripts Library, Chennai):

> *Yathā mālatikāyām vīthyām —*
>
> Mālatikā — *ko viṣamaḥ saṁsāre, ko vā duḥkhena pāryate taritum*
>
> Rājā — *kusumaśaraḥ taralākṣi. Viyogaduḥkhāmbudhiścaiva.*

Udghātyaka is a series of questions and answers and the given example fits in suitably. When Mālatikā asks what is the most troublesome thing in the world and what cannot be crossed, the king replies by saying that the arrows of cupid are a source of great trouble and that it is very difficult to cross the ocean of misery arising out of separation from the beloved. Dhanika, in his *Avaloka*, quotes the following passage from the same play as an illustration for the same *vīthyaṅga*.

> Mālatikā — *ka eṣa kāmaḥ, yena tvamapi dūyase, kiṁ puruṣah ahosvit strī itī* ।
>
> Rājā — *manojātiranādhīnā sukheṣveva pravartate* ।
> *snehasya lalito mārgaḥ kāma ityabhidhīyate* ॥
>
> Vidūṣakaḥ — *vayasya, evamapi na jāne* ।
>
> Rājā — *icchāprabhavassaḥ* ।
>
> Vidūṣakaḥ — *kim yo yamicchati, sa tasya kāma iti* ।
>
> Rājā — *atha kim?*
>
> Vidūṣakaḥ — *tat jñātam, yathā aham sūdakāraśālāyām bhojanamicchāmi* ।
>
> Rājā — *tatha bhavatu* ।

Mālatikā asks the king to explain what is love. Is it a man or a woman? The king replies by saying that love is born in the mind and that it is independent. It contributes to only happiness. It is a gentle way of (expressing) mutual attraction. The *vidūṣaka* is not able to understand. The king further explains by saying that it arises out of desire. *Vidūṣaka* asks — that means whoever likes somebody (also meaning something), it is love for him? The king says — yes. *Vidūṣaka* says that he has understood. It is like his desire for food. The king says — let it be so.

It may be noted that *Avaloka* as well as *Bhāvaprakāśa* say that it is from the play *Vikramorvaśīya,* which is wrong. It is from *Mālatikā Vīthī* as proposed by Bhoja.

Another quotation from the same *vīthī* is quoted by Bhoja while illustrating the *vīthyaṅga, nālikā. Nālikā* is an enigmatic remark made with a hidden meaning and it is meant for evoking laughter. The Prākr̥t verse quoted in this context is badly mutilated in the manuscript edited by V. Raghavan and it has not been possible to reconstruct it.

The account of the *Mālatikā Vīthī* given above is based on V. Raghavan's book on *Śr̥ṅgāraprakāśa* and we are not able to gather any more information about the play. The author of the play is also not known from the existing sources. All that we can say is that it must have been a popular *vīthī* till about twelfth century after which it was lost unfortunately.

Indulekhāvīthī

INDULEKHĀ

Indulekhā, another anonymous *vīthī,* is known only through quotations and references. Bhoja refers to it in Chapter XII of *Śr̥ṅgāraprakāśa* and quotes a verse from it to illustrate the *vīthyaṅga* called *trigata.* Only one verse has thus come down to us. The hero is a king and the heroine is probably Indulekhā, after whom the play is named. The king calls his friend, quite likely, the Vidūṣaka and says,

Rājā — *vayasya,*

kintu kalahaṁsanādo madhuro madhupāyinām tu jhaṅkāraḥ ।
hṛdayagṛhadevatāyāḥ tasya nu sanūpuram caraṇam ॥

Is the sound made by the royal swans sweet? Or the humming of the bees? As for the presiding deity of the heart, the jingling sound of the anklets of the sweetheart is the refuge.

Here, there is triple explanation for the sound heard, namely that of the swans, the bees and the anklets and hence the *vīthyaṅga trigata.*

Bhāvaprakāśana refers to this *vīthī* twice. While citing a model play for *vīthī,* the author refers to it. Again, while giving an illustration for *trigata,* the author quotes the same verse cited above. In fact, the correct reading in the verse, *madhupāyinām tu jhaṅkāraḥ,* is supplied by Śāradātanaya. Bahurūpamiśra (as also the authors of *Nāṭyadarpaṇa*) also quotes the same verse in the same context in his commentary on the *Daśarūpaka.*

All these evidences go to prove that Indulekhā was a popular *vīthī* during the time of these authors. The loss of the text has deprived us of a good example of *vīthī.*

Līlāvatīvīthī

LĪLĀVATĪ

Līlāvatī is one of the few specimens of the *vīthī* that are available to us. The author, Rāmapāṇivāda, hails from Kerala and has contributed quite a few plays in Sanskrit. Though written during the eighteenth century, the society and the culture it represents dates back to the medieval period. The sweet *vaidarbhī* style adopted in the play and its remarkable similarity with *Ratnāvalī* make it appear as though it belonged to the seventh or eighth century. The play not only satisfies the definition of *vīthī* as given in the dramaturgical texts and as proposed by the author himself but also in his other *vīthī*, Candrikā. He says,

> *pātradvayaprayojyā bhanavadekāṅkikā dvisandhiśca* ।
> *ākāśabhāṣitavatī kṛtrimamitivṛttamāśritā vīthī* ॥

> A *vīthī* is a one act play with an imaginary plot, having two characters, two junctures (the *mukha* and the *nirvahana*) and displaying *ākāśabhāṣita* Technique.

Befittingly, *Līlāvatī* is a one-act play with a well-knit plot and a delectable blend of *rasas*. The main sentiment is *śṛṅgāra* supported by *adbhuta*. There is also scope for *hāsya* coming under the domain of *vidūṣaka*. We have a fair sprinkling of the *vīthyaṅgas* that add variety and charm to the play.

THE AUTHOR AND HIS WORKS

The author Rāmapāṇivāda hails from Kerala and he belongs to the eighteenth century. He is a prolific writer in both Sanskrit and Prākṛt. *Uṣāniruddha* and *Kaṁsavaho* are his full-fledged Prākṛt *kāvyas*. Rāmapāṇivāda has shown his mastery over the Prākṛt language by writing a commentary on the Prākṛt *sūtras* of Vararuci. His contributions to Sanskrit range from *mahākāvya* to *stotra* literature. He has two *mahākāvyas* to his credit — *Rāghavīya* in 20 cantos and *Viṣṇuvilāsa* in eight cantos. In the field of drama, he has contributed *Sītārāghava*, a *nāṭaka*, *Madanaketucarita*, a *prahasana* and two *vīthīs*, *Candrikāvīthī* and *Līlāvatīvīthī*. He has also composed a *campū kāvya* called *Bhāgavatacampū*. His mastery over music is revealed by his works *Gītārāma*, a *nṛtyaprabandha*, *Śivagīti*, a musical lyric on the lines of the *Gīta Govinda* and *Tālaprastara*, a work dealing with the musical beats.

It is clear from the references he makes to a number of kings (a king Devanārāyaṇa by name is mentioned in *Līlavatīvīthī*) and feudal lords that Rāmapāṇivāda moved from place to place in search of recognition and patronage. Rāmapāṇivāda was a disciple of one Nārāyaṇa Bhaṭṭatiri whom he refers to with reverence in his works. The poet also refers to his native village, Maṅgalagrāma, in some of his works. There is a bitter controversy among the Kerala scholars on the question of the identification of Rāmapāṇivāda with the well-known Malayalam poet Kuñcan Nambiar. But the arguments against this theory seem to carry more weight.

THE TEXT OF LĪLĀVATĪVĪTHĪ

The present account of the *Līlāvatīvīthī* is based on the edition brought out by the University Manuscripts Library, Thiruvanantapuram in 1948 (Manuscript No. 958A, of the Curator's collection in the Library, procured from Narayanan Elayatu, Vempanatillam, Ambalapuzha, North Thiruvanantapuram. According to the editor, the manuscript in Malayalam script was in good condition and was free from mistakes).

THE DRAMATIC PLOT

Dramatis Personae

King Vīrapāla

Vidūṣaka

Other characters who do not appear on the stage:

Līlāvatī, the heroine

Kalāvatī, the queen

Siddhimatī, a *yoginī*

Bhadrasiddhi, the snake charmer

Tāmrākṣa, the demon

The brāhmaṇas

Kelimālā, Līlāvatī's friend

Kandalikā, Queen's maid

Stage manager and an actress (appearing in the prologue).

Līlāvatī is the daughter of the king of the Karṇāṭa country. The father fears that his daughter may be abducted by the enemies and so he entrusts her custody in the hands of Kalāvatī, the queen of King Vīrapāla of Kuntala country. Kalāvatī zealously guards Līlāvatī for she fears that the king may fall in love with her if they were to meet each other. But somehow, they meet and fall in love with each other at the first sight. The *vidūṣaka,* who always keeps company with the king, wants to bring about their union through the help of a *yoginī* by name Siddhimatī who would employ a magical spell for this purpose. In the meantime, Līlāvatī, pining to meet her lover, sends a love letter along with the signet of her ivory ear ring. Unfortunately it falls in the hands of the queen's maid who reports about it to the queen. The queen wants to meet the king and take him to task, but she falls into the web of magic cast by the *yoginī*. A cobra spreads its poison with the effect that the queen becomes unconscious. The *vidūṣaka* appears in the disguise of a snake charmer and pretends to revive the queen. Meanwhile the magic spell disappears and the queen regains her consciousness. She thinks that it is due to the timely act of the snake charmer and being pleased she grants him a boon. He cleverly says that he would claim it when needed and departs. The queen then meets the king, shows the love letter written by Līlāvatī and reprimands him severely. Siddhimatī works her magic again and prevents estrangement between the king and the queen. The queen has a dream that night in which Lord Śiva appears before her and tells her that it was he who appeared in the form of a snake charmer and saved her life. He also advises her that she should organize the wedding between the king and Līlāvatī. By the power of Līlāvatī's horoscope, the king would become an Emperor. Getting up from her slumber, the queen meets the king, narrates the entire dream and requests him to accept the hand of Līlāvatī. On the day of the wedding, Līlāvatī goes to the temple to offer the customary worship to the deities. On the way she is caught by the terrible demon, Tāmrākṣa, sent by the king of Kaliṅga, the enemy of her father. King Vīrapāla fights with him and kills him ultimately. Subsequently, the wedding between the king and Līlāvatī takes place. At the end, *vidūṣaka* reveals the trick played by him. The king appreciates Siddhimatī for her magical skill and spell and thanks the *vidūṣaka* also. The play ends with the usual Bharatavākya.

CHARACTER STUDY

Vīrapāla, the king of the Kuntala country is the hero of the play. He is a replica of such kings seen in plays like *Mālavikāgnimitra* and *Ratnāvalī*, a *dakṣiṇa nāyaka*. He is deeply in love with Līlāvatī, the princess of the Karṇāṭa country. His love for her is revealed in his anxious enquiry about her. He is reminded of her lovely charms. He asks *vidūṣaka*:

अपि खलु कुशलं मे नेत्रयोरायतानामपि च जघनभारे दूरविस्तारभाजाम्।
कुचसरसिजयुग्मे चोन्नतानां घनानां दशनवसनबिम्बे चारुणानामसूनाम्॥२२॥

When he learns that the queen, becoming suspicious has kept Līlāvatī under special security, he loses all hopes of meeting her. He pines for her and explains his condition to his friend *vidūṣaka* and seeks his help in his love affair. The breeze carrying the fragrance of full blown jasmine flowers adds to his misery. He says:

विकचकुटजमल्लीफुल्लनिर्यन्मधूलीपरिमलपरिवारे वाति सन्ध्यासमीरे।
लुठति धरणिपृष्टे दीर्घमुष्णञ्च भूयः श्वसिति वहति मूर्छां तीव्रतापः सखा मे॥२३॥

In his anxiety, he addresses the cupid very much like the hero of *Vikramorvaśīya* by saying,

बाणान् संहर, पञ्चबाण! मधुपज्यावल्लरीसंहितान्
मुञ्चामुं च शरासमैक्षवमहो व्यर्थस्तवायं श्रमः।
केकाभिश्च शिखण्डिनामविरलश्च्योतत्परागोत्करै-
र्मालत्याः प्रसवैश्च केवलममी दूयामहे यद्वयम्॥१७॥

According to him his lady love was created by cupid with the best of all ingredients available in all the three worlds. When will he be able to see her?

लोकत्रयप्रथितमोहनवस्तुसार्थैः स्पृष्टं स्वयं भगवाता मकरध्वजेन।
तस्याः सखे! निरुपमं वदनारविन्दं भूयः कदाचिदपि नाम विलोकयेयम्॥४८॥

His love for the queen is equally strong. He feels that the queen's anger about his love affair is fully justified. Her angry mood is always present before his eyes, as he says:

किमपि चपलं जानत्या मे सुखेन सखीमुखा-
दरुणिमगुणो देव्या नाद्यापि मुञ्चति लोचने।
कुचकलशयोः कोपोदीर्णो न शाम्यति वेपथु-
र्गलतलगलद्बाष्पो रुन्धेतरां परुषाक्षरम्॥२५॥

When he comes to know that the queen is bitten by the serpent, he swoons immediately unable to bear the intensity of the calamity. When he gets up, he laments that it is useless to live without her.

दष्टा चेदणकभुजङ्गमेन देवी कष्टं भो विफलमिदं हि जीवितं मे।
कर्णाटक्षितिपतिकन्यकानुरक्तं हे चेतो जहिहि शतं मनोरथानाम्॥३९॥

When the queen is revived, he heaves a sigh of relief and says:

यत्ते बालशिरीषनूतनदलस्पर्धालु मुग्धं वपुः
कष्टं दष्टमभूत्करालगरलज्वालेन कालाहिना।
तेनानेन जनेन सुन्दरि! चिरं मूर्च्छायितं साम्प्रतं
शान्ते तत्र विषोष्मणि श्वसितमित्येतन्महत्कौतुकम्॥४४॥

His condition as he is torn between the love for two women is very well brought out by himself:

> कालोऽयं खलु नीलकण्ठनटनाटोपप्रियंभावुकः
> पान्थान्तःस्मयपश्यतोहरतटिद्वल्लीसुखाकारकः।
> देवी च प्रणयानुरोधविमुखी लीलावती चेदृशी
> कामो वामतरो विधिश्च विषमो हा हन्त का मे गतिः ॥३१॥

He has great regard for his bosom friend, *vidūṣaka*. He seeks his help in all his activities, especially in the love affair. When the king and the queen prepare to go out, the *vidūṣaka* hesitates to join them. But the king says "you are not different from me" (*abhinno hi bhavān asmattaḥ*, p. 25). He praises his friend after achieving success in his endeavour:

> दोर्भ्यामेव सनक्रचक्रजटिलं वारान्निधिं सन्तरेत्
> पद्भ्यामेव स लङ्घयेदपगतालम्बं नभोमण्डलम्।
> दुस्साधाखिलकर्मसाधनविधौ पाण्डित्यमत्यूर्जितं
> बिभ्राणा सुहृदां कटाक्षलहरी जागर्त्ति यस्योदये ॥५९॥

It is not that he is always engrossed in love affairs. He rises to the occasion if the situation demands. For example, he gets into action immediately on hearing that Līlāvatī is abducted. He chases the demon and kills him, showing extraordinary valour. He shows great dignity when the queen herself offers him the hand of Līlāvatī. He simply says *yadādiśati devī*. On another occasion, he brings out the nature of the world beautifully with a philosophical outlook. 'It is very rare to find an assembly where the noble alone will be present. It is mixed with jealous people also. It is difficult to see the river whose waters do not carry the slush and dirt from the banks. Likewise, it is difficult to find happiness that is unmixed with misery in this world.

> गोष्ठी सा विरला न यत्र घटते सत्ता पुरोभागिनां
> नारी सा खलु दुर्लभा न कुसृतिश्लिष्टं यदीयं मनः।
> दुष्प्रापं च तदम्बु तीरजरजोराजिर्न यद् दूषयेद्
> दुस्साधञ्च सुखं तदाविलयते दुःखानुवृत्तिर्न यत् ॥५८॥

The *vidūṣaka* in the play is called by the name Vaibhāsika. True to his name (a hilarious person) he is full of wit, humour and satire. He has a twofold task — to carry out the wishes of his master and to provide comic relief to the audience through his witty remarks. He is referred to as *narmasaciva* (a witty minister) of the king. He has no hesitation in boasting about his credentials.

यथेष्टमष्टादशवेदवेदी चतुष्पुराणोदधिपारगामी।
वैहासिको नाम महीसुरोऽहम् न पूजितः कस्य घटयामि कार्यम्॥१०॥

I am a scholar in eighteen Vedas and I have crossed the ocean of four Purāṇas. I am called as Vaihāsika and I belong to the Mahīsura country. If requested, whose job shall I not accomplish.

By this statement he only parades his own ignorance of the scriptures. Actually the Vedas are only four in number and the Purāṇas are eighteen. He says that he can put in extraordinary effort in his pursuits (*yatra asādhāraṇa-prayāso vaihāsika-brahmaṇaḥ* — p. 24). But in reality he is very careless in his activities. He drops the signet ear ring given by Līlāvatī to be passed on to the king. He says *uttarīya dṛḍhabaddhamapi tad danta tāṭaṅkam prabharaṣṭam* (p. 12). He is rightly ridiculed as *pramādanidhi* (a heap of errors). His deceitful means are well known to everybody. Kelimālā, the friend of the heroine says *kaḥ punaste kapaṭanāṭakam na janatīti* (p. 7). (Who is not aware of your deceitful tricks?). Kandalikā, the queen's attendant is also of the same opinion. She says *sarvam mayā jñātam yuṣmākam kapaṭanāṭakam* (p. 14) (I know everything about your deceitful tricks). Though he fumbles often, he proclaims that nobody can excel him in keeping secrets (*ko anyo mama mahābrāhmaṇasya samaśīrṣam udvahati rahāsyacintāyām* — p. 6). He also boasts that he is a man of strong mind (*dṛḍhahṛdayaḥ khalu vaihāsikabrāhmaṇaḥ* — p. 8). But just on hearing that a serpent has entered the harem, he raises hue and cry saying that he has fallen into the twin tongues of the serpent *bho vayasya, duṣṭa-viṣadhara-jihvā-yugalāntara-patitam mām paritrāyasva* (p. 17). For all his foolhardiness, he is resourceful. In order to help the king in his love affair, he seeks the help of the *yoginī* and this step proves to be the turning point in the play. Then again, coming in the disguise of a snake charmer, he pretends to save the queen and thereby wins her favour. He boasts that he can cure anybody of any kind of serpent bite by his pronouncement of the Tāntric mantras.

> आअद्ढणुञ्चाडणर्ततरूहं वहामि तिक्खाण वि पण्णआणम्।
> वेसंठपळ्लङ्कमअं महाहिं विद्दावएउं वि ण मे पआसो ॥४० ॥

Even the king is not in a position to identify him though observing closely.

> आवीतमलिनवसनो दण्डाग्रग्रथितसर्पपेटीकः।
> अविरलशङ्खाभरणो मुखविलिखितरोचनातिलकः ॥४२ ॥
>
> Being clad in a dirty cloth, holding a serpent-box through a club, wearing a garland of conches and sporting a *tilaka* mark on his forehead.

His cryptic remarks sound appropriate to the situation. He advises the king to go ahead with his love affair unmindful of the possible protest from the queen. He says "Who will refrain from taking a pearl for the fear of breaking the nacre?" (*kaḥ śuktibhañjanabhayena muktāvalimujjhati* — p. 12). It is no wonder that the king is very fond of him. He cannot remain without him even for a moment. When the king reaches a breaking point out of love lorn condition, he diverts his attention to something else and saves him. His communication skills are very good. He somehow extracts the secret from the mouth of Līlāvatī's friend. While tackling the queen's friend also, he shows his ingenuity. Though generally speaking in Prākr̥t he can switch over to Sanskrit when the situation demands.

He is presented as a *vidūṣaka* of the cleverer type as we find one in *Mālavikāgnimitra*.

Līlāvatī, the heroine of the play remains incognito for the audience throughout the play. Yet one can feel her presence by the force of the dramatic action and the references made about her by the other characters. She is described as one possessing extraordinary beauty (*asādhāraṇa rūpalāvaṇyā* — p. 7). She is the daughter of the king of Karṇāṭa country. But she is in exile at the Kuntala country forced by the circumstances. She is in love with the king to whom she sends a love letter along with the signet of her ear ring. She shows considerable ingenuity in designing the letter. At the outset it appears as though she is addressing the royal swan. But the term 'rājā' refers to the king and 'pañkaja' (lotus) to herself indirectly.

राजहंस मम पङ्कजिन्या दर्शयित्वा क्षणमात्मविलासम् ।
साम्प्रतं पुनर्घनोत्कलिकां मे केवलं करोषि युक्तमिदं ते ॥२७ ॥

O Royal Swan, having 'shown your splendour for just a moment, you desert me to suffer like this. Is it proper ?'

Her subsequent words are more explicit. She says:

उत्तानीकृतभोगमण्डलचलज्जिह्वाकरालाकृति-
र्दंष्ट्राकोटिपरिस्रवद्विषकणश्रेणीनिषिक्तावनिः ।
वेत्रोदञ्चितपाणिभिर्भयवशान्मुक्तान्तिको वेत्रिभिः
कष्टं कोऽपि महोरगः स्वयमसावन्तःपुरं गाहते ॥३७ ॥

Be it the cloud dotted with water drops, be it the lightening, be it the breeze carrying the fragrance of *ketakī* flower, be it cupid who tortures the love lorn women, O Noble One, on account of you, (they) just make me bear my name (lifeless).

Her love lorn condition is pitiable.

गभीरपयोधरस्तनितान्मदमेदुरमयूरमिथुननिधुवनान् ।
कथमपि गमयति वराकी तव प्रणयालम्बना दिवसान् ॥२३ ॥

She does not care for a bath or food. She is spending sleepless nights. She does not mind about the daily routine, nor does she listen to the words of friends. She lies in the couch always undergoing the pangs of separation.

> न स्नाने न च भोजने न शयने धत्ते मनागादरं
> नादत्ते करणीयवस्तुघटनायत्तं सखीनां वचः।
> पर्यङ्कं विरहय्य पल्लवमयीं शय्यां सदा सेवते
> कष्टं सम्प्रति वीरपालविरहाल्लीलावती दूयते॥११॥

Her nobility and patience pay ultimately as she is finally united with her lover.

The queen is presented in a two-dimensional fashion. On the one hand, she is possessive, as every woman is and would not like to share her husband's love with anybody else, but at the same time she is prepared to make any sacrifice for the welfare of her husband. Knowing fully well the weakness of her husband for pretty women, she zealously guards Līlāvatī from the eyes of the king. She becomes angry when she comes to know of his love affair. But due to the effect of the magical powers of the *yoginī*, she changes her mind and offers the hand of Līlāvatī to her husband since that would fetch him the title of "supreme monarch" as per the astrological predictions. She is the replica of such queens we find in plays like *Mālavikāgnimitra* and *Ratnāvalī*.

RASAS IN THE PLAY

The main *rasa* in the play is *śṛṅgāra* as is quite evident from the theme. It is actually *vipralambha śṛṅgāra* as we find the hero and heroine pining for each other throughout the play. The love lorn condition of Līlāvatī is very well brought out by her friend:

> श्रयति गरलच्छायं भूयः पयोधरमण्डली-
> विवरगलितानिन्दोः पादानसौ विरलानपि।

कथमपि पुरोवातानेतान् विकस्वरकेतकी-
परिमलभृतो दावासेवं सखी मम सेवते ॥१२॥

The *vipralambha śṛṅgāra* as brought out in the character study of the king and Līlāvatī go to prove the ability of the dramatist in depicting this *rasa* delicately yet poignantly.

With the *vidūṣaka* being the only character other than the king presented on the stage, there is bound to be scope for *hāsya* and the play does have humour in a good measure. But it never hinders the progress of the main *rasa*. On the other hand, it supports the main *rasa* in the process of *praśamana* whenever the *śṛṅgāra* reaches its peak. In fact, the main *rasa* should never be taken to the breaking point. It should be delineated in the pattern of a wave, taken to great heights and immediately brought down to normal level with the help of a secondary rasa. The *hāsya* in the play helps in this process. There is humour in the boasting of the *vidūṣaka*, his topsy-turvey reference to the number of the Vedas and the Purāṇas, his foolhardiness in losing the signet of Līlāvatī and in his appearance as the disguised snake charmer. When the queen's attendant recovers the signet, carelessly dropped by the *vidūṣaka*, she says sarcastically "I think it got dropped from the ear of the presiding deity of the gardens" (*manye udyānalakṣmyāḥ śravaṇapāśat prabhraṣṭamiti* — p. 14). When the queen offers the hand of Līlāvatī to the king, the latter asks for the opinion of the *vidūṣaka* who makes a cryptic remark by saying "Who will forsake the food when invited?" (*āmantritaḥ ko miṣṭabhojanam parityajyati* — p. 27). The dramatist has, in fact, exhibited a very dignified sense of humour throughout the play.

We have a fair element of *adbhuta* in the play. We are in for it from the moment the *vidūṣaka* thinks of seeking the help of the *yoginī*. The wonderful dream witnessed by the queen, in which she has seen Lord Śiva appearing before her and the description of it evokes *adbhuta*.

दृष्टः स्वप्ने फणिवलयिना पाणिना पाणिनालं
मन्दं मृद्नन्नचलदुहितुर्बालचन्द्रावतंसः ।
पादन्यासप्रचलनवलद्भोगिनिश्वासवात-
क्षुभ्यद्गङ्गासलिलमुखरीभूतकोटीरभारः ॥५० ॥

The *adbhuta* is revealed in the serpent bite scene as well.

We have an instance of *vīra* in the act of the king's destruction of the demon which is described vividly in the following verse.

प्रहरसि मदिराक्षि प्रेमभाजं किमेवं
जनमिममतिकोपक्रूरतारैरपाङ्गैः ।
तव सुमुखि शपेऽहं पादपङ्केरुहाभ्यां
यदि भवति मदीयं जातु चेतोऽन्यदास्थम् ॥४६ ॥

There is an element of *bhayānaka* in the description of the demon. The appearance of the terrible serpent is equally frightful:

उत्तानीकृतभोगमण्डलचलज्जिह्वाकरालाकृति
र्दंष्ट्राकोटिपरिस्रवद्विषकणश्रेणीनिषिक्तावनिः
नेत्रोदञ्चितपणिभिर्भयवशान्मुक्तान्तिको वेत्रिभिः
कष्टं कोऽपि महोरगः स्वयमसावन्तःपुरं गाहते ॥३७ ॥

DRAMATIC TECHNIQUE

(i) *Nāndī* : The *nāndī* verse is dedicated to Lord Śiva and Goddess Gaurī in a conventional way.

तत्पादपद्मयुगलं गिरिकन्यकाया
लोकातिशायिचारितं भवतः पुनातु ।
उल्लासयन्ति यदिदं मुहुरीश्वरस्य
चूडानिशाकरकिशोरमयूखलेखाः ॥१ ॥

"May the two lotus like feet of Gaurī protect you — the feet that possess the glory surpassing the entire world; the feet which the streaks of rays of the crescent moon existing on the head of Lord Śiva gladden ever and anon."

The *nāndī* not only provides the purpose of benediction, it also makes an indirect reference to some of the incidents of the play. The term *lokātisayicaritam* indirectly refers to the dream sequence in the play and the reference to Lord Śiva indicates his appearance in the dream of the queen.

(ii) *The Prologue* : In the prologue the stage manager enters and says that he has been ordered by the assemblage to present a play. The members of the assemblage are beholden to King Devanārāyaṇa whose heart is always engrossed in analysing the intricacies of all the scriptures, the mythology, the dramas and other forms of literature.

The play is intended to be a *vīthī* which evokes simple and sweet *rasa*s and which consists of wonderful episodes. It should be composed in a new style with new expressions. The stage manager then asks his wife to render music. He says that he has become a little nervous before the assembly consisting of scholars who are steeped in the dramatic art and who have dived deep into the various art forms. In the course of the conversation, the stage manager reveals that he is going to present a play called *Līlāvatīvīthī*, composed by Rāmapāṇivāda, a nephew of Raghava Panivada and a resident of Maṅgalagrāma. The attainments of the poet are set forth in a verse form (v. 5) wherein the poet pays his tributes to King Devanārāyaṇa once again.

नित्यं नृत्यति यस्य नाम रसनारङ्गे स्वयं भारती
चित्ते यस्य च भासते सुरधुनीनाथो रथाङ्गायुधः ।

यं भूयो बहुमन्यते नरपतिः श्रीदेवनारायणः
सोऽयं मे हृदये चकास्तु सततं भूदेवचूडामणिः ॥५॥

The stage manager then talks about the season (the monsoon) and asks his wife to render a song which she obliges (v. 7). He appreciates her for the song. She then poses a question "Sir, my sister Raṅgamallikā by name, has a daughter who has fallen in love with a dancer Saṅgītamalla by name. But his first wife by name Raṅgamālā, who is filled with jealousy objects to it. Now, may I ask the brāhmaṇas assembled here to suggest a way out by which they could be united?" The narration has a veiled reference to the main story where the heroine falls in love with the king who is already married. The queen is naturally overcome with jealousy when she comes to know of her husband's love affair. Asking the brāhmaṇas for help points to the king seeking help from the *vidūṣaka* who is also a *brāhmaṇa*.

The stage manager recites a verse in praise of the worship of great personalities and justifies the act of seeking their help in getting the problems solved.

In the meantime the *vidūṣaka* boasts of his capabilities from behind the screen. The stage manager announces that the *vidūṣaka* is about to enter and so he vacates the stage along with his wife.

Thus, the prologue has many significant points and it kindles the interest of the audience as well and it induces them to witness the play in full.

(iii) *Viṣkambhaka*: In the beginning of the play proper, we have a *viṣkambhaka*. As we know, *viṣkambhaka* is a technique by which some of the incidents that need not be/cannot be represented on the stage, are made known to the audience. In the beginning of the present *viṣkambhaka*, we have a soliloque by the *vidūṣaka* in which he states that the king had fallen in love with Līlāvatī who is guarded by the queen out of jealousy. He also vows to liberate her from the clutches of the queen and unite her with the king. In this endeavour, he would seek the help of the *yoginī*. He sees that Līlāvatī's friend Kelimālā is coming in that direction and he indulges in a conversation with her in the *ākāśabhāṣita* style. The previous history of Līlāvatī and her present state are revealed through the conversation. The *viṣkambhaka* ends when the king enters reciting a verse explaining his love-lorn condition.

We find that almost half of the story is narrated in the *viṣkambhaka* and hence its usefulness.

(iv) *Bharatavākya*: The conventional Bharatavākya appearing at the end of the play has many noteworthy points.

> काव्ये नव्यपुराणभेदगणनाहीना धियो धीमतां
> सङ्गृह्णन्तु गुणानणूनपि तथा दोषानपाकुर्वताम्।
> लोकानामवधूतमत्सरकथामैत्री तथोज्जृम्भतां
> भक्तिर्नश्चिरमेधतां गुरुपदाम्भोजे जगन्मङ्गले ॥६२॥

> May the intellect of the great who are averse to the distinction between the old literature and the new one appreciate even an iota of merits in the *kāvya*, setting aside the demerits. Let amity surpass jealousy in the world. Let the devotion to the lotus feet of the preceptors grow for auspiciousness of the world.

The verse which is secular in nature is quite significant, since it indirectly refers to the joy expressed by the king, Līlāvatī and the queen as the latter let off her jealousy and united the two lovers.

VĪTHYAṄGAS IN THE PLAY

In the verse 10, where the *vidūṣaka* makes a topsy-turvey reference to the Vedas (as 18 in number) and the Purāṇas (as 4), we have an instance of the *vīthyaṅga, chala* since he heaps unworthy praise on himself by saying that he had mastered the scriptures.

Avalagita is an unexpected turn of events. The *vidūṣaka* loses the love letter and the signet ear ring. But it is recovered by the queen's maid. She taunts the *vidūṣaka* by saying that it must have fallen from the ear of the presiding deity of the garden. Here we have an instance of *avalagita*.

Asatpralāpa or incoherent talk is another *vīthyaṅga*. We have an example for this in the scene where the *vidūṣaka*, on hearing about the serpent, imagines that he had already fallen into the tongue of the serpent.

DESCRIPTIVE POWERS OF THE POET

The poet-dramatist carries on the legacy of the earlier poets in describing nature in all its beauty. We have a beautiful account of the rainy season in the verse,

गम्भीरनीरदमृदङ्गरवाभिरामं भृङ्गाङ्गनामधुरगीतकलासनाथम् ।
विद्युत्प्रदीपकलिते विपिनान्तरङ्गे नृत्तोत्सवं वितनुते ननु नीलकण्ठः ॥६॥

> Deep in the forests with light provided by the lightning, the peacocks render a dance recital to the tune of sweet music provided by the female bees and the percussion provided by the water laden clouds.

Even the *vidūṣaka*, who generally does not pay much attention to the beauties of nature, is captivated by the charm of the season and sings in praise of cupid in a beautiful verse studded with metaphors.

बाणा यस्य विकसितचूतकलिका ज्या च भृङ्गावली
मित्रं वा शशलाञ्छनो रणचमूसार्थो विदग्धस्त्रीजनः।
सोऽयं शङ्करनेत्रपावकपुरोडाशोऽपि पञ्चायुधो
धीराणामपि मनांसि नयति न क्षणाद्धंहो दशां कीदृशीम् ॥१५॥

The cupid's arrows are the mango sprouts. The bow-string, the swarm of bees; his friend is the moon; his soldiers are beautiful young women; thus the cupid, though roasted in the fire emanating from the eyes of Lord Śiva, still torments the minds of even the brave ones.

POETIC MERITS

Rāmapāṇivāda has a natural gift of poetic talents which he exhibits vividly in the play. The alliterations occurring in the text are spontaneous. In the last line of the first verse, there is an evidence.

Similarly, in the *vidūṣaka*'s statement (p. 18), cursing the serpent, there is a good *anuprāsa*:

मा मा कालरूपकालकाकोदरकरालकाकोलजलनिधौ पततु।

In the verse *rajahaṁsa. . .* (v. 17) quoted already, there is an instance of *samāsokti*. We have the same *alaṁkāra* in another verse:

दिगङ्गनासूढपयोधरासु यन्न्यलायि कान्तेन मयूखमालिना।
निमज्जते वारिणि लज्जमानया सरोरुहिण्या किमनेन हेतुना ॥३३॥

We have an example of *dṛṣṭānta* in the following verse:

निर्व्याजनिर्मलधियां विधुरेषु मन्ये वीताभिसन्धिकणिकः करुणानुषङ्गः।
किं चातका विदधते हितमम्बुदेभ्यः किं तर्पयन्ति न पयोभिरमून् पयोदाः ॥६०॥

Great men out of compassion are favourably disposed towards everybody. Do the *cātaka* birds request favour from the clouds? Do not the clouds offer water to them of their own accord?

We have a simile in the line

अत्रोद्याने वल्मीकरन्ध्रमुखस्थितं सर्पनिर्मोकमिव घनपाण्डुरमेतत दन्तताटङ्कं मया गृहीतम्।

— p. 14

I got this ivory ring from the mouth of the anthill like getting a gem from the hood of a serpent.

The *arthāntaranyāsa* or general statements are the favourite figure of speech of the poet. Some examples can be quoted:

नहि वृष्टिरेव खादयति सस्यम्। — p. 6

The rain does not eat the grains by itself.

(The *vidūṣaka* justifies that he is capable of protecting a secret and that he will not cause harm to the king himself since he is his close associate.)

अथवा दुग्धसागरमुज्झित्वा कुतो लक्ष्मीरुद्गच्छति। — p. 7

Where else will Lakṣmī stay disregarding the milky ocean.

(The *vidūṣaka* justifies the nobility of birth of Līlāvatī.)

अमथ्यमानं दधि न नवनीतं मुञ्चति। — p. 8

The unchurned curds will not give rise to butter.

(The *vidūṣaka* says that it requires great efforts to get Līlāvatī released from the clutches of the queen.)

कः शुक्तिभञ्जनभयेन मुक्तावलिमुज्झति। — p. 12

Who will leave the pearl for the fear of breaking the shell?

(The intention of the *vidūṣaka* is that the king should not mind about the queen's anger while seeking the love of Līlāvatī.)

को दुग्धस्नानपानसमये आरनालं चिन्तयति। — p. 15

Who will think of a small channel while getting a chance to bathe and drink in the milky ocean?

(The *vidūṣaka* encourages the king to read the love letter without worrying about the queen.)

गच्छतु भवान्। अहं पुनरनुपदमागच्छामि, यतो द्वयोस्तृतीयत्वं जुगुप्सितं भवति। — p. 25

With two persons, if one more is added, it does not augur well.

(There is a belief that if a group of three persons sets out together for a work it will spell doom.)

कुतः पङ्कजिनी विना राजहंसस्य निर्वृतिः। — p. 26

Where is the relief for the royal swan without resorting to the lotus?

(When the queen approves the wedding of the king with Līlāvatī.)

INFLUENCE OF THE EARLIER POETS ON RĀMAPĀṆIVĀDA

Sanskrit is a language of such rich tradition that no later poet can write a new work without the influence of the earlier poets like Kālidāsa. Rāmapāṇivāda is no exception to this general rule. We find traces of influence of some of the earlier poets in the *Līlāvatīvīthī*. For example, the verse,

चतुर्मुखमुखाम्भोजचतुष्टयाविहारिणि!।
कविलोकाश्रिते। देवि। सरस्वति नमोऽस्तु ते ॥४॥

reminds us of Daṇḍin's verse,

caturmukhamukhāmbhoja kalahaṁsavadhūrmama ।
mānase ramatāṁ nityaṁ sarvaśuklā sarasvatī ॥
— *Kāvyādarśa*, I.1

The verse

रहयति महामोहग्रन्थिं धिनोति मनोऽधिकं
जनयाति पुनः कार्ये कार्ये परिश्रमलाघवम्।
वितरति शरज्जयोत्स्नाशुभ्रं यशश्च निरङ्कुशं
किमु न कुरुते नृणामेतन्महाजनपूजनम्॥९॥

is on the lines of the *subhāṣita* stanza.
jāḍyam dhiyo harati siñcati vāci satyam . . .

The Bharatavākya verse, quoted already, reminds one of Kālidāsa's verse,

purāṇamityeva na sādhu sarvam na cāpi kāvyam navamityavadhyam — *Mālavikāgnimitra*, I.7

SPECIAL FEATURES OF THE PLAY

With the non availability of the early pieces, the *Līlāvatīvīthī* of Rāmapāṇivāda serves as a good specimen of a *vīthī* play. The poet has written another *vīthī* called *Candrikā* but an analysis of it is not taken up here in order to avoid repetition of a work from the same author.

Rāmapāṇivāda has also written a *prahasana* called *Madanaketucarita,* which has been analysed in detail in Chapter 4 of the present work. In that play, a *yogin* Śivadāsa by name, performs miracles. He enters his soul into the body of a *gaṇikā* and behaves in a peculiar fashion in order to mend the ways of a wayward Buddhist monk. In the present play we have a *yoginī* performing miracles. Rāmapāṇivāda seems to be fond of introducing *adbhuta* as a subordinate to the main *rasa* in his plays.

In order to restrict himself to just two characters, as per the rules of the *vīthī*, Rāmapāṇivāda has used many techniques. He has employed the *ākāśabhāṣita* technique at many places in the play. The *vidūṣaka*'s conversation with the ladies of the harem in this style is quite interesting. In fact, none of the lady characters appear on the stage, neither the heroine nor the queen. Whenever they have to speak they do so from behind the screen (*nepathya*). Another technique adopted by the poet is *svagatam*. When the *vidūṣaka* comes in the disguise of the snake charmer, no character in the play recognizes him but he lets the audience know of it by a *svagata* speech in which he says "Salutation to the friendship by the power of which I, a brāhmaṇa, is made to wear such a despicable dress". Similarly, the dramatist uses the *janāntika* technique quite purposefully. For example, when queen offers the hand of Līlāvatī, the king asks the *vidūṣaka* "What shall I do now?" in the *janāntika* for which the *vidūṣaka* also replies in the same vein.

The *vidūṣaka* occupies major portion of the time on the stage, quite understandably so, since he is the kingpin of the play. *Vidūṣaka*s generally speak in Prākṛt but the *vidūṣaka* of the present play often resorts to Sanskrit. This is a ploy adopted by the poet to exhibit his poetic talent, his scholarship, his knowledge of the scriptures and his command over the language. For example, when he describes the love-lorn condition of the king, the *vidūṣaka* resorts to Sanskrit (v. 13). Again women characters generally speak in Prākṛt. But when the queen describes (from behind the screen) her wonderful dream she switches over to Sanskrit.

The dramatist employs dramatic irony too in a few places. The narration of her niece's predicament by the *naṭī* in the prologue is similar to that of the heroine in the play. The veiled reference to the king in the love letter is also significant. The verses (33 and 35) recited by the two *bard*s also refer indirectly to the king's love towards Līlāvatī.

The dramatist has not proclaimed any message directly like the Polonius' advice in Shakespeare's Hamlet. But he has indicated certain lofty ideals in a suggestive fashion. He seems to emphasize the idea "More things are wrought by prayer than the world dreams of" through the *vidūṣaka*'s prayer to the *yoginī* in the beginning of the play. Accordingly, miracle after miracle occur and ultimately the king gets his wish fulfilled. The *vidūṣaka*'s optimism is another significant point in the play. If one is steadfast in his endeavours, one can achieve success in the end. One is reminded of the famous *Rāmāyaṇa* statement,

> *kalyāṇi bata gātheyam laukikī pratibhāti me* ।
> *yāti jīvantam ānandam naram varṣaśatādapi* ॥

Sītākalyāṇavīthī

The *vīthī* has the facility of representing both the Purāṇic theme as well as an invented theme developed by the author, as contrasted with most of the other minor playforms (excluding two major plays *nāṭaka* and *prakaraṇa*). *Bhāṇa* and *prahasana* never have a Purāṇic theme; *ḍima*, *vyāyoga* and *samavakāra* have only a Purāṇic theme. But *vīthī* can have both types of themes. The *Dūtavākya* of Bhāsa has a Purāṇic theme. But the dramatist himself has not mentioned anywhere that it is a *vīthī*. *Premābhirāma*, a later *vīthī* of Ravipati Tripurāntaka, perhaps has a Purāṇic theme as suggested by the title of the play. But the work is not available. The play under discussion has the *Rāmāyaṇa* theme and hence it makes an interesting study on how a Purāṇic theme can be fitted into a *vīthī* type of play.

THE AUTHOR

The author, Venkappiah, who belongs to the eighteenth century hails from the state of Karnataka. He has contributed works in both Sanskrit and Kannada. He was also known as *pradhāna venkāmātya* on account of his involvement in politics (*pradhāna* means chieftain and *amātya* a minister). He was a minister under Haider Ali who ruled the Mysore State in the second half of eighteenth century (see also page 256 above).

He was the son of Vāmāmbā and Hampāmātya (*History of Mysore*, p. 178, ed. L. Hayavadana Rao). He belonged to the family of ministers as suggested by the term *amātya* attached to his father's name as well. He was from the Aruveli Niyogi sect of *brāhmaṇas*. He must have received good education in his early days as is revealed by his works. Over the year, he gained several titles such as Veṅkasūri and Veṅkaṭabhūpati. He entered governmental service during the reign of Rānī Vīrammājī of the Mysore State around the year 1757. According to records available in the State Archives, he was transferred to a place called Hosangadi in the South Canara district of Karnataka. Later when Haider Ali ruled over the state also, he continued to be a minister. He became *dīvāna* (similar to a chief minister) of the state. Haider Ali was so impressed with his service that he took him to Śrīraṅgapatan and conferred on him the title *pradhānī*. He also entrusted the administration of Bedhur area to Venkappiah. A faithful administrator as he was, Venkeppiah improved the trade and commerce of the area and earned the confidence of the people within a short time. He was a strict disciplinarian; he found out the fraud committed by an official called Thimmappa in Mysore and brought him to books. Hyder Ali had so much confidence in him that he sent him to Pune to negotiate a Peace Treaty with Raghunath Rao, a Mahraṭṭa chieftain in the year 1774. He was no less efficient as a warrior in the battlefield. In 1770, he took an expedition to Hassan, Beḷūr and other places and put down with a firm hand the uprising against the state. In 1771, he fought against the Maharaṭṭas, near Melkoṭe, beat them back and saved the life of prince Ṭīpū. But towards the end of his career, Venkappiah had a turbulent life. Haider Ali whom he faithfully served for several years, charged him with misuse of power and even imprisoned him. Fortunately for Venkappiah, an officer called Appaji Ram, took pity on him, spoke to the Sultan about his innocence and arranged for his release. He died a sad man in the year 1782.

We do not know much about the personal life of Venkappiah. His first wife probably died at a young age. He married a second wife in 1771. He seems to have been a devotee of Śrī Rāma as revealed in the prologue of his work *Lakṣmīsvayamsvara Samavakāra*. In the midst of all his political and administrative life, Venkappiah somehow found time to make a powerful impression on the literary side as well.

Venkappiah has contributed a large number of works both in Sanskrit and Kannada. He has contributed as many as eight dramatic pieces. They are:

(i) *Kāmavilāsa* — a *bhāṇa*

(ii) *Mahendravijaya* — a *ḍima*

(iii) *Lakṣmīsvayamsvara* — a *samavakāra* (published)

(iv) *Vīrarāghava* — *vyāyoga*

(v) *Sītāsvayaṁvara* — *vīthī* (published)

(vi) *Rukmiṇī Svayaṁvara* — *aṅka*

(vii) *Kukṣimbharibhaikṣava* — a *prahasana*

(viii) *Urvaśī Sārvabhauma* — an *īhāmṛga*

The other works of the author are:

(i) *Alaṁkāra Maṇidarpaṇa*,

(ii) *Hanūmajjayam*,

(iii) *Kuśalavacampū*, and

(iv) Rāmakathāmṛtasāraḥ

THE TEXT

The present analysis of the work is based on the printed edition of the text published by R. Raghavendra Rao (Oriental Research Institute, Mysore, 1989) from Mysore, under the guidance of Panditaratnam, R.G. Malagi, Dy. Director of ORO, Mysore. The edition is based on five MSS from ORI, Mysore and one from Maharaja's Sanskrit College, Mysore. Of the six manuscripts, three are in Telugu script and one each in Grantha, Devanāgarī and Nāndīnāgarī.

An analysis of variant readings in the MSS reveals that, by far, Text 6, remains unique and is the purest of the lot. It has very few mistakes and wherever it has corrupt readings, they are copied as it is in most of the other manuscripts. The most corrupt text seems to be the Text 1. It is probably derived from for Text "T" which was less corrupt. Almost 25 per cent of corrupt readings in Text 1, either individually or in comparison with one or the other Texts. Texts 2, 3, 4 and 5 have average level corruptions. Texts 1 and 2 bear a strong resemblance to each other. It is probable that the

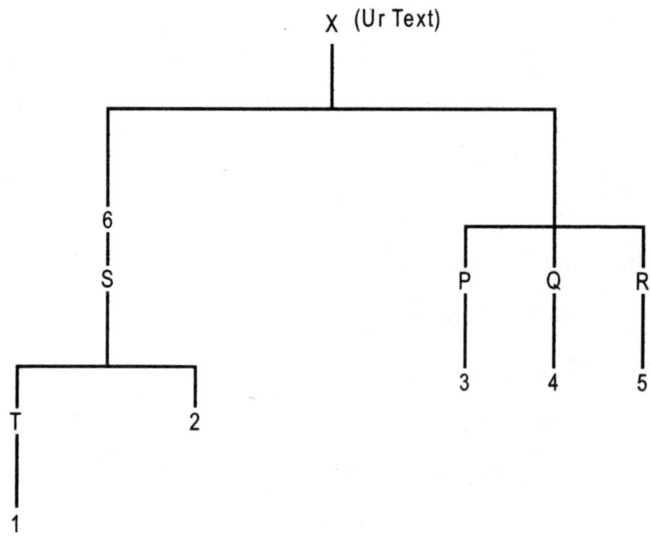

mother text of "T" and 2 was derived from a common text, say, "S". Texts 3, 4 or 5 do not seem to have much of a connection with any of the other texts. They are probably derived independently from three other texts, say, "P", "Q", "R". The Texts 1, 2 and 6 seem to have some relationship. The stemma codicum may be drawn as given above:

THE PLOT

Dramatis Personae

Sūtradhāra

Naṭī

Nārada

Disciple

Rāma

Viśvāmitra

Lakṣmaṇa

Śatānanda

Kausumbhaka

Kaulūtaka

Sītā

Her friend

THE PLAY

In the Prologue, the *sūtradhāra* and the *naṭī* appear on the stage and discuss about seasons, the nature of *vīthī*, name of the author and his works.

The play proper begins with a *śudddha viṣkambha* in which Sage Nārada and his disciple engage themselves in a conversation, through which we come to know that King Janaka is planning to conduct the *svayaṁvara* of his daughter and that he has invited all the kings from various corners of the country. Janaka has also announced that one who is able to bend the bow of Śiva will win the hand of Sītā. The disciple wonders whether anybody will be able to pick-up the bow at all, leave alone bending it. Nārada says that it should be possible for Rāma. On the request of the disciple, Nārada narrates the story of Rāma's birth and his exploits. He then points out that Rāma and Lakṣmaṇa as also Sage Viśvāmitra are entering the hall while King Janaka and his family priest, Śatānanda get ready to receive them.

In the next scene we see Rāma entering the outskirts of Mithilā. On seeing the camps spread over the area Lakṣmaṇa mistakes them to be those of the enemies of King Janaka and prepares to take up a war against them. Rāma points out that they are the camps of princes of various states that have come to attend the wedding. Moving further Viśvāmitra shows the wedding hall that had been got ready. On entering the hall, they see princes sitting in different corners and discussing about their chances. They also see King Janaka seated along with sage Yājñavalkya. As they approach him, King Janaka gets up from his seat and heartily welcomes them. Sage Viśvāmitra introduces them to Janaka, Śatānanda and other important dignitaries. The contest then gets started and a number of princes who try to lift the bow fail miserably. When his turn comes, Rāma very easily lifts up the bow, bends it and wins the contest.

In the next scene, we see two bards by the names Kausumbhaka and Kaulūtaka enter and discuss the incidents that took place after the breaking of the bow. Sītā garlanded Rāma and all the people assembled at the arena blessed them. Janaka immediately sent his ambassadors to bring Daśaratha and his family to Mithilā. The guests arrive in time and arrangements are made for the wedding. But suddenly there appears Paraśurāma, the enemy of the kṣatriyas. Rāma however subjugates him and takes away the bow of Viṣṇu as a mark of his victory. Paraśurāma is pleased with the valour and grace of Rāma, blesses him and leaves. The two bards leave the stage after narrating all these incidents.

In the last scene we see a joyous mood all around. The newly-wed couples (Rāma, Lakṣmaṇa, Bharata and Śatrughna married Sītā and her cousins, Urmilā, Māṇḍavī and Śrutakīrti respectively) enjoy the fun along with their friends. They all bow down to the sage who prepares to leave. Then Daśaratha, Rāma and other members of the family take leave of Janaka. The moon rises in the horizon and adds to the pleasant atmosphere. The play ends on a happy note at this stage.

CHARACTER STUDY

Rāma, the hero of the play, is presented as a representative of the *dhīrodātta* type. Even as he is introduced in the play he comes with the background of heroic exploits of having protected sage Viśvāmitra's sacrifice from the demons and of having killed the terrible demoness Tāṭakā.

यस्ताटकेयमदभेदनशौण्डकाण्डो येनैव कौशिकमखस्सुखनिर्मितोऽभूत्।
यत्पादरेणुरगमन्मुनिकूकुदत्वं यस्य त्रिलोकविजयश्शिशुकेलिकल्पः ॥१८॥

Nārada has no doubt that he will bend the bow of Śiva and take the hand of Sītā, which is eventually accomplished by Rāma.

आरोपितं धनुरनेन सलीलमस्मिन्नारोपिता क्षितिभुवा च मधूकमाला।
आपूरितुं त्रिभुवनं निनदेन तस्य प्रापूरितो जनकराजमनोरथोऽपि ॥४२॥

Rāma's valour is very well brought out by Sage Viśvāmitra himself.

विश्वामित्रः - मखविघ्नकृतस्त्वया निरस्ता महिजा तापि च कन्यकोपलब्धा।
जमदग्नितनूभवो जितोऽभूत् जनकादेर्हृदयानि तोषितानि ॥५७॥

You destroyed the demons who obstructed the sacrifice. You won the contest and took the hand of Sītā. You subjugated Paraśurāma. Indeed you are the favourite of everybody.

As brought out by Śatānanda, Rāma's holy feet brought redemption for Ahalyā.

शतानन्दः - नाम्ना प्रत्यभिजानामि राममव्याजवत्सलम्।
यदस्मन्मातरं योसावरक्षत्पादपांसुभिः ॥४०॥

The true mark of heroism lies in humility. Rāma is a standing example of humility. He acknowledges his respect to his *guru* Viśvāmitra on many an occasion.

In contrast with Lakṣmaṇa who is rather exuberant, Rāma observes patience and forbearance. When Lakṣmaṇa mistakes the camps to belong to the enemies, he points out to him that they are the camps meant for kings who have come for the *svayaṁvara.*

सञ्चार कृत्पौरजनानुकूलं सल्लापसम्मर्द्दसहिष्णुयोधम्।
अभ्युच्चलत्पुष्परथावलीकं आलम्बते सौम्यपदं बलं तत् ॥२८॥

The tender feeling of his love for Sītā is also very well brought out by the poet. While entering Mithilā, Rāma wonders whether Sītā will love him.

api nāma jānakī mayyanurāgam badhnāti — p. 17, line 2

Lakṣmaṇa is rather subdued in the play when compared to his characteristics as we know from Vālmīki and other poets. He follows his elder brother like a shadow and takes an active part in all his heroic exploits. He is in perfect unison with Rāma as we gauge from the number of dialogues they utter together. Janaka sees a majesty and grandeur in both.

पाणी कोदण्डाङ्कौ तूणीयुगधारिणौ भुजावनयोः।
स्थितिरपि गम्भीरेयं कथयति राजन्यजन्यतामेव ॥३६॥

With their hands holding the *kodaṇḍa* bows and the shoulders bearing the arrow pouch and presenting a majestic look — it speaks of their royal lineage.

Śatānanda brings out the contrast between the two brothers in an excellent fashion. Rāma is like the moon while Lakṣmaṇa is like cupid. Rāma presents a calm look while Lakṣmaṇa exhibits a youthful exuberance.

नवसर्गकेलिरसिकात्मना त्वया शशिमन्मथाविव पुनर्विनिर्मितौ।
कतमाविमौ करभृतासिकार्मुकौ कमनीयतूणभृतदिव्यसायकौ ॥३८॥

Lakṣmaṇa mistakes the army camps to be those of the enemies of Janaka and vows to kill them all.

शतधा विभिन्नरथवाजिकुञ्जरं पतदस्त्रशस्त्रपटलास्तुतावनि।
अहमाकलय्य रिपुराजमण्डलं जनकानुमोदनमुपैमि शाश्वतम् ॥२७॥

I will break into hundred pieces, this group of enemies along with their variegated chariots, horses, elephants, the weapons and missiles, and bring lasting happiness to King Janaka.

Of course, he is calmed by Rāma. Like Rāma, Lakṣmaṇa also has great regard for this guru Viśvāmitra.

भवदनुग्रह एव कृतार्थतां प्रकटयत्यकलङ्कतयाद्य नः।
न हि जनाक्षिगणस्य विसारिता मिहिरदिव्यकरप्रसराद्दते ॥५८॥

It is only your grace that has proclaimed blemishless success for us. But for the light of the Sun, the eyes of the people have no value.

In a short play like this, there is no scope for developing every character, but one must admit that Sītā's role is very much downplayed in the *vīthī*, more so since her name and her wedding make the name of the play itself. She gracefully meanders along, playing in the company of her friends and feeling shy now and then on the remarks made by her friends. The garland scene is appropriately described.

कटाक्षनीलोत्पलदाम कन्यया समर्पितं यत्परितोऽपि राघवम्।
मधूकमालार्पणमद्यमन्महे पुनस्तदेतपुनरुक्तिभाजनम्॥४३॥

> Having surrounded Rāma with the garland made out of the blue lotuses in the form of her eyes, the garland of flowers presented to him seemed to do an act of repetition only.

She is very much worried when Paraśurāma appears in an angry mood and attacks Rāma. She is relieved when Rāma overpowers his opponent.

[हला। दिष्टया तादृशक्षत्रियकुलहरणचणोऽपि परशुधरः प्रतिनिवृत्त इति आश्वासितमिव मे हृदयम्।] — line after v. 56

When the friends remark that it is because of the *saubhāgya* she brought to the family that the conflict ended in Rāma's favour, Sītā is overcome with bashfulness. When Viśvāmitra blesses the couple, she, in all humility, says that everything ended auspiciously on account of the grace of the sage.

Sage Viśvāmitra is present almost from the start to the finish in the play. It was he who had brought Rāma and Lakṣmaṇa to the forest for the protection of his sacrifice. He then brings them to Mithilā and bids Rāma to break the bow and take the hand of Sītā. Janaka heaps a lot of praise on him.

For Śatānanda, the sage is inevitable creator himself.

नवसर्गकेळिरसिकात्मना . . . . । — v. 37 quoted already

Rāma and Lakṣmaṇa says that all good things happen because of the grace of the sage.

King Janaka is presented as a noble king true to his nature. He is called as an incarnation of "Yoga" (v. 33). Without giving room for any fear or favour, he announces a context for giving away his daughter in marriage. Whoever breaks the bow of Śiva would become the claimant for the hand of his daughter. Yet on seeing Rāma he feels that Sītā will be a befitting bride for him.

> जनकः - (शतानन्दं प्रत्यपवार्य) अहो। किमेतद्रामाभिधानमालोकयतः मे
> वत्सा सीता तदनुरूपतया विभाति।
>
> — lines after vv. 38 and 40*

He is impressed by the exploits of the two princes as he recounts them.

> सुतौ दशरथस्यैतौ शुभलक्षणलक्षितौ।
> माद्यत्सुबाहु मारीच मदखण्डनपण्डितौ ॥ इति ॥३९॥

For all his stature as a Rājarṣi, he is very humble. He welcomes Sage Viśvāmitra and addresses him with reverence. He is always associated with his Gurus Yājñavalkya and Śatānanda whom he adores. He is pleased to see his palace buzzing with the assemblage of the princes.

> जनकः - अयमक्षिमहोत्सवः प्रहर्षो मनसश्चाप्यसमानसम्प्रसारः।
> स्वयमभ्युपयाति यन्मदीयं सदनं सानुग एष नव्यधाता ॥३४॥

His joy knows no bounds when Rāma breaks the bow. He arranges for the wedding on a grand scale.

There are a few other characters like Nārada in the play. In course of his conversation with his disciple the sage gives a brief account of the story till Rāma's arrival at Mithilā. Paraśurāma makes a brief appearance. He opposes Rāma vehemently but gets subdued and accepts his defeat gracefully. The appearance of the two bards gives a bit of dramatic relief

---

* जनकः - "साश्चर्यं स्वगतम्" अपि नाम चापमारोपयिष्यत्येष रामः।
अपि नाम वत्सायास्सीतायाः करग्रहणमङ्गलमनुभविष्यति।

in the midst of the short scenes of the play.

RASAS IN THE PLAY

According to the definition given by *ālaṁkārikas*, there should be a show of many *rasas* in a *vīthī*. The poet, in fact, calls his *vīthī*, the *Navarasavīthī*.

अलमलमन्यालापैरसमानाधीशवृत्तरसलोपैः ।
नवरसचङ्क्रमवीथी नववीथी सम्प्रयुज्यतां भवता ॥६ ॥

Śṛṅgāra, of course, dominates the play but it always remains suggestive. Rāma's worry whether Sītā will choose him and Sītā's bashfulness when teased by her friends unmistakably suggest *śṛṅgāra*. The play culminates in the wedding assuring the place of *śṛṅgāra* in it. Rāma and Sītā represent the *ālambana vibhāva*. The wedding scene and the description of marriage in the end contribute to *uddīpana vibhāva*. The statements of Sītā like "I have lost control of myself" act as the *vyabhicāri bhāva*. We may also see the presence of *anubhāva* in the lines,

किन्नु खल्वेतत् अङ्गानामपि अनीशत्वं प्राप्तमिति ।
(सीता शृङ्गारलज्जां निरूपयति ।)
— Lines after vv. 58 and 60

The sentiment of *vīra* is represented in the scene where Rāma lifts Śiva's bow, a feat which is unthinkable for others. Likewise, in the conquest of Paraśurāma there is an element of *vīra*. The breaking of the bow also leads to *adbhuta*. In the conversation between Sītā and her friends there is gentle *hāsya*. Paraśurāma himself represents the *raudra*. Kausumbhaka gets terrified on seeing Paraśurāma wherein we have element of fear. The presence of Sage Viśvāmitra, Janaka and Śatānanda and their speeches evoke *śānta*.

DESCRIPTIVE POWERS

In a short play form like the *vīthī*, there is not much scope for a poet to exhibit his descriptive powers. Yet Veṅkāmātya has suceeded in this respect because of his innate skill and imaginative spirit. The description of Mithilā is quite appealing.

संदृश्यन्ते पताकाः सकनककलशाः स्पर्धमानाः पटैः स्वैः
स्वर्गङ्गामच्छपूरां समुदितकनकाब्जातजातां सुजाताम्।
वप्रानुस्यूतवज्रद्युतिततितिरियमप्यात्तदृग्भित्तिरास्ते
संस्फायत्पट्टणश्रीहसितसितविभामञ्जरीपुञ्जरीतिः ॥१४॥

The description of the moonrise towards the end of the play adds to the delight.

रामः - आनन्दकन्दतुलनामखिलस्व कुर्वन्
अभ्येत्ययं गगनमण्डलमेष चन्द्रः।
आहृत्य सर्वजगतावलितान्धकार-
व्याजाधिसन्ततिमिवोत्सवदानशौण्डः ॥६८॥

Even Sage Viśvāmitra is enchanted by the sight of the moon. He says:

आभाति वारुणहरिद्वनितानितान्तलीलापरिष्कृतशिरोमणिवद्विवस्वान्।
सायंतनातपमपूर्वपदं विलोक्य पेयं तमूहति नवेन्दुरुचिं चकोरः ॥६३॥

POETIC MERITS

Veṅkāmātya seems to be a poet of reasonably good skill and merits. There is an element of suggestion (that Rāma is going to break the bow) in the words of Nārada.

जयत्येषा सम्पञ्जयति मिथिलैषा च नगरी
जयत्येषा सीता जयति जनको राजतिलकः।
यदायाति श्रीमाननुजसहितो गाधिजनुषा
स्वयं रामः कामक्षपणधनुरारोपणकृते ॥२१॥

There is *vyṅgya* element in vv. 23 and 25. The reference is to the sunrise and the blooming of the lotus in v. 23. But the words used in it are suggestive of the incidents that are going to take place in the play. The description of the sun hurriedly reaching out to the red (as well as "possessed of love" — *rāga*) lotus (deliberately the word *ambujinī* — in feminine gender is used) is indicative of a love sport. The lotus possessed of a garland of bees in her hand is suggestive of a wedding scene.

अभ्यागतं सरभसाग्रकरप्रसारव्यक्तानुरागमिनमम्बुजिनी चिरेण।
सद्योऽभियन्मधुकरोत्पलमालिकाङ्का सत्यं स्वयं विकसदुत्कलिका वृणीते ॥२३॥

In the other verse (25), there is reference to removal of darkness by the light of the sun. This suggests the subjugation of Paraśurāma by Rāma.

तमः प्रसारराहित्यविकसन्मुखपंङ्कज(म्)।
भुवनं भाति सर्वत्र सुकरप्रकराद्दतम् ॥२५॥

The poet has employed a good number of *alaṁkāra*s in the play. There is a simile in the description of the princes arranged for the *svayaṁvara*. They have forgotten their enmity and are enjoying their stay in Mithilā just as animals moving about in perfect peace in the penance grove forgetting their mutual enmity.

सपत्नभावात्सपदि व्यपेताः स्वयंवरस्थानमुपेत्य भूपाः।
तपोवनं तावकमेत्य भान्ति यथा मृगाः प्रच्युतवैरभावाः ॥३०॥

The union of Rāma and his brothers with their respective wives is akin to the mango tree with Mādhavī creeper and the moon with the stars.

सहकारमिवात्तमाधवीकं
शशलक्ष्माणमिवोढरोहिणीकम्।
— 2 lines of v. 62

In the words of *sūtradhāra* (*phalitam asmat tapolatābhiḥ* — The fruits are borne by the creeper of my penance) and in the verse following, we have metaphor:

रसिकाग्रेसरनिबिडैरवैरसमानसरस्वतीभृतप्रमदैः।
इयमियमाभाति सभा नयनयुगीसुकृतमञ्जरीसुलभा ॥५॥ (*sic*)

We have an instance of pun in the following verse:

अनुरक्तमरावपि प्रियायामभवच्चक्षुरमुष्य चित्रमेतत्।
स च सा च विलोक्य राममग्रे सद्दशं प्रापतुरेव भीरुभावम् ॥५३॥

Here, there is pun on the words *anurāga* (meaning "love" and a "dear damsel") and *bhīrubhāva* (meaning "fear" and "an enemy").

There is a good *dṛṣṭānta* in the verse (quoted already — v. 58) where Sage Viśvāmitra's grace is described.

We have poetic fancy in the verse (60) where a friend congratulates Sītā for obtaining Rāma as her husband. She says that under the pretext of shedding tears of joy, Sītā appeared to be sending out her joyful mind itself towards Rāma.

सखि! एवमेतत् -
भुवनाद्भुतरूपसौकुमार्यं जननेत्राभ्युदयप्रदं मनोज्ञम्।
रघुवंशललामकं हि नाथं लब्धा प्राणसमं त्वं विलक्ष्या ॥६० ॥

The poetic fancy set out in the description of the moonrise is quite appealing. It appeared as if in the guise of the evening twilight, the submarine fire was drinking away the entire darkness.

जनकपाददिदृक्षुरिवाम्वुधिं विशाति विष्णुपदं द्युमणिर्महान्।
लसति सान्ध्यरुचिर्बहिरङ्गण-प्रतिनिविष्टरुचामिव संहतिः ॥६४ ॥

The general statements offered by the poet are quite interesting.

सा विद्या या हृद्या सरसोऽपि स एव यः परवशोऽत्र।
अनभिज्ञाः स्वां विद्यामरसामन्योन्यतः प्रशंसन्ते ॥१३ ॥

The ignorant praise their own works even if they are devoid of poetic charm.

संकल्पकल्पभूजातसान्निध्यमहिमा महान्।
यस्य यद्विषयं चेतः तस्य तत्प्रतिभासते ॥२४ ॥

A mind which is absorbed in a subject will definitely master it.

There is a striking statement that describes Paraśurāma in a nutshell.

सोऽयं सर्वनृपालपङ्कजवनीसायं समुज्जृम्भते ॥५१ ॥

He is a veritable night to the lotus-woods of kings.

There are a few *anuprāsa*s also in the play.

अनुसरति नदद्वीणामनुरूपो मर्दलालापः ।
अनुसरति चूतलतामयमपि च पिकः कलालापः ॥४ ॥

अलमलमन्यालापैः. . . .
नवरस. . . .
नववीथी. . . . ॥६ ॥

कौटिल्यमयता येन कौटिल्यममरद्विषाम् ।
अहारि कस्य तच्चापमारोपविषयो भवेत् ॥१७ ॥

अरोपितं. . . .
आरोपिता. . . .
आपूरितुं. . . .
प्रापूरितो. . . . ॥४२ ॥

In a short play the poet has to resort to brevity of expression. One example can be given here:

असौ दशरथादभूदजसुरादिभिः प्रार्थितः समस्तभुवनावलीसमवनैकतानो हरिः ।
मखद्विडपनोदने तमभयं ययाचे नवत्रिविष्टपविधानतो प्रकृतकृत्यमानी मुनिः ॥१९ ॥

DRAMATIC TECHNIQUE

The dramatic techniques used by the poet are admirable. Even in the plot, which is adopted from the *Rāmāyaṇa*, the poet has introduced some innovation. For example, he has introduced Paraśurāma episode in the middle of the wedding ceremony obviously to increase the dramatic effect of the play and also to offer a mix of *vīra* and *bhayānaka rasa*s thereby enhancing the effect of *śṛṅgāra* as is evident from Sītā's statement expressing her relief that her husband has overcome the danger.

The introduction of Nārada and his disciple in the beginning of the play is an innovation. One may remember that in the original *Rāmāyaṇa* it is Nārada who first introduces Rāma to the question "who is a perfect human being?" We have two bards in the play. The mixture of mythological characters and imaginary characters gives an element of realism to the play.

The play consists of two benedictory stanzas. The first one is the conventional *nāndī* verse. In the second verse, the poet expresses his devotion to Hanumān.

Contrary to the general practice is such play forms, *Sītākalyāṇa* has a fairly long prologue, The *sūtradhāra* pays tributes to poet Vālmīki (*śl*. no. 3). He pays tribute to the music party and the audience (*śl*. nos. 4 to 5). Then we have a verse where the assembly directs the stage manager to present a *vīthī* (v. 6). Then there is a long conversation between the stage manager and his wife in which the life history and the merits of the poet are brought out in as many as four verses (9, 10, 11, 12). We come to know that the poet has contributed works to every form of *rūpaka*. His parents were Vāmāmbikā and Ramapuri Hampayya. He enjoyed the confidence of the king and he also won the admiration of the poets and literary critics.

In the main part of the play the poet has employed many dramatic techniques. There are six scenes big and small. (i) We have a *śuddhaviṣkambhaka* where Nārada and his disciple discuss the circumstances leading to Rāma's arrival at Mithilā, (ii) *Svayaṁvara* scene, (iii) Interlude with two bards, (iv) Paraśurāma scene, (vi) Departure of the guests. The poet has employed techniques like *nepathya, janāntika* and *ātmagatam* effectively. Another technique employed by the poet is the *cūlikā* scene (behind the curtain). For example, the Paraśurāma episode takes place behind the screen only. Similarly, the scene of kings trying to bend the bow also takes place behind the screen.

Some incidents are let known to us though the conversation between two characters. For example, the scene of Sītā garlanding Rāma is told to us by two bards.

The poet has employed *kaiśikī vṛtti* with a telling effect. The play consists of as many as 71 verses which is quite unusual for a *vīthī*, but the style of the author is simple and attractive. He has employed all the important metres.

In the Bharatavākya, the poet expresses the desire that poets should get rid of poverty and that they should become rich. It is also suggested here that they should rise above poverty of imagination and their expressions should be rich with poetic embellishments.

SĪTĀKALYĀṆA AS A VĪTHĪ AND THE PRESENCE OF VĪTHYAṄGAS

As per the norms of *vīthī*, the present work also consists of only one act. Generally, *vīthī*s have one or two characters only though this play has quite a few characters, but it is still not a disqualification for being called as a *vīthī*. With *śṛṅgāra* as its main sentiment and with a sprinkling of a few other *rasa*s, *Sītākalyāṇavīthī* satisfies this condition of a *vīthī*. *Vīthī* should have only *mukha* and *nirvahaṇa sandhi*s and the play follows it. A number of incidents are described using *cūlikā* (behind the curtain) technique (e.g. failure of kings to break the bow, Rāma's success, King Daśaratha's arrival for wedding, Paraśurāma's sudden appearance and Rāma's victory over him). The *vīthī* may have all the *arthaprakṛti*s and so does have the present play. Rāma's arrival at Mithilā is *bīja*; Rāma's words that Sītā perhaps loves him is the *bindu*. The Paraśurāma episode may serve as *patākā*. The presentation of Viṣṇu's bow by Paraśurāma may be *prakarī* and the departure scene in the end is the denouement.

The play consists of all the elements of *kaiśikī*, namely *narma, narmasphūrja, narmasphoṭa* and *narmagarbha*. The pleasant entry of Rāma in Mithilā is *narma*. Rāma's hope that Sītā loves him *narmasphūrja*. The garland scene and the mutual love between Rāma and Sītā is *narmasphoṭa* and their union after Paraśurāma scene is *narmagarbha,* because a number of *vīthyaṅgas* are present in the play. We have *udghātyaka* used as a device to bring out the main theme of the play in a contrived manner in the following verse:

पर्यायनामधेयं स्यात् किं वा लाङ्गलपद्धतेः।
काञ्चनस्यापि किं वा स्यात् वेङ्कामात्यकृतिश्च का ॥८॥

What is the synonym of *lāṅgala* (the plough — the answer is "Sīta") that of *kañcana* (gold — the answer is *kalyāṇa*). What is the work of Veṅkāmātya?

The answer is *Sītākalyāṇavīthī*.

Mṛdava lies in presenting the merits as demerits and vice versa. The *naṭī* tells about this in the prologue:

सा विद्या या हृद्या सरसोऽपि स एव यः परवशोऽत्र।
अनाभिज्ञाः स्वां विद्यामरसामन्योन्यतः प्रशंसन्ते ॥१३॥

eṣa khalu svabhāva āryasya yaddoṣo 'pi guṇatva apādānamiti

It is the nature of your goodself to present even a demerit as a merit.

Avalagita is an expression where a different interpretation is given for a normal statement. When Sītā mentions that she has a strange feeling, her friends interpret that it is of her husband staying by her side. There is an element of *chala* in an indirect praise of Paraśurāma by the bard while referring to his anger against kṣatriyas. *Gaṇḍa* is an abrupt remark. We have an instance of it when the bard describes Paraśurāma's entry as equivalent to ghosts entering a place where holy rites are performed.

INFLUENCE OF OTHER POETS ON VEṄKĀMĀTYA

The knowledge of the vast resources of Sanskrit literature brings about an influence of the earlier poets on the later poets, either consciously or unconsciously. Veṅkāmātya is no exception to this.

sā vidyā yā hṛdayā. . . . (v. 13) reminds one of Upaniṣadic statement, sa *vidyā yā vimuktaye.*

सखी - सहि! तहएंव सोहंगलंछीए पहावो एसो।
[सखि! तवैद्य सौभाग्यालक्ष्म्याः प्रभाव एषः।]
(सीता सलज्जं माल्येन ताडयति।)

— p. 35

This scene reminds one of Kālidāsa's statement from *Kumārasaṁbhava* — *mālyena tām nirvacanam jaghāna.*

AN OVERALL ASSESSMENT OF SĪTAKALYĀṆAVĪTHĪ

It is heartening to note that an administrator of the calibre of Veṅkāmātya could shine as a poet-dramatist as well. It shows that a poet within a man can always flash forth irrespective of his avocation otherwise. Veṅkāmātya had to weather many a storm in his life. He had to serve under a Hindu king as well as a Muslim ruler. He had to do a lot of balancing act in his political life. He was always under pressure to perform. But all the turmoil taking place outside did not diminish his poetic skill. His choice of the *Rāmāyaṇa* theme for the *vīthī* is to be appreciated. The innovations he has introduced in the theme are praiseworthy. His poetic skill is admirable. But for the demands of his official life, he would have made a still more significant contribution to Sanskrit literature. His general statements are very appropriate and are suited to the occasion. There are a few drawbacks in the play. The prologue is far too long and it may test the patience of the audience. The poet has introduced too many characters into the play to claim a place in the category of *vīthī*. But it has helped the author to introduce liveliness into play. The number of verses in the play are again too many. Some of the verses can be replaced by appropriate dialogues. A mythological theme is all right for a *nāṭaka*. But in a *vīthī* where there is provision for an invented theme, the poet could have devised an imaginary theme. But again, it is not a defect as such. Taking into consideration the merits of the play, the drawbacks are only a few, and hence we can safely say that Veṅkāmātya has succeeded in providing an interesting *vīthī*.

8

The Vīthyaṅgas in Sanskrit Drama

THE *vīthyaṅgas* are invariably present in almost all types of Sanskrit Drama. Some of the *vīthyaṅgas* form part of the prologue as stated by the dramaturgical texts. As pointed out earlier, some of the *vīthyaṅgas* have comic element in them. But it is not correct to say that wherever there is a comic element there is also a *vīthyaṅga*. There can be comedy scenes that can not be brought under any of the *vīthyaṅgas* and there are also a few *vīthyaṅgas* that do not contain any comic element at all.

The *vīthī* and the *prahasana* have much in common between them and so do the *vīthyaṅgas* and the *prahasanāṅgas*. It may also be pointed out that while the *vīthyaṅgas* are recognized by all ālaṁkārikas right from Bharata, the *prahasanāṅgas* were developed by a later writer, namely Siṁhabhūpāla. But their features are widely prevalent in plays other than *prahasanas* also. So, in the discussion on the *vīthyaṅgas*, illustrations on *prahasanāṅgas* will also be included.

Vīthyaṅgas in Bhāsa's Plays

Bhāsa has a natural sense of humour and it is reflected in his plays. They are replete with *vīthyaṅgas* also. Ānandavardhana says that great poets do not take any extra effort for including the *alaṁkāras* in their *kāvyas*. They come and fall at appropriate places spontaneously without any conscious effort on the part of the poet. Likewise, the *vīthyaṅgas* also get naturally fitted into the scheme of things in the works of great poets. That is what we find in the plays of Bhāsa as shown in the following pages.

CĀRUDATTAM

In the prologue of *Cārudattam* (ref. Poona Oriental Series No. 65, 1962) we have an instance of the *vīthyaṅga, vyāhāra* which is a humorous conversation between the two. The stage manager asks his wife "what do we have?" The wife says "There is *ghee,* sugar, curd and rice". The husband asks again "In the house?". The wife replies by saying "No sir, in the market". Then the wife says that she is fasting. The manager asks for the reason. She says that it is for begetting a good husband. He is startled but she says that it is meant for the next birth.

सूत्रधारः - आर्ये किमस्त्यभ्यर्थितम्?
नटी - अस्ति।

सूत्रधारः - आर्ये किं किम्?
नटी - घृतं, गुडो दधि तण्डुलाश्चास्ति।

सूत्रधारः - एतत् सर्वमस्माकं गेहेऽस्ति?
नटी - नहि नहि अन्तरापणे।
नटी - अद्य ममोपवासस्यार्यो सहायो भवतु।

सूत्रधारः - किन्नामधेय आर्याया उपवासः?
नटी - अभिरूपपतिर्नाम।

सूत्रधारः - किमन्यजात्याम्?
नटी - आम्।

— Act I, passages 26-50

We have a very good example of *asatpralāpa* (incoherent talk) in the following verse:

किं वासुदेवः शव पट्टनेशः कुन्तीसुतो वा जनमेजयो वा।
अहं त्वा गृहीत्वा केशहस्ते दुश्शासनः सीतामिवाहरामि॥

— I.12

> Let it be Vāsudeva, the Lord of the city of the dead. Let it be Janamejaya, the son of Kuntī. I am going to carry you away by your hair like Duḥśāsana did to Sītā.

Here there are many incongruent things. The Lord of the city of the dead is Yama and not Vāsudeva who was the Lord of Mathurā. Janamejaya was not the son of Kuntī. It was Rāvaṇa who carried away Sītā and not Duḥśāsana. Hence we have *asatpralāpa* here.

We have another instance of *asatpralāpa* in the scene where Śakāra says that he can hear the smell with his ears but he could not see it because of darkness (I, passage 21.44 ff.)

शृणोमि गन्धं श्रवणाभ्याम्। अन्धकारपूरिताभ्यां। नासपुटाभ्यां सुष्टु न पश्यामि।

In the third act also we have an example for the same *vīthyaṅga*. When the maid says that the thief has cut a hole in the door, the *vidūṣaka* asks "What a hole has entered cutting the thief?" (III, passage 14.11)

चेटी	-	. . . सन्धि छित्त्वा चोरः प्रविष्टः।
विदूषकः	-	चोरं छित्त्वा सन्धिः प्रविष्टः।
चेटी	-	हताश, सन्धि छित्त्वा चोरः प्रविष्टः।

We have *chalam* (deceit) in the following scene where Śakāra and the *viṭa* chase Vasantasenā (Act I, passage 15.12 ff).

शकारः	-	वसन्तसेने, अहं भर्तृपुत्रः कामयितव्य
गणिका	-	शान्तोऽसि।
शकारः	-	शृणु भाव शृणु। एषा वसन्तसेना मां शान्तोऽसीति भणति।
विटः	-	(आत्मगतं) आकृष्टमात्मानं न जानाति मूर्खः। ध्वंस इत्युक्ते शान्त इत्यवगच्छति।

Śakāra demands that Vasantasenā should make love to him since he is a prince. But Vasantasenā simply says "rest in peace", in other words, he may die. But Śakāra takes "resting in peace" to mean "taking rest". Śakāra is thus deceived by the idiomatic sentence of Vasantasenā and hence we have here *chalam*.

The *prahasana* element *anṛtam* consists of false praise. The *vidūṣaka* praises his own intellect according to which right will appear as left and vice versa as in a mirror (Act I, passage 21.5 ff).

नायकः	-	मैत्रेय। गच्छ। चतुष्पथे बलिमुपहर मातृभ्यः।
विदूषकः	-	न मे श्रद्धा। अन्यो गच्छतु।
नायकः	-	किमर्थम्
विदूषकः	-	मम बुद्धिरादर्शमण्डलगतेव छाया वामेषु दक्षिणा दक्षिणेषु वाम भवति।

The *prahasana* elements *bhaya* and *vipralambha* as well as the *vīthyaṅga chalam* are present in the passage where Śakāra scares the maid by catching hold of her and threatening to kill her (I.22.2 ff).

Udghātyaka is a series of questions and answers with a hidden meaning. We have an example for this in the beginning of the second Act of *Cārudattam*. With a series of clever questions, the maid finds out what is in the mind of her mistress, that she is in love with Cārudatta.

गणिका	-	ततस्ततः?
चेटी	-	अम्महे, न किञ्चिन्मया भणितम्। किं ततस्ततः इति?
गणिका	-	हञ्जे, किं मया मन्त्रितम्?
चेटी	-	अज्जुके, स्नेहः पृच्छति न पुरोभागित किं चिन्त्यते?
गणिका	-	हञ्जे, त्वं तावत् किमिति तर्कयसि?
चेटी	-	अप्रयोजनतया गणिकाभावस्य अज्जुका कमपि कामयति इति तर्कयामि।

PRATIJÑĀYAUGANDHARĀYAṆA
(Ed. C.R. Devadhar, Poona Oriental Agency, 1967)

The element *gaṇḍa* consists in an abrupt remark that may serve as a dramatic irony. For example, when the king and the queen are discussing about a suitable bridegroom for their daughter, Vāsavadattā, the chamberlain enters abruptly and says "King of Vatsa". He later explains by saying that the king of Vatsa has been held as a captive. As the plot develops, Vāsavadattā gets married to the king of Vatsa in the later part of the story.

देवी - . . . किमिदानीं विस्तरेण, यत्र दत्त्वा न सन्तापयामहे तत्र दीयताम्।
राजा - . . . कस्ते वै एतेषां पात्रताम् याति राजा . . . (प्रविश्य)
काञ्चुकीयः - वत्सराजः
राजा - किं वत्सराजः
काञ्चुकीयः - प्रसीदतु प्रसीदतु महासेनः। . . . तत्र भवतामात्येन शालङ्कायनेन गृहीतो वत्सराजः।

— II. 8.6 ff

In the same context, a series of questions and answers occur between the king and the chamberlain which may form an example for the *vīthyaṅga, udghātyaka*.

राजा - उदयनः?
काञ्चुकीयः - अथ किम्?

राजा - शतानीकस्य पुत्रः?
काञ्चुकीयः - दृढम्।

राजा - सहस्रानीकस्य नप्ता?
काञ्चुकीयः - स एव

राजा - कौशाम्बीशः?
काञ्चुकीयः - सुव्यक्तम्

राजा - गान्धर्ववित्तकः?
काञ्चुकीयः - एवं ब्रुवन्ति।

राजा - वत्सराजो नाम?
काञ्चुकीयः - अथ किं वत्सराजः।

— pp. 40-41

The *vīthyaṅga* called *mṛdava* consists in presenting merits as demerits or vice versa. We have an example for it when the king presents Udayana's merits as demerits. He says that Udayana's noble birth (belonging to the dynasty of Bharata) makes him conceited, his knowledge of music makes him proud, his youth and beauty make him vain and the people's attachment makes him egoistic. Actually, Udayana is popular on account of these qualities but the king of Avanti views them as demerits out of jealousy.

राजा - उत्सेकयत्येनं प्रकाशराजर्षिनामधेयो वेदाक्षर-समवायप्रविष्टो भरतो वंशः। दर्पयत्येनं दायाद्यागतो गान्धर्वो वेदः। विभ्रामयत्येनं वयस्सहजं रूपम्। विस्रम्भ यत्येनं कथमप्युत्पन्नोऽस्य पौरानुरागः।

— p. 45

We have another instance of *mṛdava* in the first verse of Act IV where taking to liquor is presented as a merit:

धन्याः सुराभिमत्ता धन्याः सुराभिरनुलिप्ताः।
धन्याः सुराभिः स्नाता धन्याः सुराभिः संज्ञापिताः॥

Blessed are they that are drunk with wine; blessed are they that are smeared with wine; blessed are those that bathe in wine and blessed are those that are killed by wine.

When Yaugandharāyaṇa appears as a madman in the third Act, and prattles at will in keeping with the role he was playing, we have an example for *asatpralāpa*, that is, incoherent talk. He says:

अं ऐरावणोऽहम्। न खलु तावद् देवराजो ममासन्नमारोहति। श्रुतं च मया पादपाशिकैरिन्द्रो बद्ध इति। धरणिगलैः विद्युन्मयोभिः कशाभिस्ताडयित्वा

वटोद्भ्रमेण परिभ्रमता भिद्यते मेघबन्धनम्। — pp. 54 ff

I am Airāvaṇa; but Indra does not ride on my back. And I have heard that Indra is bound by chains. Then striking with the lashes of lightning, that restrained the showers, and whirling around with the whirlwind, he burst through the clouds that bound him.

SVAPNAVĀSAVADATTĀ
(Ed. M.R. Kale, Motilal Banarsidass, 2002)

Udghātyaka is a series of questions and answers with a hidden meaning. In the first Act of *Svapnavāsavadattā* we have an example for it in the opening scene itself. Yaugandharāyaṇa and Vāsavadattā appear in the disguise of a recluse and a countrywoman respectively. They were driven away by the guards, since Princess *Padmāvatī* was visiting the hermitage. The ensuing conversation brings out their agony.

वासवदत्ता	-	आर्य, क एष उत्सारयति
यौग.	-	भवति, यो धर्मात् आत्मानं उत्सारयति।
वास.	-	आर्य, न हि एवं वक्तुकामा। अहमपि नाम उत्सारयितव्या भवामीति।
यौग.	-	भवति, एवं अविज्ञातानि दैवतान्यपि अवधूयन्ते।

— p. 4

Vāsavadattā:	Sir, Who is this that is driving us away?
Yau:	Madam, he who drives himself away from religious merit.
Vāsavadattā:	Sir, I did not mean to ask that. It is a pity that even I am ordered to clear the way.
Yau:	Madam, even deities are insulted when their real form is not known.

(Instead of a direct reply that the guards are driving them away, he says in disgust that they are driving themselves away from *dharma*.)

Avasyandita is uttering something inadvertently and then giving a new interpretation to it in order to hide the original intention. We have an example for it in the second Act (p. 20). Padmāvatī's maid reveals that the princess is interested in getting married to Udayana but wants to know whether he is good-looking. She asks Vāsavadattā "Supposing he is ugly?" In a hurry Vāsavadattā says "Not indeed, not indeed, he is quite handsome". Realising her mistake (that she was in disguise and that she should not mention anything about her husband Udayana), she says that she had heard from people about Udayana's handsomeness)

चेटी - भर्तृदारिके, यदि स राजा विरूपो भवेत्
वासवदत्ता - नहि नहि, दर्शनीय एव।
पद्मावती - आर्ये कथं त्वं जानासि?
वासवदत्ता - (आत्मगतम्) आर्यपुत्रपक्षपातेन अतिक्रान्तः समुदाचारः। किमिदानीं करिष्यामि? भवतु दृष्टम्। (प्रकाशं) हला, एवमुज्जयिनीयो जनो मन्त्रयते।

In the next scene again (p. 20), there is another instance of *avasyandita*. The nurse announces about the wedding of Udayana with Padmāvatī. Vasavdattā, inadvertently again, says that a mishap has occurred. Then correcting herself, she says that the king, having grieved at the so-called demise of his first wife, should have agreed to a second marriage so soon.

वासवदत्ता - अथ कुशली स राजा
धात्री - कुशली स इह आगतः। तस्य भर्तृदारिका प्रतीष्टा च।
वासवदत्ता - अत्याहितम्।

धात्री - किमत्र अत्याहितम्
वासवदत्ता - न खलु किञ्चित्। तथा नाम सन्ताप्य उदासीनो भवतीति।

Avasyandita figures again in the scene (p. 29) where Padmāvatī embarrasses Vāsavadattā by asking whether Udayana loved Vāsavadattā as much as he did herself. Vāsavadattā inadvertently replies by saying that he loved his former wife more. Padmāvatī asks her how she knew about it. Vāsavadattā manages the situation by saying that had her love been slight she would not have forsaken her relatives.

पद्मावती - एकः खलु मे सन्देहः।
वासवदत्ता - किं किम्?
पद्मावती - यथा मम आर्यपुत्रः तथैव आर्याया वासवदत्ताया इति।
वासवदत्ता - अतोऽप्यधिकम्।
पद्मावती - कथं त्वं जानासि?
वासवदत्ता - (आत्मगतम्) हं, आर्यपुत्रपक्षपातेन अतिक्रान्तः समुदाचारः। एवं तावद् भणिष्यामि (प्रकाशं) यद्यल्पः स्नेहः स स्वजनं न परित्यजति।

There is another instance of *avasyandita* in the fourth Act (p. 34). On seeing her husband after a long time, Vāsavadattā's eyes are filled with tears. When asked, she explains it away by saying that it was because of the pollen dust that had fallen into the eyes.

चेटी - भर्तृदारिके साश्रुरूपता खलु आर्याया दृष्टिः।
वासवदत्ता - एष खलु मधुकराणां अविनयात् काशकुसुमरेणुना पतितेन सोदका मे दृष्टिः।

The element *gaṇḍa* (abrupt remark) is seen in the passage in Act III (p. 24) where there is an interesting conversation between Vāsavadattā and the maid. The maid starts describing Udayana as a new Cupid. Vāsavadattā stops her from describing him further, since it is embarrassing for her to listen to the description of her own husband. But she gives some other reason by saying that a girl should not describe the husband of another girl. Then the maid wants her to wreathe a garland of flowers called "the co-wife destroyer". Vāsavadattā declines since she herself is agreeable to her husband marrying Padmāvatī. But she cannot tell the real reason. So she gives another reason by saying that since Udayana's first wife is dead there is no question of co-wife status for Padmāvatī.

वासवदत्ता	-	हला, भण, भण, किं दर्शनीयः?
चेटी	-	शक्यं भणितुं शरचापहीनः कामदेव इति।
वासवदत्ता	-	भवत्वेतावत्।
चेटी	-	किन्निमित्तं वारयसि?
वासवदत्ता	-	अयुक्तं परपुरुषसंकीर्तनं श्रोतुम्।
चेटी	-	इदं (औषधं) गृह्णत्वार्या।
वासवदत्ता	-	इदं तावदौषधं किं नाम्?
चेटी	-	अविधवाकरणं नाम
वासवदत्ता	-	(आत्मगतं) इदं बहुशो गुम्फितव्यं मम च पद्मावत्याश्च। (प्रकाशं) इदं तावदौषधं किं नाम?
चेटी	-	सपत्नीमर्दनं नाम
वासवदत्ता	-	इदं न गुम्फितव्यम्।
चेटी	-	कस्मात्
वासवदत्ता	-	उपरता तस्य भार्या तन्निष्प्रयोजनमिति।

In the beginning of Act IV, the *vidūṣaka* appears and describes the pleasures of the life at the palace. The cosy bed and the delicious food of the palace are indeed merits, but being not used to them they are too much for him and so considers them to be demerits. Hence, we have the *vīthyaṅga mṛdava* here. He says:

अनप्सरस्संवासो मया अनुभूयते। एकः खलु महान् दोषः। मम आहारः सुष्ठु न परिणमति सुप्रच्छादनायां शय्यायां निद्रान्न लभे।

In the scene (Act V, p. 43) where the *vidūṣaka* mistakes the garland for a snake, we have the *prahasana* element called *bhayam*.

In the same Act (p. 46), we have an instance of the *vīthyaṅga asatpralāpa* (incoherent talk) where the *vidūṣaka* starts telling a story. He says "There is a town called Brahmadatta ruled by a king Kāmpilya by name". Actually the name of the town is Kāmpilya and the king's name is Brahmadatta.

BĀLACARITA

Bhāsa is fond of personifying abstract things. In *Dūtavākya* the disc and other weapons of Kṛṣṇa are personified. In *Bālacarita*, the curse of Kaṁsa is personified. Kaṁsa is preparing to enter into the inner chamber. Just then the curse steps in and prevents him from entering by saying, "Where are you entering now? This house has become mine". Kaṁsa wonders who it could be

> कोऽयं विनिष्पतति गर्भगृहं विगाह्य
> उल्कं प्रगृह्य सहसाञ्जनराशिवर्णः।
> भीमोग्रदंष्ट्रवदनो ह्यहिपिङ्गलाक्षः
> क्रोधो महेश्वरमुखादिव गां प्रपन्नः।। — II.4

> Who could this be thus emerging from within the house? Looking dark like collyrium, keeping burning charcoal (in hand), showing frightening face with protruding terrible teeth, with brownish eyes like those of a serpent and looking like the anger of Lord Śiva that has entered the earth. The curse introduces itself as that of sage Madhuka, one carrying thunderbolt. He says that he has emerged from the cremation ground to enter Kaṁsa' heart.

Kaṁsa challenges it by saying that he is trying to do the impossible. Can the Meru mountain be shaken by the flappings of the wings of a crow? Can anybody drink up the waters of the ocean and dry it up? The curse disappears after saying that Kaṁsa would face the music in due course. After this encounter, Kaṁsa goes to sleep and the curse promptly enters into his body and begins to act. Following this, there is an altercation between curse and the personification of Royal Glory. The Royal Glory tries to prevent the entry of curse but the curse warns her to keep off. The Royal Glory again challenges it like her master. But the curse tells Royal Glory to leave the body of Kaṁsa since it is the command of Lord Viṣṇu. On hearing this, Royal Glory leaves Kaṁsa regretting that she had to desert the sole monarch of the world. After her departure, the curse gets elated and invites its companions — Alakṣmī (misfortune), Khalati (wickedness), Kālarātri (fatal night), Mahānidrā (deep slumber) and Piṅgalākṣī (brown-eyed demoness).

In the boastful conversations between the curse and Kaṁsa, and again between curse and Royal Glory, we have an instance of "Adhibāla".

MADHYAMAVYĀYOGA

Madhyamavyāyoga is again an interesting play. Ghaṭotkaca meets a family — a husband, his wife and their three sons. He wants one of the sons to be taken by him as a meal for his mother. The father is not prepared to spare the elder son and the mother the younger son but the middle one offers himself as the scapegoat. Ghaṭotkaca calls him by the name *madhyama* (middle one). Meanwhile Bhīma hears it and comes there since he is also the middle one (among the three sons of Kuntī).

He says:

मध्यमोऽहमवध्यानामुत्सिभानां च मध्यमः।
मध्यमोऽहं क्षितौ भद्र भ्रातॄणामपि मध्यमः।। — 28

> I am the middle one among the immortals, middle among the proud ones. Born of earth, I am the middle and I am the middle among the brothers too.

The further conversation results in the reinterpretation of the term *madhyama* and hence and we have an example of *avasyandita*.

Avalagita or unexpected twist is presented in the following scene. Bhīma asks Ghaṭotkaca, "Why have you pounced on the brāhmaṇa boys like Rāhu?" He expects Ghaṭotkaca to be provoked but he coolly says, "Yes, I am Rāhu". He refuses to release the boy since he has to be offered as a meal to his mother. Bhīma appreciates within himself, his love for his mother but is also surprised at his adamant nature. He asks for the name of his mother and Ghaṭotkaca says her name as Hiḍimbā. Bhīma now recognizes Ghaṭotkaca as his own son through Hiḍimbā whom he had married long back. The twist in the proceedings is an example of *avalagita.*

In continuation of the same scene, Ghaṭotkaca asks Bhīma, "Don't you know me?" Bhīma says, "I know that you are my son?". The bewildered Ghaṭotkaca asks him "So you say that I am your son?" Bhīma in return says that as a kṣatriya he is used to addressing all the subjects as his sons. The case of reinterpretation is very clear here and thus we have an instance of *avasyandita*.

PĀÑCARĀTRA

Pāñcarātra is yet another play based on an episode from the Virāṭa-Parva of the *Mahābhārata*. We have a *vīthyaṅga* in the very first verse of the play. It runs thus:

> द्रोणः पृथिव्यार्जुनभीमदूतो
> यः कर्णधारः शकुनीश्वरस्य ।

दुर्योधनो भीष्मयुधिष्ठिरः स
पायात् विराडुत्तरगोऽभिमन्युः ।।

> May Lord Kṛṣṇa save you, the Lord who is dark in complexion like a *droṇa* (crow), who served as a charioteer on Earth, who is a steersman (*karṇadhāra*) when he rides on the bird (Śakuni) (Garuḍa) who is invincible (Duryodhana), a steadfast warrior (Yudhiṣṭhira). He is also the terrific (Bhīṣma), the most honoured in sacrifices (Abhimanyu) who sets a noble path (Uttaraga), the primordial one (Virāṭa).

It is clear that the poet has punned on the names of characters appearing in the play. Hence it can be cited as an example for *udghātyaka* (statement with a hidden meaning) or *nālikā* (riddle).

In the first scene itself, there is lot of dramatic irony while describing the fire sacrifice performed by Duryodhana. The young disciples of the priests put out the fire hurriedly before oblations are fully consumed by fire resulting in the spreading of smoke all over the place. The poet says that the smoke attacks the house like an elephant the lotus. The brāhmaṇas leave the place like kinsman being driven away out of fear of ill repute. The *ghee* drenched in water continues to burn like the grief of a mother over the loss of her child. Similarly there is reference to inauspicious things like the five senses leaving a man on his death and the vital breath leaving off, a forest being burnt down due to a single dried up tree that catches fire, fortunes of man changing into a calamity, a noble man falling into ignominy due to the contact of immoral women, a man given to vices selling away his clothes and so on. All these references indicate the impending calamity of the great war. The descriptions refer to an abrupt end of the sacrifice conducted for the benefit of Duryodhana and hence we classify it under *gaṇḍa*.

In the same play Śakuni praises Duryodhana (1.28) and says that he must subjugate all rulers and bring them to his capital as Jarāsandha did. Jarāsandha kept hundreds of rulers whom he defeated under bondage. He was known for his wickedness. The demerit is presented as a merit by Śakuni. Hence we have an example of *mṛdava* here.

In continuation of the same scene, Duryodhana wants to honour his preceptor Droṇa who sheds tears being reminded of Pāṇḍavas' plight and says that his (Duryodhana) efforts are futile. This sudden turn in the midst of celebration mood may be cited as a example of *gaṇḍa*. After much persuasion, Droṇa suggests that Duryodhana should share the kingdom with his cousins which is of course rejected by Duryodhana.

In the course of further discussions, Duryodhana throws a challenge that Droṇa should produce the Pāṇḍavas before him in five days' time. Droṇa wonders how it would be possible since the brothers were living incognito. Just then a messenger comes from Virāṭa country and renders a news which gives a clue to Droṇa and Bhīṣma on the whereabouts of the Pāṇḍavas. Since the messenger's remarks bring about a sudden twist to the proceedings it can be brought under *gaṇḍa*. The messenger says that the hundred brothers of Kīcaka who were close to the Virāṭa king were killed without any weapon. Bhīṣma guesses that it would be possible only for Bhīma and confides it to Droṇa and thus a clue is obtained.

PRATIMĀNĀṬAKA

The opening scene where Sītā wears the bark garment out of curiosity is full of twists and turns, and so it can serve as an example of *avalagita*. When the maid carries away the bark garment Sītā first chides her for taking it from the green room. She aks her to restore it at the proper place. On second thought, she asks the maid to bring back the bark and wears it herself.

She is also happy to know from the maid that it fits her quite well. As it turns out, with the same bark garment Sītā prepares to leave for the forest along with Rāma when the coronation was stopped.

Similarly on hearing the sound of drums getting stopped abruptly Sītā guesses that the coronation was stopped. This sudden remark is again an instance of *avalagita*. It is followed by statement *bahuvṛttāntāni rājakulāni nāma* (many unexpected things happen in the royal household). This adds to the effect of the previous statement.

Then when Rāma hears piteous wailings of men and women in distress, he remarks that fate has struck at the roots to demonstrate its impressive powers. Just then the chamberlain enters by saying "protection protection". In the course of the conversation he reveals about the two terrible boons of Kaikeyī and the precarious position of the king.

Here we have a case for *gaṇḍa*.

In the wailing scene of Daśaratha (Act II) also we have a few abrupt remarks and reinterpretation of statements made pointing to the employment of *avalagita* to increase the dramatic effect. After speaking to Kausalyā, Daśaratha is unable to identify the one standing near her and so asks her who she is. Kausalyā starts by saying Lakṣmaṇa but stops abruptly at that. The king is reminded of Lakṣmaṇa and asks where he is. Kausalyā reinterprets her statement by saying that she was referring to Sumitrā, the mother of Lakṣmaṇa. Now it is reported that Sumantra has returned. Daśaratha is curious to know whether he has come back along with Rāma but he is shocked to know that Sumantra has come back with the empty chariot.

A series of questions and answers with a hidden meaning occurs in the beginning of the Act III proper. For all the enquiries of Bharata, the charioteer gives an indirect reply. This is an instance of *udghātyaka*.

Bharata — What affects my father?

Charioteer — A grand affliction of the heart.

Bharata — What do the doctors say?

Charioteer — They are not experts in that field (to treat the heart).

Bharata — Does he sleep?

Charioteer — Yes, on the ground.

Bharata — Food?

Charioteer — No food.

Bharata — What hope?

Charioteer — Fate alone.

In Act V, we have an interesting scene that speaks volumes about Bhāsa's innovative techniques. Rāma asks Rāvaṇa who has come in the disguise of brāhmaṇa about the ingredients for a *śrāddha*. Rāvaṇa lists a few things but stops by saying "or". This arouses the curiosity of Rāma who wants to know about the special delicacy to be offered at the ceremony. Rāvaṇa says that it is a golden deer available in the vicinity of the Himalayas. Rāma wants Lakṣmaṇa to go and fetch it but is informed that he had gone to receive a sage. Rāma goes in search of the golden deer himself leaving Sītā alone. Rāvaṇa carries her away. The abrupt remark beginning in "or . . ." can be classified under *gaṇḍa*. It is a significant scene in the play leading to the abduction of Sītā and subsequent developments in the plot.

In the Act VI (following verse 10), there is an instance of *avasyandita* or reinterpretation. Sumantra who is asked to get information about Rāma comes back and narrates the incidents to Bharata. He says that Sugrīva who had lost his wife and kingdom to Vāli has met Rāma who is also similar in grief. Bharata is startled and asks — How equal in grief? Sumantra repents within himself that he had revealed the truth but manages the situation by saying that he had meant that both Sugrīva and Rāma had lost their worldly wealth and prosperity. But Bharata compels him to tell the truth and is shocked to know that Sītā had been abducted by Rāvaṇa.

AVIMĀRAKA

Avimāraka has a theme that is developed by the poet himself. It is the story of a prince who had to live the life of an outcaste in another country due to a curse. He saves the life of the princess of the country and both fall in love with each other. Ultimately they are united in wedlock as the curse also comes to an end.

The king (heroine's father) wants to know who has rescued his daughter from the clutches of the infuriated elephant. The minister starts by saying "a handsome . . ." but stops in the middle. (Here we have the element *gaṇḍa*.) The king wants him to continue by saying that accidents do occur beyond anybody's control. The minister then describes the magnificent personality of Avimāraka and says that it was he who saved the princess.

The maid of Princess Kuraṅgī is in search of a brāhmaṇa. The *vidūṣaka* offers himself but the maid insists that she is on the look out for one who knows scriptures. *Vidūṣaka* says that he does have a good knowledge of scriptures and says *asti rāmāyaṇam nāma nāṭyaśāstram*. He says that he had studied five verses from it for a whole year. We have *asatpralāpa* or incoherent talk, here.

The maid says that she knows the *vidūṣaka* to be a *medhāvin* or a genius. This is a case of unworthy praise or *prapañca*.

In the same scene, the *vidūṣaka* says that he is well read. The maid points to the signet ring and asks him to read. But the *vidūṣaka* who is actually an illiterate, covers it up by saying that what is written on the ring is not there in the books that he had read. The maid then says that she would invite him for a dinner but wants to look at the ring. As *vidūṣaka* gives it to her, she dupes him and takes to her heels. This scene is an example of *chalam* or deception.

In Act II, the hero comes in search of his lady love. The maids of the princess meet him and ask him "what are you pondering over, Sir?". He says, "about science". The girls ask "what science". He says "it is *yoga*". The girls interpret it as "union" and reveal that the princess is also longing for union. The reinterpretation of the word *yoga* as union results in the *vīthyaṅga avasyandita*.

We have two more cases of *avasyandita* in the play. In the beginning of a the Act III, the heroine thinking about the hero, suddenly asks the maid "what did he say?"

The maid — Who, princess?

Heroine — (to herself) Ah, I am letting out the secret. (Aloud) the attendant of the inner apartment.

The maid — He did not say anything.

Heroine — I shall report to the queen that he has not fabricated the parrot's cage yet.

Maid — Your Highness, the parrot's cage is already installed.

Heroine — No, I am asking about the second one. Thus the heroine diverts the topic and asks about the time.

In the beginning of Act IV, we have a sweet conversation between two maids.

Maid 1 — Wait, Wait!

Maid 2 — Don't stop me. I am carrying the jewellery for the princess.

Maid 1 — Does the princess require jewellery?

Maid 2 — Don't talk inauspiciously.

Maid 1 — No, what I mean is, her fine form itself is the ornament for her.

This reinterpretation is an example of *avasyandita*.

The Vīthyaṅgas in the Plays of Kālidāsa

All the three dramas of Kālidāsa have *vidūṣaka* as one of the principal characters and hence there is a lot scope for humour in his plays. But the presence of *vidūṣaka* alone does not guarantee the availability of the *vīthyaṅga*s. There could be light-hearted comedy through the *vīthyaṅga*s with or without a *vidūṣaka* in a play. Kālidāsa is one who does not chain himself to any theoretical aspects. He does not employ any particular *aṅga* or an *alaṁkāra* just for the sake of it. They do not overstep into the realm of *rasa* nor do they hinder the progress of the main theme. There are no contrived situations in his plays in order to include a particular theoretical aspect, but they get fitted into the situations spontaneously and help to enhance the beauty of the respective scenes. (The references to verses and passages in the three plays are from *Works of Kālidāsa*, vol. I, ed. C.R. Devadhar, Motilal Banarsidass, Delhi, 1977.)

MĀLAVIKĀGNIMITRA

The *lāsyaprayoga* scene, quoted already, is an illustration of the *vīthyaṅga, vyāhāra*, a humorous conversation.

Avalagita is an unexpected turn of events. The king happens to see the picture of Mālavikā and wonders who it could be. The queen gives an evasive reply. The king tries to probe further but nobody gives a suitable reply. Ultimately, the little girl Vasulakṣmī lets the cat out of the bag, by saying that it is the picture of Mālavikā whom the queen had been guarding from the eyesight of the king (I. 3. 45ff; p. 6).

Prapañca is unworthy praise. When the *vidūṣaka* arrives, the king says: *ayamaparaḥ kāryāntarasacivaḥ asmān upasthitaḥ* — p. 16; I.8.11ff. (Here comes the minister who looks after another branch of our office.) The *vidūṣaka* does not deserve to be called as a minister and the job that he does is to look after the love affair of the king, which is not an official work. Hence, we have an instance of false praise here.

The scene where Gaṇadāsa and Haradatta fight a pitched battle is an example of *adhibala* (p. 18, l. 6 ff.). Haradatta says that Gaṇadāsa is not even equal to the dust of his feet. Gaṇadāsa had told Haradatta "You are to me what a puddle is to the ocean":

गणदासः - सोऽहममुना हरदत्तेन प्रधानपुरुषसमक्षं अयं न मे पादरजसाऽपि तुल्य इति अधिक्षिप्तः

हरदत्तः - देव, अयमेव मयि प्रथमं परिवादकारः। अत्र भवतः किल मम च समुद्रपल्लवयोरिवान्तरमिति।

In continuation of the same scene, the *vidūṣaka* touches the ego of Gaṇadāsa by saying "Why should you trouble yourselves with this competition in which you are certainly going to be defeated". Gaṇadāsa falls into the trap and vehemently argues that the competition should be held which was exactly what the *vidūṣaka* wanted. Hence we have here *chala* or deceit:

देवी - विरम निरर्थकारम्भात्।
विदूषकः - सुष्टु भवती भणति। भो गणदास, संगीतापदेशेन सरस्वत्युपायनमोदकानि खादतः किं ते सुलभ निग्रहेण विवादेन।
गणदासः . . . श्रूयतां अवसरप्राप्तामिदम्।
लब्धास्पदोऽस्मीति विवादभीरोस्तितिक्षमाणस्य
परेण निन्दाम् यस्यागमः केवलजीविकैव
तं ज्ञानपण्यं वणिजं वदन्ति॥ — I. 17

Avalagita is an unexpected answer to a genuine question and we have an example for this in the second Act (p. 46, lines 12 ff.). When Mālavikā finishes her recital *vidūṣaka* appreciates her performance, removes the bracelet from the king's arm and presents it to her. The queen stops him by saying that the competition is not yet over. The other performance is yet to be witnessed. "How can you bestow the ornament on her?" for which the *vidūṣaka* says "because it belongs to another".

विदूषकः - यदि भगवत्या शोभनं भणितं तत इदमस्यै पारितोषिकं प्रयच्छामि।
देवीः - तिष्ठ तिष्ठ, गुणान्तरमजानन् किमिति त्वं आभरणं ददासि?
विदूषकः - परकीयमिति कृत्वा।

We have another example for *avalagita* in the following scene in the conversation between Bakulāvalikā and Mālavikā in Act III (p. 76, ll. 9-18).

बकुलावलिका - सखि, अरुणशतपत्रमिव शोभते ते चरणम्। सर्वथा भर्तुरङ्कपरिवर्तिनी भव।
मालविका - हला, अवचनीयं मन्त्रयसे।
बकुलावलिका - मन्त्रयितव्यमेव मया मन्त्रितम्
मालविका - प्रिया खल्वहं तव।

बकुलावलिका - न केवलं मम।
मालविका - कस्य वा अन्यस्य?
बकुलावलिका - गुणेषु अभिनिवेषिणो भर्तुरपि।
मालविका - अलीकं मन्त्रयसे। एतदेव मयि नास्ति।

Bakulāvalikā: My friend, your foot looks so lovely like a red lotus. May you, by all means, sit on the king's lap.

Mālavikā: Well, you are chattering absurdly.

Bakulāvalikā: I have said what I ought to say.

Mālavikā: Surely you love me!

Bakulāvalikā: Not only I but . . . .

Mālavikā: Who else?

Bakulāvalikā: The king also, who loves good qualities.

Mālavikā: You are uttering a lie. It does not pertain to me.

After Mālavikā's performance *vidūṣaka* wants to prevent the other performance since his idea is not to witness the competition but to make the king see the beauty of Mālavikā which has already been achieved. Fortunately, the bard announces the noon time. Immediately the Vidūṣaka says (p. 48, ll. 3-5),

अविहा, अविहा, ब्राह्मणस्य भोजनवेला संवृत्ता।
अत्र भवतोऽपि। उचितवेलातिक्रमे चिकित्सका दोषमुदाहरन्ति ।

Fie fie, it is time for this brāhmaṇa to feed himself, so likewise for your majesty. And the physicians warn us that it is a grave mistake to transgress proper time for lunch.

By this trick, the *vidūṣaka* argues for the postponement of Haradatta's performance. Hence we have an example of *chalam* here.

Avasyandita is a reinterpretation of what is already said in some other sense. We have an example here (p. 80. ll. 17-19)

बकुलावलिका - एष उपारूढराग उपभोगक्षमः पुरतस्ते दृश्यते।
मालविका - किं भर्ता?
बकुलावलिका - (सस्मितं) न तावद्भर्ता। एष अशोकशाखावलम्बी पल्लवगुच्छः।

Bakulāvalikā: Here before you stands one flushed (of increased redness, passion) and fit to enjoy.

Mālavikā: What? The king?

Bakulāvalikā: (smiling) Not the king, but a spray of leaves on a bough of the Aśoka.

In the fourth Act (p. 122, ll. 63ff.) we have an interesting scene, where Nipuṇikā throws a stick on the *vidūṣaka* who is half asleep. He gets up and shouts by saying that a serpent has bitten him. Here we have a case for the *prahasanāṅga, bhayam.*

VIKRAMORVAŚĪYAM

In the scene (I.10, p. 14, ll. 2-5) where King Purūravas recovers Urvaśī from the clutches of the demon and brings her back, we have an example of *avalagita*. Looking longingly at the king, Urvaśī says "Equal in suffering, seems to drink me up with thirsty eyes". Citralekhā puts a significant question "Who my dear?" The expected reply is "the king", but Urvaśī hides it and says "This group of my friends".

उर्वशी - समदुःखः पिबतीव मां नयनाभ्याम्।
चित्रलेखा - (साकूतं) अयि कः?
उर्वशी - सखीजनः

Again when Urvaśī takes leave of the king, her necklace gets entangled in the thicket of creepers. Citralekhā sarcastically remarks that the entanglement is too deep. She indirectly refers to her entanglement in love which is deep. Urvaśī chides her for the remark. Here again we have scope for *avalagita*. (I. 15, ll. 14-24, p. 20)

उर्वशी	-	(उत्पतनभङ्गं रूपयित्वा) चित्रलेखे, मोचय तावदेनम्।
चित्रलेखा	-	(सस्मितं) दृढं खलु लग्ना। दुर्मोचनीयेव प्रतिभाति। भवतु यतिष्ये तावत्।
उर्वशी	-	स्मर तावत् एतत् आत्मनो वचनम्।

In the second Act (from the beginning, ll. 37ff., p. 26) we have an example for *chalam*. On seeing the *vidūṣaka*, Nipuṇikā, the queen's attendant is able to guess that he is trying to suppress some secret. She tells him that the queen is angry since the king uttered the name of some lady while addressing the queen. *Vidūṣaka* gets excited and asks her whether it is Urvaśī. Since she has extracted the truth by deceit we have the *vīthyaṅga chalam* here.

विदूषकः	-	स्वस्ति भवत्यै। (आत्मगतं) इमां दुष्टचेटिकां दृष्ट्वा तत् राजरहस्यं हृदयं भित्त्वा निष्क्रामति। (प्रकाशं) निपुणिके संगीतव्यापारमुज्झित्वा क्व प्रस्थितासि?
निपुणिका	-	देव्या वचनेन आर्यमेव द्रष्टुम्।
विदूषकः	-	किं तत्र भवती आज्ञापयति
निपुणिका	-	देवी भणति, सदाप्यार्यो मयि पक्षपाती न मां अनुचितवेदनादुःखितं उपेक्षत इति।
विदूषकः	-	(सवितर्कं) किं वा वयस्येन तत्रभवत्याः प्रतिकूलमाचरितम्?
निपुणिका	-	आर्य, यन्निमित्तं भर्ता उत्कण्ठितस्तस्याः स्त्रिया नामधेयेन भर्त्रा देवी आलपिता।
विदूषकः	-	(स्वगतं) कथं स्वयमेव तत्रभवता रहस्यभेदः कृतः। (प्रकाशं) किमामन्त्रिता तत्र भवती उर्वशीति? तस्य दर्शनेन उन्मादितस्तत्रभवान् न केवलं तत्र भवतीं ममापि विनोदविमुखो दृढं पीडयति।

निपुणिका - (आत्मगतं) कृतं मया भेदनं भर्तः रहस्यदुर्गस्य। (प्रकाशं) आर्य किं तावत् देव्यै निवेदयामि?

विदूषकः - निपुणिके, विज्ञापय तत्र भवतीं यत्ते तावत् मृगतृष्णिकाया निवर्तयितुं वयस्यं ततो देव्या मुखं द्रक्ष्यामीति।

The *prahasana* element *upapatti* consists in misinterpretation; giving a different reply, concealing the truth also forms part of it. We have a few examples for it in *Vikramorvaśīya*. The *vidūṣaka* had, inadvertently, let out the secret of the king's love affair to the queen's maid. Suddenly the king asks him whether he had kept the secret. The startled *vidūṣaka* keeps quiet. The king gets alarmed and asks him as to why he is keeping mum. The *vidūṣaka* manages the situation by saying "I have so effectively restrained my tongue that I cannot answer off-hand even your inquiries". (II.2, ll. 3 ff., p. 30)

राजा - अपि रक्ष्यते रहस्यनिक्षेपः।

विदूषकः - (सविषादमात्मगतं) हा धिक्, हा धिक् अभिसंहितोऽस्मि दास्या। अन्यथा न वयस्य एवं पृच्छति।

राजा - (साशङ्कम्) किं भवान् तूष्णीं आस्ते?

विदूषकः - एवं मया निमन्त्रिता जिह्वा यत् भवतोऽपि सहसा प्रतिवचनं न ददामि।

The last part of the second Act (pp. 60-64) is full of humorous situations. Many *vīthyaṅga*s can be identified in this section. Among them, *upapatti* figures prominently. The *vidūṣaka* carelessly drops the love letter written by Urvaśī to the king. The queen who comes there by chance, picks it up and takes the king to task.

निपुणिका	भट्टिनी। एतस्यैव अन्वेषणा वर्तते	Mistress, they are searching this very thing
देवी	पश्यामि	I see
विदूषकः	म्लायमानकेसरच्छविना मयूरपिच्छेन विप्रलब्धाऽस्मि	O, I was deceived by a peacock-feather of the colour of a faded *keśara* flower.
राजा	सर्वथा हतोऽस्मि	So I am ruined anyway.
देवी	(उपेत्य) आर्यपुत्र, अलमावेगेन, एतत् तद् भूर्जपत्रम्	(approaching) Noble lord, do not grieve. Here is the *bhurja*-leaf.
राजा	(ससंभ्रमम) अये, देवी, स्वागतं देव्यै	(confusedly) Oh, the Queen, Welcome, Queen!
विदूषकः	(अपवार्य) दुर्गतमिदानीं संवृत्तम्	But now it is the reverse of welcome.
राजा	(जनान्तिकं) सखे, किमत्र प्रतिविधेयम्	(aside) Friend, how to meet the present situation?
विदूषकः	लोत्रेण गृहीतस्य कुम्भीरकस्य अस्ति वा प्रतिवचनम्	How can a thief answer for himself when caught with a portion of the stolen article on his person?
राजा	देवि नेदं मया मृग्यते। स खलु परसमन्वेषणार्थं आरम्भोऽयम्।	Queen, this was not the object of my search. I was searching for some other object.
देवी	युज्यत आत्मनः सौभाग्यं प्रच्छादयितुम्	It is but proper to conceal one's good fortune.
विदूषकः	भवति। त्वरयास्य भोजनं यत् पित्तोपशमनसमर्थं भवति	Madam, quickly get ready his dinner which will effectively remedy his bile problem.
देवी	निपुणिके। शोभनं खलु ब्राह्मणेन आश्वासितो वयस्यः	Nipunikā, how well has the brāhmaṇa consoled his friend.
विदूषकः	भवति। ननु पश्य आश्वासितः पिशाचोऽपि भोजनेन	Madam, don't you see even a ghost is laid by dinner?
राजा	मूर्ख, बलादपराधिनं मामापादयसि	Fool, how falsely you represent me as guilty.
देवी	नास्ति भवतोपराधः। अहमेव अत्र अपराद्धा	It is not your fault. Only I am at fault.
राजा	अपराधी नामाहं . . . (इति पादयोः पतति)	I confess my guilt . . . . (falls at the feet)

देवी	(आत्मगतं) मा खलु लघुहृदयाऽहं अनुनयं बहु मन्ये। किन्तु अदाक्षिण्यकृतात् पश्चात्तापात् बिभेमि। (राजानमपहाय सपरिवारा निष्क्रान्ता)	(to herself) I am not so light hearted to take his appeasement seriously. But I am afraid of the remorse that would be caused by my inactivity.
विदूषकः	प्रावृण्णदीव अप्रसन्ना गता देवी उत्तिष्ठ	Like a turbid river in the rains the Queen, being unhappy has gone off. Rise.
राजा	(उत्थाय) वयस्य नेदं उपपन्नम्। पश्य	(rising) Friend, this is not unreasonable. Look. . . .
विदूषकः	अनुकूलमत्र भवतः एतत् न खलु अक्षिदुःखितः अभि मुखे दीपशिखां सहते।	This is quite agreeable to you. For a person whose eyes are dazzled will not bear the lampflame in his face.
राजा	मा मैवम्।	Do not think so. . . .
विदूषकः	तिष्ठतु भवतो धीरता। *bubhukṣitasya brāhmaṇasya jīvitam avalambyatām bhavan* ।	Enough of bravery. Courage! But please do sustain the life of a famished Brāhmaṇa.

In the *unmatta purūravas* scene of Act IV, there are a number of instances of the *vīthyaṅga asatpralāpa* (incoherent talk) or the *prahasana* element *vibhrānti* (delusion). One example may be cited here:

हंस प्रयच्छ मे कान्तां गतिरस्यास्त्वया हृता।
विभावितैकदेशेन देयं यदभियुज्यते॥ — Verse 17

O swan, give me my Love; you have stolen her gait; He who is proved guilty as regards a part should restore the whole of what is claimed.

ABHIJÑĀNA-ŚĀKUNTALAM

In the first Act (p. 26), there is plenty of scope for gentle humour when the three friends make fun of each other and also when the king joins them in the conversation. Observing the demeanour of both Duṣyanta and Śakuntalā, the friends remark "Dear Śakuntalā, if only father were here today. . . ."

Feigning anger Śakuntalā asks "What would happen then?" The friends say "He would make this distinguished guest happy even if it took the most valuable possession of his life". They mean that the father would be ready to give her away in marriage to Duṣyanta. This is an instance of *avalagita* where a twist is given towards an intended meaning.

सख्यौ - (उभयोराकारं विदित्वा, जनान्तिकं) हला शकुन्तले यद्यत्र अद्य तातः सन्निहितो भवेत् -

शकुन्तला - ततः किं भवेत्?

सख्यौ - इदं जीवितसर्वस्वेन अपि अतिथिविशेषं कृतार्थं करिष्यति।

शकुन्तला - युवामपेतम्। किमपि हृदये कृत्वा मन्त्रयेथे। न युवयोर्वचनं श्रोष्यामि।

In the second Act, while the army officer praises hunting as a good sport, the *vidūṣaka* despises it. Depending upon one's own view whether hunting can be taken as a sport or not, either of the statements of the two (*vidūṣaka* and the army officer) can be taken as an example of *mṛdava*, where merit is presented as demerit or vice versa.

Udghātyaka is a series of questions and answers with a hidden meaning. The *vidūṣaka* is not interested in hunting. So feigning as though he is sprained and crippled he welcomes the king without lifting his hand. When the king asks him what has happened, he relies by saying "Having yourself troubled my self you are asking why there are tears?" The king is not able to understand what he meant. The *vidūṣaka* asks him again "If the *kubja* plant is bent is it of its own accord or is it due to the current of the river?" The king says "it is due to the current of the river". Still the king does not understand. Then he explains by saying that due to the strain of the hunting expedition he has been immobilized.

विदूषकः - भो वयस्य, न मे हस्तपादं प्रसरति। तदवाङ्मात्रेण जापयिष्यामि।

राजा - कुतोऽयं गात्रोपघातः?
विदूषक - कुतः किल स्वयं अक्षिणी आकुलीकृत्य अश्रुकारणं पृच्छसि।
राजा - न खलु अवगच्छमि। भिन्नार्थमभिधीयताम्।
विदूषक - वयस्य, यद्वेतसः कुब्जलीलां विडम्बयति तत् किं आत्मनः प्रभावेण? ननु नदीवेगस्य?
राजा - नदीवेगस्तत्र कारणम्।
विदूषक - ममापि भवान्
राजा - कथमिव?
विदूषक - राजकार्यमुज्झित्वा एतादृश आकुल प्रदेशे वनचरवृत्तिना त्वया भवितव्यम्। यत्सत्यं प्रत्यहं श्वपादानुसरणैः संक्षोभित सन्धिबन्धनं मम गात्राणां अनीशोऽस्मि संवृत्तः। तत् प्रसादयिष्यामि विसर्जितुं मां एकाहमपि तावद् विश्रामितुम्।

Gaṇḍa is an abrupt remark which serves as a dramatic irony as well. We have an example for this in the fifth Act (p. 152). When the king indirectly accuses Śakuntalā of uttering a lie of having got married to him, Śārṅgarava becomes enraged and throws the blame on the king by saying that only kings adopt deception calling it to be a strategy. The king asks "What do I gain by deceiving her?" for which Śārṅgarava replies angrily "damnation". As it happens, the king comes to know of the truth later and undergoes untold suffering for having forsaken his wife.

Rājā: *bhoḥ satyavādin, abhyupagataṁ tavadasmābhirevam* । *kiṁ punaḥ imāṁ atisandhāya labhyate?*

Sārṅgaravaḥ: *vinipātaḥ* ।

The fisherman scene in the beginning of Act VI is an excellent example of the *adhibala* (outvying) or *vyāhāra* (humorous conversation).

In the same Act (pp. 176-77) we have an example of *chala* or false praise. The king complains about the effect of the mango shoots which are considered as the arrows of Cupid.

The *vidūṣaka* says "Wait a bit . . . I shall destroy Love's arrows with my stick". He then tries to strike down the mango shoot. The king says "Enough. I have seen a brāhmaṇa's powers".

In the scene where the king and *vidūṣaka* are witnessing a picture of Śakuntalā bothered by the bee (pp. 190-91), there is the *prahasana* element *vibhrānti*, that is delusion. Both of them mistake it to be a real bee and try to drive it away.

Mṛcchakaṭikam (of Śūdraka)

Mṛcchakaṭikam is an excellent specimen of a *prakaraṇa*. It is quite a long play consisting of as many as ten Acts. The play is also known for its innate humour that runs throughout the play. Normally there will be only one comedian in Sanskrit plays. But in *Mṛcchakaṭika* there are many, each having his own way of evoking laughter. Parts of the play can serve as independent pieces. For example, the *dyūtakarasaṁvāhakāṅka* may very well serve as a small *prahasana*. Illustrations for the *vīthyaṅga*s are available in plenty in this play.

In the scene where Śakāra chases Vasantasenā along with the *viṭa* we have a number of comic interludes. In the following verses (I.25, 29, 47) we have an example of *asatpralāpa*:

झणझणायमान बहुभूषणशब्दमिश्रं
किं द्रौपदीव पलायसे रामभीता।
एष हरामि सहसेति यथा हनूमान्
विश्वावसोर्भगिनीमिव यथा सुभद्राम्॥

Here the references to Draupadī running away being afraid of Rāma and Hanumān carrying away Subhadrā, mentioned as the sister of Viśvāvasu — are all wrong and hence it is a case of incoherent talk.

किं भीमसेनो जमदग्निपुत्रः
कुन्तीपुत्रो वा दशकन्धरो वा।

एषोऽहं गृहीत्वा केशहस्ते
दुश्शासनस्यानुकृतिं करोमि ॥

Be it Bhīmasena, the son of Jamadagni, be it Rāvaṇa, the son of Kuntī (nobody can save you). Seizing you by your hair, I am going to do what Duḥśāsana did.

शूरो विक्रान्तः पाण्डवः श्वेतकेतुः
पुत्रो राधाया रावण इन्द्रदत्तः।

आहो कुन्त्यां तेन रामेण जातः
अश्वत्थामा धर्मपुत्रो जटायुः ॥

Is he Śvetaketu, the brave and valiant son of Pāṇḍu? Or is he Rāvaṇa, the Indra-given son of Rādhā? Or is he Aśvatthāmā, born of Kuntī from that well-known Rāma? Or is he Jaṭāyu, the son of Dharma?

In both the verses, the incoherent talk is quite evident. The third verse quoted above is Śakāra's assessment of Cārudatta.

Vākkelī consists in two persons trying to outwit each other. In the scene where there is an altercation between Śakāra and the *vidūṣaka* (Act I, p. 55) we have an example.

शकारः - अरे.... उपविश। उपविश (Sit down ... sit down)

विदूषकः - उपवेशिता एव वयम् (We have been already made to sit)

शकारः - केन (By whom?)

विदूषकः - कृतान्तेन (By fate)

शकारः - उत्तिष्ठ उत्तिष्ठ (Well, get up ... get up)

विदूषकः - उत्थास्यामः (We shall get up)

शकारः - कदा (When?)

विदूषकः - यदा पुनरपि दैवेन अनुकूलं भविष्यति। (When destiny will again become favourable)

शकारः - अरे रुद्धि रुद्धि (Eh weep ... weep)

विदूषकः - रोदित एव वयम्। (We have been already made to weep)

शकारः - केन (By whom?)

विदूषकः - दुर्गत्या (By poverty)

शकारः - अरे। हस हस (Eh, laugh ... laugh)

विदूषकः - हसिष्यामः (We shall laugh)

शकारः - कदा (When?)

विदूषकः - पुनरपि ऋद्धया आर्य चारुदत्तस्य। (When the noble Cārudatta attains prosperity again)

In the second Act (II.8), there is a scene where the keeper of the gambling-house praises gambling. This is a case of *mṛdava*.

द्रव्यं लब्धं द्यूतेनैव दारा मित्रं द्यूतेनैव।
दत्तं भुक्तं द्यूतेनैव .... ॥

Money is obtained by gambling only. Wife and friends are acquired through gambling alone. Gifts are given and things enjoyed by means of gambling alone.

The elements *chala*, *vākkeli* and *adhibala* are all present in the conversation between the gambling-hall keeper and *saṁvāhaka* (Act II, pp. 81ff.). The entire scene is so hilarious that it cannot be explained. One has to enjoy the scene when it is represented on stage.

The *prahasana* element *avalagita* is decrying something out of delusion. In the third Act (between verses 3 and 4) we have a scene where the *vidūṣaka* makes a remark about a music performance. Actually it was a good performance as attested by Cārudatta, who is knowledgeable in music, but the *vidūṣaka* decries it because of his lack of knowledge in music.

मम तावत् द्वाभ्यामेव हास्यं जायते। स्त्रिया संस्कृतं पठन्त्या मनुष्येण वा काकलीं गायता। स्त्री तावत् संस्कृतं पठन्ती दत्तनवनस्येव गृष्टिरधिकं सुसुशब्दं करोति। मनुष्योऽपि काकलीं गायन् शुष्कसुमनोदामवेष्टितो वृद्धपुरोहित इव मन्त्रं जपन् दृढं मे न रोचते।

I become hilarious on account of two things; by a woman reading Sanskrit and by a man singing in a low tone. For, when a woman speaks in Sanskrit, she noisily snuffles (making a *su su* sound) like a young cow that has had a new rope put through the septum of her nose. A man too when he is singing in a low tone, is not to my liking like an old priest repeating *mantras*.

There is an example for *prapañca* (false praise) when the *vidūṣaka* proclaims that he is the greatest brāhmaṇa among all brāhmaṇas like the *dundubha* (harmless and despised) among all the serpents (Act III, p. 108):

यथा सर्वनागानां मध्ये दुन्दुभस्तथा सर्वं ब्राह्मणानां मध्ये अहं ब्राह्मणः।

The *prahasana* element *anṛtam* is also similar to *prapañca* as both are based on false praise. We can find an example for it in verse 21 (Act III) where the thief praises his own capabilities.

भुजग इव गतौ गिरिः स्थिरत्वे
पतगपतेः परिसर्पणे च तुल्यः।
शश इव भुवनावलोकनेऽहं
वृक इव च ग्रहणे बले च सिंहः॥

In movement I am quick like a snake; in steadiness, like a mountain; in flying, I resemble the lord of the birds. In surveying the entire space I am like a hare; in effecting a capture I am like a wolf; and in strength, a lion.

In the scene (Act III, p. 123), where Cārudatta praises the thief for his excellent skill in breaking the wall, we have another example for the element *prapañca*.

When a statement is made in a hurry and then revised out of emotion, there is a case for *avasyandita*. We may find an example for it in the fifth Act (v. 9).

यस्यार्थस्तस्य सा कान्ता
धनहार्यो ह्यसौ जनः।
(स्वगतं) न गुणहार्यो ह्यसौ जनः।

Cārudatta first says that Vasantasenā, being a *gaṇikā*, is to be bought with money. But within himself he feels that she has to be bought with merits since both of them are in love with each other.

In the conversation between the *ceṭa* and the *vidūṣaka*, (pp. 186-87) there is the element *vākkeli*, which is based on a wordy duel.

In the same Act (Act V, pp. 187-88) we have an example for *nālikā* or a riddle. The attendant wants to convey to the *vidūṣaka* that Vasantasenā has come. Here he puts a riddle. "When does the mango tree blossom?" The *vidūṣaka* gives the wrong answer as "summer" but after consulting Cārudatta, he says "*vasanta*" (spring). The next question is "who affords protection to the rich villages?" As before after an initial fumble, the *vidūṣaka* says "*senā*" (army). Then he is asked to put the two together. The *vidūṣaka* says *senāvasanta*. He is asked to turn it around. After some more fumbling, he arrives at the correct answer "Vasantasenā".

The Act VI of the play is full of dramatic action. Āryaka an ally of the hero, escapes from the prison. The soldiers search for him. There is a question on who could have rescued him, for which one of the soldiers Candanaka by name replies in a riddle style (vv. 9 and 10). One who has the Sun in the eighth place, or the Moon in the fourth, or Venus in the sixth or the Mars in the fifth. According to astrology all these zodiac signs signify calamity, death, disease, loss or mental disorder.

(There is a battle of wits between the two soldiers Vīraka and Caṇḍanīka in the same context — Act VI (pp. 236 ff.) — which can serve as an example of *adhibala*.)

In Act VIII (v. 2) also, we have an example for *nālikā*. A mendicant appearing in the first scene says,

पञ्चजना येन मारिता
स्त्रियं मारयित्वा ग्रामो रक्षितः।
अबलश्य चण्डालो मारितः
अवश्यं स नरः स्वर्गं गाहते॥

That man most surely attains heaven, who has killed five men and after killing a woman has guarded the town and has also killed the helpless caṇḍāla.

After killing so many people one can never attain heaven. So the inner meaning has to be looked into here. The "five men" refers to the "five senses". The "woman" refers to *avidyā* or "Nescience". The "town" refers to the "body". *Caṇḍāla* refers to the "egotism". The real meaning is that one who protects his body well and conquers the five sense organs, the nescience and the egotism can hope to attain heaven.

The scene in the same Act (pp. 254 ff.) involving the mendicant, the Viṭa, Ceṭa and Śakāra may be noted for the *vīthyaṅgas vākkeli, nālikā asatpralāpa, chala* and *adhibala*. When enacted on the stage, the entire scene would be hilarious. Similarly, when Śakāra is praised for his musical skill there is *chala* or deceit (p. 252). He himself says that he has taken a mixture of cumin seeds, asafoetida, etc., all of which portend only a harsh voice.

Further, in the same Act, the Viṭa requests Śakāra to keep Vasantasenā as a *nyāsa* — a pledge. Śakāra promises to keep her as a *nyāsa* taking it in the sense of death. (The word has a double meaning.)

In verses 35, 36, 37 and 45, there is mismatch between the Purāṇic characters in the words of Śakāra as in the first Act. All these can be taken as examples for *asatpralāpa*.

The court scene of the ninth Act is very interesting. While testifying before the judges, Śakāra says "Vasantasenā must have been killed by somebody with the noose of his arms; but not by me" — Then realizing his mistake he says "What I was saying was that her body was seen by me". This is an example of *avasyandita* or "reinterpretation".

Mudrārākṣasa (of Viśākhadatta)

Mudrārākṣasa of Viśākhadatta is unique in several aspects. In the first place, it is a play of political manoeuvres. After the defeat of Nandas, Candragupta is installed on the throne of Māgadha. But Cāṇakya who engineered the victory of Candragupta is not satisfied since he knows that Rākṣasa, the faithful minister of the Nandas, is still active. Until he is brought under control, there will be no peace for Candragupta. The play unfolds the political plot laid by Cāṇakya to capture Rākṣasa and make him accept ministership under Candragupta. The other peculiarity of the play is that it has no woman characters all.

The first verse of the play is in the form of a series of question and answers between Pārvatī and Lord Śiva. There are hidden meanings and witty remarks in the verse. It is an excellent example for *udghātyaka* which is defined as *gūḍārtha pada paryāya mālā*. It runs thus:

धन्या केयं स्थिता ते शिरसि शशिकला किं नु नामैतदस्या
नामैवास्यास्तदेतत् परिचितमपि ते विस्मृतं कस्य हेतोः।
नारीं पृच्छामि नेन्दुं विजया न प्रमाणं यदीन्दु -
र्देव्यादु-निह्नोतुमिच्छोरिति सुरसरितं शाठ्यमव्याद्विभोर्वः॥

The conversation runs thus:

Pārvatī — Who is this blessed one placed on your head?

Śiva — It is Śaśikalā.

Pārvatī — What? Is that her name?

Śiva — That indeed is her name. How did you forget it? It is familiar to you.

Pārvatī — I ask about that woman and not the Moon.

Śiva — If you do not believe in the Moon let Vijayā tell you.

"May the skill in equivocation of Lord Śiva displayed in thus concealing the Gaṅgā from his consort, protect you."

Pārvatī is jealous since Śiva has given place to another lady namely Gaṅgā, that too on his head. On being questioned, Śiva diverts her attention to the Moon who is already known to her and which can be verified with her friend Vijayā.

The clever counter arguments given by Śiva are indicative of clever manoeuvres that take place in the play. The word "Indu" which is a synonym of *candra* is indicative of Candragupta. "Gaṅgā" refers to the sovereignty of Candragupta and "Pārvatī" that of the Nandas.

In the prologue involving humorous conversation between the stage manager and his wife, we may have *vyāhāra*. The wife says that she is preparing a grand dinner since the moon is going to be eclipsed (by Ketu). The words indirectly refer the Candragupta and Malayaketu, who are two of the main characters in the play.

We have the element of *gaṇḍa* just after the conversation between Cāṇakya and his pupil in Act I. Cāṇakya gives certain instructions to his pupil and wonders how Rākṣasa can be taken. Siddhārthaka, the spy, suddenly enters and says: "Taken Sir", Cāṇakya asks "What is taken?" Siddhārthaka replies by saying that the master's instructions are taken.

We have seen that *ākāśabhāṣita* is one of the features of the *vīthī*. In fact, it can be taken as an element of *vīthī*. A question may arise here. *Ākāśabhāṣita* is the main feature of *bhāṇa*. So, if there is such a scene in other playforms, can it be taken as *bhāṇa* element or a *vīthī* element? The question can be answered taking into consideration the other features of these playforms. If an entire act is laid only in *ākāśabhāṣita* style, it can be called *bhāṇa* element. If there are characters other than the one employing *ākāśabhāṣita* figuring in an Act, then it can be termed as an element of *vīthī*. The logic behind this conclusion is that *bhāṇa* is a monologue play and *vīthī* has more than one character.

In any case, we have at least two places where *ākāśabhāṣita* technique is adopted in *Mudrārākṣasa*. In the beginning of Act II, one of the agents of Cāṇakya appears as a snake charmer and reveals his intentions to the audience through the *ākāśabhāṣita* mode. In the beginning of Act III, the chamberlain converses with the officials of the palace employing the same technique.

In Act IV, Rākṣasa calls for an astrologer to fix the day for the marching against Candragupta. The doorkeeper enters and announces that an astrologer has come. Rākṣasa asks "who is it?" The doorkeeper says "a monk with a well-shaven head". Rākṣasa feels that it is an ill omen, since it is said that one should avoid sighting a shaven-headed man while setting on an important task. On Rākṣasa's remark, the door keeper announces the name of the astrologer, that is Jīvasiddhi (which again refers to death indirectly). This can be quoted as an example of *avasyandita*. As for fixing the time, the astrologer says that they should start when the moon has arisen (indirectly when Candragupta is all powerful) in conjunction with Budha or the Mercury (referring to Cāṇakya) and when Ketu has set (portending the fall of Malayaketu).

The *vīthyaṅgas* play an important role in the play dominated by the intense political activity and strategic moves.

Veṇīsaṁhāra (of Bhaṭṭanārāyaṇa)

Veṇīsaṁhāra of Bhaṭṭanārāyaṇa is one of the rare plays that have a *rasa* other than *śṛṅgāra* as the main *rasa*. It has *vīra*, to be specific, as its predominant sentiment. It derives its theme from the *Mahābhārata* and the main incidents centre around the duel between Bhīma and Duryodhana.

In the prelude scene of Act I, in the course of the discussion between the stage manager and his assistant, we have an instance of *avasyandita* or reinterpretation. The stage manager says:

सत्पक्षा मधुरगिरः प्रसादिताशा मदोद्धतारम्भाः ।
निपतन्ति धार्तराष्ट्राः कालवशान् मेदिनीपृष्ठे ॥ — I.6

The main idea is that the sons of Dhṛtarāṣṭra will fall flat (dead) on the ground. The assistant hurriedly says "Sir, may evil be averted, let not any untoward event happen". The stage manager reinterprets his statement and says that he has described the onset of autumn. Apparently there is pun on the words employed in the verse. "Dhārtarāṣṭra" also means a swan. The entire verse means that (with reference to autumn) "The swans, spreading their wings and enjoying the season will land in the gardens and sport in various ways in an unrestrained fashion." The second half of the next verse also affords scope for reinterpretation.

रक्तप्रसाधितभुवः क्षत्रविग्रहाश्च ।
स्वस्था भवन्तु कुरुराजसुताः सभृत्याः ॥

First meaning: May the sons of Dhṛtarāṣṭra together with their folks be the occupants of heaven (die), having painted the earth red with their blood and their bodies shattered.

Reinterpretation: Let the sons of king of Kurus restore the portion of the earth to the Pāṇḍavas attached to them and stop all hostilities.

In the beginning of Act II, the *ākāśabhāṣita* technique is resorted to when the chamberlain describes the battle scenes resulting in the deaths of Bhīṣma and Abhimanyu.

In the same Act when Duryodhana mentions about the slaying of Abhimanyu by Droṇa, Karṇa, Jayadratha and others, the chamberlain wonders by saying "What is great in it?" Duryodhana gets angry and says that there is same greatness as the Pāṇḍavas got when they killed Bhīṣma placing Śikhaṇḍī in the front (II.4). Noticing the annoyance of the master, the chamberlain reinterprets his statement by saying that they had never witnessed any obstruction to the prowess of Duryodhana. This reinterpretation can be brought under *avasyandita*.

In the same act, in the course of the *śṛṅgāra*-oriented scene, Duryodhana, in the company of his wife, mentions about his thigh. Just then the chamberlain enters and says, "Broken, Broken". When asked to explain he says "Broken by Bhīma". What he meant was that the post of Duryodhana's chariot was broken by a terrible (Bhīma) wind. The abrupt remark made here is a definite instance of *gaṇḍa*.

In Act III, there is a bitter quarrel between Karṇa and Aśvatthāmā. Both try to outwit each other by their bragging resulting in *adhibala*. When he was led to believe that his son Aśvatthāmā had been killed (which was a wrong information), Droṇa dropped his weapons and stood still. Making use of this opportunity, the Pāṇḍava army killed him. According to Karṇa, Droṇa should not have stopped fighting at that stage. Aśvatthāmā vows to kill all the enemies at one stroke. Karṇa tauntingly says that there are many in the Kaurava army to achieve the feat. Aśvatthāmā claims that, arising out of the grief of the death of his father, his anger will fly hard on the enemies.

कर्णः - मूढ, दुःखितस्य अश्रुपातः कुपितस्य च
आयुधद्वितीयस्य
सङ्ग्रामावतरणमुचितं नैवंविधाः प्रलापाः।

अश्वत्थामा - (सक्रोधं) अरे रे, राधागर्भभारभूत, सूतापसद . . .

कर्णः - (सक्रोधं) अरे रे, वाचाट,
वृथाशस्त्रग्रहणदुर्विदग्ध . . .

अश्वत्थामा - (सक्रोधं) अरे रे रथकारकुल कलङ्क, . . .
आयुधानभिज्ञ . . .

The quarrel goes on in this vein and Duryodhana finds it hard to pacify them. Aśvatthāmā refuses to fight under the leadership of Karṇa. The infighting among the Kaurava ranks was one of the reasons for their downfall.

Uttara-Rāmacarita (of Bhavabhūti)

Bhavabhūti's plays may lack dramatic action but the lyrical beauty that is enshrined in them is unparalleled. *Uttararāmacarita* is the classic play with *Karuṇa* as the predominant *rasa*.

The abrupt remark made by the spy Durmukha has already been quoted as an example of *gaṇḍa*. This is a significant point in the play since Rāma decides to abandon Sītā in the forest in order to put an end to the public scandal. There are a few more examples of the *vīthyaṅga*s in the play.

In Act III, Rāma comes to *janasthāna* and on seeing the lovely places in the forest he is reminded of the good old days he spent in the company of Sītā. Sītā also comes there by chance but she is able to remain invisible to the eyes of others by the power of Bhāgīrathī. Whenever Rāma loses his consciousness due to unbearable grief, Sītā gives a soothing touch and revives him. He wonders:

आश्च्योतनं नु हरिचन्दनपल्लवानां
निष्पीडितेन्दुकरकन्दलजो नु सेकः।
आतप्तजीवितमनः परितर्पणोऽसौ
सञ्जीवनौषधिरसो हृदि मे नु सिक्तः — III.11

> Is this the oozing of sandal sprouts on my chest? Or is it the juice of curshed twigs of moon beams? Or is it the juice sprinkled in my heart, of the *sañjīvanī* herb which gives solace to my tortured soul and mind?

We have an instance of *trigata* here since there is triple explanation for the touch of Sītā as the juice of sandal, moon beams and the *sañjīvanī* herb.

In the beginning of Act IV, we have a humorous conversation between two hermit boys. On seeing the sages visiting the hermitage, one of them remarks "Welcome to all the grey beards because of whom we have a holiday today". The other boy ridicules him by saying "unique is your reason for regard towards elders". This can serve as an example for *prapañca* or false praise.

As Lava and Candraketu meet (Act V) they marvel at each other by saying:

> When this person is seen, my heart clings to him. Is it the power of his numerous virtues? Or is it an old acquaintance closely formed in a previous birth? Or is it certain relationship of his kept in the dark by Destiny?

Since there is a threefold explanation for the affection developed, it can become under *trigata* (triple explanation).

In the wordy duel between Lava and Candraketu we have *adhibala*. Lava objects to the proclamation regarding Rāma's greatness printed in the plate tied to the horse sent in connection with *aśvamedha*. Candraketu is surprised to see that Lava cannot tolerate the valour of even Rāma, the conqueror of Paraśurāma. At this Lava makes a sarcastic remark, "What is great in conquering Paraśurāma, a brāhmaṇa warrior?" Candraketu becomes angry and says that Lava does not know about the heroic exploits of Rāma. Lava criticizes Rāma's action in killing of Tāṭakā, a woman and Vālin. Candraketu gets infuriated and a pitched battle ensues between them.

On seeing Lava, Rāma wonders:

त्रातुं लोकानिव परिणतः कायवानस्त्रवेदः
क्षात्रो धर्म श्रित इव तनुं ब्रह्मकोशस्य गुप्त्यै।

सामर्थ्यानामिव समुदयः सञ्चयो वा गुणानां
प्रादुर्भूय स्थित इव जगत्पुण्यनिर्माणराशिः॥ — VI.9

Is it the science of archery having taken a human form for protecting the worlds? Or is it the characteristic valour of kṣatriyas having put on a body for preserving the Universe? Or is it an accumulation of all powers or aggregation of all good qualities? Or is it a combination of the fruits of the meritorious actions of the people that stands manifesting itself?

Any three of the statements can be taken to form *trigata*.

Mālatīmādhava (of Bhavabhūti)

Mālatīmādhava is a social play of Bhavabhūti. It is the story of love between two main characters of the play, namely, Mālatī and Mādhava, the impediments they come across and their ultimate union is wedlock with the blessings of elders. Both of them are the offspring of ministers of two different countries. Mālatī's father is pressurized to get his daughter married to Nandana, a favourite of the local king. This puts road blocks in the path of the lovers. Into this main theme is woven another love story between Makaranda, a friend of the hero and Madayantikā, the sister of Nandana.

After he had a first glimpse of Mālatī, Mādhava describes her thus:

sā rāmaṇīyakanidheradhidevatā vā
saundarya sārasamudāyaniketanam vā

Three explanations are possible here:

i. Creation of god of love

ii. Guardian deity of the treasures of beauty

iii. The abode of the essence of loveliness.

Hence this can be an example of *trigata.*

Act I is a delightful piece. The prelude tells us about the attempt of Kāmandakī, the Buddhist female ascetic in bringing about the union of Mālatī and Mādhava. The main scene is laid in the grove of cupid. Mādhava sees Mālatī for the first time and is enraptured by her beauty. Mālatī also betrays signs of love. One of the maids of Mālatī approaches Mādhava, gives him the family details of Mālatī and takes away from him the *bakula* — wreath as a souvenir for his mistress. Meanwhile a painting of Mādhava drawn by Mālatī is brought to him which confirms her love for him. Mādhava paints the picture of his sweetheart on the same board, to be sent to her. The Act ends with a description of Mādhava's love pangs.

The Act is suitably named as *bakula vīthī.* We have seen that the features of *vīthī* can be incorporated into other playforms.

Here is an example of it. The commentator Jagaddhara quotes the definition of *vīthī* from Bharata in this context.

> *'nānārasa samāyuktā sandhidvaya-vibhūṣitā* |
> *arthaprakṛtibhiḥ pūrṇā syādekaṅkā tu vīthikā* | |
>
> *tribihi pātraiḥ prayojyeyamuttamādhama madhyamaiḥ* |
> *kartavyā nāyikā cātra śṛṅgāradvaya samyutā* | |

In the beginning of Act II, Lavaṅgikā hands over to Mālatī, the garland woven by Mādhava. Mālatī finds that the weaving is uneven in one part. Lavaṅgikā says that Mālatī herself is responsible for the fault. On being questioned by Mālatī, Lavaṅgikā explains by saying that on seeing the extreme loveliness of Mālati, Mādhava got unnerved and so he could not concentrate on the weaving of the flower. This is an instance of *avalagita*.

The altercation between Mādhava and Aghoraghaṇṭa, a tāntric man in the cemetery (Act V) can be cited as an example of *adhibala*, where they try to outwit each other by boastful arguments.

Prabodhacandrodaya (of Śrī Kṛṣṇa Miśra)

Prabodhacandrodaya of Kṛṣṇamiśra is to drama what *Meghasandeśa* was to poetry. Just as *Meghasandeśa* gave rise to a separate class of poetry called *sandeśa kāvyas*, *Prabodhacandrodaya* stands as a forerunner for allegorical plays in Sanskrit. We have seen that right from Bhāsa's times, some abstract concepts are personified and presented as characters in a play. In *Bālacarita*, the curse of Kaṁsa appears as a character, but in an allegorical play, all the characters are personifications of abstract ideas.

The main philosophical concept that forms the theme of *Prabodhacandrodaya* is Advaita. It also recognizes Viṣṇu as the

Supreme Deity at the *vyāvahārika* level. The *ātman* is longing for liberation but it is suppressed by *māyā*. The soul is kept down in the false sense of plurality which is called *saṁsāra* which is aided by *moha* (confusion), *dambha* (vanity), *mithyāsiddhi* (false perception) and so on. The virtuous characters like *viveka* (discrimination), *vidyā* (spiritual knowledge) and *śraddhā* (faith) help the struggling soul in its advancement. With the help of Viṣṇu-*bhakti*, the soul realizes its true self and attains final emancipation through *prabodha* (true knowledge).

The very first verse which is highly philosophical gives a clue to the proceedings. It says that the Inner Light which is intense, bliss and pure is to be known as one's own self. All the manifestations of the five elements will disappear like the illusory snake, appearing initially on a garland or a rope, disappearing finally.

In the Act II, the egoism boasts of itself (II.9). It says:

नास्माकं जननी तथोज्ज्वलकुला सच्छोत्रियाणां पुन-
र्व्यूढा काचन कन्यका खलु मया तेनास्मि ततोधिकः।

अस्मच्छालकभागिनेयदुहिता मिथ्याभिशप्ता यतस्-
तत्संपर्कवशान्महा स्वगृहिणी प्रेयस्यपि प्रोज्झिता॥

My mother did not belong to a noble family but I married a girl from a respectable family. In this respect I am superior to my father. The daughter of the nephew of my brother-in-law was falsely accused but on account of her relation to this person, I left my wife though beloved to me.

This being an unworthy praise, may be termed as *prapañca*.

Replying to the *ahaṁkāra* (egoism), *dambha* (deceit) says that he once visited Brahmā's abode and that all the sages rose up from their seats and honoured him. This is again a case of *prapañca*.

In the words of the *mahāmāyā* (grand delusion) we have the *prahasana* element *avalagita*, which is decrying the accepted concepts out of delusion; it says (II:16):

आत्मास्ति देहव्यतिरिक्तमूर्तिर्भोक्ता स लोकान्तरितः फलानाम्।
आशेयमाकाशतरोः प्रसूनात् प्राथीयसः स्वादुफलप्रसूतौ ॥

The view, that there is a soul separate from the body which on reaching the other world enjoys rewards, is like the hope to get tasty fruits from the big flower of a tree in the sky.

The *mahāmāyā* gives again an absurd interpretation of the Cārvāka concept of materialism and justifies courting any woman at will and coveting the wealth of others. This is an instance of the *prahasana* element *avaskanda*.

हिंसायामथवा यथेष्टगमने स्त्रीणां परस्वग्रहे
कार्याकार्यविचारणा हि यदमी निष्पौरुषाः कुर्वते ॥ — II.18

In fact, most of the statements of the Cārvāka decrying the ascetic life, the Vedas and penance are instances of the *prahasana* elements *avalagita* or *avaskanda*.

In the boastful statements of anger and greed also we have these elements. The anger, for example, says:

केयं माता पिशाची क इव हि जनको भ्रातरः केऽत्र कीटा
वध्योऽयं बन्धुवर्गः कुटिलविट सुहृच्चेष्टिता ज्ञातयोऽमी। — II.33

Who is this demoness, my mother, who is my father, who are my worm-like brothers? Relations are fit to be slain and also the people of the family who are influenced by these wicked friends.

In Act III, there is a battle of wits between the Kāpālika, the Jaina and the Buddhist, where we have scope for *adhibala* and *vākkeli*.

Karpūrmañjarī (of Rājaśekhara)

In the prologue where the assistant coins a riddle while referring to the name of the poet (I.5), we have an instance of *nālikā*. "Who is called 'Moon crowned'? — *rajanī-vallabha-śikhaṇḍī* — and who is the teacher of Mahendrapāla, the crest jewel of the race of Raghu?" The moon is also *rāja* and the crest is *śekhara*. Hence the answer is "Rājaśekhara" (The references here pertain to the Harvard Oriental Series edition, Motilal Banarsidass, 1963).

In the presence of the king and the queen and her attendant, the *vidūṣaka* declares that he is the only scholar in the group since his father-in-law's father-in-law used to browse through books at the neighbour's house (between verses 18 & 19, ll. 3 ff.). Here we have *chalam* which is based on false praise.

In the same Act (Act I, ll. 14ff. after v. 20), the queen's maid tells *vidūṣaka*: "You, though unlettered as the iron beam of a goldsmith's balance, are employed while I, though lettered, like the common balance, am not employed". Here again there is false praise. The goldsmith's balance will be small and there will be no space for any letters to be engraved. But the beam of a common balance used in a grocery shop will be big enough to accommodate the name of the manufacturer, etc.

In the course of the same conversation, the *vidūṣaka* and the maid abuse each other through indirect references to limbs, punning of words, etc. All these have the element of *nālikā*. The *vidūṣaka* says that he will cut her limb that goes by the name of Yudhiṣṭhira's elder brother (Karṇa which also means "ear"). The maid says that she would break that part that goes by the name of the star following Uttaraphālgunī (which is Hastā that also means "hand"). Again she says that he may take himself off to the place where her first swaddling clothes went (that is, devil's place). The *vidūṣaka* retorts by saying that she may go the place where his mother's first set of teeth went (devil's place). There are also some indirect references to a kick by the foot or a push by the neck. Thus we have *nālikā* here. In fact, the entire conversation is replete with *vīthyaṅga*s such as *vākkeli* and *adhibala*.

In verses 22, 23 and 24 (Act I), where the magician boasts of his credentials, there is *mṛdava* which is presenting merits as demerits and vice versa. He says that his teacher had excused him from the practice of trance and that he took to drink and women as a means to salvation. What better religion could there be?

In the second Act (after verse 11, passages 7 to 22) there is an interesting conversation between the maid and the king on how the heroine was anointed and decorated. There is a reinterpretation by the king on what the maid says. It can serve as an example of *avasyandita*.

Maid — Her limbs were anointed with a paste of saffron essence until they were yellow.

King — That was polishing a golden doll till it was beautifully bright.

Maid — A pair of emerald anklets were put on her feet.

King — That was surrounding a pair of lotuses with swarms of bees.

Maid — A jewelled girdle was tied to her hips.

King — That was making a peacock dance on the cliffs of golden mountain.

Maid — Then bracelets were put on her forearms.

King — That was decorating the inverted arrow of the Cupid.

Maid A necklace was placed around her neck.

King That was giving to the moon of her face an ample retinue of stars.

Maid A pair of gem studded earrings were put on her ears.

King That was transforming her face into a chariot of Cupid with two wheels.

Maid Then collyrium was applied to her eyes.

King That was putting a bee on the fresh blue lotus.

Maid Then her curly locks of hair were arranged.

King That was the spotted antelope appearing on the moon's disk.

Maid Her tresses of hair were adorned with flowers.

King That was letting one see a contest between Rāhu and the Moon.

Maid Thus the Queen adorned that girl.

King That was adorning the pleasure garden by the spring season.

After the heroine vacates the swing and goes away (Act II, after v. 40, ll. 3 ff.), the king and the *vidūṣaka* give their own view of her disappearance. According to the *vidūṣaka*, it is like the lightning that has come and gone. According to the king it is like the mirage. Since there are three concepts — the heroine, the lightning and the mirage, we can take it as an example of *trigata* or triple explanation.

We have an example for *udghātyaka* in the third Act (vv. 9 ff).

Vidūṣaka What is it that they call "love . . . love"?

King	The knot of attachment wich exists between a mutually united pair and which has grown strong under the dictates of Cupid is called "love".
Vidūṣaka	And of what sort it is?
King	Love is based on sincerity, is devoid of blemishes of suspicion and it creates longing between the lovers. It is imparted by Cupid and enhanced by amorous play.
Vidūṣaka	How is it recognised?
King	By restless glances, etc.

On seeing the king, the heroine wonders (ll. 19 ff. after v. 20, Act III) whether he is the full moon descended from heaven or Cupid that has come in a bodily form or someone who has stolen my heart? Here again, we have an instance of *trigata* on account of threefold explanation of the king's form.

Vīthyaṅgas in the Prahasanas

It has already been pointed out that the *vīthī* and the *prahasana* have much in common between them. It is no wonder that the *vīthyaṅga*s are present in a good measure in the *prahasana*s. Moreover, the main sentiment in the *prahasana*s is *hāsya*. A number of *vīthyaṅga*s being *hāsya* oriented, they find scope in the *prahasana*s.

(i) The *Bhagavadajjukīya* of Bodhāyana Kavi

The story is about the reformation brought into the mind of a wayward disciple by a *yogin*. For this purpose, the *yogin* gets into the body of a *gaṇikā* and talks of philosophy instead of love. In the meantime, the body of the *yogin* is infused with the life of the *gaṇikā*. Accordingly, the *yogin* behaves in an odd fashion. The disciple who was earlier enamoured of the *gaṇikā*, gets convinced about the transient nature of the world and becomes a true disciple. The souls are exchanged again and both the *yogin* and the *gaṇikā* behave their usual self. (References are from edition of the text by Anujan Achan, Cochin, 1925.)

The opening dialogue of the disciple where he repents for his life of asceticism and states the reason for his leaving Buddhism (since he cannot get food after midday) is an instance of the *prahasana* element *avalagitam* which is "decrying something out of delusion". It can also be brought under the *vīthyaṅga mṛdava*, that is, considering merits as demerits or vice versa. The conversation between the teacher and the disciple in the garden may be cited as an instance of the *vīthyaṅga, udghātyaka*. The scene where the disciple mistakes a peacock to be a tiger (p. 37) is an instance of the *prahasanāṅga bhayam*. The comparison of the *gaṇikā* to a *parivrājaka* (p. 71) is an example of the *vīthyaṅga prapañca* (or *prahasanāṅga, anṛtam*) which is based on false praise. We have a quack doctor in the play. When he is asked to quote the relevant rules of the medicinal science, he struggles at the very first step and mutters some unintelligible sounds (p. 84). This is called *asatpralāpa*.

(ii) *Mattavilāsa-prahasana* of Mahendravarma Pallava:

This *prahasana* is full of comic situations created by degraded ascetics in the form of a Kāpālika, his fiancé, a Pāśupata, a Buddhist monk and a lunatic. (References are from the edition by N.P. Unni, College Book House, Trivandrum, 1974.)

Prapañca which is based on false praise figures prominently in this play. The Kāpālika praises his companion thus:

> *priye devasome, satyameva etat — tapasā kāmarūpatā prāpyate iti* । *yat tvayā praramavratasya vidhivat anuṣṭhitena eva rūpātiśayaḥ ksanāt pratipannaḥ* —p. 42
>
> My dear Devasoma, it is indeed true that loveliness of form is obtained by penance. By observing the austerities according to the rules, you have just attained the beauty.

The licentious life of the Kāpālikas is praised in another place.

> *peyā surā priyatamāmukhamīkṣitavyam*
> *grāhyaḥ svabhāvalalito vikṛtaśca veṣaḥ* ।
>
> *yenedamīdṛśamadṛśyata mokṣavartma*
> *dīrghāyrastu sa bhagavān pinākapāṇiḥ* ॥ — v. 7

The comparison of the liquor shop to a sacrificial hall (pp. 45-46) also belongs to the same variety (*prapañca*).

The opening scene (p. 42) where the Kāpālika and his fiancé talk incoherently due to intoxication is an instance of *asatpralāpa*. The prattlings of the lunatic too fall under the same category.

> *grāmasūkaramāruhya gaganamutpatitena sāgareṇa prabhañjya rāvaṇam balāt gṛhītaḥ śakrasutaḥ timiṅgalaḥ* । . . . *yasya vā kasya vā bhāgineyaḥ khalvaham bhīmasenasya ghaṭotkaca iva.*
> — pp. 62-63

Terming a merit as a defect or vice versa is called *mṛdava*. The Kāpālika's criticism of the celibacy observed by the Buddhist monks (pp. 44-45) is an instance of this *vīthyaṅga*. Chance coincidence of reference to something and its actual happening is called *avalagita*. When the Kāpālika knows that his bowl is missing, he says *priye, tarkayāmi śūlyamāmsagarbhatvāt śākyabhikṣuṇā śunā vā gṛhītam iti* (p. 48). Enters then the Buddhist monk with a bowl hidden inside his garment arousing the suspicion of the Kāpālika and his companion. Hence we have here *avalagitam.*

When the Buddhist monk says that the original texts, permitting wine and women for the monks have been deliberately suppressed by the old monks of the order (pp. 48-49), we have the *prahasana* element *upapatti,* that is, misinterpretation. Other instances of the *upapatti* in the play are the Kāpālika's accusation that the Buddhists have compiled their scriptures from portions stolen from the Vedānta and the *Mahābhārata* (v. 12),

> *vedāntebhyo gṛhītvārthān yo mahābhāratādapi* ।
> *viprāṇām misatāmeva kṛtavān koṣasañcayam* ॥

and the Buddhist monk's salutation to the Buddha for having prescribed shaven head when he escaped being caught by hair by Devasomā (p. 55).

The *prahasana* element *vyāhāra* refers to the humorous conversation between two or three. An instance of this can be found in the conversation between the Kāpālika and the Buddhist monk (pp. 51-52). The same can illustrate the *vīthyaṅga, vākkeli* also. Another example for the same can be found in the conversation between the Kāpālika, the Buddhist monk and the lunatic (p. 66).

The *prahaana* element *pralāpa* consists in showering praise on an unworthy or trivial object. Devasomā's praise of the begging bowl (p. 59) can be cited as an instance for the same.

> *hā hatāsmi, mandabhāgā* । *sarvalakṣaṇasampannatayā kamalāsana-śīṛsakapālānubhavasya paurṇamāsīsomadarśanasya nityasurā-gandhinaḥ etasya malinapaṭasamsargeṇeyam īdṛśamavasthā saṁvṛttā.*

9

Conclusion

Having thus surveyed the origin and development of the *prahasana* and the *vīthī* literature from several aspects, we may note in conclusion that though the beginning was very interesting and promising, the tempo had been slowly lost in course of time. Let us first take up the case of the *prahasanas*. The sublimity of thought and style, and restraint, witnessed in the *Bhagavadajjukīya* and a few other works of this class, slowly and inevitably gave place to decadence in diction and decency. The decline in the taste of the *prahasana* writers reflects the trend of the society for which they composed. Though the poets cannot altogether be blamed for what they gave us, since very often they are found to cater to the needs of the society in which they live, the tendency to overdo things should be attributed to them only. The criticism of men in high offices, respectable professions and orders of life, like kings, priests, ascetics and physicians, though started originally with all good intentions of mending the ways of erring men and educating the society against the exploitation by evil men and women, has been overdone in the later *prahasanas*. *Prahasana* has thus become an excuse for a writer to criticize very often in unparliamentary language, religious sects, personalities and practices which are not acceptable to him. Such works must have had a limited appeal only even in the days of their composition; and much more so now, when in a secular society like ours, all religious and linguistic barriers are broken, or are in the process of being snapped, if not completely wiped out. Thus, if a poet is really serious, he can reform the society by his thought-provoking themes, sober language and original approach. No one can prevent him from doing so. Thus, even in a late period we have the *Madanaketucarita* of Rāmapāṇivāda upholding the high traditions of *prahasana*. One salient feature of the *prahasana*s from the seventh century to the modern times is that they reveal, in some form or the other, the social and cultural life of certain sections of the Indian society during different periods of history. It is also partly true that some of the *prahasana*s need not be taken seriously as projecting different cultural and social conditions.

Some of the *prahasana*s are novel and original in their general set-up and characterization. Thus the *Kuhanābhaikṣava* and the *Lokarañjana* have introduced Musalmans in their cast and the *Kukṣimbharabhaikṣava* has two Europeans. The *Gaurīdigambara* is unique in that it has only divine beings in its cast. There was thus scope for innovations in the *prahasana*s, though many of the later writers allowed themselves to be swayed away by the irresistible temptation to imitate the popular *prahasana*s colourlessly.

As for the practical aspect of the stage-worthiness, it may be pointed out that barring a few stereotyped pieces of the later times, several of the *prahasana*s can be staged. There is evidence that the *Bhagavadajjukīya* and the *Mattavilāsa* have been quite popular with the Kerala stage from very early times. The *Hāsyacūḍāmaṇi* and the *Madanaketucarita* have been staged even in recent times. The *saṁkīrṇa* type of *prahasana*s can also be staged by removing some of the objectionable passages. Several of the twentieth-century *prahasana*s, which have been listed in the Appendix, were specifically written for the stage. The *prahasana* allows itself to be easily staged because of its shortness, being confined to just one or two acts. While long *nāṭakas* and *prakaraṇas* are presented only in parts, short and humorous plays will have a better reception on the present-day stage. It may be stated that *prahasana* could be a very effective means of popularizing Sanskrit among the general public, especially the younger generation.

Prahasanas in Sanskrit thus form an important and interesting field of study. The account presented in the foregoing chapters is representative but not exhaustive. Several aspects of the *prahasanas* can still be studied in detail with advantage. For instance, a comparative study of the Sanskrit *prahasanas* with those of the Indian vernaculars, and the farce in English and other European languages could be quite interesting and rewarding. A comparison of the *prahasana* with the *bhāṇa* in Sanskrit itself, in terms of their interaction and influence, could again be another field of study. The present account, it is hoped, may kindle interest among scholars to undertake such pursuits with an advantage and conviction.

The *vīthī* represents one of the earliest stages of Sanskrit drama. Having lent its characteristics to the other play forms like *prahasana* it went into oblivion. As most of the dramaturgical writers refer to it, it must have existed at least to a limited extent during their times. The non-availability of early specimens is indeed a handicap to the study of *vīthī* but the citations from *Mālatikā* and *Indulekhā* found in dramaturgical texts is a small solace. Though *Dūtavākya* has been included in the study, its credentials as a *vīthī* are still waiting for its universal recognition. But seeing the other minor play-forms being represented, e.g. *Madhyamavyāyoga, Karṇabhāra* (an *aṅka*) it is reasonable to suppose that Bhāsa intended *Dūtavākya* to be a *vīthī*.

In the fast-changing scenario of present-day life, it may be difficult to stage long plays like *Uttararāmacarita.* Long descriptions and slow dramatic action may not appeal to the present-day audience. But short play-forms like *vīthī, prahasana* or *bhāṇa* can be staged often to attract the audience. They have simple themes and lesser characters when compared to other play-forms. Being social play-forms they do not require elaborate scene settings or costumes. The modern-day dramatists may, therefore, write and produce such play-forms for the benefit of the audience. It could serve as a means of popularizing Sanskrit as well. On an experimental basis one may introduce Hindi or the regional languages in the place of Prākṛt. But while doing so, one may resort to the Sanskritized form of the vernaculars rather than the colloquial form of the same.

There is every reason to believe that *vīthī* started as a street play. It may very well be revived to create awareness among the people on the social issues that are plaguing the country. This is the best way of taking Sanskrit to the masses and preserving it for the posterity. The case of forgotten tradition is not peculiar to Sanskrit alone. A number of village traditions are dying in every part of the country. The folk dramatic traditions which are akin to a *vīthī* are also facing the same fate in several parts of the country. They were once popular forms of entertainment in the villages. They have everything an Indian audience wants, songs, dance, action, comedy, social relevance and so on. They were invariably staged in villages during all festivals and celebrations. But they are losing ground even in villages. There was, no doubt, an element of religious fervour in them as the themes were chosen from the Purāṇas and the epics. But the message was Universal — the good will ultimately win, the evil will get punished. In the name of secular state, such message-rendering mechanism has been dumped to dust with the result that there is widespread violence, religious intolerance and erosion of values in the society today.

Is Vīthī a Forerunner for Indian Folk Theatre?

India presents a colourful assortment of folk culture, best portrayed through the unique art of folk theatre. Variously known as the *jātrā* (Bengal, Orissa, Eastern Bihar), *tamāśā* (Maharashtra), *nauṭaṅkī* (Uttar Pradesh, Rajasthan and Punjab), *bhavai* (Gujarat), *yakṣagāna* (Karnataka) and *terukkūttu* (Tamil Nadu), folk theatre reaches out to a large cross-section of the population.

The decline of Sanskrit drama saw the emergence of folk theatre in various regions from the fourteenth century through the nineteenth century. Maintaining the basic conventions like stage preliminaries, the *sūtradhāra*, the *vidūṣaka*, the opening prayer song, etc. pertaining to the Sanskrit theatre, the folk theatre resorted to the regional languages and made rapid strides by taking it to the masses. The themes were also taken from the epics and the Purāṇas but they were given a regional outlook to attract the masses. In fact, the folk theatre played a major role in maintaining the cultural unity of India. They also imparted moral values in a way that was appealing to the rural masses so much so that even the commonest of the people knew of *dharma, puṇya, pāpa,* etc. Heroes like Rāma, Kṛṣṇa and Arjuna wielded a great influence on them.

In the folk plays generally, the actors perform in the open ground with gangways attached to the makeshift stage. This helps immensely since the actors frequently converse with the audience in the course of the play. Audience participation is an essential part of the Indian Folk Theatre. The stage is often a huge empty space which the actors deftly manipulate according to their roles, singing or dancing or rendering dialogues in a stylized manner with symbolic gestures. Loud music, dance, gaudy costumes, heavy make-up, masks and chorus-singing are the hallmarks of folk theatre, making it so different from the modern theatre.

Folk theatre provides a valuable insight into the local practices, traditions, customs, dialectical usages and native humour. Although mythological and medieval romances are their main thrust, folk theatre acquires a timeless appeal by improvizing with symbolic relevance to the current social and political happenings.

*Jātrā*s are usually long plays (running to about four hours) featuring epic themes, music, gesticulation and witty dialogues. *Jātrā*s are often very melodramatic with a stylized delivery of dialogues and exaggerated gestures. Earlier religious and moral values were communicated to the masses through the powerful medium of *jātrā.*

The original Oriya and Bengali *jātrā*s are quite hazy and the historians and theatre critics have widely divergent views on their origin and development. Nevertheless, they have drawn attention to the mention of *jātrā* in the *Nāṭyaśāstra*. They have also attributed the beginnings of dramatic presentation in Bengal, Bihar and Orissa in Jayadeva's *Gīta Govinda*.

In Bengal there was a form of singing called *carya* which was popular between the ninth and twelfth centuries. The commentaries on the *Amarakośa* mention its existence and some fragments from them are quoted in copperplate grants. The language of these songs is considered to be a creation of sections of the people who were trained in local dialects, traditions and customs. It is also clear that it was a kind of a musical drama which was probably prevalent during that time both in Bengal and Orissa.

Caitanya, the great Bhāgavata and social reformer and his followers contributed a reawakening of *carya* and were responsible for bringing about national integration in many parts of India at the cultural level at a time when all Indian regions were affected by political and economic devastation. They were the creators and directors of their own musical dramas. They self-consciously used the vehicle of drama for socio-religious purposes. History owes them the first definite presentations of theatrical spectacle where Caitanya himself played the role of Rukmiṇī. This then was perhaps the beginning of *Kṛṣṇa Jātrā*. So he is undoubtedly the predecessor of the present-day *jātrā* of Bengal and Orissa.

Today the style of writing plays for *jātrā* has undergone changes. *Jātrā* plays are now no longer limited to the mythological or historical subjects. They include social themes to suit modern tastes.

Jātrā is performed on a simple stage with the spectators surrounding it on all sides. The chorus and the musicians take their positions off stage. There are no stage properties except a single seat meant to serve various functions — a throne, a bed or a wayside bench. On stage the actors move in a very theatrical manner. They deliver their dialogue in high-sounding words and have to be loud enough to be audible to the spectators seated on all sides. Consequently they adopt an exaggerated style and exhibit a heavy make-up. They sport dazzling costumes, their swords blaze and their words boom to the accompaniment of the crashing cymbals. Sometimes the actors depict subtle emotional moods like love, sorrow, pathos but the element of exaggeration is always present, as they have to project themselves as larger than life figures.

The northern Oriya and Bengali theatres of the present day owe their origin to the *jātrā*.

Yakṣagāna translated as celebration of the celestials is a complete theatre which includes song, dance and drama and is extremely popular in Malanadu, Uttara and Dakshina Kanara districts of Karnataka. It is essentially a stage form which entertains and educates the rural folks. A *yakṣagāna* team consists of 15-20 actors who carry their bag and baggage on their heads and walk from one village to another covering 20-30 km. a day. They camp in a temple and erect an extremely simple stage by using just four poles and many leaves for decoration. People with their families walk or ride their bullock carts to witness a performance. An episode from the *Rāmāyaṇa* or *Mahābhārata* is selected and accordingly the team does its own make-up and wear very attractive and colourful costumes. There are no women in any team and hence men wear *saris* and act as women.

A performance commences with a *pūjā* to Śrī Gaṇeśa followed by a buffoonery by *kodaṅgīs*. A loud background music is provided by *chanda* and *maddala* (various types of drums) and a *tāla* (cymbals) handled by a team of three. Seated among them is a Bhāgavata who is the producer, the director and the master of the ceremonies. Every actor must have good physique and excellent stamina and should sing, dance, act and converse the whole night. He should have sound knowledge of the scriptures. In every act there will be gods, goddesses, Kirātas, Kimpuruṣas and demons.

Tamāśā is a traditional folk play-form performed often with singing and dancing. It was performed by local or travelling groups, in Maharashtra. It probably got evolved during sixteenth century and became popular subsequently. The themes were selected suited to the times. It consisted of lively dialogues and witty conversation.

Nauṭaṅkī is named after the Punjab princess who was known for her exceptional beauty. There are several stories connected with her. *Nauṭaṅkī* is staged in courtyard and *maidāns*. The music has a pattern of its own which does not vary much from drama to drama. The poetry is written in various metrical patterns and sung according to a special convention. A single-faced kettledrum called *nagāḍā* is played during the performance. The *sāraṅgī*, harmonium and *ḍholaka* are also played. The language employed is generally Hindi but the actors resort to the local dialects depending upon the place of performance. Themes from traditional stories were originally employed. Over the years, contemporary themes have been incorporated.

Bhavai meaning strolling actors, is a popular folk theatre of Gujarat. They are called by other names like *veṣa*s (meaning costumes) and *svāṅga*. The origin of *bhavai* dates from the fourteenth century. It is said that a village chief by name Hemala Patel had a beautiful daughter by name Gaṅgā. She was kidnapped by a Muslim *sūbedār*. Their family priest, Asait Thakkar, a resident of Siddhapur, rushed to the *sūbedār* claiming Gaṅgā to be his own daughter. The *sūbedār* asked Thakkar to eat with Gaṅgā in the same plate to prove that she is his daughter. Thakkar did that but he incurred the wrath of his own caste men and was excommunicated as he had taken food with a low caste girl. He started earning his livelihood by performing plays which later came to be known as *bhavai*.

The caste of performers of *bhavai* came to be known as *tragala*. In one of his long poems, Thakkar has given the date of his composition as CE 1360. Thus it seems that *bhavai* as a dramatic form emerged in the later fourteenth century. Thakkar wrote about 360 plays out of which some 60 have survived. Some of these plays bear his name. It is clear from the *bhavai*'s performance that this form must have evolved from earlier known forms of folk entertainment. The word *bhavai* in the sense of a show of spectacle occurs in a thirteenth-century Apabhraṁśa Jaina religious verse. It says "In a treeless tract, even a branch of *eraṇḍa* (castor oil plant) makes (*bhavai*)". Abu'l Faẓl's *Āin-i-Akbarī* also mentions *bhavai* while referring to some communities.

Bhavai is as much a form of entertainment as it is a kind of a ritual offering made to Goddess Ambā in the courtyard of the Ambājī temple near Mount Abu where the Navarātri festival is celebrated with *bhavai* performances. Ambā is the presiding deity of *bhavai*. *Bhavai*, according to some scholars, is made up of two words *bhava* and *aai*. *Bhava* means universe and *aai* is mother, together it means mother of the universe, Ambā.

Subtle social criticism laced with pungent humour is the speciality of *bhavai*. The pompous behaviour of the high caste people is scoffed at in *bhavai*. Probably the anger over the injustice suffered by the originator, Asaita Thakkar got permeated into the mood of *bhavai*. Some of the *bhavai* plays present scattering review of the caste-ridden social structures. People belonging to different levels of social strata ranging from king to knave are portrayed in *bhavai*. *Bhavai veṣa*s portray people from all walks of life. The barbers, blacksmiths, robbers, bangle sellers, economic and social offenders, fake *sādhu*s and deceitful people figure in them. The idea is to warn the unwary public of the divine designs of unscrupulous people.

Humour plays a vital part in any *bhavai* performance and it comes into play even while dealing with mythological personages. This element makes *bhavai* unique among the folk arts of India.

The chief of the *bhavai* troupe is called *nāyaka*. He first marks the performing area, then offers *kumkum* to the oil torch which is a symbol of Goddess Ambā and sings prayer songs in her praise. Then enters an actor covering his face with a plate. He is Lord Gaṇeśa, the remover of obstacles. Goddess Kālī is the next to enter and after she departs comes the brāhmaṇa. After these preliminary appearances, the *veṣa* actually starts.

The *nāyaka* and the jester always remain on the stage directing the course of action with their commentary and intervention. Through songs, dialogues, speeches, prose and verse, the story unfolds. There is lot of dancing and singing in *bhavai*. Men wear suitable dress and make-up and adorn the role of women. The language of *bhavai* is a blend of Gujarati, Hindi, Urdu and Marwari. *Veṣa*s were published for the first time in nineteenth century. Past performances were linked to their predecessors, through practice and the oral tradition.

The *bhavai* performance is accompanied by the playing of several musical instruments. One such instrument is the *bhuṅgal* which is a 4 ft long copper pipe that provides a strong note and is unique to *bhavai*. The *bhuṅgal*s are played during dance sequences and otherwise to indicate important characters. Other musical instruments that form part of *bhavai* are *pakhāwaj* (drums), *jhāñjha* (cymbals), the *sāraṅgī* (one-stringed instrument) and the harmonium. The style of music is always Hindustani interspersed with local tunes.

Bhavai is also prevalent in Rajasthan as a folk dance comprising of spectacular performance. The dance form consists of veiled women dancers balancing up to seven or nine brass pitchers as they dance nimbly, swaying with the soles of their feet perched on the top of a glass or on the edge of the sword. There is a sense of cutting-edge suspense and nail-biting acts in the dance.

A few words about the ancient Tamil theatre of *therukkūttu* may not be out of place in the context of the study of *vīthī*. The Tamil literature speaks of three types of art, namely *iyaḷ* (literature), *isai* (music) and *nāṭakam* (drama). The term *nāṭakam* was probably borrowed from Sanskrit at a much later period. Ancient Tamil literature refers to drama by the term *kūttu; theru* meaning "street" is added to it to refer to the street play. Till the late 1940s and 1950s the *kūttu* was a popular folk theatre in the villages. The *kūttu* performance would start around 8 p.m. and go on till about midnight. Episodes from the epics and the Purāṇas would be generally selected for representation. Themes from Tamil literature like *Kovalan* and *Kaṇṇaki* would also be presented. It would have all men cast. The role of women characters would also be played by men. The make-up and the costumes would be gaudy looking from general theatre standards but it would be attractive for the village audience. The plays would be staged on a plain ground with a makeshift screen serving the purpose of a green room. The players would adorn many roles, changing their costumes in quick succession. The integral point of a *kūttu* (also spelt as *koothu*) will be the jester called "Komāḷi". He will be appearing every now and then providing the much needed comic relief. The interesting point of the *kūttu* was the introduction of current topics in a veiled fashion, into the theme of the play. Thus during the independence struggle, when congregations were banned the actors would cleverly weave dialogues condemning foreign rule into a Purāṇic theme.

With the change in social system after the Independence, the *kūttu* format lost its patronage. Earlier the wealthy landlords of the villages used to foster the folk arts in order to establish their own prestige in the society. The change in the social set-up very badly affected the folk arts. The *kūttu* troupes languished without proper support. The onslaught of cinema and cable TV have added to the woes of the folk arts. Most of the *kūttu* troupes have been disbanded and the rest are just lingering in poverty.

There is also another point that added to the degradation of the folk arts. Though the stage artists had popularity and recognition there was always a stigma attached to the profession. The artist of the *kūttu* were called *kūttādi*s in a derogatory sense. They had to move from place to place like gypsies and so they could not set up a permanent dwelling. They were living like nomads wandering all over the country. They were spending most of their time away from the families and many of them could not afford a family life at all. Having to face uncertainties all through their life the actors generally fell prey to temptations of life. This also led to the loss of respect in a society. Parents would not allow their children to take to acting however talented they were.

Aesthetic appeal and artistic talents can never be suppressed. There were several instances of young boys running away from their families and joining drama troupe, out of their love for the art. When professional acting became a difficult proposition amateur actors turned up to fill the gap. In the *therukkūttu* format generally the actors came from the washerman families. They performed during temple festivals and auspicious occasions. In return they got respect and remuneration and that established their social status. But the collapse of the system in the later half of the twentieth century undermined their status. They returned back to their washerman's job.

There are still a few islands of excellence. We have for instance Purvasi Therukkūttu Mandram which is still functioning though not as gloriously as it was in the past. The leader of the group, Kāśī, says that they get only about one programme a month but still they keep going for the love of the art (see article "The Colours are Fading", published in *The New Indian Express*, 28 September 2008). Their troupe gave performances even in foreign countries. They participated in the 5th International Theatre Festival held in Bogota in 1996. The troupe has been performing for over 50 years and has gone abroad six times so far. A number of awards and titles have been conferred on Kāśī by several organizations.

According to Kāśī, *therukkūttu* is an interactive form of play and it engages the audience also in brief conversations in the course of the play. The players turn to the audience at times and ask them, "What do you say about it?" Invariably there is huge response from the audience. The play-form has attracted many foreign scholars, like Hanne M. de Brulin, who have documented the art form. Hanne has married a *therukkūttu* expert, Rajagopalan, and has founded a Koothu Theatre in Kāñcīpuram, which runs a residential school. The students pay a nominal annual fee of Rs. 1,000. After school hours the students learn the nuances of *kūttu* from her husband, Rajagopalan. The main grievance of the *kūttu* artistes is that while artistes of classical forms of dance are respected, the *kūttu* artistes do not receive their due recognition from the society.

In recent years the art has received attention and encouragement from the art-loving people and also the state and central governments who are promoting the folk arts. The artistes feel that frequent workshops must be conducted in cities and towns to attract people.

They also feel that the government should come forward to arrange for *kūttu* showing in metropolitan towns and allow the artistes to perform at the government-owned theatres. They should waive the theatre charges for the troupes and pay the artistes reasonably well.

The artistes also agree that innovations are needed in their style of performance, the theme and the theatrical devices, without altering the basis of the form, in order to make it appealing to the people of the present-day generation. The present-day audience will not have the patience to sit for the whole night to watch the traditional *kūttu*. The plays should be of shorter duration and fast moving. The number of songs should be kept at a minimum and the story part should move at a brisk pace. Who knows? Just as the world is now turning to vegetables grown from organic farms, so also it may turn to traditional arts. Every village may turn back to see once again the *therukkūttu* with its robust rhythms and vivid costumes.

The *vīthī* playform of Sanskrit theatre has all the problems of the *therukkūttu* described above. In *therukkūttu*, at least the language is not a barrier or a problem. Tamil is the spoken tongue of the state of Tamil Nadu and a *therukkūttu* play can be staged anywhere in the state. But with respect to *vīthī*, it can only attract a small audience in well-known cities. If *vīthī* has to be revived, its language, that is, Sanskrit itself has to be revitalized. It needs governmental support and recognition. Rashtriya Sanskrit Sansthan is conducting a Sanskrit drama competition every year. The Sansthan may earmark each year for representing *nāṭaka*, *prahasana*, *bhāṇa* or *vīthī* respectively.

The present-day Sanskrit dramatists may be encouraged to write and present *vīthī* plays employing modern themes and techniques. In fact, a street play-form of *vīthī* will be helpful in popularizing Sanskrit itself. An interesting representation may encourage the audience to take to serious study of Sanskrit itself. It is fondly hoped that the present work may serve as a small step in this direction.

Appendices

Appendix A

A List of Non-available Sanskrit Prahasanas and Vīthīs

Non-available Prahasanas

1. *Ānandakośa* : (Anon.)
   Probable date : Fourteenth century or earlier.
   Reference : *Rasārṇavasudhākara*, TSS edn., 1916, pp. 40-41, 50, 291-95.

2. *Bṛhatsubhadraka* : (Anon.)
   Probable date : Fourteenth century or earlier.
   Reference : *Rasārṇavasudhākara* (According to M. Krishnamachariar, *HCSL*, p. 699)

3. *Devadurgati*
   Author : Rammoy Vidyābhūṣaṇa.
   Probably date : Eighteenth century.
   Edition : Calcutta, 1884.
   Reference : *HCSL*, p. 700, Sten Konov, pp. 186 following.

4. *Dhūrtacarita* : (Anon.)
   Probable date : Fourteenth century or earlier.
   Reference : *Sāhitya-Darpaṇa*, ch. VI, bet. *śls.* 265-67.

5. *Hāsyaratnākara* : (Anon.)
   Reference : M. Krishnamachariar (see *HCSL*, p. 699)
   says that the work is referred to

in *Daśarūpaka* but it could not be traced in the available editions of the text.

6. *Hāsyasāgara*
   Author : Rāmānanda.
   Probable date : Seventeenth century.
   Reference : *Sāgarikā,* Sanskrit Journal, vol. XV, p. 186.

7. *Hṛdayavinoda*
   Author : Kavipaṇḍita.
   Probable date : Eighteenth or ninteenth century.
   Reference : Peter Peterson, 1031, *CC,* II, 234, Schuyler, p. *62.*

8. *Kalikeli* : (Anon.)
   Probable date : Twelfth century or earlier.
   Reference : *Bhāvaprakāśana,* GOS edn., p. 247.

9. *Kandarpakeli* : (Anon.)
   Probable date : Fourteenth century or earlier.
   Reference : *Sāhitya-Darpaṇa,* ch. VI, bet. *śls.* 265-67.

10. *Payodhimathana* : (Anon.)
    Probable date : Fourteenth century or earlier.
    Reference : *Rasārṇavasudhākara,* III.264.

11. *Pāṣaṇḍaviḍambana* : (Anon.)
    Probable date : Eighteenth or nineteenth century.
    Reference : CC, I, 336 ; Schuyler, p. 73.

12. *Sairandhrikā* : (Anon.)
    Probable date : Twelfth century or earlier.
    Reference : *Bhāvaprakāśana,* GOS edn., p. 247.

13. *Sāgarakaumudī* : (Anon.)
Probable date : Twelfth century or earlier.
Reference : *Bhāvaprakāśana*, p. 247.

14. *Śaśivilāsa* : (Anon.)
Probable date : Thirteenth century or earlier.
Reference : *Nāṭakalakṣaṇaratnakoṣa*, Chowkhamba edn., 1972, p. 276.

Non-available Vīthīs

1. *Bakula Vīthī* : Probably it refers to the first act of *Mālatīmādhava* which carries the same name.
Probable date : Twelfth century or earlier.
Reference : *Bhāvaprakāśana*, GOS edn., ch. 8, section 122.

2. *Indulekhā Vīthī* : (Anon.)
Probable date : Tenth century or earlier.
Reference : *Śṛṅgāraprakāśa*, Josyer ed., Mysore, 1963, ch. XII.

3. *Mādhavī Vīthī* : (Anon.)
Probable date : Thirteenth century or earlier.
Reference : *Rasārṇavasudhākara*, TSS edn., 1916, III.265-67.

4. *Mālatikā Vīthī* : (Anon.)
Probable date : Tenth century or earlier.
Reference : *Śṛṅgāraprakāśa*, Josyer edn., Mysore, 1963, ch. XII.

Appendix B

Modern Sanskrit Prahasanas and Vīthīs

Prahasanas

A NUMBER of *prahasana*s have been written by contemporary writers in the last century. Original and creative writing marks the beginning of the new era in *prahasana* literature. New themes and ideas have replaced some of the old conventions and norms. The association of the *prahasana* with the ridiculing of the degraded life led by pseudo-religious men has been severed for its own good. Vulgarity which pervades the medieval *prahasana*s is happily absent, almost totally, in the modern *prahasana*s. In short, the twentieth-century *prahasana*s show a welcome change in the outlook of the *prahasana* writers. A noteworthy feature of these *prahasana*s is that most of them have been written specifically for the stage and some of them have been staged more than once.

Day-to-day problems of the common man and social evils are touched upon in the modern *prahasana*s. We have, for instance, the dowry problem in the *Ubhayarūpakam,* and the theme of widow-rehabilitation in the *Cāmuṇḍa Prahasana*. Some of the *prahasana*s have novel themes, as for instance, *Śṛṅgāranāradīyam* (change of sex) and *Manoharam Dinam* (students clamouring for a holiday). Allegorical themes have also been taken up, on the model of *Sahṛdayānanda* of Harijīvanamiśra. Raghavan's *Vimukti* is an attempt in this direction. Some of the modern *prahasana*s are translations and adaptations of English or French farces (e.g. *Vaidyabandhu*).

The hero of a modern *prahasana* is not necessarily an *adhama* character. We have modern young men with progressive ideas as heroes (as in *Ubhayarūpakam*). Divine characters also figure in some of the *prahasana*s. Historical figures like Hitler, Mussolini and Stalin too appear in one of the *prahasana*s (viz., *Caṇḍatāṇḍavam*). There are, of course, conventional *prahasana* characters like the gluttons, fake doctors and ill-equipped *purohita*s.

In the field of dramatic technique too, inevitable changes have taken place. Prākṛt is almost totally dispensed with and there is increasing tendency among the modern playwrights to use the local vernaculars.[1] Not much attention is paid to *prastāvanā*, *viṣkambhaka*, etc. There is an increasing tendency to divide the plays into Acts and Scenes on the model of Western plays.

The language in modern *prahasana*s has undergone slight changes so as to suit the needs of the modern times. New words and phrases have been coined to denote objects like telephone, radio, train, newspaper and the like.

Both, conventional and modern techniques are adopted for arousing *hāsya*. We have, for instance, a glutton, giving out a long list of eatables liked by him (Kauṇḍinya in *Kauṇḍinya Prahasana*) which is evidently an influence of *Dhūrtasamāgama*. There is then the old style of misquoting and misinterpreting well-known sayings and rules of scriptures. *Ekaḥ svādu na bhuñjīta*, according to a glutton, means that he must take a large number of sweets and not just one.

There is a parody on the famous song of Sadāśivabrahmendra, in

चिन्ता नास्ति किल तेषां
चिन्ता नास्ति किल

---

1. Cf. Usha Satyavrat, *Twentieth Century, Sanskrit Dramas*, Introdution.

परगृहभोजनपरितुष्टानां ।
नित्यातिथ्योत्सवनिष्ठानां । (चिन्ता . . .)
— *कौण्डिन्यप्रहसन*

Humorous similes are also employed to evoke *hāsya*, for example,

माषापूपः सुहृदिव शठः क्लेशदायी विपाके
साधारण्यात् परिचित इवानादरस्सक्तुपिष्टे ।

अस्त्युद्वेगो मधुरविकृतिष्वाप्तवाक्येषु यद्वत्
सेवाक्लेशो रसविधुरता शष्कुलीदुष्प्रबन्धे ॥ — *कौण्डिन्यप्रहसन*

This is how an irrate lady angrily replies when asked why her husband is delaying, *rātrau bandhanabhraṣṭo mahiṣaḥ kutra gata iti kena kena śakyam vaktum?* (*Cāmuṇḍa Prahasana*). For one of the characters who is not interested in listening to the Purāṇic discourses, *ślokāḥ śokatvamāgatāḥ* has become a fact. Wrong pronunciation of words or wrong splitting of *sandhi* is another source of *hāsya*, for example,

भवाङ्कुरङ्गे यतमं कैवल्य फलदायकम् ।
न मामि माम कैशानपादपं केरु हंपरम् ॥

instead of

भवाङ्कुरं गेयतमं कैवल्यफलदायकम् ।
नमामि मामकैशानपादपंकेरुहं परम् ॥ — *लीलाविलासप्रहसन*

Thus, we find a happy blend of both convention and originality in the modern *prahasana*s and they are a significant contribution to the *prahasana* literature at large. A bibliographical account of some of these *prahasana*s is given below:

SELECT BIBLIOGRAPHY OF THE TWENTIETH-CENTURY PRAHASANAS

1. **Anukūlagalahastakam**[2] by Vishnupada Bhattacharya,

2. Vide "A Bibliography of Modern Sanskrit Plays" by C.S. Sundaram and V. Raghavan, *Saṁskṛta Raṅga Annual*, volume III, Madras.

Calcutta: Manjusha, 1959.

Theme: Divyendrasundara telephones to his friend Yāminīkantā but gets a wrong number. The person at other end, a girl by name Yāminī wants to play a practical joke on the caller. As a result, Divyendrasundara goes to her house in Ranchi and is mistaken to be a thief and arrested by the servants in the absence of their mistress. When she comes to know of this, Yāminī apologizes to him and at the suggestion of a friend, agrees to become his life-partner.

2. **Caṇḍatāṇḍavam**[3] by Srijiva Nyayatirtha, Calcutta: Oriental Press Limited, 1953.

   Theme: This is on the horrors of Second World War, introducing Hitler, Mussolini, Stalin and other European leaders on its cast. Allegorical characters like greed, anger and violence are also featured.

3. **Caura-Cāturīyam**[4] by Srijiva Nyayatirtha, Calcutta: Sanskrit Sahitya Parishad, 1951.

   Theme: This play deals with how cheats and thieves thrive on the vulnerability of the common man.

4. **Cāmuṇḍaprahasanam**[5] by K.L. Vyasaraya Sastri, Madras: K.V. Ramakrishna Rao, 1937.

   Theme: This is about how a village hypocrite Cāmuṇḍa, who hates a widow for growing long hair and for going to London (for her higher studies in medicine), becomes repentent later, on coming to know of her noble qualities.

---

3. Vide, "A Bibliography of Modern Sanskrit Plays" by C.S. Sundaram and V. Raghavan, *Saṁskṛta Raṅga Annual*, volume III, Madras.
4. Vide, *Saṁskṛta Raṅga Annual*, vol. III.
5. See *Sāgarikā*, Saṁskṛta Journal, vol. XVI-i, p. 76.

5. **Cipiṭaka Carvaṇa**[6] by Srijiva Nyayatirtha, Calcutta: Manjusha, 1959.

   Theme: This deals with the nature of the misers.

6. **Daridradurdaivam**[7] by Srijiva Nyayatirtha, Calcutta: Sanskrit Sahitya Parishad, 1968.

   Theme: The evils of greed and jealousy are dealt with in this play. A greedy man, though blessed by an angel with a desire-yielding dice, brings his own downfall because of jealousy for others.

7. **Dhruvāvatāra**[8] by Skanda Sankara Khot, Nagpur: Kamala Khot.

   Theme: Depicts how the present-day boys have funny ideas about the legendary figures like Dhruva.

8. **Hā Hanta Śārade**[9] by Sankara Khot, Nagpur: Kamala Khot.

   Theme: Deals with the difficulties faced by scholars married to illiterate women.

9. **Kauṇḍinya Prahasana**[10] by Y. Mahalinga Sastri, Madras: the author, 1930.

   Theme: A farcical episode of how a gluttonous brāhmaṇa cheats householders and dines at their cost.

10. **Kāñcanamālā**[11] by Surendra Mohan Panchatirtha, Calcutta: Manjusha, 1955.

---

6. Vide, *Saṁskṛta Raṅga Annual*, vol. III.
7. See *Sāgarikā*, vol. XVI-i, p. 39.
8. Cf. *Saṁskṛta Raṅga Annual*, vol. III.
9. Cf. ibid.
10. Cf. Usha Satyavrat, *Twentieth Century Sanskrit Dramas*, p. 175.
11. Cf. *Saṁskṛta Raṅga Annual*, vol. III.

Theme: This deals with how a woman, greedy after gold, finally realizes the futility of money.

11. **Kṣutakṣemīya**[12] by Srijiva Nyayatirtha, Calcutta: Manjusha, 1956.

    Theme: A niggard who has amassed much wealth by blackmarketing and other underhand dealings outwits even Yama in the other world and obtains a fresh lease of life.

12. **Līlāvilāsa Prahasana**[13] by K.L. Vyasaraya Sastri, Palghat (Kerala): Subramanya Vadyar and Sons.

    Theme: Deals with how certain parents want to wash their hands off their daughter by getting her married to somebody without looking into the attainments of the bridegroom.

13. **Manoharam Dinam**[14] by A.R. Hebare, Calcutta: Sanskrit Sahitya Parishad, 1941.

    Theme: Concerns with how school boys try to get a holiday declared by the headmaster.

14. **Maṇikāñcanasamanvayaḥ**[15] by Vishnupada Bhattacharya.

    Theme: Deals with the exploits of two rogues.

15. **Navoḍhā Vadhūḥ Varaśca**[16] by Pattabhiram Sastri, Calcutta: Calcutta University.

    Theme: The nuptials of a newly-wedded couple is delayed due to various reasons. At last when it takes place the

12. Cf. *Saṁskṛta Raṅga Annual*, vol. III.
13. See Usha Satyavrat, *Delhi University Journal*, vol. II, 1973.
14. Cf. *Saṁskṛta Raṅga Annual*, vol. III.
15. See *Sāgarikā*, vol. XVI-i, p. 113.
16. See *Sāgarikā*, vol. XVI-i, p. 196.

husband is shocked to find that his wife is an eunuch.

16. **Nāṭye ca Dakṣā Vayam**[17] by Kshirasagara.

Theme: The stage director of a drama troupe arranges for a performance of *Vikramorvaśīya*. But he is faced with mumerous problems. When the situation becomes utterly hopeless, he prays to the presiding deity of drama to save him.

17. **Rāga-Virāga**[18] by Srijiva Nyayatirtha, New Delhi: Sanskrit Pratibha Sahitya Academy, 1959.

Theme: Deals with how a king who is averse to music, banishes all those who sing from his country and how he is reformed on hearing the captivating music of a couple.

18. **Svargīyaprahasana**[19] by Chattopadyaya.

Theme: Describes an imaginary situation on how there is clamour for power even among gods in heaven.

19. **Śṛṅgāranāradīyam**[20] by Y. Mahalinga Sastri, Madras: the author, 1956.

Theme: Based on the Purāṇic story of change of sex of Nārada.

20. **Tīrthayātrāprahasana**[21] by Ramkuber Malaviya, Benares.

Theme: Describes the funny experiences of people going on a pilgrimage.

---

17. See *Sāgarikā*, vol. XVI-i, p. 205.
18. Cf. *Saṁskṛta Raṅga Annual*, vol. III.
19. See *Sāgarikā*, vol. XVI-i, p. 68.
20. See *Saṁskṛta Raṅga Annual*, vol. III and *'Twentieth Century Sanskrit Drama'* by Usha Satyavrat.
21. See *Sāgarikā*, vol. XVI-ii, p. 203.

21. **Ubhayarūpakam**[22] by Y. Mahalinga Sastri, Madras: the author, 1962.

    Theme: A villager wants to get his college educated son married to illiterate daugher of a wealthy man, for a huge dowry. The boy, however, is interested in one of his own classmates. The farcical element of the play is best revealed in the scene where the passage 'To be or not to be', of Shakespeare's *Hamlet* is mistaken to be a suicide letter left by the boy. All ends well when the actual letter left by the boy is traced.

22. **Vaidya-bandhuḥ**[23] by V. S. Venkataraghavachariar, Madras: the author.

    Theme: This is adapted from Molieres' 'The physician in spite of himself', dealing with the eccentricities of a quack doctor.

23. **Vana-bhojanam**[24] by Srijiva Nyayatirtha.

    Theme: Six boys go on an excursion to the woods nearby and prepare their lunch there. On hearing some peculiar noise, the boys mistake it to be that of a tiger and run away. One of the boys, who is the cause of the mischief, comes in the disguise of a *saṁnyāsin* in the evening and eats away the delicious dishes.

24. **Vimuktiḥ**[25] by V. Raghavan, Sanskrit Pratibha, vol. IV, pt. 1.

---

22. *Ubhayarūpakam*, See *Saṁskṛta Raṅga Annual*, vol. III and also Usha Satyavrat's *Twentieth Century Sanskrit Dramas*. p. 179.
23. Cyclostyled copy of the play *Vaidya-bandhuḥ* is available with the author.
24. *Vanabhojanam*, see *Sāgarikā*, vol. XVI-i, p. 40.
25. On *Vimuktiḥ*, see Usha Satyvrat's *Twentieth Century Sanskrit Plays*, pp. 194 f.

Theme: An allegorical play describing how a brāhamṇa succeeds in bringing his quarrelsome wife, wagabond sons and others, under his control. The allegory is in the identification of the brāhmaṇa with the soul, his six sons with the six sense organs (including the *manas*) his wife with "nature" and his mother-in-law with the *māyā* (illusion). His ultimate success indicates the liberation of the soul from the worldly bondages.

25. **Vivāha-viḍambana**[26] by Srijiva Nyayatirtha, Sanskrit Pratibha.

    Theme: A one act farce dealing with an old man's craving to look young and vigorous and to get married with the help of a broker. In the end, his plans are foiled by the broker himself.

26. **Veṣṭana-vyāyoga**[27] by Virendrakumara Bhattacharya, Calcutta: Sanskrit Sahitya Parishad, 1971.

    Theme: Deals with the *gherāo* and the difficulties faced by the employers and employess in the process.

Vīthīs

Mordern writers in Sanskrit, in keeping with the times, do not specify the type of play. But short one-act (sometimes two acts) plays with social themes and employing a mixture of *rasa*s may be classified as *vīthī*s. Some of them are listed below:

1. **Dambhasāmrājyam** by Visveswar Dikshit (b. 7.7.1924), ref.: Ranganath, Modern Sanskrit Dramas of Karnataka, Net source (henceforth referred as Net source 1).

---

26. Cf. *Saṁskṛta Raṅga Annual*, vol. III.
27. See *Sāgarikā*, vol. XXV-i, p. 72.

2. **Dāmpatyakalahaḥ** by H.V. Nagaraja Rao (b. 10.9.1942), ref.: Net source 1.
3. **Dharmavyādhadarśanam** by Jaggu Shingararya (b. 20.11.1891), ref.: Net source 1.
4. **Kalikāluṣyam** by Jaggan Alwar lyengar (b. 1902), ref.: Net source 1.
5. **Lalitā** by Krishnan Thampi, a twentieth-century writer, ref.: N.P. Unni, Net source 2.
6. **Lobhasāmrājyam** by Visveswar Dikshit, ref.: Net source 1.
7. **Mādaracchannaḥ** by M.C. Nanjundaradhya, ref.: Net source 1.
8. **Mādhavīvāsantīyam** by T. Ganapati Shastri, ref.: Net source 2.
9. **Maireyapāraṁparyam** by Jaggan Alwar Iyengar, Net source 1.
10. **Peṭikā Saṁnyāsī** by Krishnan Thampi, ref.: Net source 2.
11. **Pratikriyā** by Krishnan Thampi, ref.: Net source 2.
12. **Ratnāṅgulīyakam** by Vighnesvara Sharma (b. 9-8-1908); ref.: Net source 1.
13. **Śrāddham** by S. Jagannath (b. 12-10-1956) ref.: Net source 1.
14. **Yakṣapraśnam** by Jaggu Shingaraya, ref.: Net source 1.

Appendix C

Prahasanas in Other Indian Languages

Prahasanas are of very late origin in the Indian vernaculars, and the earlier ones among them are clearly influenced by the Sanskrit *prahasanas*. In Hindi for instance, we have a nineteenth-century *prahasana* named *Andhera-Nagarī* (Dark City) by Bharatendu Harischandra.[1] The hero of the play, a foolish king, Caupaṭṭarāja by name, is a replica of King Anayasindhu of Hāsyārṇava. One of his subjects complains that his goat was killed by the collapse of the wall of the neighbour's house. The neighbour puts the blame on the mason who had built his house; the mason blames his assistant and so on. The charge finally falls on the *kotwāl* (a petty officer) who is sentenced to death by hanging. But when the executioners report to the king that the noose is too big for the lean *kotwāl*, the king orders his men to get hold of anyone in the city whose neck fits in the noose. The soldiers catch hold of an innocent young student and are about to hang him. The teacher of the student, an ascetic, arrives along with another disciple of his and volunteers to hang himself in lieu of his student. Meanwhile, the king comes there. The ascetic teacher tells the king that he, along with his two disciples, would like to be hanged that very day, since one who dies that day would directly go to *vaikuṇṭha*. The minister, the *kotwāl* and everybody else clamour to get hanged now. But the king silences them all and says

1. See, *Bhāratendu Granthāvalī*, vol. 1, Benares: Vrajaratnadass edn., 1950, p. 355.

that being the first citizen, he alone would get hanged and go to *vaikuṇṭha*. So saying, he goes to the gallows.

Vaidikī Hiṁsā Hiṁsā Bhavati is another play by the same author.[2] The title itself is in Sanskrit and a number of quotations from the Smṛtis and other texts are found in the body of the play.

King Gṛdhrarāja feels like eating a very delicious fish and his *purohita* also joins him. On being asked how he could take fish, being a brāhmaṇa, the *purohita* replies:

केचिद् वदन्त्यमृतमस्ति सुरालयेषु
केचिद् वदन्ति वनिताधरपल्लवेषु ।
ब्रूमो वयं सकलशास्त्रविचारदक्षाः
जम्बीरनीरपरिपूरितमत्स्यखण्डे ॥

He also quotes *pañca pañcanakhāḥ bhakṣyāh* in support. The king then orders that a big *bali* of goats and birds be made at a sacrifice to be held the next day in his palace. The *purohita* is overjoyed at the prospect of his having a sumptuous feast.

Enters then a Bengali Vaiṣṇava announcing:

पतिहीना तु या नारी पत्नीहीनस्तु यः पुमान् ।
उभाभ्यां षण्डरण्डाभ्यां न दोषो मनुरब्रवीत् ॥

Among the several persons that attend the *yajña* is a Vidūṣaka. He tells the Vedāntin that he being a *be-dāntin* (one without teeth), cannot relish the meat served on the occasion. The Bengali maintains that fish-eating is not prohibited in scriptures. The king and his minister extol liquor, explaining the *Gītā* passage *madyājī māṁ namaskuru* as *madya-ājī*, instead of *mad-yājī*. The next scene is laid in the court of Yama, God of

2. See, *Bhāratendu Granthāvalī*, vol. 1, Benares: Vrajaratnadass edn., 1950, p. 70.

Death, where the king and his retinue are seen. Citragupta lists their misdeeds and they misquote several scriptural passages profusely to justify their own deeds while on earth.

These comedy-oriented plays of Bharatendu Harischandra are actually called *prahasanas*. Apart from these there is a large number of humorous short plays in Hindi. Farcical element is evident in a number of modern Hindi plays.

The *prahasanas* of Rajasekhara Bose are very popular in contemporary Bengali literature. The farce *Viriñci Bābā* for instance, deals with the atrocities of hypocrite in the guise of a saint. There is another farce by the same author, the *Cikitsā Saṅghāt*, in which a middle-aged bachelor millionaire is troubled by an unknown malady. No doctor could cure him. Ultimatly, a lady doctor diagnoses the case and prescribes that he needs a partner of life. She herself offers to marry him.

***

In the Marathi literature also *prahasanas* are of a later origin. In one *prahasana* a few brāhmaṇas, including a Station Master, pose as very orthodox people. They, however, stealthily open an unclaimed railway parcel and eat up the sweets therein. Later some Harijans come there and claim that parcel as theirs. The parcel contained the left-over sweets of a grand dinner held in the Nizam's palace at Hyderabad, sent to them by their relative employed in the palace. The so-called orthodox people simply shake off their heads and refuse to believe in what they heard.

***

Stage drama had a revival during the twentieth century in Tamil Nadu. Farcical plays have a good reception on the present-day stage. For example, the *Honeymoon Couple* (English title) is a modern farce about a middle-aged man forcing his wife to make a honeymoon trip, several years after their marriage.

***

The era of *prahasana*s in Telugu was started in the nineteenth century by Kandukuri Viresalingam Pantulu, who has to his credit nearly fifty *prahasana*s. These plays deal with contemporary social evils like child-marriage, dowry, licentiousness and drunkenness. His *Lokottara Vivāhamu* and *Kanyāśulkamu* depict how a young girl is married to a dying rich old man by her greedy parents. His *Kautakavardhani* points out another social evil, viz. debauchery. His *Veśyāprahasanamu* also belongs to this category. His *Vinodataraṅgiṇi* stresses the need of widow-remarriage.

Cilakamarti Lakshminarasimham, another prolific writer with about seventy *prahasana*s to his credit, touches similar social problems in his plays. His *Varakatnam* is on the evil of paying a heavy dowry to the bridegroom. Other *prahasana* writers in Telugu include Panuganti Laksminarasimha Rao, Bhamidipati Kameshvara Rao and Veturi Prabhakara Shastri, the last of whom translated the Sanskrit *prahasana*s *Bhagavadajjukīya* and *Mattavilāsa* into Telugu.

***

Prahasana is not totally unknown to Kannada literature, the earliest one being the *Vivāhaparahasana* of Iggappa Heggadeya. As in Telugu, the *prahasana* in Kannada is also used as a means of social reformation.

***

In Kerala, where Sanskrit *prahasana*s like the *Bhagavadajjukīya* and *Mattavilāsa* were popularly staged, the influence of Sanskrit *prahasana* is quite evident. For instance, the *Hāsyacūḍāmaṇi* appeared in Malayalam under the title *Kapaṭakeli*. A number of farces mark the modern Malayalam literature.

***

It is thus clear that *prahasana* in both the north and south indian languages is very late in origin. They bear influences of the Sanskrit *prahasana*s and to some extent, the farce of English language and literature. They were written for the stage, with a definite motive of bringing out the ugly and dark side of human life in contemporary society. They go a long way in eradicating the social evils, ushering in a freer social order, carrying conviction to the masses that witness them on the stage, or read them in print.

Appendix D

The Farce in English Literature

A FARCE is usually considered to be a boisterous comedy involving ludicrous action and dialogue.[1] In its most elementary form it is found in the gestures and tricks of the circus clown and the baffoonery of the pantomime, which provoke ready laughter among the greatest number of people.[2] The plot in a farce depends upon a carefully exploited situation rather than upon character development.[3] The purpose of the farce is to evoke simple hearty laughter. To do so it commonly employs highly exaggerated or caricatured character types, puts them into improbable and ludicrous situations and makes free use of broad verbal humour and physical horseplay.[4] The physicality of farce may not always qualify as humorous, but it is always anti-romantic, a kind of parody of the solemn idealization that is involved in romantic notions of love or strife.[5]

Origin of Farce in English Literature

Comedy was the general term referring to the farce and other types of humour, in the early European literature. Aristotle, in his *De Poetica* defines comedy thus, "comedy is an imitation

---

1. *A Dictionary of Literary Terms*, by Harry Shaw.
2. *Dictionary of World Literary Terms*, by Joseph T. Shipley.
3. *A Dictionary of Literary Terms*, by Harry Shaw.
4. *A Glossary of Literary Terms*, ed. M.H. Abrahams.
5. Margery M. Morgan, *The Shavian Playground*, p. 34.

of an action that is ludicrous and defective of adequate magnitude in language variously embellished, the several kinds of embellishment being severally used in different parts of the play carried on by agents, as in the form of narrative, through pleasure and laughter for its mother". This may be compared with the definition of *prahasana* by Bharata.

"Comedy", according to some, is derived from "Komos". Ancient Greeks used to sing "Komos songs" in honour of a Greek deity by name Dioninosus. These songs might have been the early form of comedy. Butcher, who commented on *De Poetica*, offers the following exaplanation. "Comedy is an imitation of character of a lower type, not however, in the full sense of the word bad, the ludicrous being merely a sub-division of the ugly. It consists is some defect or ugliness which is not painful or destructive."

It may be relevant to note here the views of George Meridith on comedy. (An essay on comedy and the uses of the comic spirit — Westminster. Constable, 1897). "Comedy lifts women to a station offering them free play for their wit, as they usually show it when they have it, on the side of sound sense. The higher the comedy, the more prominent the part they enjoy in it." This may be compared with Bharata's view that *hāsya* is more appealing to the women (and children too).

Three stages are recognized in the development of comedy in Greek literature: (i) Old comedy which was poignant, (ii) Middle comedy which Aristotle had in his view and which might have been the earliest form of farce, and (iii) New comedies which paved the way for what are now understood to be "comedies" referring to happy-ending plays as contrasted with the tragedies. Aristotle mentions Epicharmus, Phormus and Crates as authors of comedies.

Roman authors like Plautus and Terence also wrote comedies, following the Greeks. Early English comedies are modelled on the works of these playwrights. The first comedy in English is *Ralphroister doister*. The Shakespearean comedies[6] of the Elizabethan era are, of course, quite popular. These plays were termed "Comedy of Humours" contrasted with "Comedy of Manners" which became popular later. It is the "Comedy of Manners" which gave rise to the farce in English literature. There are farcical elements in the comedies of Dryden,[7] Wilson,[8] and Mrs. Behn.[9] The tremendous popularity of Molieres' French farces[10] influenced the English playwrights during seventeenth century. Thus farce is rather a forced development in the history of English drama.

The farce had its heyday during the eighteenth century (especially in the later half). Some of the best farces belong to the period 1750–1800. The majority of the farces during this period deal with characters cast in the Johnsonian mould, but others are of the intrigue type and in some we catch a glimpse of the manners style. A few are sentimental.[11] Arthur Murphy was an important writer of farce during this period. Sheriden's "St. Patrick's Day" is also a farce.

The farce maintained its popularity during the early nineteenth century too. Of course, the farces of this period were made to order. Not much of ingenuity is seen in the

6. Shakespeare's *Comedy of Errors* may fill in as an excellent specimen of farce, without being designated so.

7. For instance, *The Wide Gallant*.

8. "Marriage of the Devil."

9. "A new way to play an old game."

10. Moliere's *The Physician in spite of Himself* has also been adapted into Sanskrit in the recent times. See p. 438, no. 22 above.

11. Allardyce Nicholl, *A History of English Drama*, vol. III, pp. 188 ff.

plays of this period.[12] Much was left to the actors who were to interpret farcical element in the plays. The language was rough in the stylistic sense. Puns of the broadest kind obviously made their appeal. Important writers of farce from this period are — Charles Dance (*The Dark Lady of the Sonnets*, etc.), Mrs Pennyfarthing (*Each for Himself*, etc.), Douglas Jerrold (*More Frightened than Hurt*, etc.) and J.M. Morton (He has contributed more than 30 farces). A short scene from *The Dark Lady of the Sonnets* may be quoted here to illustrate the farcical element in English farces.

Alphonse : The questions that I wish to ask are of so delicate a nature that I hardly know where to begin.

Sangfroid : At the beginning, I should say.

Alphonse : Yes, I know; but that's the difficulty.

Sangfroid : Then try the middle, or the end. You have no time to spare and in another scene.

Alphonse : Any communication you have to make to her now, must go through me.

Sangfroid : Must it? Then I have a favourite sword I wish to send her. Would you like that to go through you?

We have a foolish king in "The Peri who loved a prince", on the lines of the kings we come across in Sanskrit *prahasana*s.

Man : Long live the Emperor.

Emperor : Silence, villains ! stow it ! We'll not live long, unless we like — you know it. It is not for your plebeian throats to give orders to us how long you'd have us live.

---

12. Allardyce Nicholl, *A History of English Drama*, vol. IV, p. 121.

(They all prostrate themselves before him)

Sons of burnt fathers ! What means that position?
How dare you tumble down without
permission?

(They rise abruptly and stand bold upright in a line)

Now by my pigtail ! by my father's nails,
By the imperial dragon's sacred scales
My mind's so tossed about, so hurried, flurried
Bothered, perplexed, annoyed, insulted, worried,
etc.

Yes, stay, I'd best first tell you what's the matter.

What happened to Sanskrit *prahasana*s of the later times, happened to the late English farces of the nineteenth century. "The farces of this time have not much to offer us of real intrinsic merit. Some are written in a sprightly style; but even the best display a certain mechanical structure. Most of them were written for low-comedy actors who could 'put across' almost anything and consequently there is generally evident, a carelessness on the part of the authors, both as regards plot and form. Old themes are constantly being refurnished and stock situations occur with irritating frequency. We may say that neither in regard to literary form nor to inventiveness did their farces bring anything of permanent worth to the theatre."[13]

---

13. Werner Klean, *English Farce — (1800–1900) — Die English Farce*, Bern, 1946.

A number of the twentieth-century playwrights have written comical and satirical plays without designating them farces. Bernard Shaw's *Doctor's Dilemma* is a play closer to the style of farce.

It may be interesting to note, in this context, some instances of farcical elements from the relatively unknown Chinese literature belonging to the thirteenth-fourteenth centuries. We have, for instance, a Buddhist monk, Hui-Ming in the play *Hsi-hsiang-chi*, who scorns at the strict rules laid for monks, in the same way as the monk of *Mattavilāsa*.

> I can't talk about tracts and scriptures,
> Too lazy to join in meditation
> I take forbidden knife and temper it.

In an anonymous novel, *Shui-hu-chunan*, one Lu Ta becomes a monk and resides in a monastery on Wu-Tai mountain. He does not like the strictures of the monastery. He sneaks out one day from the monastery and goes to an inn and demands meat and liquor. Though the Innkeeper points out that he, being a monk, should not take to meat and wine, the monk insists on both being served to him.[14] It is quite probable that the farces and farcical elements in other forms of literature were used by the poets effectively to educate people on the atrocities of certain unscrupulous elements in the religious orders, in medieval China, as it was done in India during this period.

---

14. See Bruce E. Carpenter, "The Mark of Laughter: Satire in the 13th and 14th century Chinese Literature", *Bulletin of Tezukayama University*, no. XIII, Nare, Japan.

Appendix E

Farcical Elements in the Plays of Kālidāsa*

It has been acknowledged by poets and critics alike that the *rasa* or the sentiment is the most important factor in a literary work. But for *rasa*, a work becomes rather dry.[1] The *rasas* are nine in number — *śṛṅgāra, hāsya, karuṇa, raudra, vīra, bhayānaka, bībhatsa, adbhuta* and *śānta*. A literary composition may have one of these as its prominent *rasa* (*pradhāna-rasa*) and the other *rasas* too might find their due place but they can figure only as the *aṅga-rasas* to the main *aṅgī-rasa* or *pradhāna-rasa*. The *aṅga-rasas* should only help to heighten the effect of the *pradhāna-rasa*, but they should never impede the progress of the main *rasa*.[2] Thus, though *śṛṅgāra* or *vīra* generally figures as the *pradhāna-rasa* in a drama, the *hāsya rasa* and the farcical elements do find their due place not only to provide comic relief to the audience but also to heighten the intensity of the *pradhāna-rasa*, thereby contributing to the dramatic effect of the play. It is in this respect that *hāsya* has its place of importance in the *nāṭaka* and the *prakaraṇa*, but it figures as the *pradhāna-rasa* in *prahasanas* (farces) and to some extent in the *bhāṇas* too.

Hāsya has *hāsa* (laughter) as its *sthāyībhāva*.[3] Bharata speaks

---

* Lecture delivered at the K.S.R. Institute, Madras, on 2 October 1979, "Kālidāsa Day"; Also appeared in *Vishveshvaranand Indological Journal*, vol. XIX, parts I-II, 1981.

1. Cf. न हि रसादृते कश्चिदर्थः प्रवर्तते — *NŚ*, Ch. VI
2. Cf. प्रसिद्धोऽपि प्रबन्धानां नानारसनिबन्धने ।
   एको रसोऽङ्गीकर्तव्यस्तेषामुत्कर्षमिच्छता ॥ — *Dhvanyāloka*, III.77
3. Cf. *NŚ*, ch. VI.

of six kinds of laughter[4] — *smita* (gentle smile), *hasita* (smile), *vihasita* (gentle laughter), *upahasita* (deriding laughter), *apahasita* (excessive laughter) and *atihasita* (reeling laughter). *Hāsya* has a much wider scope than the other *rasa*s in the sense that it arises not only from its own *vibhāva, anubhāva*, etc. but also from the *anukṛti* (imitation) and *ābhāsa* (misplaced form) of other sentiments. Thus while the love between the hero and the heroine is dignified *śṛṅgāra*, that between the *vidūṣaka* and the maid attendant can be called *śṛṅgārānukṛti* or imitation of *śṛṅgāra* and this gives rise to only *hāsya* and not *śṛṅgāra*. In fact, imitation of every *rasa* leads to *hāsya* only. An illustration here may make the point clear. We have a fickle-minded, impertinent disciple — a *brāhmaṇa-vaṭu* by name Śāṇḍilya in *Bhagavadajjukīya-Prahasana*. As he enters a garden along with his teacher, he requests the teacher to lead the way since he had heard from somebody that a tiger has been roaming in that garden. Suddenly he shouts aloud,

> अविधा, व्याघ्रेण गृहीतोऽस्मि।
> मोचयथ मां व्याघ्रमुखात्। अनाथ इव व्याघ्रेण खादितोऽस्मि।
> इदं खलु रुधिरं प्रस्रवति कण्ठात्।[5] etc.

Then the teacher apprises him of the fact that it was only a peacock and not a tiger. The disciple opens his eyes now and is convinced that it was only a peacock. Then he says,

> अविधा, दास्याः पुत्रो व्याघ्रो मद्भयेन
> मयूररूपं गृहीत्वा पलायते, हीही . . .।[6]

Here the show of his heroism by the disciple is really a misplaced one in view of his earlier distress cries and so here it is not *vīra* but is only *virābhāsa* which leads to *hāsya*.

---

4. Cf. *NŚ*, ch. VI, *śl*s. 54-59, ed. Manmohan Ghosh, Calcutta, 1967.
5. *BA*, p. 37, ed. Anujan Achan, Trichur, 1925.
6. Ibid.

It may also be noted that *hāsya* is rather free from certain limitations and constraints attached to the other *rasas*. *Śṛṅgāra* is, no doubt, the noblest among the *rasas* but it finds its fullest expression only in privacy. It requires only two to make love but a hundred can join together in laughter.[7] *Karuṇa* is indeed heart-rending but it also indicates our weakness. *Raudra* and *vīra* have an element of risk and may lead to rashness and danger. *Bhayānaka* again indicates our weakness. *Bībhatsa* causes the mind to shrink. *Adbhuta* has a thrill in it, but it presupposes our incapacity to understand and explain the nature of such a phenomenon. *Śānta* has very little appeal to the youth. But *hāsya* seems to be free from such limitations and has a wider application. Humour has a place even in grim places like the hospital, the judiciary or even the battlefield (cf. "Humour in Uniform", *Reader's Digest* volumes). Other sentiments cannot compete with *hāsya* in terms of universal appeal.

In their treatment of *hāsya* most of the *ālaṁkārikas* have followed the model of Bharata but have given their own illustrations. But the *Rasārṇavasudhākara* of Śiṅgabhūpāla deserves special attention for its treatment of *hāsya*. The author gives a list of ten new elements called *prahasanāṅgāni* or farcical elements. It does not, however, mean that *prahasanāṅgas* were totally a new creation of Śiṅgabhūpāla. Many of the *prahasanāṅgas* given by Śiṅgabhūpāla come under the *vīthyaṅgas* and even Bharata has stated that the thirteen *vīthyaṅgas* may figure prominently in a *prahasana*. The thirteen *vīthyaṅgas* are:

उद्घात्यकावलगिते प्रपञ्चत्रिगते छलम्।
वाक्केल्यधिबले गण्डं अवस्यन्दित-नालिके।
असत्प्रलाप-व्याहार-मृद्वानि त्रयोदश ॥[8]

---

7. Cf. Satindranath Sengupta, "The Sentiment of Laughter", *Journal of Bihar Research Society*, vol. XXXIX, pt. 4, p. 377.

8. *NŚ*, ch. XVIII, *śls*. 104-05.

It may be laborious to define each one of them and give illustrations now here. I shall just point out only one, by way of a specimen sample.

Vākkelī is defined thus:

वाक्केली हास्यसम्बन्धो द्वित्रि प्रत्युक्तितो भवेत्।[9]

Vākkelī arises from a comic dialogue comprising two or three sets of questions and answers. *Sāhitya-Darpaṇa* quotes the following verse as an illustration:

भिक्षो मांसनिषेवणं प्रकुरुषे? किं तेन मद्यं विना
मद्यं चापि तव प्रियं? प्रियमहो वाराङ्गनाभिः सह।
वेश्याप्यर्थरुचिः, कुतस्तव धनं? द्यूतेन चौर्येण वा
चौर्यद्यूतपरिग्रहोऽपि भवतो? नष्टस्य काऽन्या गतिः॥[10]

The ten *prahasana* elements listed out by *RS* are:

अवलगितमवस्कन्दो व्याहारो विप्रलम्भ उपपत्तिः।
भयं अनृतं विभ्रान्तिः गद्गदवाक् च प्रलापश्च॥[11]

The author defines them and gives illustrations from a *prahasana* called *Ānandakośa* which is unfortunately lost to us. I shall again refrain from quoting definitions and illustrations of these here but only point out their general nature. The element *anṛtam* in this group is similar to the *vīthyaṅga-prapañca*. False praise is the basis for both. The illustration given is also the same:

रण्डा चण्डा दीक्षिता धर्मदारा मद्यं मांसं पीयते खाद्यते च।
भिक्षा भोज्यं चर्मखण्डं च शय्या कौलो धर्मः कस्य नो भाति रम्यः॥[12]

from *Karpūramañjarī*. The element *gadgadavāk* again is the same as the *vīthyaṅga asatpralāpa*. The term *vyāhāra* is found in both

---

9. *SD*, p. 218, Motilal Banarsidass edn., 1977.
10. Ibid.
11. *RS*, ch. III., pp. 290 ff., Trivandrum Sanskrit Series, no. l, 1916.
12. *Karpūramañjarī*, I.23.

the groups. The *prahasana* elements may be based on pun and other types of word-play in the form of *prahelikā*s and arise due to vain quarrel, improper speech, impertinence, roundabout talk, incoherent talk, humorous interpretation of religious codes, etc., misquoting of scriptural passages or well-established sayings out of context, exaggeration, vain boastings, deceptive words and actions, feigned *paścāttāpa*, etc.

It may however be necessary to point out the difference between the general *hāsya* and the *prahasana* elements. A passage is said to contain a *prahasana* element only if it is *hāsyaprāya*. But the contrary is not true. Not all passages which are *hāsya*-oriented can be said to have a *prahasana* element. A *prahasana* element is that which, while being *hāsya*-oriented, is dramatic in nature and is full of action and gesticulations. *Hāsya*, plain and simple, may evoke *smita* (gentle smile) or *hasita* (smile), but a *prahasana* element is boisterously farcical evoking *apahasita* (excessive laughter) or *atihasita* (reeling laughter).

Kālidāsa, being a complete dramatist as he is, has handled the sentiment of *hāsya* very creditably and to the fullest advantage in embellishing the *pradhāna-rasa* in his plays. There are very many humorous scenes and passages in his plays illustrative of both plain humour and farcical elements. I shall just place before you a few passages belonging to the latter type only.

The farcical element *avasyandita*[13] is utterances of certain words with a hidden meaning. The following scene in the first Act of *Abhijñānaśākuntala* illustrates this.

When Śakuntalā shows sings of love on seeing Duṣyanta, her friends taunt her thus:

हला शकुन्तले, यद्यत्र अद्य तातः संनिहितो भवेत् . . . ।

13. Cf. *DR*, pp. 65 ff., Nirnaya Sagar Press edn., 1941.

Śakuntalā: (सरोषं) ततः किं भवेत्?
The friends: इमं जीवित-सर्वस्वेन अतिथिं कृतार्थं करिष्यति।

The poor Śakuntalā simply says: युवामपेतम्। किमपि हृदये कृत्वा मन्त्रयेथे। न युवयोर्वचनं श्रोष्यामि।[14]

The farcical element *avalagitam* consists in decrying (*dūṣaṇa*) or abandoning (*tyajana*) one's earlier dicision, out of delusion.

पूर्वमात्मगृहीतस्य समाचारस्य मोहतः।
दूषणं त्यजनं चात्र द्विधा अवलगितं मतम्॥[15]

The *praveśaka* scene in the second Act of *Abhijñānaśākuntala* may serve as an illustration for this. The *vidūṣaka* repents for having accompanied the king for the hunting expedition.

एतस्य मृगयाशीलस्य राज्ञः वयस्यभावेन निर्विण्णोऽस्मि

and later he says

गण्डस्योपरि पिण्डिका संवृत्ता[16]

(a new pimple growing on the old boil).

The farcical element *udghātyaka* is a series of questions and answers so as to bring about a point, in a roundabout way, which is humorous. The following conversation between the king and the *vidūṣaka* in the second Act of the same play illustrates this point.

विदूषकः - भो वयस्य। न मे हस्तपादं प्रसरति। तद् वाङ्मात्रेण ज्ञापयिष्यामि। जयतु जयतु भवान्।

राजा - कुतोऽयं गात्रोपघातः

विदूषकः - कुतः किल स्वयं अक्षिणी आकुलीकृत्य अश्रुकारणं पृच्छसि।

---

14. *Abhijñānaśākuntala*, Act I, between *śl*s. 21 and 22.
15. Cf. *DR*, p. 65 fn., Nirnaya Sagar Press edn., 1941.
16. *Abhijñānaśākuntala*, Act II, Praveśaka scene.

राजा - न खलु अवगच्छामि।

विदूषकः - भो वयस्य। यद्वेतसः कुब्जलीलां विड़म्बयति। तत्किमात्मनः प्रभावेण उत नदीवेगस्य

राजा - नदीवेगस्तत्र कारणम्।

विदूषकः - ममापि भवान्।[17]

The king still does not catch the point and the *vidūṣaka* proceeds to explain that due to inexperience, he had become totally emaciated while accompanying the king in this hunting expedition.

Then we have a farcical element called *bhayam* which can be illustrated by the following scene. The hermits in Kaṇva's hermitage request Duṣyanta that he may guard the hermits from the fear of demons. Duṣyanta agrees and the hermits depart. Then after some time, the king asks the *vidūṣaka* whether he is interested in seeing Śakuntalā. The *vidūṣaka* replies,

प्रथमं सपरीवाहं आसीत्।
इदानीं राक्षसवृत्तान्तेन बिन्दुरपि नावशोषितः।[18]

The king assures him that he need not have any fears. The king then receives the call from the capital, but he wants to send the *vidūṣaka* with the message that the king has other duties to be discharged at the hermitage at the request of the hermits. The *vidūṣaka* gladly agrees to go back but then says,

मा खलु मां रक्षोभीरुं गणयसि।[19]

I shall go but don't think I am afraid of the demons.

These farcical scenes in second Act introduced in between the *śṛṅgāra*-dominated Acts I and III serve to heighten the effect

17. *Abhijñānaśākuntala*, Act II, between *śls*. 2 and 3.

18. Ibid., Act II, between *śls*. 16 and 17.

19. Ibid., Act II, between *śls*. 17 and 18.

of the *pradhāna-rasa* (i.e. *śṛṅgāra*).

The farcical element *vipralambha* (deception) is deceiving others by tricks and the like. An illustration for this can be found in the *praveśaka* scenes in the second Act of *Vikramorvaśīya*. The King Purūravā has entertained love for Urvaśī and the *vidūṣaka* is expected to keep this matter, a well-guarded secret. But the queen senses some foul play and sends Nipuṇikā to find out the truth. Nipuṇikā straightaway comes to the *vidūṣaka* and informs him that the queen seeks his counsel in a particular matter. *Vidūṣaka* asks what it is. Nipuṇikā says, "Sir, the king addressed the queen by the name of the very woman who has been the source of his anxiety". The *vidūṣaka* wonders whether the king himself had let the cat out of the bag and so asks Nipuṇikā, "What, did he call the queen by the name Urvaśī, ever since he saw her he has been out of his senses". Having thus extracted the secret by clever deception, Nipuṇikā departs to convey the same to her mistress. Thus here we have the farcical element *vipralambha*.

The farcical element *vyāhāra*, a *vīthyaṅga* is defined thus:

अन्यार्थं एव व्याहारो हास्यलोभकरं वचः ।[20]

Vyāhāra is a remark made with a different purpose while it is understood by others as having a different motive. *DR*, *ND*, and *SD* — all three offer the same illustration, namely the *vidūṣaka*'s remark from the *lāsya-prayoga* scene of *Mālavikāgnimitra*.

After her dance performance is over Mālavikā wants to go. But *vidūṣaka* stops her by saying

भवति, तिष्ठ, किमपि वो विस्मृतः क्रमभेदः ।[21]

---

20. *Daśarūpaka*, III.20.

21. *Mālavikāgnimitra*, Act II, between *śls*. 5 & 6.

When Gaṇadāsa asks him as to what blemish he found in Mālavikā's dance, the *vidūṣaka* says,

प्रथमं ब्राह्मणस्य पूजा कर्तव्या, सा ननु वो विस्मृता।[22]

On hearing this, Mālavikā smiles and thus the *vidūṣaka* wins some more time for the king to observe the charming beauty of Mālavikā. Moreover, here what *vidūṣaka* means by *upadeśaśuddhā* is that he must be honoured first while Gaṇadāsa thinks that the *vidūṣaka* had actually noted a blemish in Mālavikā's dance and hence *anyārtha* leading to the farcical element *vyāhāra*.

The farcical element *anṛtam* is an utterance of false praise or flattery —

अनृतं भवेद् वाक्यं असत्यस्तुतिगुम्फितम्।[23]

An instance for this could be found in the third Act of *Mālavikāgnimitra*.

The king and the *vidūṣaka* observe from a hiding place, *Mālavikā* performing a *dohada* act under orders from the queen. The king remarks that the girl deserves to smite two objects — the *aśoka* awaiting its blossoms and the lover who might have offended her in *praṇaya-kalaha*. The *vidūṣaka* quickly says, "May you soon commit such an offence to her so that you will have the pleasure of being kicked by the feet of this beautiful girl". The king then says,

प्रतिगृहीतं वचः सिद्धिदर्शिनो ब्राह्मणस्य।[24]

The reference to the *vidūṣaka* that he is a *siddhapuruṣa* is merely

---

22. *Mālavikāgnimitra*, Act II, between *śls*. 9 and 10.
23. *RS*, Ch. III, pp. 290 ff., Trivandrum Sanskrit Series edn., 1916.
24. *Mālavikāgnimitra*, Act III, between *śls*. 12 and 13.

an exaggerated praise showered on him in a humorous way and hence we have the element *anṛtam* here.

The farcical elements from Kālidāsa's plays that I have selected and presented here are not exhaustive but only representative in nature. Many more such instances could be found by discerning readers.

Appendix F

Elements of Farce in the Plays of Harṣa*

A PRAHASANA (*pra+has+lyuṭ*) is that which causes one to burst into laughter. The elements of farce in the three plays of Harṣa are very much proportionate and appropriate tending to help the main sentiment of the play. The author in this paper, after illustrating the *prahasanāṅga*s and *vīthyaṅga*s as dealt with by other dramaturgists, has tried to present similar specimens from Harṣa's *Nāgānanda, Ratnāvalī* and *Priyadarśikā*.

After Bhāsa and Kālidāsa, it is Harṣa who handles the sentiment of *hāsya* in an effective way in his plays. The humour of Harṣa is always dignified and straight. He never indulges in the so-called slapstick comedy. His *hāsya* never looks out of place but always has a purpose to serve in the dramatic sequence of the play. Providing comic relief to the audience in the midst of gripping scenes is not the only purpose of the humorous scenes. The *hāsya* in Harṣa's plays always serves as a supplement to the *pradhāna-rasa* and helps to heighten it, thereby contributing to the overall dramatic effect of the play. Looking from this angle the farcical elements do have a leading role to play in the three plays of Harṣa.

The *prahasanāṅga*s or the elements of farce form an indispensable part of a *prahasana* (farce). They are, however, widely employed in *nāṭaka*s and *prakaraṇa*s too. It may be necessary here to point out the difference between "general

---

* Appeared in *Journal of the Ganganatha Jha Kendriya Sanskrit Vidyapeetha*, vol. 10 parts 1-4, Jan.-Dec. 1984.

hāsya" and the "*prahasana* element". A passage is said to contain *prahasana* element only if it is *hāsyaprāya*. But the contrary is not true. Not all passages which are *hāsya*-oriented contain a *prahasana* element. A *prahasana* element is that which, while being *hāsya*-oriented, is dramatic in nature and is full of actions and gesticulations. *Hāsya*, plain and simple may evoke *smita* (gentle smile) or *hasita* (smile), but a *prahasana* element is boisterously farcical, evoking *apahasita* (excessive laughter) or *atihasita* (reeling laughter). The *prahasana* elements may be based on pun and other types of word play or may arise from vain quarrel, improper speech, impertinence, roundabout talk, incoherent talk, humorous interpretation of the religious codes, etc., misquoting of scriptural passages or well-established sayings out of context, overexaggeration, vain boastings, deceptive words and actions, feigned *paścāttāpa*, etc.

Śiṅgabhūpāla was probably the first author of dramaturgy to deal with the *prahasana* elements at length. He has named ten of them and has offered illustrations from a *prahasana* called *Ānandakośa* which is unfortunately lost to us. But Śiṅgabhūpāla's list does not seem to be complete. He has probably included only those for which he could offer illustrations from *Ānandakośa*. Some of the *prahasana* elements mentioned by him overlap with some of the *vīthyaṅgas*, either in their name or by their content. He has failed to include some of the other *vīthyaṅgas*, which are fit to be called *prahasanāṅgas* as well. Thus the *prahasanāṅga anṛtam* mentioned by Śiṅgabhūpāla is the same as the *vīthyaṅga prapañca* which is based on "false praise" or "flattery". Likewise *gadgadavāk* is similar to *asatpralāpa* (*vīthyaṅga*) since both arise due to incoherent talk. The term *vyāhāra* occurs in both the groups though their definitions differ from one another. Hence, the *prahasana* elements may not be restricted to just ten which are mentioned by Śiṅgabhūpāla, but may include the majority of the *vīthyaṅgas* which are also farcical in nature. The term *prahasanāṅga*s mentioned by Śiṅgabhūpāla in *Rasārṇavasudhākara*[1] are:

(i)	*avalagita*	-	Slipdown
(ii)	*avaskanda*	-	Scooping
(iii)	*vyāhāra*	-	Jocular dialogue
(iv)	*vipralambha*	-	Deception
(v)	*upapatti*	-	Reasoning
(vi)	*bhayam*	-	Consternation
(vii)	*anṛtam*	-	Falsehood
(viii)	*vibhrāntiḥ*	-	Misconception
(ix)	*gadgadavāk*	-	Choking
(x)	*pralāpa*	-	Prattling

The 13 *vīthyaṅga*s, first mentioned by Bharata[2] and later adopted by other dramaturgists are —

(i)	*udghātyaka*	-	Abrupt dialogue
(ii)	*avalagita*	-	Continuance
(iii)	*prapañca*	-	Complement
(iv)	*trigata*	-	Triple rendering
(v)	*chalam*	-	Deception
(vi)	*vākkeli*	-	Repartee
(vii)	*adhibala*	-	Outvying
(viii)	*gaṇḍam*	-	Abrupt remark

1. *Rasārṇavasudhākara* (*RS*), III.274-76; Adyar Library Series edn.; 1979, Madras.
2. *Nāṭyaśāstra* (*NS*), ch. XVIII, 168; Nirnaya Sagar Press edn., 1942, Bombay.

(ix)	*avasyandita*	-	Humorous interpretation
(x)	*nālikā*	-	Enigma
(xi)	*asatpralāpa*	-	Incoherent talk
(xii)	*vyāhāra*	-	Humorous talk
(xiii)	*mṛdava*	-	Euphemism

It may be difficult to give below the illustrations for all of the *prahasanāṅga*s as dealt with in *Rasārṇavasudhākara* and for the *vīthyaṅga*s as given in works like *Avaloka*. But still as a sample case, one or two illustrations from the works quoted above may be seen here, before we take up similar specimens from the plays of Harṣa.

The *prahasana* element *pralāpa* (prattling) is defined thus by Śiṅgabhūpāla —

प्रलापः स्यादयोग्यस्य योग्यत्वेनानुमोदनम् ।[3]

Pralāpa amounts to endorsing another's inappropriate words or action. The following illustration from *Ānandakośa* is cited by Śiṅgabhūpāla.

राजा - (सौदार्योद्रेकम्) — अये बिडालाक्ष,
अस्मदीये नगरे विषये च —
पतिहीना च या नारी जायाहीनश्च यः पुमान् ।
तौ दम्पती यथाकामं भवेतामिति घोष्यताम् ॥
बिडालाक्षः - देवः प्रमाणम् ।
गुह्यग्राही - (सश्लाघागौरवम्)
मन्वादयो महीपालाः शतशो गामपालयन् ।
न केनापि कृतो मार्ग एवमाश्चर्यसौख्यदः ॥

The *vīthyaṅga vākkeli* is defined thus by Viśvanātha.[4]

3. *RS*, III.283.

4. *Sāhitya-Darpaṇa*, (*SD*), ch. VI, 269, Nirnaya Sagar Press edn., 1936.

वाक्केलिर्हास्यसम्बन्धो द्वित्रिप्रत्युक्तितो भवेत्।

With this bird's-eye view of the *prahasanāṅga*s and the *vīthyaṅga*s, we shall now take up a few illustrations from the three plays of Harṣa.

Nāgānanda

The first portion of the third Act in *Nāgānanda* is replete with *prahasana* elements. The comic element thus introduced in the central Act brings about a parity between the *śṛṅgāra*, depicted in the first two Acts and the *karuṇa* delineated in the last two Acts and thereby helps to heighten the effect of these two *rasa*s. This particular scene, if taken out from the main play and enacted separately, may itself serve as a model *prahasana*. It has two important *prahasana* characters in the *viṭa* and the *vidūṣaka*, who are merrymaking during the marriage celebrations of Jīmūtavāhana and Malayavatī. The opening verse of this Act is cited by *Avaloka* as an instance of the *vīthyaṅga-prapañca*. *Prapañca* is based on false praise and is defined thus:

असद्भूतं मिथः स्तोत्रं प्रपञ्चो हास्यकृन्मनः।[5]

The undue praise placed by the *viṭa* on Baladeva's drinking habits in the following verse, is thus an illustration of *prapañca*.

नित्यं यः पिबति सुरां जनस्य प्रियसङ्गमं च यः करोति।
मम तौ द्वावेव देवौ बलदेवः कामदेवश्च ॥[6]

The next verse in the same Act,

वक्षःस्थले दयिता दत्तोत्पलवासिता मुखे मदिरा।
शीर्षे च शेखरं नित्यमेव संस्थितानि यस्य ॥[7]

5. *Daśarūpaka* (*DR*), ch. III, 15cd, Nirnaya Sagar Press edn., Bombay, 1941.

6. *Nāgānanda*, III.1.

7. *Nāgānanda*, III.2.

is an instance of the *vīthyaṅga chalam* which is defined thus:

प्रोक्तं छलं ससोत्प्रासैः प्रियाभासैर्विलोभनम् ।[8]

Chalam is based on flattery or boasting without merit which we find in the verse quoted above. Another instance of the same element can be found in the boasting of the *vidūṣaka* about his personality to the *ceṭī* when they see the hero describing the charm of his newly married wife.[9]

चेटी - श्रुतं त्वया कथं वर्णिता इति ।

विदूषकः - चतुरिके, मैवं गर्वमुद्वह । अस्माकमपि मध्ये दर्शनीयो जनो अस्त्येव । केवलं मत्सरेण कोऽपि न वर्णयति ।

The *ceṭī* promised to redress his grievance by saying,

आर्य अहं ते वर्णयामि ।

Blackening his face with the juice of *tamāla* sprouts, she says

ननु वर्णितोऽसि ।

Then we find the *viṭa* mistaking the *vidūṣaka* in feminine dress, for Navamālikā. It turns out to be an absolutely ridiculous situation with the drunken *viṭa* forcibly dragging the *vidūṣaka* and embracing him and all that. Hence, this scene may serve as an illustration for the *prahasana* element *vibhrāntiḥ* which is defined thus

वस्तुसाम्यकृतो मोहो विभ्रान्तिरिति गीयते[10]

A series of humorous exchanges between two or three is called *vyāhāra* (also called *vyavahāra*) another *prahasana* element.

8. *DR*, III.17ab.

9. *Nāgānanda*, Act III, pp. 86-89, ed. C. Sankara Rama Sastry, Madras, 1946.

10. *RS*, ch. III, 282cd.

व्यवहारः स्वसंवादी द्वित्राणां हास्यकारणम्[11]

The following scene[12] may illustrate this:

The *viṭa* offers a cup of wine, tasted first by Navamālikā, to the *vidūṣaka*. The *vidūṣaka* hesitates to accept it.

विदूषकः - शेखरक, ब्राह्मणः खल्वहम्।

विटः - यदि त्वं ब्राह्मणः, क्व ते ब्रह्मसूत्रम्

विदूषकः - तत् खल्वमुना चेटेन आकृष्यमाणं छिन्नम्।

चेटी - (विहस्य) यद्येवं, वेदाक्षराण्यपि कतिचित् उदाहर।

विदूषकः - भवति, सीधुगन्धेन मम वेदाक्षराणि नष्टानि।

This dialogue may serve as an illustration for व्याहार

Ratnāvalī

Ratnāvalī has always had the reputation of being the model play for dramaturgists. *Avaloka* quotes major portion of the play while illustrating the *sandhyaṅga*s and other dramaturgical aspects. It is in *Ratanāvalī* that the poet is at his best as a humorist. Thus most of the dramaturgists, like Bhoja, Śāradātanaya, Rāmacandra and Guṇacandra and of course Dhanika, quote profusely from *Ratnāvalī* while illustrating the several *vīthyaṅga*s.

In the first Act when the king wonders whether the festival belongs to Kāma or to himself the Vidūṣaka remarks:

अहं पुनर्जानामि, न भवतो।
न च कामदेवस्य, ममैवैकस्य ब्राह्मणस्यायं महोत्सवः[13]

This passage can be illustrative of the element *chalam*.

11. *RS*, ch. III, 279ab.

12. *Nāgānanda*, Act III, pp. 77-78.

13. *Ratnāvalī*, Act I, p. 14, ed. M.R. Kale, Booksellers Pub. Co., Bombay, 1964.

The following passage[14] is quoted in *Avaloka* as an example of the element *vākkeli*.

विदूषकः - भवति मदनिके, भवति चूतलतिके। मामप्येतां चर्चरीं शिक्षयताम्।

उभे - (विहस्य) हताश, न खल्वेषा चर्चरी।

विदूषकः - तत् किं खल्वेतत्।

मदनिका - द्विपदीखण्डं खल्वेतत्।

विदूषकः - (सहर्षम्) किमेतेन खण्डेन मोदकाः क्रियन्ते

चेट्यौ - (विहस्य) न हि न हि। पठ्यते खल्विदम्।

ND defines *vyāhāra* thus,

अन्यार्थां भाविदृष्दिर्वा व्याहारो हास्यालेशगीः[15]

and draws the illustration from *Ratnāvalī* for the second type, i.e. *bhāvidòṣṭiḥ*. The verse quoted is,

उद्दामोत्कलिकां विपाण्डुररुचं प्रारब्धजृम्भां क्षणा-
दायासं श्वसनोद्गमैरविरतैरातन्वतीमात्मनः।
अद्योद्यानलतामिमां समदनां नारीमिवान्यां ध्रुवं
पश्यन्कोपविपाटलद्युतिमुखं देव्या करिष्याम्यहम्॥[16]

अत्र राज्ञा वासवदत्तां प्रति भाव्यर्थदर्शनं हास्येनोभमिति। says *ND*. Then when the king and the *vidūṣaka* hear the words of Sārikā, the *vidūṣaka* is frightened and shouts.

भो वयस्य, एहि पलायावहे। एतस्मिन् बकुलपादपे किमपि भूतं प्रतिवसति।[17]

This is an instance of a *prahasana* element *bhayam*.

We have the *prahasana* element *vibhrāntiḥ* in the following

---

14. *Ratnāvalī*, Act I, p. 22.
15. *Nāṭyadarpaṇa* (*ND*), II. 31ab, GOS edn., 1959.
16. *Ratnāvalī*, II.4.
17. Ibid., Act II, p. 66.

passage.[18]

विदूषकः - भोः एषा खलु दास्याः पुत्री चतुर्वेदीव ब्राह्मणः ऋचः पठितुं प्रवृत्ता।

राजा - वयस्य, किमनयोक्तं, किमप्यन्यचेतसा मया नावधारितम्।

विदूषकः - एतत्खल्वेतया मन्त्रितम् —

दुर्लभजने नु रागो लज्जजा गुर्वी च परवश आत्मा।
प्रियसखि विषमं प्रेम मरणं शरणं केवलमेकम्॥

राजा - महाब्राह्मणः खल्वसि, कोऽन्य एवमृचामभिज्ञः।

विदूषकः - किं खल्वेतत्।

राजा - ननु गाथेयम, कयापि श्लाघ्ययौवनया प्रियजनमनासादयन्त्या जीवितनिरपेक्षयोक्तम्।

BP defines *avasyandita* as उक्तस्य अन्यथा व्याख्या[19] and draws the illustration from the famous "Citraphalaka" scene.[20]

सुसङ्गता - सखि, यस्य कृते त्वमागता सोऽयं पुरतस्तिष्ठति।

सागरिका - (सासूय) सुसंगते कस्य कृतेऽहमागता

सुसङ्गता - (विहस्य) अलमन्यशङ्कितेन, ननु चित्रफलकस्य, तद्गृहाणैतम्।

The same passage is quoted in *SP* as an instance of *avalagita* which is defined by him thus

यत्र अन्यस्मिन् समावेश्य कार्यमन्यत् प्रसाध्यते।[21]

Viśvanātha, however, quotes the same passage as an instance

18. *Ratnāvalī*, p. 72.
19. *Bhāvaprakāśana* (*BP*), p. 232, GOS edn., 1930.
20. *Ratnāvalī*, Act II, p. 84.
21. *Śṛṅgāraprakāśa* (*SP*), ch. XII, pp. 492-96, ed. Josyer, Coronation Press, Mysore, 1963.

of *nālikā* which is defined by him thus

प्रहेलिकैव हास्येन युक्ता भवति नालिका ।[22]

and according to him *prahelikā* is

संवरणकार्युत्तरम्

In the same Act (II) of *Ratnāvalī* we find Susaṅgatā threatening the king that she would inform the queen about "Citraphalaka" episode. But by this feigned threatening she only wants to help her friend. Hence, this is an instance of *prapañca*, according to *Nāṭyadarpaṇa*.

The element *gaṇḍa* is an abrupt remark which caused a flutter in the hearts of the listeners because of its application in a matter in progress. When the king is trying to pacify the feigned anger of Sāgarikā, *vidūṣaka* makes an abrupt remark

भो एषा खल्वपरा देवी वासवदत्ता ।[23]

Sāgarikā and Susaṅgatā take to their heels immediately fearing that Vāsavadattā has actually arrived. The abrupt remark made by the *vidūṣaka* here is an instance of the element *gaṇḍa*. Another illustration for the same element can be found in Act III,[24] when the king rejoices over the sudden meeting of Sāgarikā and says

वयस्य सेयमनभ्रावृष्टिः ।

Vidūṣaka remarks

एवमेतत् यद्यकालवातावलीव देवी आगत्य अन्यतो नेष्यति ।

and actually it so happens that Vāsavadattā comes there and observes the act of infidelity of her husband.

Then we have an instance of *chalam* in the same Act, with a glitter of hope still lingering in his mind the king.

22. *Sāhitya-Darpaṇa*, ch. VI, 261b.

23. *Ratnāvalī*, Act II, p. 94.

24. *Ratnāvalī*, Act III, p. 140.

Appendix G

Elements of Farce in the Plays of Murāri and Jayadeva*

HĀSYA has a twofold role to play in a drama: first, to provide comic relief to the audience in an otherwise serious play and secondly, to heighten the effect of the main sentiment *śṛṅgāra* or *vīra*. Though *hāsya* is the predominant sentiment in the *prahasana*, the elements of farce (*prahasanāṅgas*) are found in a large measure in the other types as well.

Śiṅgabhūpāla, in his *Rasārṇavasudhākara*, has listed the *prahasanāṅgas* thus:

avalagita āvaskandau vyavahāro
vipralambha upapattiḥ ।

bhayam anṛtaṃ vibhrāntir
gadgadavāk ca pralāpaś ca ॥[1]

The ten elements of farce are: *avalagita* (decry), *āvaskanda* (absurdity), *vyavahāra* (outrage), *vipralambha* (deceit), *upapatti* (deviation), *bhaya* (fear), *anṛta* (flattery), *vibhrānti* (delusion), *gadgadavāk* (incoherent talk), and *pralāpa* (prattling). In studying the elements of farce, we may have to take into consideration the thirteen *vīthyaṅgas* also, which have been recognized by Bharata himself and which are also farcical in nature. The *vīthyaṅgas* are:

---

* Appeared in *The Adyar Libray Bulletin*, vol. 56, 1992, pp. 13-21.

1. *Rasārṇavasudhākara*, III.276, Adyar Library edn., 1979, Madras.

udghātyakāvalagite prapañcatrigate chalam ।
vākkelyadhibale gaṇḍam avasyanditanālike ॥
asatpralāpavyāhāramṛdavāni trayodaśa ॥[2]

Udghātyaka (speech with a hidden meaning), *avalagita* (unexpected turn), *prapañca* (unworthy praise), *trigata* (triple explanation), *chala* (deception), *vākkeli* (witty retort), *adhibala* (outvying), *gaṇḍa* (abrupt remark), *avasyandita* (re-interpretation), *nālikā* (riddle), *asatpralāpa* (incoherent talk), *vyāhāra* (guile), and *mṛdava* (euphemism) make up the list.

Even a cursory glance at the two lists will reveal that some of them are identical either in name or by nature. For example we have *avalagita* in both the lists. The *prahasanāṅga anṛta* is the same as the *vīthyaṅga prapañca* since both are based on false praise or flattery. Similarly *gadgadavāk* and *asatpralāpa* are identical since both arise due to incoherent talk. It is therefore justifiable in including the *vīthyaṅga*s also into the fold of the *prahasanāṅga*s.

It may not be possible to define and illustrate all the ten *prahasanāṅga*s and all the thirteen *vīthyaṅga*s here. But as a sample case, one from each of the two groups may be taken up for discussion. The *prahasanāṅga vibhrāntiḥ* is defined thus:

vastusāmyakṛto moho vibhrāntir iti gīyate

An illustration for this may be drawn from the *Bhagavadajjukīya Prahasana*.[3] We have a noble teacher who has to deal with an impertinent and fickle-minded disciple. As the two enter into a garden, the disciple shouts loudly, closing his eyes,

avidhā । *vyāghreṇa gṛhīto 'smi* ।

---

2. *Nāṭyaśāstra* ch. XVIII, *śls*. 104-05, Manmohan Ghosh edn., Calcutta, 1967.

3. *Bhagavadajjukīya*, pp. 35 ff., Anujan Achan edn., Trichur, 1925.

mocayatha māṃ vyāghramukhāt ।
anātha iva vyāghreṇa khādito 'smi ।
idaṃ khalu rudhiraṃ prasravati kaṇṭhāt . . . etc.

The teacher assures him that nothing untoward has happened. He points out that what he saw was only a peacock and not a tiger. The disciple slowly opens his eyes now and is convinced that it was indeed a peacock and not a tiger. Then he says,

avidha, dāsyāḥ putro vyāghraḥ madbhayena mayūrarūpam gṛhītvā palāyate hi hi . . .

Here, the disciple's delusion in mistaking the peacock to be a tiger is a source of *hāsya* and hence we have the *prahasanāṅga vibhrāntiḥ* here.

The *vīthyaṅga vākkeli* is defined thus:

vākkeli hāsyasambandho dvitripratyuktito bhavet

Vākkelī arises from a comic dialogue comprising two or three sets of questions and answers. *Sāhitya-Darpaṇa*[4] quotes the following verse as an illustration.

bhikṣo māṁsaniṣevaṇaṁ prakuruṣe
kiṃ tena madyaṁ vinā
madyaṁ cāpi tava priyaṁ priyaṁ aho
vārāṅganābhiḥ saha ।
veśyāpyartharuciḥ kutas tava dhanam,
dyūtena cauryeṇa vā
cauryadyūtaparigraho 'pi bhavato,
bhraṣṭasya kānyā gatiḥ.

We may now take up for discussion a few illustrations of farcical elements from the plays of Murāri and Jayadeva. In this context, we have to note that both Murāri and Jayadeva are rather serious writers and there is not much scope for

4. *Sāhitya-Darpaṇa*, p. 218, Motilal Banarsidass edn., 1977.

humour even in the theme they have chosen.

In the beginning of the third Act of the *Anargharāghava*, the Kañcukin laments about his debility due to old age on similar lines of his counterpart in the *Śākuntala*. He says,

gātrair girā ca vikalaś caṭum īśvarāṇām
kurvannayam prahasanasya naṭaḥ kṛto 'smi |
tattvām punaḥ palitavarṇakabhājam enam
nāṭyena kena naṭayiṣyati dīrgham āyuḥ ||[5]

The one whom we meet in the *Anargharāghava* is a typical Kañcukin. Due to old age, his limbs as well as speech are faltering, but still he has to do the duty of amusing his master. But what is significant here is that he has been reduced to the status of an actor in a *prahasana*, according to his own version,

prahasanasya naṭaḥ kṛto 'smi

The commentator explains further:

prahasanapraṇetā naṭaḥ varṇakena haritalādinā vapuḥ ālipya dhavalīkṛtakeśaḥ prabhūṇām pramodāya nṛtyati, tadvad aham api dīrghāyuṣā pravartitaḥ bahūni tāni tāni kāryāṇi kartum utsahe yaiḥ prabhavaḥ mudam anubhavantīti madāyuḥ mām prahasanapātramiva naṭayatīti tātparyam.

In the sixth Act of *Anargharāghava*, a few minor characters are discussing about the prospects of the war. Mālyavān, a minister of Rāvaṇa, is elated at the arrival of Kumbhakarṇa and Indrajīt. He wants to wish them victory. He says,

svasti vijayetāṃ rāmalakṣmaṇau kumbhakarṇa-meghanādau

Another character by name Śuka says,

śāntam śāntam! katham aviśiṣṭakartṛkarmabhāvam ubhayatra dvivacanam prayuktam āryeṇa?

---

5. *Anargharāghava*, III.1, Chowkhamba edn., Varanasi, 1960.

In the statement of Mālyavān, it is not clear whether Kumbhakarṇa and Meghanāda are to be victorious over Rāma and Lakṣmaṇa or vice versa, since both the nominative and accusative duals have similar forms in Sanskrit and the order of the words, generally, does not guarantee the subject-object order in Sanskrit. In fact, such a sentence comes under an *arthadoṣa* called *sasaṁśaya*.

The illustration quoted above can be brought under the *vīthyaṅga* called *gaṇḍa*. It is defined thus:

gaṇḍaṁ prastutasambandhi bhinnārthaṁ sahasoditam

Gaṇḍa is a statement suddenly introduced in the middle of another statement as a sort of dramatic irony which has some connection with the context on hand. The *Avaloka* quotes the following passage from the *Uttararāmacarita*[6] as an illustration:

Rāmaḥ: *iyaṁ gehe lakṣmīr iyam amṛtavartir*
nayanayorasāvasyāḥ sparśo vapuṣi
bahulaś candanarasaḥ, ayam bāhuḥ
kaṇṭhe śiśiramasṛṇo mauktikasaraḥ kim
asyā na preyo yadi param asahyas tu
virahaḥ.

Pratihārī: *deva, upasthitaḥ*

Rāmaḥ: *ayi kaḥ?*

Pratihārī: *devasyāsannaparicārakaḥ durmukhaḥ*

There is a dramatic irony in Rāma's utterance of *viraha* and the Pratihārī's word *upasthitaḥ*. As we know, the *viraha* does take place later. Similarly, in the *Anargharāghava*, the statement

vijayetāṃ rāmalakṣmaṇau kumbhakarṇameghanādau

6. *Uttararāmacaritam*, I.38 ff., Motilal Banarsidass edn., 1971.

has dramatic irony in it and it is suggestive of the impending death of Kumbhakarṇa and Meghanāda. Hence we have the *vīthyaṅga* called *gaṇḍa* here.

We have another farcical element called *nālikā* which is defined thus:

sopahāsā nigūḍhārthā nālikaiva prahelikā[7]

Nālikā is a riddle or an enigmatic remark made with a hidden meaning in order to evoke laughter. It is of two kinds: (i) *bahirlāpā* and (ii) *antarlāpā*. For the type, *antarlāpā*, *Rasārṇavasudhākara* quotes a verse from the first Act of *Prasannarāghava*.

***pra**tyaṅkam aṅkurita**sa**rvanavāvatāra-*
***nna**vyollasatkusumar**ā**ji-virājibandham* ।
***gha**rmetarāṁśum iva **va**kratayātiramyam*
nāṭyaprabandham atimañjulasaṁvidhānam ॥[8]

The antique letters in the verse combine to give the name of the work in a contrived manner. Since the answer to the riddle is found within the verse itself, we have the variety called *antarlāpā* here. If the answer is found by other methods, then it is called *bahirlāpā*. (E.g. Which is the carpet that can never be rolled? Ans: the sky.)

We have the element called *udghātyaka* which is in the form of a series of questions and answers with a hidden meaning.

gūḍhārthapadaparyāyamālā praśnottarasya vā ।
yatrānyanyaṁ samālāpo dvedhodghātyam tad ucyate ॥[9]

The *Avaloka* quotes the following passage.

---

7. *Daśarūpaka*, pp. 65 ff., N.S. Press edn.
8. *Prasannarāghava*, I.7, Chowkhamba edn., Varanasi, 1977.
9. *Daśarūpaka*, pp. 65 ff.

vidūṣakaḥ: *bho, vayasya, ka eṣa kāmo yena tvam api dūyase? sa kim puruṣaḥ athavā strīti?*

rājā: *sakhe,*

manojātir anādhīnā sukheṣveva pravartate,
snehasya lalito mārgaḥ kāma ity abhidhīyate.

vidūṣakaḥ: *evam api na jānāmi*

rājā: *vayasya, icchāprabhavaḥ sa iti.*

vidūṣakaḥ: *kiṃ yo yadicchati, sa tat kāmayati?*

rājā: *atha kim,*

vidūṣakaḥ: *tajjñātam — yathāhaṃ sūpakāraśālāyāṁ bhojanam icchāmi*

Though not so striking, the following passage from *Prasannarāghava*[10] may stand as an illustration of this element. A *tāpasa* and a *bhikṣu* are discussing about Tāṭakā's arrival.

tāpasaḥ: *kva punaḥ samprati tāṭakā?*

bhikṣuḥ: *purīm praviṣṭā.*

tāpasaḥ: *tat kim daśarathasya?*

bhikṣuḥ: *nahi nahi, antakasya.*

tāpasaḥ: *kena punaḥ pratihārāyitam antakapuripraveśe tasyāḥ?*

bhikṣuḥ: *rāmabāṇenaiva*

The *prahasana* element *anṛta* and the *vīthyaṅga* called *prapañca* are both based on false praise. These elements are found in the following conversation in the third Act of *Prasannarāghava*.[11] We have two minor characters Vāmanaka and Kubjaka

10. *Prasannarāghavam*, Act II, Viṣkambhaka, pp. 103 ff., Chowkhamba edn., Benares, 1977.

11. Ibid., pp. 149 ff.

entering the stage. They are attendants of Rāvaṇa. Kubjaka is hunchbacked by nature, but Vāmanaka assumes the hunchback so that he does not shatter the welcome arch erected on the road. The fact is that he is a dwarf and does not have to bend even while entering the arch.

vāmanaka: *aho aṅgānām me tuṅgatvam. api nāma īdṛśaiḥ aṅgaiḥ atra sañcaratā mayā dvāraśikharam bhajyate? tat kubjo bhutvā sañcariṣyāmi (tataḥ praviśati kubjakaḥ)*

kubjaka: *vayasya, vāmanaka, idānīm sakalaguṇasamyukto 'si tvam.*

vāmanaka: *katham iva?*

kubjaka: *prathamam eva vāmanaḥ, idānīm punaḥ kubjatvam prāptaḥ.*

vāmanaka: *(sakrodham) aye mūrkha, katham ātmanaḥ kubjatvam parasmin āropayasi, nanu tvameva kubjakaḥ. mayā punaḥ dvāraśikharabhaṅgaṁ śaṅkitena ātmani kubjatvam āropitam.*

kubjaka: *katham vitastimātreṇa tavāṇgena dvāraśikharam bhaṅkṣyate? (punaḥ sakrodham) are, alīkavācāla, kena tava kathitam aham kubjaka iti?*

vāmanaka: *nanu anenaiva dṛptavṛṣabhakakudasadṛ śena pṛṣṭhasthitena māṁsastabakena udvāhitena.*

kubjaka: *(vihasya) aye matiśūnya, katham ayam māṁsastabako 'pi punaḥ saubhāgyalakṣmyā upadānagendukaḥ.*

The conversation goes on in this vein, with the hunchback maintaining that the protruding flesh on his back is an ornamental piece and the dwarf ridiculing him by saying that *tanur iva matir api te vakrā* — "is your mind also crooked like your body?"

Such light-hearted comedy will have a better effect on the stage than when it is read. The *prahasana* elements themselves are action-oriented and their effect could be hilarious. Realizing this, perhaps, Murāri and Jayadeva have introduced the *prahasana* elements, though in a limited way, in their otherwise serious plays.

Bibliography

I. Sanskrit Prahasanas

Adbhutataraṅga of Harijīvanamiśra, Ms from Anup Sanskrit Library, Bikaner.

Bhagavadajjukīya of Bodhāyanakavi, ed. Anujau Achan, Cochin, 1925.

Caṇḍānurañjana of Ghanaśyāma, Ms from Tanjore.

Dāmakaprahasana (Anon.), Punjab Sanskrit Series, Motilal Banarsidass edn., 1926.

Dhūrtanartaka of Sāmarāja Dīkṣita, Ms from Bodleian Library, Oxford.

Dhūrtasamāgama of Jyotirīśvara, photostat copy of the ed. Lassen, 1838.

Dhūrtaviḍambana of Amareśvara, copy of Ms from BORI, Poona.

Ghṛtakulyāvalī of Harijīvanamiśra, copy of Ms from Anup Sanskrit Library, Bikaner.

Gaurīdigambaraprahasana of Śaṅkaramiśra, Chowkhamba edn., 1969.

Hāsyacūḍāmani of Amātya Vatsarāja, in Rūpakaṣṭaka, G.O.S. edn., no. 8, 1918.

Hāsyakautūhala of Viṭṭalakṛṣṇa, copy of Ms from Anup Sanskrit Library, Bikaner.

Hāsyārṇava of Jagadīśvara, Chowkhamba edn., 1963.

Kāleyakautūhala of Bharadvāja, copy of Ms from BORI Library, Poona.

Kuhanābhaikṣava of Tirumalanātha, printed in Malayamāruta, Delhi: Rashtriya Samskrit Samsthan, 1978.

Lambodaraprahasana of Veṅkaṭeśvara, Mysore: Vidyatarangini Press, 1890.

Laṭakamelaka of Śaṅkhadhara, Chowkhamba edn., 1962.

Lokarañjanaprahasana of Śrīnivāsācārya, copy of Ms from Oriental Research Institute, Mysore.

Madanaketucarita of Rāmapāṇivāda, Trivandrum: University Manuscripts Library, 1948.

Mattavilāsaprahasana of Mahendrapallava, ed. N.P. Unni, Trivandrum: College Book House, 1974.

Mithyācāra of Vaidyanātha, xerox copy of Ms from Bombay University Manuscripts Library, Bombay.

Muṇḍitaprahasana of Śivajyotirvid, copy of Ms from BORI Library, Poona.

Nātavāṭaprahasana of Yadunandana, Bombay: Nirnaya Sagar Press, 1888.

Palāṇḍumaṇḍana of Harijīvanamiśra, Printed in Malayamāruta, vol. III, Delhi: Rashtriya Samskrit Samsthan.

Prāsaṅgika of Harijīvanamiśra, copy of Ms from Anup Sanskrit Library, Bikaner.

Sāhṛdayānanda of Harijīvanamiśra, copy of Ms from Anup Sanskrit Library, Bikaner.

Sāndrakutūhala of Kṛṣṇadatta, copy of Ms from BORI Library, Poona.

Somavallīyogānanda of Aruṇagirinātha, copy of Ms from Oriental Research Institute, Mysore.

Subhagānanda of Vāsudevakavīndra (Śrīvatsāṅka), Copy of Ms from Sarasvati Mahal Library, Tanjore.

Unmattakavikalaśa of Veṅkaṭeśvara, copy of Ms from Sarasvati Mahal Library, Tanjore.

Vibudhamohana of Harijīvanamiśra, Printed in Malayamāruta, vol. I.

Vinodaraṅga of Sundaradeva, copy of Ms from India Office Library, London.

II. Books in Sanskrit

Abhinavabhāratī of Abhinavagupta, along with the *Nāṭyaśāstra*, GOS edn., vols. I-IV, 1926-34.

Arthaśāstra of Kauṭilya, vols. I & II, Lahore: Motilal Banarsidass, 1923-24.

Atharvaveda, in 4 vols., Bombay Sanskrit Series, 1895-98, no. 54, Poona, 1951.

Bhagavadajjukīya of Bodhāyana Kavi, Anujan Achan edn., Cochin, 1925.

Bhagavadgītā, Poona: Ānandāsrama Press, 1896.

Bhāsanāṭakacakram, ed. C.R. Devadhar, Poona Oriental Series no. 54, Poona, 1951.

Bhāvaprakāśana of Śāradātānaya, GOS edn., no. 45, Baroda, 1930.

Bṛhadāraṇyaka Upaniṣad, Madras: Ramakrishna Math, 1968.

Chāndogya Upaniṣad, Madras: Ramakrishna Math, 1956.

Daśarūpaka of Dhanañjaya, (i) ed. Parab, Bombay: Nirnaya Sagar Press, 1941, (ii) with English Translation, C.O. Haas, New Delhi: Motilal Banarsidass, 1962. (iii) ed. Hall, Asiatic Society of Bengal, 1865.

Dhvanyāloka of Ānandavardhana, ed. K. Krishnamurthy, Dharwad: Karnatak University, 1974.

Dūtavākya of Bhāsa, ed. R.S. Vadyar & Sons, Palghat, 1973.

Hāsyacūḍāmaṇi Prahasana of Amātya Vatsarāja, GOS, no. 8, 1918.

Kamsavaho of Rāmapāṇivāda, ed. A.N. Upadhya, Delhi: Motilal Banarsidass, 1963.

Kāmasūtra of Vātsyāyana, Chowkhamba edn., 1964.

Karpūramañjarī of Rājaśekhara, Motilal Banarsidass edn., 1963.

Kaṭhopaniṣad, Madras: Ramakrishna Math edn., 1916.

Kālidāsa's Works (Works of Kālidāsa), vol. I (Dramas), Delhi: Motilal Banarsidass, 1977 tr. C.R. Devadhar.

Kāvyāprakāśa of Mammaṭa, Delhi: Motilal Banarsidass 1966.

Kāvyānuśāsana of Hemacandra, Kāvyamālā-71, Bombay: Nirnaya Sagar Press edn., 1934.

Kauṣītaki Upaniṣad, Bombay: Nirnaya Sagar Press edn., 1948.

Kirātārjunīya of Bhāravi, Bombay: Nirnaya Sagar Press edn., 1917.

Kumārasambhava of Kālidāsa, Cantos I-VIII, ed. M.R. Kale, New Delhi: Motilal Banarsidass.

Laṭakamelaka Prahasana of Śaṅkhadhara, Chowkhamba edn., 1962.

Līlāvatī Vīthī of Rāmapāṇivāda, Trivandrum: University Manuscripts Library, 1948.

Madanaketucarita of Rāmapāṇivāda, Trivandrum: University Manuscripts Library, 1948.

Mānavadharmasūtra, J. Jolly, London: Trubner & Co., 1887.

Mālatīmādhava of Bhavabhūti, ed. M.R. Kale, Motilal Banarsidass, 1967.

Mattavilāsa Prahasana of Mahendra Pallava, ed. N.P. Unni, Trivandrum: College Book House, 1974.

Mṛcchakaṭika of Śūdraka, ed. M.R. Kale, Motilal Banarsidass, 1972.

Muṇḍaka Upaniṣad, ed. R.K. Math, Madras, 1949-50.

Naiṣadham of Śrīharṣa, Haridass Sanskrit Series edn., no. 205 Benares, 1954.

Nāgānanda of King Harṣa, Madras: Balamanorama Press, 1967.

Nāṭaka Candrikā of Rūpakagosvāmin, Chowkhamba edn., 1964.

Nāṭakalakṣaṇaratnakośa of Sāgaranandin, Chowkhamba edn., 1972.

Nāṭyadarpaṇa of Rāmacandra and Guṇacandra, GOS edn., no. 48, 1928.

Nāṭyaśāstra of Bharatamuni, (i) Kāvyamālā-42, Nirnaya Sagar Press, 1942; (ii) GOS in 4 volumes, 1926-34; (iii) Kashi Sanskrit Series, 1929; (iv) Manmohan Ghosh, Calcutta: Manisha Granthalaya, 1967.

Prabodhacandrodaya of Kṛṣṇamiśra, Motilal Banarsidass edn., 1971.

Pratāparudrīya of Vidyānātha, ed. V. Raghavan, Madras: Sanskrit Education Society, 1979.

Prākṛtaprakāśikā of Vararuci, Madras: Adyar Library, 1946.

Priyadarśikā of King Harṣa, Motilal Banarsidass edn., 1977.

Rasagaṅgādhara of Jagannātha Paṇḍita, in 3 vols., Chowkhamba, 1960.

Rasārṇavasudhākara of Śiṅghabhūpāla, TSS edn., no. L, 1961.

Raghuvaṁśa of Kālidāsa, Bombay: Nirnaya Sagar Press, 1904.

Ratnāvalī of King Harṣa, Madras: Balamanorama, 1938.

Ṛgveda, ed. Max Müller, London: India Office, 1849-74.

Sāhityadarpaṇa of Viśvanātha, Delhi: Motilal Banarsidass, 1977.

Sītākalyāṇa Vīthī of Veṅkappayya, ed. R. Raghavendra Rao, Mysore: Oriental Research Institute, 1989.

Subhāṣitāvalī of Vallabhadeva, Bombay: Govt. Central Book Depot, 1886.

Śatapatha Brāhmaṇa, Lahore: Motilal Banarsidass, 1926.

Śṛṅgāraprakāśa of Bhoja, ed. G.R. Josyer, Mysore: Coronation Press, 1963 (vols. I-II)

Tāṇḍya Brāhmaṇa, Benares: Chowkhamba, 1935-36.

Uttararāmacarita of Bhavabhūti, Motilal Banarsidass edn., 1971 (tr., Notes etc. P.V. Kane).

Vedāntaparibhāṣā of Dharmarājadhvarīndra, Madras: Adyar Library Series edn., 1942.

Veṇīsaṁhāra of Bhaṭṭanārāyaṇa, ed. M.R. Kale, Motilal Banarsidass, 1977.

III. Books in English and Other Languages

A New Bibliography of Sanskrit Drama, by R.V. Tripathi, Delhi: Pratibha Prakashan, 1998.

Bhāsa: A Study, by A.S.P. Ayyar, Madras: M.L.J. Press, 1942.

Bhoja's Śṛṅgāraprakāśa, by V. Raghavan, Madras, 1978 (revised edition), 1st edn. 1961.

Bibliography of Sanskrit Drama, by Montgomery Schuyler, Columbia University Press, 1906.

Catalogus Catalogorum, vols. I-III, by Aufrecht.

Contribution of Kerala to Sanskrit Literature, by K.K. Kunjunni Raja, Madras: University of Madras, 1958.

Critical Study of Sanskrit Dramas by Kerala Authors, by S. Subramanya Iyar, Unpublished Thesis, Kerala University, 1971.

Critiques of Sanskrit Drama, by S.A. Dange, Delhi: Aryan Books International, 1994.

Dhvani Theory in Sanskrit Literature, by Mukunda Madhava Sarma, Benares: Chowkhamba Sanskrit Series, 1968.

Dictionary of Literary Forms, by Harry Shaw, USA: McGraw Book Company,1972.

Dictionary of World Literary Terms, by Joseph T. Shipley, London: George Allen and Unwin Ltd.

Drama and Ritual in Early Hinduism, by Natalia Lidova, Delhi: Motilal Banarsidass, 1994.

Drama in Sanskrit Literature, by R.V. Jagirdar, Bombay: Popular Book Depot, 1947.

Dūtavākya of Bhāsa, Palghat: R.S. Vadyar & Sons, 1973

Epigraphica Indica, vol. IV.

Glossary of Literary Terms, by M.H. Abraham, Holt, Rinechart and Winston, United States of America.

Greek Tragedy and Sanskrit Drama, by Robert Antoine, Calcutta: Writers Workshop, 1995.

History of Classical Sanskrit Literature, by M. Krishnamachariar, New Delhi: Motilal Banarsidass, 1974.

History of Dharmaśāstra, by P.V. Kane, Poona: BORI, 1930-68.

History of English Drama, by Allardyee Nicolt, Cambridge, England (vols. I-VI).

History of India, K.A. Nilakanth Shastri, Madras: Oxford University Press, 1958.

History of Prostitution in India, ed. Sinha and Basu, Calcutta: The Bengal Social Hygiene Association, 1933, vol. I.

History of Sanskrit Literature (Classical period), by S.N. Dasgupta and S.K. De, Calcutta, 1947.

History of Sanskrit Literature, by A.B. Keith, Oxford University Press, 1973 (revised edition).

History of Sanskrit Poetics, by S.K. De, Calcutta: Firma KLM Limited, 1976.

History of Sanskrit Poetics, by P.V. Kane, Delhi: Motilal Banarsidass, 1971.

How Urvasi was Won, by V. Narayan Rao and D.D. Schuman, New York: New York University Press, 2009.

Indian Drama, by Sten Konow (tr.), Calcutta: General Printers and Publishers Ltd.

Indian Kavya Literature, by A.K. Warder, Delhi: Motilal Banarsidass, vols. I-III.

The Indian Theatre, by C.B. Gupta, Delhi: Munshiram Manoharlal, 1991.

Indian Theatre, by F.P. Richmond et al., Honololu, Hawaii: University of Hawaii Press, 1990.

Introduction to Prākṛt, by A.C. Woolner, Delhi: Motilal Banarsidass, 1975.

Jagannātha Paṇḍita: A Study, by V.A. Ramaswamy Sastri, Annamalai University Series, 1942.

Kāpālikas and Kālāmukhas, by David Lorenzen, University of California Press.

Kutiyattam: The Sanskrit Theatre of India, by F.P. Richmond, Michigan: University of Michigan Press, 2002.

Law and Practice of Sanskrit Drama, by S.N. Sastri, Benares: Chowkhamba Sanskrit Series, 1971, vol. I.

Malavika and Agnimitra, by Daniel Balogh, New York: Eszter Somogyi, 2009.

New Catalogus Catalogorum, vols. I-X, Madras University.

Number of Rasas, by V. Raghavan, Madras: Adyar Library Publications, 1940.

Philosophy of the Aesthetic Pleasure, by P. Panchapagesa Sastri, Annamalai University, 1940.

The Playworld of Sanskrit Drama, by R.E. Goodwin, Delhi: Motilal Banarsidass, 1998.

Post Independence Sanskrit Drama, by S. Ranganath, Bangalore: H. Venkataramiah, 1994.

The Quartet of Causeries, by C. Dezso, New York: New York University Press, 2009.

The Rise of Wisdom Moon, by Mathew Kapstein, New York: New York University Press, 2009.

Sanskrit Drama: Essays in Revaluation, by Madusudan Pati, Delhi: Amar Book Prakashan, 1991.

Sanskrit Drama: Its Aesthetics and Production, by V. Raghavan, Chennai: Sarada Raghavan, 1993.

Sanskrit Drama: Problems and Perspectives, by G.K. Bhat, Delhi: Ajanta Books, 1995.

Sanskrit Drama, by G.K. Bhat, Dharwar: Karnatak University Publications, 1975.

Sanskrit Drama and Dramatists, by K.P. Kulkarni, Poona, 1927.

Sanskrit Drama in Theory and Practice, by S.S. Janaki, Delhi: Rashtriya Sanskrit Samsthan, 1995.

Sanskrit Drama: Its Origin and Decline, by J. Sekhar, Leiden: E.J. Bill, 1960.

Sanskrit Theatre, by B. Sinha, Delhi: Raj Publications, 2005.

Shakespearean Comedy and Sanskrit Drama, by Asif Anwar, Delhi: Janaki Prakashan, 2005.

Silappadikāram (Tamil), Saiva Sidhanta Society, Tirunelveli, 1970.

Social Play in Sanskrit Literature, by V. Raghavan, Reprint from Indian Institute of World Culture, Bangalore.

Sociology of Sanskrit Drama, by B. Biswas, Delhi: India Publishers and Distributors, 1999.

Some Aspects of Sanskrit Drama, by S.S. Janaki, Chennai: Kuppuswami Shastri Research Institute, 2005.

Stories from Sanskrit Drama, by Anant Pai, Mumbai: India Book House, 2000.

Studies in Sanskrit Literary History, by Gode, Poona, 1953.

Studies in the Nāṭyaśāstra, by G.M. Tarickar, Motilal Banarsidass, 1975.

Studies in Sanskrit Dramatic Criticism, by T.G. Mainkar, Motilal Banarsidass, 1971.

Studies in Some Concepts of Alaṅkāra Śāstra, by V. Raghavan, Adyar Library, 1942.

Survey of Sanskrit Literature, by C. Kunhan Raja, Bombay: Bharatiya Vidya Bhavan, 1962.

Taking a Ride on the Clay Cart, by B. Bernhard et al., New York: Insight Media, 1995.

Tantras: Studies on their Religion and Literature, by Cintaharan Cakravarti, Calcutta: Punthi Pustak, 1963.

Theatre in Ancient India, by S. Chattopadhyaya, Delhi: Manohar, 1993.

Theatre of the Hindus, by H.H. Wilson, vols. I & II, London, 1871.

Theories of Rasa and Dhvani, by A. Sankaran, University of Madras Publication, 1973.

The Traditional Sanskrit Theatre, by C. Rajendran, Kolkata: University of Calicut, 1999.

Types of Sanskrit Drama, by D.R. Mankad, Karachi: Urmi Prakasan Mandir, 1936.

Vidūṣaka in Theory and Practice, by J.T. Parikh, Surat: Sarvajanik Education Society, 1953.

IV. Research Journals

Adyar Library Bulletin, Madras, vol. XV, 1951.

Annals of Bhandarkar Oriental Research, Poona, vol. XXII.

Bhāratīya Vidyā, Bharatiya Vidya Bhavan, Bombay.

Indian Historical Quarterly, vols. III-VII.

Journal of the Asiatic Society of Bengal, Calcutta.

Journal of the Asiatic Society, Bombay.

Journal of Bihar Research Society, vol. XXXIX.

Journal of Bihar and Orissa Research Society, March-June, 1924.

Journal of Ganganatha Jha Research Institute, Allahabad.

Journal of Oriental Research, Kuppuswamy Sastri Research Institute, Madras, vols. VI-VII.

Journal of the University of Bombay.

Journal of the University of Delhi, vol. II.

Journal of the Universtiy of Poona.

Our Heritage, Sanskrit College, Calcutta vol. III.

Poona Orientalist, vol. VII.

Prācī Jyoti, Kurukshetra University, Kurukshetra.

Sāgarikā, Sagar University, vol. V.

Saṁskṛta Raṅga Annual, vols. I-VII.

The Mysore Orientalist.

Vishveshvaranand Indological Quarterly.

नामपदानुक्रमणी

Index